Karel Reisz

Manchester University Press

BRITISH
FILM
MAKERS

Karel Reisz

COLIN GARDNER

Manchester University Press
MANCHESTER AND NEW YORK

distributed exclusively in the USA by Palgrave

Published by Manchester University Press
Oxford Road, Manchester M13 9NR, UK
and Room 400, 175 Fifth Avenue, New York, NY 10010, USA
www.manchesteruniversitypress.co.uk

Distributed exclusively in the USA by
Palgrave, 175 Fifth Avenue, New York, NY 10010, USA

Distributed exclusively in Canada by
UBC Press, University of British Columbia, 2029 West Mall,
Vancouver, BC, Canada V6T 1Z2

British Library Cataloguing-in-Publication Data
A catalogue record for this book is available from the British Library

Library of Congress Cataloging-in-Publication Data applied for

ISBN 0 7190 7548 3 hardback
EAN 978 0 7190 7548 3

First published 2006

15 14 13 12 11 10 09 08 07 06   10 9 8 7 6 5 4 3 2 1

Typeset in Scala with Meta display
by Koinonia, Manchester
Printed in Great Britain
by Bell & Bain Ltd, Glasgow

Contents

List of plates

Every attempt has been made to obtain permission to reproduce the figures illustrated in this book. If any proper acknowledgement has not been made, copyright holders are invited to inform the publishers.

Series editors' foreword

The aim of this series is to present in lively, authoritative volumes a guide to those film-makers who have made British cinema a rewarding but still under-researched branch of world cinema. The intention is to provide books which are up-to-date in terms of information and critical approach, but not bound to any one theoretical methodology. Though all books in the series will have certain elements in common – comprehensive filmographies, annotated bibliographies, appropriate illustration – the actual critical tools employed will be the responsibility of the individual authors.

Nevertheless, an important recurring element will be a concern for how the oeuvre of each film-maker does or does not fit certain critical and industrial contexts, as well as for the wider social contexts which helped to shape not just that particular film-maker but the course of British cinema at large.

Although the series is director-orientated, the editors believe that reference to a variety of stances and contexts is more likely to reconceptualise and reappraise the phenomenon of British cinema as a complex, shifting field of production. All the texts in the series will engage in detailed discussion of major works of the film-makers involved, but they all consider as well the importance of other key collaborators, of studio organisation, of audience reception, of recurring themes and structures: all those other aspects which go towards the construction of a national cinema.

The series explores and charts a field which is more than ripe for serious excavation. The acknowledged leaders of the field will be reappraised; just as important, though, will be the bringing to light of those who have not so far received any serious attention. They are all part of the very rich texture of British cinema, and it will be the work of this series to give them all their due.

Acknowledgements

For someone who usually finds the writing process to be excruciatingly painful, this book turned out to be (relatively speaking) a pleasure to write. Now, either I have finally mastered the art of critical self-expression (highly unlikely) or I was surrounded by a wealth of research and editorial talent that at least minimized the book's shortcomings and allowed me to take full responsibility for my own creative urges (a much more likely scenario). First of all I would like to thank my editor at Manchester University Press, Matthew Frost, who was such an enormous support on my previous book on Joseph Losey and gave the green light for this project. Series editors Brian McFarlane and Neil Sinyard read the proposal in its earliest stages and provided invaluable input on chapter organization and the overall balance of the book, while Brian was also very generous in sharing his insights on Reisz's early film criticism in *Sequence* magazine. Georg Gaston's 1980 book on Reisz proved to be extremely useful, not only because of the author's rigorous close readings of the films themselves but also because until now it has been the only book-length study of the director (up to and including *Dog Soldiers*), thus helping to give my own work some overall historical shape and perspective.

I also owe a great deal of gratitude to Sarah Athanas, my fabulous research assistant at the University of California, Santa Barbara and a talented film-maker in her own right, who diligently fed me with a steady supply of primary and secondary sources over a period of eighteen months, and to my esteemed colleague Helen Taschian, who generously read each of the early drafts of the book and provided important insights into readability and narrative continuity. Her constant e-mails urging me to send her the next chapter also inspired me to stay on schedule for fear of incurring her considerable wrath (just kidding!).

My research made extensive use of several libraries and archives and I would like to acknowledge the extremely helpful librarians and staff at the following institutions: Ann Stephenson in the Stills, Posters and Designs department at the British Film Institute; BFI's Research Viewing Service and Stills Archive; the University of California, Los Angeles (UCLA) Film and Television Archive; the UCLA University Research and Arts Libraries;

the Margaret Herrick Library of the Academy of Motion Picture Arts and Sciences; the Davidson and Arts Libraries at the University of California, Santa Barbara; the Main Library at the University of California, Berkeley, and Claire at 'Eddie Brandt's Saturday Matinee' in North Hollywood where most of the book's film stills were acquired. These stills are reproduced by kind permission of the British Film Institute; Graphic Films Ltd. (London); MGM/Sony; Turner Entertainment Co.; Warner Bros. Entertainment Company; StudioCanal (Paris); Universal Studios and Paramount Pictures. Every attempt has been made to contact the copyright holders. In the event of any misattribution please contact the publishers.

The writing of the manuscript was significantly aided and abetted by a sabbatical leave from the University of California, Santa Barbara, which accounted for two thirds of the final project. Many thanks to Kip Fulbeck, Art Department Chair, and David Marshall, Dean of the Humanities, for approving the leave of absence. I would also like to acknowledge the professional and moral support of my usual gang of academic and artistic cohorts: Peter Bloom, Trudy Bolter, Jane Callister, Alain Cohen, Dick Hebdige, Steve Mamber, Lary May, Warren Neidich, Tony Shaw, Janet Walker, Samuel Weber and John Welchman. Finally, love and appreciation to my wife, Louise, and my Golden Retriever, Nicky, whose endless cookie mooching and burp-filled interruptions were an endearing annoyance throughout.

Introduction: Karel Reisz, 'The last great man in England'

The way my films all work ... they try first of all to document and make real the spiritual and emotional life of a central character. That's not to say that the central character isn't subjected to some criticism; he's not idealized. It's in the clash between the character's inner desires and what the society demands of him – in that clash is the content of my films ... I have very definite political views, but in that way the films don't raise the political questions – they provide, if you like, certain emotional information from which political discussion can usefully start. (Karel Reisz)[1]

Mid-way through Karel Reisz's international hit, *Morgan: A Suitable Case for Treatment* (1966), fervent Trotskyite and erstwhile painter Morgan Delt (David Warner) and his equally ardent Stalinist mother (Irene Handl) visit Karl Marx's grave in Highgate Ceremony to mark the occasion of the great Communist philosopher's birthday. As Morgan reverentially places his bunch of flowers beneath Marx's stony countenance, his sentimental Cockney mother recalls her late husband and the good old days of the revolutionary Old Left. 'Your dad used to love comin' 'ere', she recalls. 'You know, 'e wanted to shoot the royal family, abolish marriage, and put everybody who'd been to public school in a chain gang?' She leans back, sighs wistfully, and adds the kicker: 'Yes, he was an idealist your dad was'. Then, as a solo trumpet plaintively picks out the refrain of 'The Red Flag', she asks Morgan to read the inscription on the grave, Marx's famous dictum: 'Philosophers have tried to understand the world. Our problem, however, is to change it'. As Morgan reads, mother and son, Stalinist and Trotskyite, find a common bond in the call to praxis, their emotional truce transcending their generational and sectarian divide. However, as Morgan makes eye contact with Marx's bust, he undergoes an extremely strange metamorphosis. Almost imperceptibly, Morgan's look of profound respect transforms into a simian smirk. Suddenly, he emits a basso grunt, like a highly agitated gorilla. Then, horror of horrors, he starts pounding his chest, provoking the reified Marx like a jungle rival jealously protecting his territory. Not surprisingly, Mrs Delt is horrified by this atavistic spectacle: 'Morgan! That's disrespectful!' Then, in a massive understatement of the obvious, she adds: 'You 'ave grown into a peculiar sort of a feller, Morgan'. *Very* peculiar, for Morgan, it turns out, is certifiably insane, 'a suitable case for treatment' indeed. Significantly, the cemetery scene ends on a slapstick *and* allegorical note as Morgan offers to give his footsore mother a piggyback ride home. As they weave their merry way through the gravestones to his mum's delighted squeals, Morgan triumphantly shouts, 'Up the Revolution!' as Marx stares expressionless from his pedestal, eschewing editorial comment. However, although the Father of Communism remains significantly mute, Reisz makes it clear that Morgan's cry is nothing but windy rhetoric, for the young man is obviously as much in need of a psychological revolution as a political one (it's easy to recall John Lennon's telling line from The Beatles' *Revolution* (1968) – 'You tell me it's the institution! Well, you know, you better free your mind instead'). Moreover, we can also read the scene symbolically, as a still-born New Left (Morgan) carries the crippling Golem of the Old Left on its shoulders, creating a dialectical impasse that can only be resolved internally, through withdrawal into the schizophrenic line of flight that Gilles Deleuze and Félix Guattari call 'becoming-animal'.

During a 1966 interview with *Morgan*'s screenwriter, the playwright David Mercer, an anonymous London *Times* correspondent summarized the film's position succinctly:

> To Mercer, Morgan is the defeated revolutionary – a Marxist turned inside out. Incapable of further allegiance to the belief in revolutionary social change, and haunted by the tragic deterioration of revolutionary ideals in countries where revolutions have taken place, he asserts an 'internal revolution.' The debris of political faith gives rise to a new, subjective mythology – a world where the innocence of animals is a counterpoint to the corruption of men, where the gorilla, which rarely uses its great strength in aggression, becomes a tragic-comic image of Morgan's alter-ego.[2]

Although based on an earlier 1962 teleplay, Mercer's shooting script was heavily influenced by the existential psychoanalysis of radical psychiatrist R. D. Laing, particularly the idea that schizophrenia may be a function of the breakdown of personal relationships in families. This is compounded in Morgan's case because his parents also represent the idealism but subsequent corruption of the Old Left – his mother stubbornly refuses to de-Stalinize – which has consequently destroyed his faith in the political efficacy of the counter-culture (a theme to which Reisz will return twelve years later in *Dog Soldiers* (1978), a searing examination of the inner self turned psychotic in the wake of Nixon, the drug wars and Vietnam).

Reisz claimed at the time that *Morgan* was an attempt to heal the rift between the generations. Although the Morgan character isn't Reisz's direct mouthpiece any more than, say, Isadora Duncan or Patsy Cline represent his aesthetic and subjective position in subsequent films, he did see in the character 'a divine spark which provoked the question of who is mad and who is sane, analogous to the way our older generation treats today's hippies as freaks, as "cases." The film seemed to me a way to bridge the generations'.[3] However, one could also argue that the then-unknown David Warner's quirky innocence in contrast to Irene Handl's much beloved filmic persona actually served to exacerbate the film's political and generational differences which, as Philip French percep-tively noted at the time, 'makes nonsense of the socio-political situation of which he [i.e. Morgan] is supposed to be the victim ... Somewhere between people in their sixties (Morgan's mother, the die-hard Stalinist) and those in their early twenties (Morgan himself) there is a missing generation. It is this generation that is behind the cameras'.[4]

This is an important observation because it underlines a common thread that runs through all of Reisz's films, namely his use of char-acters and contexts to represent ideological and subjective positions that are not necessarily his own. In this case Reisz himself is caught *between* generations (he was forty at the time of Morgan's release), too young to identify with (or make excuses for) the repressive pogroms of the Old Left, too old to belong to the burgeoning student movement of the 1960s. It is to Reisz's credit that he never tried to force an artifi-cial synthesis from this antinomy, but rather sustained the mounting tensions between the Old and New Left, preferring to explore the gener-ational and ideological impasse as itself a worthwhile subject of study. It also suggests that as a political refugee and Jewish émigré from Nazi persecution – the Czech-born Reisz spoke no English on his arrival in Britain at the age of twelve – the apprentice director clearly learned at first hand both the psychological and material ramifications of personal displacement. All of his major characters are in some ways expressions of this dislocation, whether as class antagonists against establishment norms (Arthur Seaton in *Saturday Night and Sunday Morning*, the psychopath Danny in *Night Must Fall*, Morgan Delt in *Morgan*); artistic and idealistic free spirits (Isadora Duncan, Patsy Cline, Sarah Woodruff in *The French Lieutenant's Woman*); or Nietzschean existentialists (Axel Freed in *The Gambler*, Ray Hicks in *Dog Soldiers*) exercising their will-to-power in the face of unpredictable fates. As the playwright John Guare perceptively noted following Reisz's death in 2002, 'I always think his view of things was essentially about freedom: the Albert Finney character at the end of *Saturday Night and Sunday Morning*, or the gambler being paralysed by his obsession. How do you find your freedom in the middle of paralysis? The day Karel's life changed, from one universe to the other, when he was 12 years old, was all about that: how do you survive when all the rules change suddenly?'[5]

Reisz expresses this alienation through a deliberate split between the understated social realism of his *mise-en-scène* and the performative expressionism of his actors. Unlike another émigré director, Joseph Losey, who resorted to an overwrought baroque stylization to draw attention to the very fabric of the cinematic device as a form of individual and historical self-justification, Reisz is visually self-abnegating to the point of seeming invisibility. Indeed, one of the main critical complaints against Reisz's oeuvre (and the resultant anathema of auteur critics such as Andrew Sarris, who accused the director of 'an ingrained reluctance to pursue passion to its lyrical extensions in time and space'[6]) is that it lacks a distinctive authorial visual signature. 'A good case can be made for Lindsay Anderson as a bilious but authentic "auteur"', notes Peter Wollen, 'but nobody has made a serious claim for the auteurist credentials of Reisz, Richardson, Schlesinger, and others'.[7] Wollen's point is well taken, but a more generous view is that Reisz creates a neutral but carefully detailed and concrete *mise-en-scène*, all the better to root his films in a specific cultural milieu and class context that both defines *and* alienates his protagonists, giving them both their identity and a reason to rebel. In one of the most incisive reviews of *Saturday Night and Sunday Morning*, for example, Alan Lovell observed in the *New Left Review* that,

> Karel Reisz gets his main effect from the style he uses. It's almost an anti-style. The camera does only enough work to tell the story as simply and directly as possible. Because of this the audience is encouraged to make judgements for itself. Just how important this is has gone unnoticed. Very few contemporary films, whatever their quality, leave their audience alone. Nearly every director, either serious or hack, tries to bludgeon his audience by his technical skill or his dramatic talents. Because of their uncertainty about their relationship with the audience, directors seem constantly to be saying 'Look I'm here and I'm good.' Very few film makers have enough confidence in the audience just to assume their co-operation. Karel Reisz does this.[8]

On one level then, Reisz can be defined as cinema's Emile Zola, a cultural determinist whose characters are inescapably (and thus passively) defined by their background. This 'trap' is all the more profound because the films' milieux are transparently 'real' and stylistically 'neutral' to the point of seeming inevitability. Against this backdrop Reisz also creates a more active, performative space defined by his characters/actors, who struggle to escape the confines and limitations of their milieu through various acts of hedonistic self-assertion (or, some might argue, self-indulgence) or outright rebellion. This is the subjective register of Reisz's cinema, where the audience identifies with the character's point of view and shares vicariously in his or her struggle.

However, Reisz adds a third layer – expressed largely through editing, sound and temporal ellipse – which allows him objectively to critique his characters, to open up an ambivalent critical and hybrid 'third' space that leaves the spectator scrambling to discern a concrete identity and psychological closure. It is at this more formal level that we discover the deeper meaning in Reisz's art. Far from engaging in a rebellious agency, Reisz's characters are themselves vicariously harnessed to a series of cultural constructions, so that their apparent will-to-identity is already interpellated (in Louis Althusser's sense) by larger social forces.[9] Thus Arthur Seaton has no real *creative* agency in *Saturday Night and Sunday Morning*, but instead channels his desire through already constructed formulas – heavy drinking, womanizing, armchair Marxism, infantile pranks – that make him ripe for his eventual assimilation into a soulless suburban marriage and the responsibilities of fatherhood. Similarly, Morgan, Isadora and Sarah Woodruff are slaves to their own clichéd fantasies, their dreams of life and love lived through a romanticized imaginary of life-as-art, which turns out to be the benign flipside of its more dangerous corollary: madness and death. Axel Freed and Ray Hicks's existentialism – their touching faith in the luck of the dice throw or their Zen-like affirmation of fate – is equally myopic insofar as they are naively unaware of the darker social forces, in this case a corrupt, unforgiving underworld economy of drugs and gambling, that have come to permeate western society as a whole, including the very counter-culture that was spawned to combat it. While country singer Patsy Cline is perhaps Reisz's most driven, life-affirming artistic force, not only is her career cut tragically short by the 1963 air crash that claimed her life, but her husband, Charlie Dick (Ed Harris), is yet another of Reisz's empty ciphers, living vicariously through the deeds of another. The result is a cinema of alienation that forces the viewer both to think *and* feel the psychological damage of an era that began with hopes of revolutionary social change and ends with the savage backlash of Reagan, Thatcherism and a new conformity fuelled by a combination of cynicism, pragmatism and indifference (the subject of Reisz's final feature, *Everybody Wins*). In this context, Reisz's return to the work of Samuel Beckett at the end of the millennium is both appropriate and telling, a sign that, stylistically at least, the theatre of the absurd is perhaps *the* last viable form of social realism.

In a pair of interviews during the 1970s, Reisz himself acknowledged this clear line of continuity in his work – he always thought of himself as a cinematic auteur – but stressed that it was a continuity of neither British nor Czech sensibilities: 'It's easier for me to say that because I'm not British anyway, and it was largely accident that I ended up in Britain and therefore began making British films. But essentially I always make the same film, wherever and however I'm working. All my films – *Saturday Night and Sunday Morning, Night Must Fall, Morgan, Isadora* – are about a central character who is in some way on the edge of sanity, seen partly from his or her own point of view, partly, none too sympathetically, from the outside. It's obsessive, so that it turns out that way even when, as in *Night Must Fall*, the subject was not initially my own choice'.[10] Then, as a necessary corollary, he also admitted: 'I don't think there is much of my Czech sensibility in my films ... I do feel myself to be an outsider in both these countries. So I suppose there is a kind of cool touch to the movies – a kind of outsider's view. It's also something perhaps which has made me identify with outsiders – with people who are outside society. All my films have been portraits of people who are in one way or another not acceptable to society, either as heroes or villains or whatever. But I've never made films about spokesmen or typical people. It's always been edgy people who've been ill at ease with their world'.[11]

Like many exiles and outsiders, Reisz was able to balance an emotional investment in his adoptive country with the ability to remain critically distanced enough to recognize and then de-familiarize the cultural tropes that make it tick. It's hardly surprising then that, speaking specifically of Morgan's political insecurities, Reisz admitted that 'The character seemed very relevant to me, since I had had a left-wing youth myself in Czechoslovakia, an allegiance swiftly broken by the Soviet-inspired purges there in 1947–50. Morgan's type has a nursery full of idealistic and ideological toys: it could have been crucifixes, it just happened to be Lenin and Trotsky. In adult life he finds them totally useless. It seems to be extremely germane to the way young people are now'.[12] Because ideology is manifested through representations, and because representations are reproduced through processes of production and circulation, a de-familiarization of these mechanisms through self-reflexive aesthetics helps to disclose the constructed nature of ideology itself. Thus, according to Althusser, 'What art makes us see, and therefore gives to us in the form of "*seeing*," "*perceiving*" and "*feeling*" (which is not the form of *knowing*), is the ideology from which it is born, in which it bathes, from which it detaches itself as art, and to which it *alludes*'.[13]

Because they are concerned with baring representations as ideological devices, one could argue that all of Reisz's films are Althusserian by their very nature.

Although Reisz's directorial career spanned forty-five years, he produced a mere nine features, two filmed television plays and two groundbreaking documentaries. 'There's no real reason for it', Reisz admitted to Brian McFarlane in a 1992 interview. 'I'm lazy. I don't find the process very enjoyable. I think it is very hard to make a film. And I have sometimes had to abandon projects because I felt I couldn't cast them. My films tend to be portrait films that revolve around a central character. There is a sense of tension and ambiguity between the *persona* of the specific actor cast in the central role and the part he plays. This is often the subject of my films. So when I haven't been able to cast a central role ideally, I've sometimes abandoned the project'.[14] Despite his relatively meagre output it would still be fair to place Reisz among the seminal figures in postwar British cinema, both as a film-maker and, as we shall examine in the next chapter, as a film writer (his early 1950s theory and criticism was at least on a par with, if less polemical than, the work of his fellow auteur theorists, Gavin Lambert and Lindsay Anderson).

Along with Anderson, Tony Richardson, Robert Vas and Lorenza Mazzetti, Reisz was a founding member of the independent Free Cinema 'movement' which attacked the prevailing parochial values of post-war British cinema (specifically Ealing comedies and Gainsborough costume dramas) with a vigorous commitment to everyday working-class subject matter and a uniquely personal film style. Deeply indebted to the poetic realism of Humphrey Jennings and the urban immediacy of Italian neo-realism (as opposed to the sociological, 1930s documentary tradition of John Grierson), Reisz's Free Cinema films, *Momma Don't Allow* (1956, co-directed with Tony Richardson) and *We Are the Lambeth Boys* (1959) laid the basis for a unique hybrid form of 'poetic social realism', a director-driven documentary-like style that culminated in the international success of Reisz's first fiction feature, *Saturday Night and Sunday Morning* (1960) starring Albert Finney. *Momma Don't Allow* (the title was derived from the lyrics of a popular skiffle song of the period) was an attempt to rehabilitate youth culture in the wake of the negatively framed Teddy-boy phenomenon through a sympathetic look at the Wood Green Jazz Club (actually a hired room in a North London pub featuring the music of the Chris Barber Jazz Band) and its predominantly teenage patrons. As Reisz's programme note pointed out, 'We felt free not to disapprove of Teddy-boys, not to patronise shop girls, not to make sensational or hysterical a subject which is neither (but is almost always shown so)'.

We Are the Lambeth Boys is a revealing look at the Alford House Youth Club in South London's predominantly working-class area of Kennington. The film features teenagers 'puttin'' on the agony, puttin' on the style' in their Saturday night dances, discussing pressing issues of the day such as the death penalty (no need to worry there – almost all the lads are 'hang 'em and flog 'em Tories'), while struggling to face (or avoid) a future of mind-numbing routine in monotonous jobs. At this time (1958–59), Reisz was also involved with the burgeoning New Left and its journal, *Universities and Left Review*, which subsequently merged with the *New Reasoner* to form the *New Left Review* and was initially edited by the Jamaican-born Stuart Hall, soon to be a key voice in the nascent field of cultural studies and postcolonial theory. This led in turn to Reisz becoming active in the Campaign for Nuclear Disarmament (CND). Along with Lindsay Anderson, Christopher Brunel, Charles Cooper, Allan Forbes and others, Reisz was one of the so-called 'production assistants' (read: cameramen/film-makers) on *March to Aldermaston* (1959), the documentary record of the 1958 CND Peace March to the now-infamous nuclear facility west of London.

Despite earning a well-deserved reputation in the field of documentary, the Free Cinema group had intended to make dramatic fiction films from the start, not documentaries. As Lindsay Anderson later recalled,

> In fact I would say our interest in films was always very much more to do with the fictional and dramatic approach ... But we weren't able to make them because at the time when we started making films it was impossible for new directors to work in British cinema, which was profoundly conservative. So in our small ways we started making films which were documentaries, which are always easier to make. I think the characteristics of the kind of films we tried to make were that they were much less theoretically political; they were much more concerned with human beings as individuals and as characters, and perhaps more concerned to be what I would call poetic than to be instruments of propaganda.[15]

Certainly Reisz's first two features followed this dictum to the letter and, along with Tony Richardson's *Tom Jones* (1963), proved to be career-making vehicles for the young Albert Finney. Adapted by Alan Sillitoe from his eponymous novel, *Saturday Night and Sunday Morning* is the quintessential 'kitchen sink' drama. It features the boozy, womanizing factory worker Arthur Seaton (Finney) as a rebel without a cause living the high life in industrial Nottingham while trying to stave off the entrapments of adult responsibility. His married mistress (Rachel Roberts) is pregnant with his child, while his upwardly mobile girlfriend, Doreen (Shirley Anne Field) promises a dismal future of semi-detached suburban life with deadly mortgage payments and yet more babies.

Despite run-ins with local censors (the film was actually banned by the Warwickshire County Council), *Saturday Night and Sunday Morning* was a critical and box-office success and the film's returns helped to finance Lindsay Anderson's own feature debut, *This Sporting Life* (1963), which Reisz produced.

The latter's second feature with Finney was supposed to be a film about the nineteenth-century Australian bandit, Ned Kelly (eventually realized by Richardson, with the Rolling Stones' Mick Jagger in the title role), but when location shooting proved to be prohibitively expensive, the pair quickly accepted an offer from MGM to remake the 1937 thriller, *Night Must Fall*. Adapted from Emlyn Williams's successful London stage play, Finney stars in the original Robert Montgomery role as the psychopathic Danny, a charming bus boy who has already committed one murder (he keeps the decapitated woman's head in a hatbox as a portable trophy) and proceeds to insinuate himself into a country house and 'seduce' the inhabitants. Reisz attempted to expand the 'penny dreadful' psychoanalysis and *grand guignol* dramatics of the original by rooting Danny's psychosis in concrete social conditions, but as Finney noted at the time, 'We meant to stick to sociology, but that damn head in the hatbox proved too powerful'.[16]

Reisz's response to the disappointing critical and box-office reception of *Night Must Fall* was a complete change of pace, for with its free-wheeling slapstick style, fast motion sequences and swinging London milieu, *Morgan* was more akin to Mack Sennett's Keystone Kops or Richard Lester's Beatles films than the gritty urban realism of Free Cinema and *Saturday Night and Sunday Morning*. As we have seen, David Warner plays Morgan Delt, a mentally deranged, alienated communist with a passion for gorillas who struggles to de-Stalinize his working-class mother. Morgan also fights the class war on a second front as he attempts to win back his aimless upper middle-class ex-wife, Leonie (Vanessa Redgrave) from the pretentious bourgeois clutches of her art dealer fiancé, Charles Napier (Robert Stephens). To add insult to injury, Napier also happens to be Morgan's dealer. As Morgan's subversive actions border on the anarchic, culminating in the disruption of Leonie's wedding reception while wearing a gorilla suit, he finds it increasingly difficult to discern the difference between fantasy and reality. The film ends with Leonie pregnant with his child as she visits Morgan in a mental institution, his revolutionary spirit heavily medicated but ultimately undimmed.

Reisz's next project was *Isadora* (1968), a film biography of the revolutionary dancer and Modernist free spirit Isadora Duncan (Vanessa Redgrave in a *tour de force* performance). The film uses a fractured flashback structure to create a dialectic between Isadora's youthful commit-ment to free love and the liberating effects of beauty and art, and the self-deprecating, more embittered fatalism of the present-day (1927), as she dictates her memoirs while in pursuit of a handsome Bugatti driver who will ultimately lead to her death by accidental strangulation. Using the chaotic mosaic of Isadora's memories as their narrative guide, Reisz and his screenwriters, Melvyn Bragg and Clive Exton, create a subjec-tive weave of Eros and Thanatos, idealism and cynicism, as they trace the dancer's career from American vaudeville to the avant- garde stage of revolutionary Russia, taking in a wide variety of lovers along the way. Although Reisz's original three-hour edit was cut by fifty minutes with the director's 'unwilling help', the film's video release features a restored director's cut of 153 minutes, allowing us to appreciate his original vision.

Following the enforced cutting of *Isadora* by Universal Pictures (it was released in truncated form in the United States as *The Loves of Isadora*), a disillusioned Reisz suffered through two abortive projects – adaptations of John Le Carré's *The Naïve and Sentimental Lover* and André Malraux's *Man's Fate* – before directing Chekhov's one-act play, *On the High Road* (1973), for BBC television. It would be six years after the release of *Isadora* before Reisz successfully teamed with screen-writer James Toback to produce his next feature, *The Gambler* (1974), a flawed but incisive portrait of an obsessive gambler. James Caan's Axel Freed teaches English in a New York City College by day, lecturing on Dostoyevsky and Nietzschean will-to-power as a theoretical justification of his own gambling addiction. By night he is in debt to the mob to the tune of $44,000. Freed borrows from his mother to pay the debt, but immediately flies to Las Vegas with his girlfriend (Lauren Hutton) in an attempt to double his money. Driven by a mixture of *amor fati* and sheer ego, Axel wins big at the craps tables but at the same time loses an equal amount betting on college and NBA basketball games. Pressured by the mob, Axel recruits one of his students, a basketball star, to shave points while playing against the college's cross-town rivals in order to square his debt. Fuelled by a mixture of self-hatred and high adrenalin, Axel then risks his own life by stage-managing a fight with a Harlem pimp and a prostitute, which culminates in his face being slashed with a knife. As he examines the brutal wound, a faint smile crosses his face: he has beaten the odds yet again. Freeze-frame.

Although the film was a commercial failure, Reisz's incisive direc-tion on *The Gambler* sufficiently impressed United Artists to entrust him with the film version of Robert Stone's National Book Award-winning novel, *Dog Soldiers* (released in the United States as *Who'll*

Stop the Rain, 1978), a dark meditation on the decline and corruption of the drug-based counter-culture in the wake of the Vietnam War. The director was immediately attracted to Stone's novel because, as he put it, 'it's a damn good *story*. It changes in unexpected ways and takes you into worlds you didn't know existed – what we used to call a rattling good yarn. Some of my best experiences in the movie theatre as a viewer have been with "The American Storytelling Cinema" – genre films like *They Live by Night, Force of Evil, Act of Violence, Treasure of the Sierra Madre*, and a lot of the [John] Ford films. They are defined by narrative confidence, which is a very American – and not European – tradition. My other films are single-character studies, so I was very tempted to have a go at one of these'.[17] One might expect the result to be Reisz's most traditionally American film – a case of plot driving character, rather than the reverse – but *Dog Soldiers* turns out to be a deconstruction of the action-hero genre, where traditional values of personal justice and strict loyalty are destroyed by a corrupt new world fuelled by a drug economy ruthlessly hostile to spiritual ideas. Nick Nolte's hippy Zen warrior is ultimately overmatched by the perverse currents of the Nixon era (the film is uncannily prescient of the corruption of Reagan and Iran-Contra), leaving the moral playing field open to Michael Moriarty's more passive pragmatism.

Reisz's 1981 film of John Fowles's *The French Lieutenant's Woman*, a self-reflexive novel about a doomed nineteenth-century love affair, is a model of creative adaptation. In true Brechtian fashion, Fowles's existential book comments on itself as it unfolds, culminating in three different endings designed to satisfy the demands of three different genre expectations. Reisz and his scriptwriter, Nobel Prize Winner Harold Pinter, overcame the cinematic limitations of this uniquely literary device by telling the story in a parallel double register, cross-cutting the melodramatic Victorian love story between the scarlet woman, Sarah Woodruff (Meryl Streep), and bourgeois archaeologist, Charles Smithson (Jeremy Irons), with modern-day actors – and adulterous lovers – Anna and Mike (also Streep and Irons) who are playing the period roles for a new movie. The modern love story thus plays out in counterpoint with the 'filmic' fiction, so that life comes to imitate art, and vice versa, albeit with radically opposed results. In their own different ways, both sets of characters become slaves to genre expectations, harnessing their individual will-to-power to a controlling fictional deceit (this *Madame Bovary*-like trope is a common theme in Reisz, as we have seen), fuelled by an almost gothic romanticism.

The director's second foray into filmed biography, *Sweet Dreams* (1985), features another artistic free spirit – ill-fated country singer Patsy

Cline (Jessica Lange) – only in this case the film is structured chronologically as a series of counterpoints between the singer and her ne'er-do-well second husband, Charlie Dick (Ed Harris). Comparisons to Michael Apted's *Coal Miner's Daughter* (1980), the filmed life of Loretta Lynn and her relationship with an equally unfaithful husband, are perhaps inevitable, but in the latter film Tommy Lee Jones's Doolittle is an active force in promoting his wife's career. Charlie in contrast lacks agency, living vicariously (and not a little jealously) through Patsy's short-lived success. The resultant fissure between compelling art and creative vacuum is never resolved, leaving Charlie at the film's end mourning Patsy's tragic death without any clear idea of what his own future holds.

Reisz's final feature, *Everybody Wins* (1990), was adapted by Arthur Miller from his own play, *Some Kind of Love Story*, his first screenplay since 1962's *The Misfits*. Nick Nolte is Tom O'Toole, a Connecticut private eye hired by the beautiful and charming Angela Crispini (Debra Winger), who claims to have crucial information that could free a man unjustly convicted of murder. Not only do the authorities have the wrong man, but the case also hints at corruption and cover-up at the highest levels of state government. Unfortunately for Tom, as he falls under Angela's seductive spell he gradually discovers that she has a personality problem – three of them in fact, each seemingly unknown to the others. As Tom delves deeper into the corrupt underbelly of the community – the main suspect is an ex-drug runner biker turned religious fanatic; the DA turns out to be Angela's ex-; even the presiding judge has designs on her – the logic of the case explodes into a series of Machiavellian alignments in which ultimately 'everybody wins' except the truth and Tom, who is left shaking his head at the corrupt absurdity of it all.

For the want of interesting and commercially viable film projects, the 1990s saw Reisz return to the theatre (he had previously directed James Woods, JoBeth Williams and Sam Waterston in John Guare's *Gardenia* in 1982 at the Manhattan Theater Club in New York), where he directed an award-winning production of Terence Rattigan's *The Deep Blue Sea* (1993), several plays by Pinter (*Moonlight*, 1995, *A Kind of Alaska*, 1998, *Ashes to Ashes*, 1998–89, *Landscape*, 2001), as well as Samuel Beckett's *Happy Days* (1996) with Rosaleen Linehan at the Lincoln Center's Beckett Festival. This extremely fruitful stage period culminated in a filmed adaptation of Beckett's *Act Without Words I* (2000) for Channel 4's 'Beckett on Film' series. Starring Sean Foley as an unnamed everyman stuck without water in a studio-bound desert, the 1956 drama takes the form of a balletic mime as the character is 'locked' into the space by an invisible wall. Life-saving water and other useful props are tantalizingly dangled by wires from the rafters but just far enough out of reach that Foley expends more energy trying to grab them than if he had passively accepted his fate. The play ends with no resolution other than an expression of humans' life-affirming spirit in the face of the overwhelming absurdity of existence, an apt metaphor perhaps for Reisz's oeuvre as a whole. Once affectionately described by director Stephen Frears as 'The last great man in England', Karel Reisz died in November 2002 at the age of seventy-six from a blood disorder following a six-month illness.

Notes

1 Karel Reisz, interviewed by Eva Orbanz, Helmut Wietz and Klaus Wildenhahn, in Eva Orbanz, *Journey to a Legend and Back: The British Realistic Film* (Berlin, Edition Volker Spiess, 1977), p. 58.
2 Anonymous, 'David Mercer on Why He Writes the Plays He Does', *The Times*, 27 July 1966, p. 6.
3 Karel Reisz, interviewed 11 December 1969, in Alexander Walker, *Hollywood, England: The British Film Industry in the Sixties* (London, Harrap, 1974 and 1986), p. 311.
4 Philip French, 'Alphaville of Admass', *Sight and Sound*, Vol. 35, No. 3, Summer 1966, p. 110.
5 John Guare, quoted in Andrew O'Hagan, ed., 'Karel Reisz Remembered', *London Review of Books*, Vol. 24, No. 24, 12 December 2002. Accessed 27 January 2005. www.lrb.co.uk/v24/n24/mult03_.html.
6 Andrew Sarris, 'Metaphor in Search of a Movie', *Village Voice*, 9–15 September 1981, p. 49.
7 Peter Wollen, 'The Last New Wave: Modernism in the British Films of the Thatcher Era', in Lester Friedman, ed., *Fires Were Started: British Cinema and Thatcherism* (Minneapolis, University of Minnesota Press, 1993), p. 37.
8 Alan Lovell, 'Film Chronicle', *New Left Review*, No. 7, January–February 1961, p. 52.
9 Interpellation for Althusser was a form of 'hailing'. Language positions the individual into a situation of passive response to the cry, 'Hey you!', so that our reply, 'Who me?', inevitably constructs us as an ideological subject into a pre-existing system of relations that we are powerless to control.
10 Karel Reisz, quoted in John Russell Taylor, 'Tomorrow the World: Some Reflections on the Un-Englishness of English Films', *Sight and Sound*, Vol. 43, No. 2, Spring 1974, p. 82.
11 Karel Reisz, quoted in Gordon Gow, 'Outsiders: Karel Reisz in an Interview with Gordon Gow', *Films and Filming*, Vol. 25, No. 4, January 1979, p. 13.
12 Reisz, quoted in Walker, *Hollywood, England*, p. 311.
13 Louis Althusser, 'A Letter on Art', *Lenin and Philosophy and Other Essays*, trans. Ben Brewster (London, New Left Books and New York, Monthly Review Press, 1971), p. 222.
14 Karel Reisz, interviewed October 1992, in Brian McFarlane, *An Autobiography of British Cinema* (London, Methuen, 1997), p. 479.
15 Lindsay Anderson, interviewed by Eva Orbanz, Gisela Tuchtenhagen and Klaus Wildenhahn, in Orbanz, *Journey to a Legend and Back*, p. 41.
16 Albert Finney, interviewed 16 September 1971, in Walker, *Hollywood, England*, p. 148.
17 Karel Reisz, quoted in Leigh Charlton, 'Who'll Stop the Director', *Village Voice*, 23, 4 September 1978, p. 63.

2

When one comes to consider films which attempt a more rigidly authentic approach to reality, it becomes obvious that here the director must be mainly in charge. The great films of the sound period – *The Grapes of Wrath, Le Jour Se Lève, Bicycle Thieves* – are all essentially 'directors' films. (Karel Reisz)[1]

It's no exaggeration to say that the *Sequence* group changed the whole way of feeling and thinking about film in England – at any rate for a few inspiring years. (Tony Richardson)[2]

Ideology is not acquired by thought, but by breathing the haunted air. (Lionel Trilling)[3]

Given his lifelong affinity for outsiders and exiles, it is clear that Reisz's personal background is crucial to any understanding of his cinema, not only because of his own exile from Nazism and subsequent displacement into a foreign culture, but also, like the directors of the French New Wave, because of his graduation into film-making from the academic world of film criticism, a realm largely alien to many of the veterans of the British film industry. It would thus behove us to examine facets of both Reisz's early life and career in more detail.

Karel was born on 21 July 1926 in the mill town of Ostrava in north-central Czechoslovakia, a few hours' walk from the southern Polish border. At the age of twelve he was sent to England as part of the Quakers' Kindertransport Programme (Children's Transport) because his father Josef, a Jewish lawyer, was fearful of the threatened Nazi invasion of the Sudetenland. Unbeknown to Reisz at that time, his escape was abetted by a young British stockbroker, Nicholas Winton (b. 1909), often referred to as the 'British Schindler', a man so modest that he kept his activities secret for another fifty years.[4] In late 1938, Winton visited Prague at the invitation of a friend at the British Embassy and was asked to help in the newly constructed refugee camps. Appalled by the overcrowded conditions and troubled by the impending Nazi invasion, he set up an office in his room at the Wenceslas Square Hotel and tried to extricate as many children to the safety of Britain as possible. Although overwhelmed by requests from concerned parents, Winton established the organizational blueprint of the Kindertransport in Prague in early 1939 before leaving for London to deal with the necessary bureaucracy at the British end. This necessitated persuading the London Home Office to issue a visa, find a foster family and provide a £50 guarantee for each child (no small change in those days), as well as raising cash for the train journey from central Europe. By the time war was declared on 3 September 1939 Winton had arranged for 669 children to escape on eight sealed trains, passing clandestinely through Germany to the Hook of Holland, and then on by boat to England. A smaller group of fifteen children were flown out to Sweden. Unfortunately, a last train, crammed with 250 children, was due to leave the day Britain entered the war and it never left Prague station. The children were never seen again. Among the children rescued was Karel Reisz, who met Winton for the first time forty-five years later at a teary-eyed reunion of the survivors. 'I had never heard of him', Reisz admitted. 'I thought the Red Cross had organised it. I took my children and grandchildren – I think it brought it alive to them to learn where their grandfather came from. It was very emotional'.[5]

Young Karel was sponsored by the Quaker-run Leighton Park School in Reading, where his brother Paul had been boarding since 1936. According to Reisz's second wife, the American actress Betsy Blair, the school had been chosen by their Uncle Franz over Harrow and Mill Hill schools 'because they don't beat the boys'.[6] The headmaster, Edgar Castle, encouraged Reisz to retain the name Karel instead of his mother's proposed assimilationist 'Charles' and also bought him a bicycle. Of course, under the emergency circumstances of the Kindertransport, Reisz was forced to leave his parents behind in Ostrava and it wasn't until the age of eighteen that he learned of their ultimate fate in Auschwitz concentration camp. In 1944 he joined the Czechoslovakian wing of the RAF as a fighter pilot but the war ended before he could see action. The following year he was repatriated to Czechoslovakia with his military unit but managed to gain a leave of absence to attend Emmanuel College, Cambridge, where he studied natural sciences, specializing in chemistry.

Politically, Reisz had been sympathetic to the left in his teens, but the Stalinist coup in Czechoslovakia in 1947 quickly left him disenchanted with the western European Communist parties and their stubborn affiliation to the Moscow party line (this, remember, was a full nine years before the British New Left's own political awakening following the Soviet suppression of the Hungarian Revolution in November 1956). After graduation Reisz remained in England, teaching at the Grammar School of Marylebone in London between 1947 and 1949. It was the latter experience, rather than organized politics in the form of strict party membership, which proved to be his formative political experience:

> Coming straight from university, the whole impact of that outside world was very, very strong. It was probably the first kind of wider community life I'd come across at all; for though I'd been happy at boarding school and university, I'd felt totally encapsulated there. Teaching was my first taste of social reality: and you can't deal daily with working-class youngsters and their parents in their own habitat and retain an archaic view of the lower classes as comic relief or criminals, the roles they traditionally filled in British films. Nor could you regard them as documentary statistics: no one has a greater contempt for these, and all the denial of diversity they imply, than the man or woman whose back is to the blackboard.[7]

Questioning Reisz on his Marylebone experience in *Punch* in 1961, Philip Oakes noted with amusement that the teacher 'maintained discipline by shouting, but he still has a recurrent nightmare in which he shepherds sixty small boys through north London to their football pitch. "It was, and still remains," he says, "my idea of hell."'[8] Despite his obvious ambivalence, it is clear that his experience as a teacher formed an indelible mark on Reisz, particularly the need to treat the working class with respect and to give them an opportunity to voice their own opinions and fears without excessive editorializing (a goal only partly realized in his subsequent Free Cinema outings, *Momma Don't Allow* and *We Are the Lambeth Boys*, as we shall see in the next chapter). 'He talks constantly of wanting to make films which are "civilized,"' notes Oakes, 'and ... his purpose as a film-maker is akin to Lindsay Anderson's, "... to make ordinary people feel their dignity and importance so that they can act from their principles."'[9]

By 1950 Reisz had abandoned formal teaching, venturing on a career in film criticism. Although his most notable work was his hugely influential 1953 book, *The Technique of Film Editing* (which, with an update by Gavin Millar, is still in print to this day), from 1950 to 1952 Reisz also wrote numerous articles and reviews for the Oxford University Film Society magazine, *Sequence* – he co-edited the final issue with Lindsay Anderson – and the British Film Institute's (BFI) *Sight and Sound* (1950–58), which at that time had been revitalized under the aegis of *Sequence* co-founder, Gavin Lambert, and his eventual successor as editor, *Sequence* alumna Penelope Houston. During 1951–52, while working at the British Film Academy, Reisz also wrote a pair of scholarly articles on the creative role of the Hollywood producer ('The Showman Producer') and the filmic adaptation of novels ('Substance into Shadow') for the annual Pelican paperback series, *The Cinema* (formerly *The Penguin Film Review*), edited by Roger Manvell and R. K. Neilson Baxter. (See the Bibliography for a complete list of Reisz's critical publications.)

How deep is the connection between Reisz's film theory and criticism and his own ideological self-evaluation as a class-conscious educator and his subsequent work as a film and theatre director? Firstly, it's important to dispel any misconception that Reisz and his peers saw a clear-cut division between cinema as an intellectual and artistic 'discipline' as opposed to a commercial and industrial 'craft' or 'business'. As Reisz explained to the London *Times* in 1960,

> This distinction between the 'intellectual' critic who starts making films and the director who graduates in the traditional way from the cutting room or from being an assistant director or cameraman is often rather misleading. It would be difficult to find any more 'intellectual' directors than people like Robert Hamer and Alexander Mackendrick, who have grown up in the industry, while on the other hand many of the outside people, the ex-critics, would have much preferred to be working practically in the industry if they had had the chance. For instance, when I came down from Cambridge I would have liked nothing better than to go and work for a few years in a cutting room, but I just couldn't; there was unemployment in the industry and no opening for new workers, so I became a critic instead. But if I had been able to do as I wanted, you would be thinking of me now as on the other side of the fence, a trained technician from inside the industry rather than an 'intellectual' from outside ... Basically what matters, I think, is a passion just for doing things with film, for using a camera, and having film in one's hands, manipulating it – which is a very different thing from just being vaguely interested in making a film.[10]

Secondly, because of their shared polemical interests, it's often very difficult to separate Reisz's evolving critical voice from those of Anderson and Lambert, not only because he was a latecomer to *Sequence*'s roster of writers – the magazine's political and aesthetic stance was already well established by its Oxford undergraduate founders – but also because Reisz's more measured, scholarly 'voice' tended to be overshadowed (if not overwhelmed) by the more wilful and strident rhetoric of his colleagues.[11] In fact, *Sequence* (like the subsequent Free Cinema 'movement') was deliberately doctrinaire and undemocratic from its inception. As Brian McFarlane points out in his invaluable survey of the magazine's development, although *Sequence* was handsomely produced, nobody got paid (including contributors) and it remained a largely inbred, amateur enterprise: 'amateur in its history, its distribution, and its sense of owing allegiance to nothing except its editors' sense of what they believed in and valued about cinema'.[12] Lambert concurs, noting that, 'In an early editorial, Lindsay announced that *Sequence* welcomed (unpaid) contributions "from anyone, on any aspect of the cinema, written from any point of view." In fact we never published anything that we disagreed with, which was why we wrote most of the articles and reviews ourselves'.[13] In short, the editors chose what should be in the journal and then decided who should write it. We can thus safely say that Reisz must have concurred with this editorial consensus otherwise he wouldn't have been invited to write for *Sequence* in the first place.

This collective accord was expressed through both negative and positive polemics. A recurring complaint in the magazine's pages was the domination of the British entertainment industry by the Americans, and its obvious corollary: the failure of British cinema to produce films of an authentic (read: working-class) national character. The ideological implications of the latter were made clear in numerous articles attacking British producers who turned out 'mid-Atlantic' product to compete with Hollywood and confused commercial success with true art (Gainsborough and Rank being the usual targets) as well as the inflated patriotism of postwar British films, especially in the work of Michael Powell and David Lean. There was begrudging praise for Carol Reed (*The Fallen Idol*, 1948, received widespread approbation), while Reisz's acknowledged 'intellectuals', Mackendrick and Hamer, invariably escaped the magazine's usual invective against home-grown talent. As Reisz later pointed out, 'You have to remember that British films were heavily dominated by country-house comedies, patriotic war epics and period melodramas. They were not concerned with contemporary British life – the changing realities were largely ignored. You have to remember, too, that this was the time of Italian neo-realism, which engaged passionately with contemporary life ... There was nothing remotely equivalent in British cinema. The British cinema seemed to us out of touch with what was going on, and stiflingly class-bound: it was due for a radical shake-up ... the general level of filmmaking was very provincial and airless'.[14] Similarly, traditional British documentary of the Grierson School – which may have been expected to provide a more self-consciously ideological perspective – was attacked for its dull didacticism and stodgy sociology, as well as, more importantly, its collective (as opposed to personal/auteurist) mode of production.

Largely ignoring the economics of film as a business (there were no articles, for example, on studio mergers and their impact on film production; no statistical analyses of exhibition and distribution), *Sequence* instead concentrated on cinema as an *art* form, as opposed to Grierson's idea of film as public education. As Anderson declared in *Sequence* No. 3, 'What is required is a cinema in which people can make films with as much freedom as if they were writing poems, painting pictures or composing string quartets'.[15] In effect, *Sequence* advocated a Leavis-ite criticism, with film replacing the study of English as '*the* supremely civilizing pursuit, the spiritual essence of the social formation'.[16] Like F. R. and Queenie Leavis and their fellow contributors to *Scrutiny* in the 1930s, the magazine stressed personal vision and style over a specific message and underlined the importance of a vibrant arts (and criticism) to the health of the broader culture. 'There is no reason to demand that every film should be a work of art', argued Lambert. 'The output of bad novels and bad plays is equally high, and the important factor is that the kind of mass relaxation accepted by any society is a pointer to the condition of that society, that mass pleasures are formed by habit, and that a debased standard of popular entertainment is dangerous both to social ease and artistic vitality'.[17]

For the editors, film had a social duty to uphold the quality of life, and the bulk of this responsibility fell on the shoulders of the film's director. He/she was seen as the medium's creative driving force, taking on the hybrid role of author-as-poet. Consequently, as Reisz notes, most of the issues of *Sequence*, 'were built around a long central article about an individual director – Ford, Carné, early Hitchcock, Disney, and so on. Much of the emphasis was on American cinema. This was a time when most literate writing on the cinema was pretty patronising about Hollywood. Russian and German silent films and French cinema were the canon of "serious" film criticism. *Sequence* concentrated on the movies we enjoyed at the Odeon – musicals, Disney, Ford, Preston Sturges, and so on'.[18] The main strength of the journal lay not in its *theoretical* base – as McFarlane rightly notes, *Sequence* was far removed from the theory-laden, semiotic approach of *Cahiers du Cinéma* or *Screen* in the 1970s, or even André Bazin's ontological theories of film published between 1945 and 1951[19] – but in its enthusiasm for good films, Hollywood or otherwise: 'All we basically knew was that we cared about personal films', recalled Lambert, 'not official ideas of "art," and *Sequence* was partly a series of love letters to directors we admired, partly a succession of hate-mail against work we despised'.[20] The focus was thus on 'emotional truth' and the compatibility of cinema style with content rather than the promotion of an aesthetic theory for its own sake – for example, *Screen*'s 1970s Althusserian-cum-Lacanian approach.[21]

In addition to the lionization of specific contemporary films – George Rouquier's *Farrebique* (France, 1946), Arne Sucksdorff's *People in the*

City (Sweden, 1947), Georges Franju's *Blood of the Beasts* (France, 1949) – most critical attention was paid to specific auteurs, with the surrealists Luis Buñuel (*L'Age d'Or*, 1930) and Jean Vigo (*L'Atalante*, 1934), poetic realist Humphrey Jennings (*Fires Were Started*, 1943; *A Diary for Timothy*, 1943–45) and Anderson's personal favourite, John Ford (especially *She Wore a Yellow Ribbon*, 1949) leading the pack because of their deep personal vision. Moreover, a focus on auteurs also necessitated a detailed discussion of *style*, for as Anderson was quick to point out, 'with a poetic artist like Ford, style is the essence'.[22] Reisz and the editors' position can best be summed up in Anderson's effusive paean to *My Darling Clementine* (1946), which featured prominently on the cover of *Sequence* No. 2:

> There was a particular warmth, a particular familiarity about the handling of the traditional atmosphere and the traditional themes. The images were masterly, the music perfectly evocative. But none of these easily identifiable excellences, singly or together, seemed really to explain the magic of the film. This emanated rather from a quality altogether more elusive and more profound, some kind of moral poetry. I knew of course that poetry could not be defined. But something impelled me to try. So I began to have some glimmerings of what is, after all, the essence of cinema: the language of style.[23]

As if to underline the point that moral poetry *is* style, Anderson attacked the highbrow press for its critical myopia, reminding his readers that, 'If you have forgotten that poetry, visual as well as verbal, is its own justification, you will call *L'Atalante* sordid and obscure and join the critic of "The Times" in condemning *My Darling Clementine* to "the graveyard of mediocrity."'[24] Not that all films by a common auteur received equal praise. *Fort Apache* (1948), Ford's first entry in the so-called 'cavalry trilogy', was vilified for its poor script, cinematography and acting, reinforcing the editors' position that the discerning critic should focus as much on distinguishing between first- and third-rate films by esteemed directors as on ferreting out artistic gems from unexpected (read: lowbrow, avant-garde or B-movie) nooks and crannies.[25]

Reisz's first major article for *Sequence* was a thoughtful analysis of *La Terra Trema* (1948), Luchino Visconti's lyrical neo-realist fable about Sicilian fishermen exploited by commercial wholesalers and boat owners. Radically different from Visconti's subsequent operatic mannerisms in *Senso* (1953) and *Rocco and His Brothers* (1960), the film's understated poetry seems tailor-made for promoting the magazine's editorial stance that cinematic style and content should fuse to form something original and strikingly individual, literally a whole greater than the sum of its parts (a critical precursor to the subsequent Free Cinema dictum that,

'A style means an attitude. An attitude means a style'). Reisz begins his analysis by acknowledging the difficulty of expressing the theme of extreme poverty, as it entails stepping outside one's own social milieu, 'to make, as it were, a film from the outside. There is the danger that the director may remain too distant from his material, may never subjectively grasp the effects of hunger and poverty'.[26] Sergei Eisenstein's *The General Line* (1929) falls into this trap with its patronizing, 'flippant atmosphere', while Robert Flaherty's *Man of Aran* (1934) 'over-prettifies' *La Terra*'s similar theme of man's eternal struggle against the sea: 'The imposition of an irrelevant pictorial style ... brings out a sort of "picturesque peasant" attitude to poverty which is little short of an impertinent sophistication', complains Reisz.[27] Visconti, an aristocrat by birth and seemingly the last person who would identify emotionally with his film's subject matter, 'avoids all these pitfalls by bringing a style to his subject, which, in spite of a continual emphasis on pictorial values, is never less than relentlessly realistic'.[28] There is no forcing of pace, few imposed dramatic climaxes. Instead 'a most penetrating feeling for situation, rather than a consciousness of dramatic highlights, dominates the style. Firm, finely observed, magnificently (and only in some rare instances too consciously) composed, Visconti's handling is that of a compassionate, sensitive observer'.[29]

On the other hand, the film's commitment to absolute verisimilitude is ultimately at the expense of filmic *art*. The film turns out to be a little *too* slow, a bit *too* harrowing, much like an objectively rendered Pathé newsreel or documentary. 'One wonders whether obeying the demands of realism to such an extent must not finally cause the director to lose control over the material and thereby indirectly lessen the film's final impact', notes Reisz. 'Unlike *The Grapes of Wrath*, with which *La Terra Trema* might reasonably be compared, there is here none of the skilful variation of dramatic tension, none of the subtly controlled pathos'.[30] Once again Ford is held up as the apotheosis of style for the sake of critical comparison because he is unafraid to manipulate concrete reality for the sake of poetic effects that might lead to a higher truth (another future watchword for Free Cinema). The touching farewell scene between Ma and Tom Joad in *The Grapes of Wrath*, for example, is probably more emotionally and ideologically authentic *because* of the hermetic claustrophobia derived from its obvious studio artificiality than in spite of it. Ultimately, *La Terra Trema* comes close to true poetry but falls into the trap of transparent mimesis. As Reisz concludes, 'The film is a deeply felt, compassionately told chronicle rather than a completely realised artistic achievement'.[31]

This lionization of Ford (and other Hollywood auteurs such as John

Huston, Preston Sturges, Charlie Chaplin and Frank Capra, who were considered to be of comparable status) is all well and good but what about the more problematic case of directors working within the commercial Hollywood studio system who didn't have control over their choice of scripts or hadn't yet reached the status of producing their own films? In 'The Showman Producer', Reisz's brief but incisive article for *The Cinema 1951*, he bucked the *Sequence* trend by approaching the subject from the other side of the coin, arguing that the voice of the director or writer is largely irrelevant in the context of the average Hollywood commercial film. In this case 'authorship' is almost entirely the responsibility of the producer. This raises another key question: is it possible for a producer to impose a personal style on a specific film or, more importantly, leave his signature on an entire body of work? Reisz argues that it is, and more often than not it is the producers – powerful creative voices personified by Samuel Goldwyn, Walter Wanger, Stanley Kramer and Arthur Freed – who exhibit a consistency of style across a studio-produced oeuvre rather than specific directors or screenwriters.

A good example is Louis de Rochemont (1899–1978), the former originator and Executive Producer of the *March of Time* documentary series from 1935 to 1943, who subsequently produced *The House on 92nd Street* (Henry Hathaway, 1945), *13, Rue Madeleine* (Hathaway, 1946), *Boomerang!* (Elia Kazan, 1947) and *Lost Boundaries* (Alfred Werker, 1949). Reisz correctly notes that these four documentary-like films, 'bear obvious affinities to factual reportage; in their sober, efficient dramatisation of real events, they are all quite distinguishably the work of a single controlling personality'.[32] In contrast, if we examine the other studio work of these films' varying directors and writers, we find little or no individual personality or stylistic consistency. To underline his point, Reisz then cites another group of films, describing them as follows: 'All these films show a markedly consistent dramatic atmosphere. They are without exception elegant, most efficiently mounted melodramas, all dealing in one way or another with themes of sadism. Most of them are concerned with the lives of neurotic, utterly amoral characters, and display a sophisticated attitude to extreme violence. There is a peculiarly vicious sting in [these] films, easily identifiable by the connoisseur'.[33] He could easily be describing the oeuvre of director Don Siegel (*The Killers, Madigan, Dirty Harry*), but he is actually discussing several films produced by Hal B. Wallis and directed by a wide range of Hollywood studio technicians including Lewis Milestone, Anatole Litvak, William Dieterle, Robert Siodmak and Anthony Mann.[34] Once again, the writers' and directors' larger resumés show no sign of consistent theme or poetic style, leaving Reisz to conclude that 'in the normal American commercial film it is the producer who sets the standard of excellence and who determines the stylistic approach to a subject. Litvak, Mann, Siodmak and countless others contribute their technical skill but little more'.[35] Even the work of a quality director like Jules Dassin can be improved by a forceful producer with a real aesthetic vision. Thus Dassin's *The Naked City* (1948) and *Brute Force* (1947), directed for Mark Hellinger, are significantly better than his crude thrillers for other producers – namely *Thieves' Highway* (1949) and the British-made *Night and the City* (1950).

Another more problematic case is the well-regarded Hollywood studio director who appears to have developed a distinct visual style but is hamstrung by the fact that he doesn't originate his own projects. A strong argument has been made (mostly by the French critics, Roger Leenhardt and André Bazin) that places William Wyler among the great artists of cinema. In 'The Later Films of William Wyler' (*Sequence* No. 13), a far more critical Reisz instead describes him as a 'technician-director' rather than a true author, although he is quick to point out that, 'It need hardly be said again that to make this distinction between the artist-director and the technician-director is not necessarily to differentiate between the director who writes his own scripts and the one who does not'.[36] The *Cahiers du Cinéma* critics believed that the latter distinction separated the true auteur from the so-called *metteur-en-scène* (directors, like Joseph Losey, who adapted pre-existing material through a distinctive visual style). Reisz and his colleagues refused to acknowledge this separation of form and content. Indeed, Reisz later described himself as an *artist*-director who just happened to be dependent on the writer/text for his raw material (with the exception of James Toback and Bob Getchell's original scripts for *The Gambler* and *Sweet Dreams* respectively, all of Reisz's features derive from literary and dramatic sources).

Wyler is a good candidate for *metteur-en-scène* analysis because so many of his films were adaptations of successful plays. How far does Wyler the technician serve his material beyond creating a form of filmed theatre, and to what extent does he impose a visual style that works in counterpoint to the play's dramatic intent? 'Opinions and personal tastes are apt to vary on the subject of filmed theatre', notes Reisz:

> The purist would have it that the cinema, by its very nature, rejects the use of stage dialogue, that the compression and simplification permissible in a stage play is unnecessarily cramping on the screen. Such theories need, however, to be tested on the evidence of actual films. Broad movement, so often to be held one of the essentials of genuine cinema, is not, surely, an absolute necessity. If a director can sustain interest by other means, if he can evolve a method which uses (the necessarily

more static) stage conventions and stage dialogues without surrendering expressive pictorial values, he is surely entitled to do so. To call his work 'theatrical' is, then, to recognise a style, rather than to imply a weakness.[37]

Wyler's adaptation of Lillian Hellman's *The Little Foxes* (1941) exemplifies this argument, for his preference for long takes, deep focus and very few close-ups produces 'a brilliantly apt fusion between pictorial style and writing'.[38] For Reisz, however, one of Wyler's major shortcomings was his tendency to over-dramatize individual scenes at the expense of the narrative whole, creating a lop-sided emotional effect that threatens to blunt character conflicts and overwhelm the nuances of plot development: 'What consistent "attitude" there is in his work shows itself in his predilection for the big scene rather than in his ability to treat a situation on its own merits. Where the material is suitable – *The Little Foxes* – that is, of course, Wyler's strength: he can bring an intensity to his scenes unequalled by any contemporary director. Where it is not – *Mrs. Miniver, The Heiress* – it is his downfall and demonstrates an inflexibility of approach which is the mark of a limited sympathy and imagination'.[39]

On a more theoretical note, Reisz also critiques the applicability of Bazin's theory of deep focus and long takes in Wyler's films as a democratization of space which allows the spectator freedom to choose what (s)he wants to see within the *mise-en-scène* as a particular sequence unfolds. 'It is entirely untrue to say that cuts destroy smooth continuity', argues Reisz.

> An 'almost effortless flow of the scene' does not necessarily require long takes. To say that deep images make for more interesting compositions *and* to say that it gives the spectator freedom to turn his attention to what he wishes, is a contradiction: the purpose of composition is, surely, to *direct* the spectator's eye, to express an emotional concept by pictorial means. Toland's camerawork is so effective in *The Best Years of Our Lives* because it gives the illusory sense of an absence of 'direction' which is precisely suitable to the contemporary urgency of the subject ... To label this 'neutral' direction is to ignore the purposive composition of the images: the director is quite plainly 'intervening' between the actor and the spectator.[40]

Wyler's problem is that having discovered deep focus he uses it as a fixed technique when conventional shot/reverse shot cutting would be more suitable (e.g. in *The Heiress*, 1949), yet another reinforcement of Reisz's ongoing dictum that style should be tailored to fit content.

Writing in *Sight and Sound*, Reisz finds similar shortcomings in the work of the theatre-turned-film director, Elia Kazan, whose predilection for uninterrupted long takes reinforces the temporal continuity of the actor's performance, as if it were taking place in real time on a theatrical stage. Citing *Panic in the Streets* (1950) as a prime example, Reisz acknowledged that the film's semi-documentary thriller style, shot entirely on location in New Orleans, added conviction to the melodramatic material, but noted that it is as a thriller that the film is least successful. Kazan crowds his backgrounds with significant detail so that we become distracted by the over-determined bric-a-brac of the locale. Moreover, the cast are 'visually overblown and theatrical', reinforced by Kazan's use of long takes, which keep the actors on screen for as long as possible without a cut. 'Throughout the film, one recalls Kazan's theatrical background', argues Reisz. 'The scenes are scripted and executed as more or less self-contained one-act plays, each with a beginning, a build-up and a climax ... But these isolated scenes never fuse into a whole: the necessary sense of continuity throughout the film is lacking'.[41] This echoes Reisz's similar complaint against Wyler, but it is particularly problematic in a film where the race against the clock is the key to building suspense: 'This Kazan fails to convey; the structure of the script is too fragmentary, the continuity not sufficiently clearly established to suggest the inexorable approach of the story's zero hour'.[42] In short, the long takes completely undermine tension in the action and chase sequences, so that the film's dramatic denouement is ultimately undercut by Kazan's slavish adherence to ontological continuity.

It's clear from the above analyses that Reisz saw 'realism' as something more than the mere spatio-temporal unity of an event (what Bazin calls 'concrete duration', where the essence of a scene's 'reality effect' demands the simultaneous presence of two or more factors within the continuity of the shot, as opposed to the 'abstract time' of montage) and was not averse to using editing creatively – whether seamlessly in the traditional Hollywood style or calling attention to itself through jump-cuts and temporal ellipses.[43] Indeed, as we discussed in the Introduction, Reisz felt that editing may be used effectively to undercut the spatial integrity of the *mise-en-scène* (and the characters' performative immersion within its ontology) in order to open a critical space for objective evaluation of ideological and cultural forces.

Although Reisz always used an outside editor to cut his own films, as a critic he was well equipped for such an evaluative task because of his first-hand knowledge of editing principles and techniques. Between February 1950 and June 1951, for example, he wrote eight regular columns on the subject for *Sight and Sound*, as well as a critical review of Eisenstein's technical treatise, *Film Form*. Then, as Reisz recalls, 'The British Film Academy advertised for someone to collate the views of distinguished British editors and directors, to produce a textbook on film editing. I got the job. It was to be a straightforward factual kind of book, not critical, more like a primer of film editing'.[44] The Academy hired Reisz in part because he had no practical editing experience of his own. Instead they 'wanted to find a journalist as Boswell to a lot of senior British directors and editors'.[45] The objective was to pick the brains of a number of film technicians but unfortunately only Thorold Dickinson (himself a talented editor and scriptwriter before turning to directing with *Gaslight*, 1940 and *The Queen of Spades*, 1949) followed through. Reisz was forced to sift through the mountain of material himself. For almost two years he ran films by D. W. Griffith, Erich von Stroheim, David Lean and Jules Dassin through the Moviola, taking them apart and putting them back together again to see how they 'worked'. When the Academy ran out of funds, Reisz finished the book on his own time for a share of the royalties. Although the book was subsequently trans-lated into Polish and Russian – 'For the Poles, at least, he is a sort of Anglo-Saxon Kuleshov', wrote the London *Times*[46] – it's important to note that the book, published in 1953 as *The Technique of Film Editing*, is *not* Reisz's academic response to the Soviet montage theorists or Bazinian realism: 'The book is built around an analysis of sequences from actual films', notes Reisz. 'It doesn't aspire to any sort of theory of montage'.[47]

Which is not to suggest that Reisz lacked fiercely held theoretical opinions. Firmly echoing Vsevolod Pudovkin's belief that 'editing is the foundation of cinematic art', Reisz constantly laments expressive montage's fall from grace since the end of the silent era: 'The tradi-tion of expressive visual juxtaposition, which is characteristic of the best silent films, has been largely neglected since the advent of sound. It will be one of the main arguments of this book that this neglect has brought with it a great loss to the cinema'.[48] Following Pudovkin, Reisz argues that editing involves three separate but interdependent functions: 1) The choice of camera set-ups, bearing in mind how they will be assembled in the final film; 2) The timing of shots to get the best dramatic effect; 3) The choice of series of shot juxtapositions – i.e. the expressive flow of images within the filmic whole. 'Here the editor is no longer solely responsible', Reisz reminds us. 'Writer, director, and, to a lesser degree, cameraman and sound crew must be integrally involved, and it will become almost impossible to assign credit to any single individual'.[49]

It's not insignificant that, echoing *Sequence*'s auteurist position, Reisz feels that the power of montage should always be under the creative aegis of the film's director: 'It is he who is responsible for planning the visual continuity during shooting, and he is therefore in the best position to exercise a unifying control over the whole production. This implies that he must also be in charge of the editing and be allowed to interpret the material in the cutting room as he visualised it on the floor'.[50] The best creative balance of poetic film-making thus tends to come from writer–director collaborations, for example the early films of Marcel Carné and his screenwriter, Jacques Prévert – *Jenny* (1936), *Drôle de Drame* (1937), *Quai des Brumes* (1938) and *Le Jour se Lève* (1939) – where the former sketched in the main lines of the visual and narrative continuity while the latter wrote the dialogue to fit this prearranged framework. For Reisz, the reverse method leads to static and overly wordy films.

Unfortunately, the latter vice is more symptomatic of today's films than the former. Pudovkin's earlier dictum has begun to ring hollow: 'Shots are joined together as smoothly as possible in order not to distract from the actors' performances. The modern editor's chief preoccupation is indeed primarily with smoothness (cutting his shots in such a way as to make the shot-to-shot transition almost imperceptible), and with timing his cuts so as to give the sequence a tempo appropriate to its mood'.[51] To make matters worse, Pudovkin himself has become one of the worst culprits, as guilty as Kazan in giving too much preference to a static *mise-en-scène* in order to fetishize and reify the actor's performance. Reisz cites Pudovkin's *Zhukovsky* (1950), a fawning biography of the Soviet aeronautics pioneer, as a prime example. The film is almost completely constructed around the verbose dictates of the great man, shot with a static camera and accentuating every word. Indeed, the camera almost never leaves the actor. 'That Pudovkin, the director who at one time preached more vehemently than anyone else the importance and virtues of the montage method, should suddenly surrender completely to the easy way out – making the actor do all the work and letting the camera merely watch – is a sobering thought indeed ... In making a film for primarily non-aesthetic reasons, Pudovkin has discarded all the forms of presentation which are aesthetically valid in the cinema. As a result, all the life has ebbed out of his film and it remains a dry piece of academicism'.[52]

Reisz instead makes an impassioned plea in another column 'for the creatively edited, visual sequence in which dialogue plays only a secondary role. This is not to say that the visual sequence is in some way better, more "climactic" than the dialogue scene. It is simply to stress that the primarily visual sequence can be made to evoke a range of emotions which are different in kind from those conveyed by the dialogue scene. If you are not convinced, go and see *Louisiana Story* again'.[53] More importantly, Reisz also argued that editing style should always fit the film's specific genre and narrative content so that, for example, comedies would require a different montage than thrillers, while the documentary as straight reportage would be cut differently from the imaginative documentary (e.g. Flaherty and Dovzhenko) or the non-fiction film of ideas (Basil Wright and Humphrey Jennings).

Here again, Reisz's views diverged significantly from Bazin. 'The primitive slapstick comedies, especially those of Keaton, and the films of Chaplin, have much to teach us on this score', notes the French theorist. 'If slapstick comedy succeeded before the days of Griffith and montage, it is because most of the gags derived from a comedy of space, from the relation of man to things and the surrounding world. In *The Circus* Chaplin is truly in the lion's cage and both are enclosed within the framework of the screen'.[54] The gag is thus predicated on the fact that the audience is convinced that Chaplin really is in danger both as a character and possibly as an actor. Reisz, in contrast, believes that audience credulity is a secondary issue (i.e. that comedic 'truth' is not ontological but a wilful artifice, a creative construction). Presaging his own subsequent approach in *Morgan*, he argues that, 'In a comedy ... it is often not necessary to convince the spectator of anything; it is only necessary to make him laugh. If this involves a harsh cut, a faulty piece of continuity or any other unrealistic distortion, then that may be all to the good. The funniest films are often those in which the editor has been absolutely ruthless in his disregard for reality and concentrated solely on extracting the maximum of humour out of every situation'.[55]

In light of the Free Cinema films to follow, Reisz's views on documentary are of obvious interest here. In the case of newsreel-like reportage, editing *is* the film. Whereas the story-film is primarily concerned with the development of a *plot*, the documentary film is concerned with the exposition of a *theme*. 'The interpretation of a theme is so much a matter of fine personal judgments', states Reisz, 'that to spread the responsibility for writing, direction and editing between three separate individuals would be to impair the film's unity: it would, for example, be nonsensical to allot the editing of a documentary to an independently working editor – as is often done with story films in Hollywood – for the acts of direction and editing are merely two stages of one creative process'.[56] Consequently, the director's skill is essentially that of an editor, and the latter process must by necessity begin long before the footage actually enters the cutting room: 'It is precisely through the purposeful selection and editing of the natural material that a convincing and significant impression of reality can be achieved'.[57]

In the case of the so-called 'imaginative documentary' – typically works by Dovzhenko, Flaherty, Joris Ivens and Basil Wright that probe beneath the surface of objective reportage in order to convey the emotional overtones and significance of natural themes – the chief problem is to produce a poetically satisfying continuity. Focusing specifically on Flaherty, Reisz discerns two main creative processes in this genre. The first priority is the selecting of the primary material, whose artistic arrangement often defies rational criticism:

> The whole complex atmosphere of the opening sequence of *Louisiana Story* is conveyed by such emotionally varied images as the still close-ups of flowers and birds, calm yet menacing shots of the alligator, and swift electrifying glimpses of a water snake. Individually, these shots convey at best only a minute fraction of the overall feeling; in juxtaposition they convey the whole awe-inspiring, magic-yet-real atmosphere of the forest. Further than this, there is little that can profitably be said. Here, one is discussing factors which are so closely dependent on the individual aesthetic judgment of the artist as to make any hard-and-fast theoretical discussion useless and indeed meaningless.[58]

The second part of the process is the organization of the shots into a series of expressive shot juxtapositions. This is conditioned by the required atmosphere, so that specific points of detail remain the decision of individual artists, feeding his or her overall vision.

Reisz's final documentary category, the non-fiction 'film of ideas', is the closest to the Free Cinema ideal and warrants some detailed scrutiny. In his February 1951 *Sight and Sound* column, Reisz discusses the curious fact that Eisenstein's famous associative montage of attractions from the 1920s has had so little lasting influence on film practice. Reisz suggest that this is partly because contemporary films are character-driven, creating exposition through the performative and psychological register of continuous narrative. Eisenstein's methods are innately unsuitable to the portrayal of characters: 'his films express ideas and the reactions of groups of people to these ideas; they only very rarely touch on personal dramatic conflicts ... Eisenstein's aim was to affect the spectator more directly: his way was to evolve more intellectually appealing continuities and let the spectator receive the ideas, as it were, straight from the director'.[59] Thus the Menshevik leader of the Provisional Government, Aleksandr Fyodorovich Kerensky, is less a real person or character in *October* (1927) than an abstract *signifier* of the odious nature of the bourgeois upstart – literally the *idea* of the pompous mechanical peacock against which he is clumsily juxtaposed in Eisenstein's dialectical montage. The main problem with such a symbolic association is that it is inherently undramatic (not to mention non-psychological) and difficult to assimilate into a smoothly unfolding film narrative where *character* development is paramount. Instead Reisz welcomes the introduction of sound into Eisenstein's later films as it forced him to generate a more contrapuntal relationship between sound and image and thus create a more complex dialectical synthesis.

For Reisz, this more sophisticated 'film of ideas' is best exemplified not through Eisenstein but rather via Basil Wright's *The Song of Ceylon* (1934) and Humphrey Jenning's *A Diary for Timothy* (1943–45). With its juxtaposition of images of native life with the clearing of the jungle and the superimposed sounds of trains, typewriters and people dictating letters,

> The theme of *Song of Ceylon* is the essential duality of life in Ceylon: on the one side the Western influence; on the other, the traditional behaviour and life of the Sinhalese. The theme itself is, in this sense, peculiarly well suited to the treatment. Wright uses – not altogether consistently – the sound and picture to evoke respectively the two different aspects of life in Ceylon. Throughout Reel 3 we are shown in the picture the routine of native life in Ceylon and in the sound-track the sounds associated with the Europeans who control it – as if unseen forces were guiding the natives' lives. It is only by making the rhythm of the sound-track conform to the rhythm of the images that a kind of physical unity is preserved.[60]

One of the obvious strengths of *The Song of Ceylon* is Wright's trust in his audience to do the necessary didactic work themselves through a more 'felt' response to sound–image relationships than through the obvious alternatives – Eisenstein's over-determined 'relational' editing or, more conventionally, voice-over narration.

The latter is a particularly sticky subject because the commentary invariably smacks of 'the voice of authority', imposing a convenient master narrative on otherwise disparate material, all the better to reinforce the film-maker's worldview. Interestingly, Jennings – the documentary darling of the *Sequence* and Free Cinema group, as we shall see in the next chapter – invariably utilized a commentary, but often to surprisingly poetic effect. As Reisz notes in his 'Editing' column, 'Jennings succeeded uniquely in his films in combining the personal values of the artist with the clear exposition of ideas. He was able, as well as any one, to construct a sequence purely by "editing" ... yet, in most cases, where he wanted to conduct an argument, he guided the spectator with a commentary. *Diary for Timothy* states its "argument" in the commentary but the visuals give it more than mere illustrations. The commentary and visuals, through a subtly contrived and timed interweaving pattern, alternately comment on each other: neither is the primary source of appeal and there is no repetition of statement'.[61]

A perfect illustration of Jennings's masterful technique in *A Diary for Timothy* can be seen in the sequence which seamlessly inter-cuts, through both image and sound, a performance of *Hamlet* at London's Haymarket Theatre with two men talking in the canteen about the deadly range of Hitler's V2 rockets: 'The inter-weaving pattern in the continuity creates an effect which is not to be described in words, for the final impact on the spectator is more complex than the mere reception of two parallel events: the construction and timing of the images fuse the two events in the spectator's mind in a manner only possible in the cinema. The passage, in other words, is so purely cinematic that a description of the way it achieves its effect cannot begin to describe the effect itself'.[62] Thus when Hamlet asks the Gravedigger: 'Ay, marry, why was he sent into England?' and the latter replies, 'Why, because he was mad: he shall recover his wits there ...', the dialogue appears to comment on the discussion in the canteen. Reisz perceptively notes that the unity between the two actions is emphasized by *smoothing out* the transitions between them, not by dialectical shock or counterpoint: 'In this way the two scenes are knit together so closely as to come over to the spectator as a complex but homogeneous continuity. In contrast with the Eisenstein approach to editing, the cuts do not so much make points themselves; they switch the argument about and keep it going at different levels'.[63]

Jennings's strength was that he realized that for complex ideas to be expressed it is not necessary to rely on images or sound alone, and that commentaries need not be voices of authority (i.e. they can act *connotatively* rather than denotatively, what Roland Barthes calls semantic 'relay' rather than 'anchor' functions). 'The point really is that Jennings's commentaries are always suggestive, never descriptive', states Reisz. They 'almost invariably deal with universals while his images deal with particulars'.[64] For Reisz this is clearly the way the intellectual film essay should develop in future, in effect sounding the death knell for relational editing: 'It may be – at least, until someone makes a film to prove the contrary – that a more complex intellectual argument cannot be expressed though "relational editing" alone; that, in fact, Jennings's approach is the one ideally suited to the expression of the intellectual film essay. It may be, that the method of "relational editing", hitherto held to be a universally applicable method for the purveyance of ideas in the film medium, is an unnecessary complication which the sound cinema has outgrown'.[65]

For Reisz, the sound cinema was principally a medium for expressing the psychology of *character*. One of the more consistent threads running through his film criticism is his passionate belief in the synchronicity between film style – editing, *mise-en-scène*, camera movement – and the role of the actor (reinforced in turn by good casting) in serving the cause of expressing and furthering character development. This is at the root of Reisz's dislike for Kazan's theatricality. Discussing what he calls the 'inflated virtuosity' of Kazan's technique in *Man on a Tightrope* (1953), Reisz admits, 'He succeeds in some cases in getting remarkable performances from his players, but in a way that makes one feel he is "good with actors" rather than that he has a real, a direct response to character'.[66] Instead, Reisz's directorial role model is John Huston – *The Maltese Falcon* (1941), *The Treasure of the Sierra Madre* (1948), *The Asphalt Jungle* (1950), *The African Queen* (1951) – and many of the future director's own ideas concerning actors seem to have been taken (unconsciously or otherwise) straight from the pages of his *Sight and Sound* interview with Huston in 1952.

Reisz notes that Huston appears to be a director who eschews cinematic style – his conception of film is primarily literary, and any discernible poetry comes from intelligent improvization on the studio floor. In fact, Huston claims that he does not 'direct' actors at all: 'The trick is in the writing and casting. If you cast the right people, using only good actors, and adjust the script to suit the actors you've chosen, then it's best to leave them to work out their own gestures and movements. Your job is to explain to them the effect you want and your skill lies in being able to do that exactly and vividly. Then, if they're good actors, it's best not to interfere in *how* they get your effect across – you'll only throw their natural performance out of gear if you try'.[67] Twenty-seven years later, in a 1979 *Films and Filming* interview with Gordon Gow, Reisz echoes Huston's comments, almost to the letter: 'Once the shooting starts, it is the relationship with the actor that is the mainspring for me. I never know where to put the camera until I've rehearsed the scene. It springs for me, after the script is done, out of that collision between what the actor can do and the way the character is conceived'.[68] And again, discussing the making of *Sweet Dreams* in 1985: 'To the actors, I never say do this or do that. I tell them what is important, and they get to do it their own way'.[69] Reisz makes a point of never imposing camera movement onto the action for the sake of dramatic punctuation, but instead lets kinaesthetics arise organically from the actors' movements observed during rehearsals, 'so the basic strokes come out of the text and the actors' feelings and intuitions. There's nothing as useful as a good actor's itch to move!'[70] This allows the film's moral (and by extension didactic) force to come out of the characters themselves, which in turn springs out of performance and situation rather than being grafted on from the outside.

An excellent example is *Umberto D.* (1952), Vittorio de Sica and Cesare

Zavattini's devastating social realist study of a retired civil servant on a fixed pension, Umberto D. Ferrari, and his dog Flick who are evicted from their Roman apartment because he has fallen behind with his rent. Forced into the streets, the pensioner first fakes an illness in order to live rent-free in hospital, turns to panhandling and finally attempts suicide, only to be distracted from the onrushing train by his beloved dog. For Reisz, the film is a model of its kind, for 'reality is not observed for the social facts it may reveal, but for its own sake – for, in Zavattini's phrase, "the love of reality", the joy and pain of observing human beings as they are'.[71] The film's non-professional actors are asked not to act but simply to 'be'. Although some of the scenes demanding strong emotional reactions find some of the players wanting and the dramatic pacing is often painfully slow, 'there is behind them a kind of passionate identification with the characters' human predicament which creates an extraordinary concentration. De Sica has brought his subject to the screen with a direction which springs from an inner conviction and faith in his characters. It gives the film, in spite of faults in execution, the unmistakable authority and completeness of a masterpiece'.[72] Reisz concludes with the ultimate compliment, describing *Umberto D.* as 'an experimental film' on a par with Visconti's *La Terra Trema*, Jean Renoir's *The River* and John Ford's *Wagonmaster*, films which employ a discursive approach to character that isn't directly dependent on dramatic narrative – 'they make their points through obliquely relevant passages of observation rather than through an organised dramatic pattern'.[73] This eschewal of causal drama in favour of moral character is an obvious forerunner of Reisz's own technique in *Saturday Night and Sunday Morning*, where he adapts the pre-existing anecdotal structure of Alan Sillitoe's source novel to construct a series of character vignettes that use Arthur Seaton as a reflection of his social situation without resort to external ideological editorializing.

Compare the above with Reisz's negative evaluation of Juan Antonio Bardem's widely acclaimed *Death of a Cyclist* (1955), where moral revolt fails to spring internally from character. A socially critical film made under the nose of the repressive Franco regime, *Death of a Cyclist* tells the story of Juan, a university professor and his socially well-connected mistress who run down a worker on a bicycle while out driving. Fearful that their illicit affair will be discovered, they drive off, leaving the man to die. The film scores most of its political points by contrasting the lifestyles of the rich and poor districts of Madrid, but state censorship forced Bardem to punish the adulterous woman in a contrived, melodramatic ending. Reisz savages the film for familiar reasons: 'Employing an ostentatious, rather hysterical editing style, Bardem's continuity covers a great deal of ground but does not allow him to get close enough to his central characters. Juan ... emerges as a sort of theoretical good man, lacking the authority the part demands: his moral revolt is grafted on to him by the director's conception, it does not spring from the character we see'.[74] Although Bardem is ruthlessly critical of the bourgeoisie, the film seems contrived and thin when dealing with the sector of society with which the film approves – Juan's mother, the students and the neighbours of the dead cyclist. In short, 'Bardem is more interested in the film's social implications than in the individuality of his characters. As a result the film makes its courageous and admirable gesture with a rather cold hand'.[75]

Reisz's tendency to focus on character and style over social context strongly echoes the *Sequence* party line of the period. Indeed, his predilection for close reading and detailed analysis of camera placement, movement and composition in relation to actors pushes much of his criticism dangerously close to formalism at times. In this sense his method is very much of its time – Clement Greenberg was producing similar formalist paeans to the New York School of abstract expressionist painters throughout the 1940s and 1950s – and provides us with an invaluable insight into the critical *Zeitgeist* of the period. However, by the same token, it would be a mistake to conclude that Reisz advocated cinematic poetry and form *at the expense* of politics and ideology. Indeed, *Sequence* and Free Cinema later came to incorporate many of the 'Griersonisms' that they had previously attacked – especially in their call for a more socially conscious realism and personal vision allied to the politics of the emergent New Left. In this context, Reisz's seminal political writings – 'Hollywood's Anti-Red Boomerang: Apple Pie, Love and Endurance Versus The Commies' (*Sight and Sound*, 1953) and 'Milestone and War' (*Sequence*, 1952) – are among his most insightful pieces. They are just as fresh and critically valid today (especially in light of the post-9/11 Patriot Act and the constant need to defend First Amendment rights, epitomized by George Clooney's 2005 film, *Good Night, and Good Luck*, detailing the media war between CBS journalist Edward R. Murrow and Senator Joseph McCarthy) as they were when they were first published in the general context of the Cold War.

Reisz begins the *Sight and Sound* essay by noting a huge increase in the number of anti-Communist films that had emerged from Hollywood over the previous six months (i.e. in 1953): 'They are, of course, not designed as public relations jobs for the United States, but that is, in effect, what they are'.[76] He observes that Nazis have now been replaced by Reds as the 'enemy du jour' and many of the actors who used to play *Gauleiters* are happily back at work playing Commies with similarly thick accents. Reisz dismisses many of the films – e.g. *The Red Danube* (George Sidney, 1949), *The Iron Curtain* (William Wellman, 1948) – as shoddy B-pictures that distort facts for political purposes: 'Their irresponsibility is applied to subjects which demand more serious treatment, but it is of a kind one has come to expect from Hollywood. On the whole, they are too unimportant to arouse much anger or protest, particularly since none of them is as blatantly dishonest as, say, the Soviet *Secret Mission*'.[77] However, the more numerous films about the communist menace within the United States are another matter entirely. Most of the films are less well-reasoned attacks on communism from an ideological or sociological perspective than formulaic thrillers in which the anti-communism element is introduced as a topical titbit for jaded audiences. The films' propaganda is therefore unsystematic and incidental to their main function as entertainment. They simply replace the hoodlums of the old gangster films – characters traditionally played by James Cagney, Edward G. Robinson and Paul Muni – with references to Commies, creating a system of paradigmatic exchange where one corrupt extreme stands in for the other instead of attacking the communist political system *as such*.

According to this easy formula, the American Communist Party is run by gang of cheap but diabolically clever crooks. Their only difference from 1930s bootleggers and gangsters is that their boss lives in the Kremlin instead of a Manhattan penthouse. Unlike their over-excitable Italian or Irish precursors, with their sentimental love for mom and the Catholic Church, Commies are hard, intellectual people, cold-blooded scientists who never form personal attachments. They have no observable private life and love is always treated with bitter disdain. Basically, there are only three ways that a normal person can become a communist: 1) He/she is temporarily discontented by a social injustice; 2) He/she is marked as Other – usually a Jew or black – but will probably leave the party in the last reel; 3) He is seduced by a conniving woman. Conveniently ignoring the Soviet Union's recent role in defeating the Nazis in World War Two, Commies are invariably depicted as closely allied to Fascists, many having come over to the Left from the German Bund. Even worse, they are anti-semitic and racist. They are almost never from proletarian backgrounds but usually blue bloods or *nouveau riche*. They therefore propagate the Moscow party line not for the sake of ideological principle but for private gain or a mania for power. They live in luxurious flats with modernist furniture and their larder invariably substitutes as a darkroom for developing microfilm. They raise money by organizing blind campaigns but end up keeping the money for themselves. Finally, once you're in the Communist Party, it's well nigh impossible to get out: they will blackmail you forever (the basic plot of *I Married a Communist/The Woman on Pier 13*). 'What makes these meretricious trimmings particularly objectionable is that they are attached to themes which demand serious treatment', bemoans Reisz who, following the Soviet take-over of Czechoslovakia, was no fan of Stalinism himself:

> Though obscured by ludicrous fabrication and bad scriptwriting, most of the contentions the films make about communists are distantly based on observed practice: communists in fact *do* violently denounce their stray sheep, *do* attract and exploit racial minorities, *do* organise fake campaigns. These things are worth reporting honestly and are 'dramatic' enough not to need the routine hoodlum patter ... And there is a practical objection too: they make anti-communism a kind of game which, being played to the rules of the penny dreadful, no one can take seriously.[78]

This game is particularly insidious when played out through the post-1945 war film – *Sands of Iwo Jima* (Allan Dwan, 1949), *Submarine Command* (John Farrow, 1951), *The Halls of Montezuma* (Lewis Milestone, 1950), *The Frogmen* (Lloyd Bacon, 1951), *Flying Leathernecks* (Nicholas Ray, 1951), *The Wild Blue Yonder/Thunder Across the Pacific* (Allan Dwan, 1951) – which Reisz sees as a new strain of gory, bloodthirsty and often inhumane action films that focus on heroism at the expense of moral self-evaluation and are clearly designed to re-fight World War Two through the distorting prism of Manichean Cold War *realpolitik*: 'It is the joy in war, the wholehearted acceptance of fighting as a desirable and admirable occupation, expressed by the recent Hollywood war films, that is open to protest. The blood-thirsty tone they adopt and the human values they assert invalidate any purpose that may be claimed for them'.[79]

Lewis Milestone comes in for considerable criticism on the latter point, particularly as his pre-Cold War films – most notably *All Quiet on the Western Front* (1930) – were exemplary in their moral even-handedness. Although for Reisz, Milestone was a director of variable talent and uneven subject matter, his war films were notable for their compassionate focus on the common recruit and his often brutal trial-by-fire in withering combat: 'Milestone brings to his war films the essential grasp of the big situation and the willingness to put over huge overwhelming effects directly', argues Reisz. 'He faces the devastating moments of horror and does not sentimentalise the occasional moments of peace and beauty. To each, his intensely personal, super-realistic style of conveying emotional stresses in compositions gives at once an individual poetry and a universal validity'.[80] Yet Milestone's latest entry into the genre, 1950's *The Halls of Montezuma*, exhibits the worst tendencies of clichéd tub-thumping and blatant war-mongering. It's significant that Reisz sees this as a symptom of Milestone's lack of personal vision, that in fact his films simply mirror the shifting *Zeitgeist* instead of taking a committed moral stand rooted in a concrete ideological stance. As Reisz notes, '*All Quiet on the Western Front*, *The Purple Heart* and *A Walk in the Sun* reflected, in their different ways, a gradual change of attitude which was representative of Western liberal opinion in general. In retrospect, one sees that Milestone's statements were not those of a reformer but of a spokesman for an intellectual climate. Perhaps *Halls of Montezuma* continues the process. If the haunted air of the cold war evokes in the same liberal groups the ideology of *Halls of Montezuma* then the thought is not depressing in the context of Milestone's career alone'.[81]

What is at stake here for Reisz, and what pushes his criticism beyond mere aesthetic discourse into the realm of moral and ethical necessity, is nothing less than a crisis of political commitment, exemplified by the necessity of finding a satisfactory hero – whether as a fictional character or the author of the text itself – who can stand up to the *Zeitgeist* (defined by Stalin, McCarthy or state terror in general) and make his ideological voice heard without compromise or distortion. Unfortunately, the precedents in both the American and British arts were not very promising, especially as the militant liberal of traditional popular discourse had proven to be a hopelessly unsatisfactory hero. 'Whether he is up against crooked fight promoters or unscrupulous editors, Hollywood producers or political racketeers, his fate is always the same', writes Reisz. 'The heroes of *The Harder They Fall*, *That Winter*, *The Producer*, *All the King's Men*, when faced with their particular authoritarian foe, rarely have the satisfaction of doing more than hissing an elaborate moral *Sucks-Boo!* into the boss's face and then getting the sack; alternatively, they sell out. None of them would be much good against the commies'.[82] Reisz bluntly argues that truly liberal or socialist western values are incompatible with a traditional dramatization through a militant action hero and 'must be allowed to emerge by the way, as standards implicit in a film's approach to its particular reality',[83] i.e. as a new form of social/poetic realism. 'And if the enemy has to be attacked direct, then let it be done honestly and with intellectual conviction'.[84] Which turns out to be a concise summary of the basic principles of Free Cinema, to which we now turn.

Notes

1 Karel Reisz, *The Technique of Film Editing*, Second Enlarged Edition with Gavin Millar (New York, Focal Press Ltd and Hastings House Publishers, 1968), p. 60.
2 Tony Richardson, *The Long Distance Runner: An Autobiography* (New York, William Morrow and Company, 1993), p. 93.
3 Opening quote from Karel Reisz, 'Milestone and War', *Sequence*, No. 14, New Year 1952, p. 12.
4 Winton's heroics are the subject of Czech director Matej Minac's documentary, *Nicholas Winton: The Power of Good* (2001). The film was scripted by Vera Gissing who, as a child, was also one of the beneficiaries of Winton's Kindertransport Programme. See also Muriel Emanuel and Vera Gissing, *Nicholas Winton and the Rescued Generation* (London, Vallentine Mitchell, 2002). For more on the Kindertransport, see Mark Jonathan Harris's Academy Award winning documentary, *Into the Arms of Strangers – Stories of the Kindertransport* (2000).
5 Karel Reisz, quoted in Louis Bülow, 'Nicholas Winton: Schindler of Britain'. Accessed 14 January 2005. www.auschwitz.dk/Winton.htm.
6 Betsy Blair, *The Memory of All That: Love and Politics in New York, Hollywood, and Paris* (New York, Alfred A. Knopf, 2003), p. 325.
7 Reisz, quoted in Walker, *Hollywood, England*, p. 36.
8 Philip Oakes, 'New Reputations: Karel Reisz, Break for Commercial', *Punch*, Vol. 240, No. 1299, 7 June 1961, p. 858. In a witty anecdote, director Clive Donner recalled an incident after the first screening of *We Are the Lambeth Boys* at the National Film Theatre (NFT), London. The teenage boys featured in the film turned up making 'a fearsome racket'. Ever the schoolteacher, Reisz mounted the stage and, with a not particularly convincing cry of 'Shut up everyone!', forced them into miraculous silence. Clive Donner, 'Memories of Karel', 'Directors Guild of Great Britain'. Accessed 21 January 2005. www.dggb.co.uk/publications/article12_127.html.
9 Oakes, 'New Reputations: Karel Reisz, Break for Commercial', p. 859.
10 Anonymous, 'From Free Cinema to Feature Film: Mr. Karel Reisz Talks About the Change', *The Times*, 19 May 1960, p. 18.
11 In all, fourteen issues of *Sequence* were published between 1946 and 1952, with Reisz joining the group for Issue 10 (New Year, 1950). Anderson co-edited twelve of the fourteen issues; Peter Ericsson co-edited eleven; Penelope Houston co-edited two before joining the BFI and subsequently editing *Sight and Sound* (from 1956); Gavin Lambert co-edited six; and Reisz co-edited the last issue with Anderson.
12 Brian McFarlane, '*Sequence*: "Saying Exactly What We Liked"', *Filmviews*, No. 135, Autumn 1988, p. 31.
13 Gavin Lambert, *Mainly About Lindsay Anderson* (New York, Alfred A. Knopf, 2000), p. 50.
14 Reisz, quoted in McFarlane, *An Autobiography of British Cinema*, p. 476.
15 Lindsay Anderson, 'A Possible Solution', *Sequence*, No. 3, Spring 1948, p. 9.
16 Terry Eagleton, *Literary Theory: An Introduction* (Minneapolis, University of Minnesota Press, 1983) p. 31.
17 Gavin Lambert, 'Your Critic – Right or Wrong!', in Roger Manvell, ed., *The Cinema 1952* (Harmondsworth, Penguin Books, 1952, reprinted New York: Arno Press, 1978), pp. 142–3.
18 Reisz, quoted in McFarlane, *An Autobiography of British Cinema*, p. 476.
19 See André Bazin, *What Is Cinema? Vol. 1*, trans. Hugh Gray (Berkeley and Los Angeles, University of California Press), 1967.
20 Gavin Lambert, 'Introduction' to Lindsay Anderson, 'John Ford: A Monograph', *Cinema*, Vol. 6, No. 3, 1971, p. 22.

21 *Sequence*'s non-academic formula paid obvious dividends insofar as it attracted luminaries such as director John Huston and cinematographer Douglas Slocombe as contributors to its pages.

22 Lindsay Anderson, *About John Ford* (London, Plexus, 1981 and 1999), p. 11.

23 *Ibid.*, p. 14. Reisz remained loyal to Ford throughout his career, always including one of the director's films among his Top Ten favourites. In *Films & Filming*'s 1963 survey it was *Young Mr. Lincoln* (1939), in *Sight and Sound*'s 2002 Top Ten he picked *They Were Expendable* (1945).

24 Lindsay Anderson, 'Angles of Approach', *Sequence*, No. 2, Winter 1947, p. 8.

25 McFarlane notes in particular the magazine's praise for MGM musicals, Robert Siodmak's *Criss Cross* (1949), Max Ophuls's *Caught* (1949), Richard Haydn's *Miss Tatlock's Millions* (1948), Michael Gordon's *The Lady Gambles* (1949), Harold Clurman's *Deadline at Dawn* (1946) and Irving Allen's *Strange Voyage* (1946) as typical examples of *Sequence*'s broad range of stylistic taste.

26 Karel Reisz, '*La Terra Trema*', *Sequence*, No. 12, Autumn 1950, p. 38.

27 *Ibid.*

28 *Ibid.*

29 *Ibid.*, p. 39.

30 *Ibid.*, p. 40.

31 *Ibid.*

32 Karel Reisz, 'The Showman Producer', in Roger Manvell and R. K. Neilson, eds, *The Cinema 1951* (Harmondsworth, Penguin Books, 1951), p. 161.

33 *Ibid.*, p. 163.

34 The films included *The Strange Love of Martha Ivers* (1946), *Sorry, Wrong Number* (1948), *Paid in Full* (1950), *The File on Thelma Jordan* (1949), *Rope of Sand* (1949) and *The Furies* (1950).

35 Reisz, 'The Showman Producer', pp. 163–4.

36 Karel Reisz, 'The Later Films of William Wyler', *Sequence*, No. 13, New Year 1951, p. 19.

37 *Ibid.*, p. 22.

38 *Ibid.*, p. 24.

39 *Ibid.*, p. 28.

40 *Ibid.*, pp. 29–30.

41 Karel Reisz, 'Editing', *Sight and Sound*, Vol. 19, No. 8, December 1950, p. 335.

42 *Ibid.*

43 For Bazin's argument, see 'The Virtues and Limitations of Montage', in *What Is Cinema? Vol. 1*, pp. 41–52.

44 Reisz, quoted in McFarlane, *An Autobiography of British Cinema*, p. 476.

45 Karel Reisz, letter to the author, 9 November 1989, in Georg Gaston, *Karel Reisz* (Boston, Twayne Publishers, 1980), p. 18.

46 Anonymous, 'Karel Reisz: Free Czech', *Films & Filming*, Vol. 7, February 1961, p. 5.

47 Reisz, quoted in McFarlane, *An Autobiography of British Cinema*, p. 476.

48 Reisz, *The Technique of Film Editing*, p. 15.

49 Karel Reisz, 'Editing', *Sight and Sound*, February 1950, p. 32.

50 Reisz, *The Technique of Film Editing*, p. 58.

51 Karel Reisz, 'Editing', *Sight and Sound*, February 1950, p. 32.

52 Karel Reisz, 'Editing', *Sight and Sound*, Vol. 19, No. 12, April 1951, p. 476.

53 Reisz, 'Editing', *Sight and Sound*, February 1950, p. 32.

54 Bazin, 'The Virtues and Limitations of Montage', p. 52.

55 Reisz, *The Technique of Film Editing*, p. 102.

56 *Ibid.*, p. 125.

57 *Ibid.*, p. 126.

58 *Ibid.*, p. 143.
59 Karel Reisz, 'Editing', *Sight and Sound*, Vol. 19, No. 10, February 1951, p. 415.
60 Reisz, *The Technique of Film Editing*, pp. 158–9.
61 Reisz, 'Editing', *Sight and Sound*, February 1951, p. 415.
62 Reisz, *The Technique of Film Editing*, p. 161.
63 *Ibid.*, p. 162.
64 *Ibid.*, pp. 162–3.
65 Reisz, 'Editing', *Sight and Sound*, February 1951, p. 415.
66 Karel Reisz, '*Man on a Tightrope*', *Sight and Sound*, Vol. 23, No. 1, July–September 1953, p. 32.
67 John Huston, cited in Karel Reisz, 'Interview with Huston', *Sight and Sound*, Vol. 21, No. 3, January–March 1952, pp. 130–1.
68 Reisz, quoted in Gow, 'Outsiders: Karel Reisz in an Interview with Gordon Gow', p. 17.
69 Karel Reisz, interviewed in Samir Hachem, '*Sweet Dreams*', *Horizon*, Vol. 28, No. 8, October 1985, p. 32.
70 Karel Reisz, quoted in Harlan Kennedy, 'Interview with Karel Reisz', *Film Comment*, Vol. 17, No. 5, September–October 1981, p. 30.
71 Karel Reisz, '*Umberto D*', *Sight and Sound*, Vol. 23, No. 2, October–December 1953, p. 88.
72 *Ibid.*
73 *Ibid.*
74 Karel Reisz, '*Death of a Cyclist*', *Sight and Sound*, Vol. 26, No. 1, Summer 1956, p. 32.
75 *Ibid.*
76 Karel Reisz, 'Hollywood's Anti-Red Boomerang: Apple Pie, Love and Endurance Versus the Commies', *Sight and Sound*, Vol. 22, No. 3, January–March 1953, p. 132.
77 *Ibid.*
78 *Ibid.*, p. 135.
79 *Ibid.*, p. 136.
80 Reisz, 'Milestone and War', p. 13.
81 *Ibid.*, p. 16.
82 Reisz, 'Hollywood's Anti-Red Boomerang', p. 148.
83 *Ibid.*
84 *Ibid.*

1 Percy struts his stuff beside the Alford House Youth Club cricket nets in Free Cinema's *We Are the Lambeth Boys*, the second in the Ford Motor Company's 'Look at Britain Series'

2 The Lambeth girls engage in some friendly banter with the lads at the beginning of *We Are the Lambeth Boys*.

42

3 Karel Reisz and cinematographer Walter Lassally set up a street scene for *We Are the Lambeth Boys*.

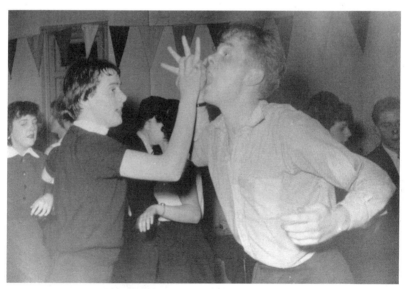

4 'Putting on the style' at London's Wood Green Jazz Club in Reisz's first Free Cinema short, *Momma Don' t Allow*.

5 'We don't care what Momma don't allow ... We're gonna' keep on dancin' anyhow!' Chris Barber's band gets the crowd boppin' in *Momma Don' t Allow*.

6 Brenda (Rachel Roberts) and Arthur (Albert Finney) enjoy a bit of casual adultery in Reisz's first feature, *Saturday Night and Sunday Morning*.

7 'Anybody would think you were ashamed to be seen with me'. Doreen (Shirley Ann Field) guilt trips Arthur into taking her to the fair in *Saturday Night and Sunday Morning*.

8 Murder most foul: Danny the psychopathic pageboy (Robert Montgomery) cuts off Mrs Bramson's telephone in Richard Thorpe's 1937 version of Emlyn Williams's classic thriller, *Night Must Fall*.

9 Mrs Bramson (Mona Washbourne) is seduced by Albert Finney's wily charms in Reisz's controversial 1964 remake of *Night Must Fall*.

10 Ideology wars: avid Trotskyist Morgan Delt (David Warner) gives his Stalinist mother (Irene Handl) a piggy-back ride across Highgate Cemetery in *Morgan: A Suitable Case for Treatment*.

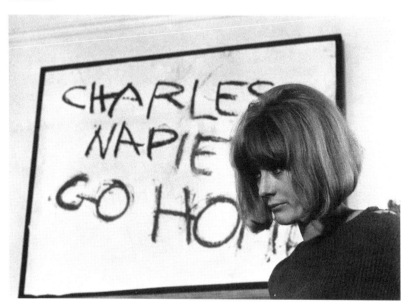

11 Leonie Delt (Vanessa Redgrave) examines some of her ex-husband's handiwork in *Morgan: A Suitable Case for Treatment*.

12 Karel Reisz directs Vanessa Redgrave during one of the Russian sequences in *Isadora*.

13 Tuck in your scarf! Isadora Duncan (Vanessa Redgrave) takes her last fateful ride with 'Bugatti' (Vladimir Leskova) in Reisz's ill-fated biopic, *Isadora*.

14 Feeling the juice: Axel Freed (James Caan) tries his luck at the Las Vegas craps tables in Reisz's first Hollywood feature, *The Gambler*.

15 Who'll stop the counterculture? Old Marine Corps comrades, newspaperman John Converse (Michael Moriarty) and merchant seaman Ray Hicks (Nick Nolte), hatch a heroin smuggling plot in *Dog Soldiers*.

16 Row your boat: Sarah (Meryl Streep) and Charles (Jeremy Irons) cement their blissful reunion on Lake Windermere at the conclusion of *The French Lieutenant's Woman*.

17 'You want a lot don't ya?' says a sassy Patsy Cline (Jessica Lange) to the sexually aggressive Charlie Dick (Ed Harris) after their first meeting in *Sweet Dreams*. 'Well, people in hell want ice water. That don't mean they get it'.

18 Between the blinds: Angela Crispini (Debra Winger) and Tom O'Toole (Nick Nolte) search for an illusive 'truth' in *Everybody Wins*.

Free Cinema and the New Left: *Momma Don't Allow* (1956), *We Are the Lambeth Boys* (1959) and *March to Aldermaston* (1959)

3

> As film-makers we believe that no film can be too personal. The Image speaks. Sound amplifies and comments. Size is irrelevant. Perfection is not an aim. An attitude means a style. A style means an attitude. Implicit in our attitude is a belief in freedom, in the importance of people and in the significance of the everyday. (First Free Cinema Manifesto)[1]

> The moment you reject the factor of interpretation you are actually rejecting your responsibility. (Karel Reisz)[2]

> A socialism that cannot express itself in emotional, human, poetic terms is one that will never capture the imagination of the people – who are poets even if they don't know it. (Lindsay Anderson)[3]

Given their common roots, the evolution from *Sequence* to Free Cinema, from Reisz's career as a critic to that of amateur film-maker, seems both logical and, with the 20–20 power of hindsight, smoothly preordained. The declaration from the first Free Cinema Manifesto excerpted above could quite easily have originated in *Sequence*'s editorial pages, while Anderson's retrospective summary of Free Cinema principles – 'Independent, personal and poetic'[4] – bears an uncanny similarity to the magazine's own definition of auteurism discerned in the work of pantheon directors such as Ford, Sturges and Buñuel. One might be forgiven then for thinking that Free Cinema and *Sequence* were cut directly from the same critical cloth. As one might expect, the truth turns out to be a little more complex. The actual phrase 'Free Cinema' was first coined in an eponymous article by TV and film director Alan Cooke in *Sequence* No. 13 (New Year, 1951), which discussed a programme of American and Canadian shorts curated by Olwen Vaughan at the New London Film Society in November 1950. The wide range of films included works by American independent film-makers – Maya Deren (*Meshes of the Afternoon*, 1943, *A Study in Choreography for Camera*, 1945), Curtis Harrington (*Picnic*, 1948, *On the Edge*, 1949), Kenneth Anger

(*Fireworks*, 1947) and Francis Lee (*1941*, 1941, *Le Bijou*, 1946) – two Canadian films by Norman McLaren (*La Poulette Grise*, 1947, *A Little Fantasy on a 19th Century Painting*, 1946), a Canadian fantasy, *The Loon's Necklace* (Radford Crawley, 1949), and Joseph Strick and Irving Lerner's *Muscle Beach* (1948). Eschewing the traditional term 'avant-garde', Cooke preferred to group the films under another heading, namely:

> Free Cinema – which has the advantage of being inclusive rather than exclusive, of indicating a genre to which we may credit all films which please or illuminate without compromise or self-mutilation. *Muscle Beach* is an example of free cinema, and so is *Fireworks*. So (amongst films discussed elsewhere in this issue) are *Wagonmaster*, *Les Dames du Bois de Boulogne*, *Orphée*. All these films, however diverse their intentions, have one achievement in common: an expressive and personal use of the medium. Free Cinema includes the acknowledged successes as well as the films *maudits*, the traditionalist as well as the experimentalist; it constitutes the real avant-garde, the true aristocracy of the cinema.[5]

In line with *Sequence*'s editorial stance, Cooke modelled Free Cinema on an eclectic heritage ranging from Surrealism and the avant-garde to American and European directors such as John Ford, Robert Bresson and Jean Cocteau. However, he refused to label it as a unified 'movement' because it had no clear definition of itself. It was, in effect, whatever stimulated the critic to a favourable (and equally importantly, pleasurable) response.

It turns out, however, that the term was less theoretical than *practical*. It was editorially imposed on Cooke's article by Lindsay Anderson, who, as he later recalled to Elizabeth Sussex, had rewritten the article 'to make it a bit more "important". I coined the phrase "Free Cinema" which I put into the last paragraph, and I called the article "Free Cinema". We always did this on *Sequence*; we were always rewriting people's things'.[6] Anderson's objective was less to colonize Cooke's ideas than to extend the magazine's basic principles – art as personal expression (later to become the Free Cinema dictum, 'No film can be too personal'); objective realism and the symbiosis between form and content; 'poetry' as the supreme stylistic quality of a film; the director as poet/artist; hostility to the constraints of commercial film-making – into creating the foundation for a new kind of filmic *practice*. However, it's also fair to say that Reisz, Anderson and Richardson lacked any real commitment to the documentary film *as such*, as their subsequent careers in directing features and plays would prove. They graduated into the genre for largely pragmatic reasons, simply because it was the easiest way for a young unknown to get into film-making. With the development of new light-weight 16mm cameras and faster film stock it was cheap and convenient and, because of Grierson's historical legacy, extremely prestigious and therefore reasonably well-funded. Alan Lovell's famous description of Free Cinema as, 'An episode in the development of a tendency'[7] is not far off the mark because, to all intents and purposes, *documentary chose Free Cinema*, not the reverse.

Given that they emerged at approximately the same time and evolved in a similar vein out of auteurist film criticism, many historians have compared Free Cinema unfavourably to the French New Wave, 'the backwash of a wave which had happened elsewhere' as John Caughie pithily puts it.[8] In contrast, James M. Welsh and John C. Tibbetts make a good case for the opposite view, noting that Anderson, Richardson and Reisz 'were writing in *Sequence* before François Truffaut published his first criticism in *Cahiers du cinéma* in 1953. Moreover, Richardson and Reisz completed *Momma Don't Allow* a year *before* Truffaut made *Les Mistons* in 1957. Rather than a backwash, the Wave was already breaking in England before it crossed the Channel'.[9] Although this argument may be good for some patriotic flag waving, the comparison is misconceived at best, or irrelevant at worst, for unlike its French counterpart, which was defined by a deliberately integrated theoretical and stylistic method, often rooted in Modernist literary sources such as the Nouveau Roman of Marguerite Duras and Alain Robbe-Grillet, '"Free Cinema" was nothing more than a label of convenience', admits Anderson.[10] 'It was never planned as anything other than a way of showing our work. It was pragmatic and opportunist'.[11] Reisz concurs: 'We made films and wrote manifestos to provide a little publicity for the movement, but the value of these films, if they have one, lies in the films themselves and not in the movement'.[12]

This is borne out by the fact that the group wrote their manifestos and compiled their six exhibition programmes *after* they had made their films. In fact, Anderson had already completed twelve short films before *O Dreamland* (1954) and *Wakefield Express* (1952) were included in Free Cinema Programme 1 (5–8 February, 1956) and Programme 3 ('Look at Britain', 25–29 May, 1957) respectively, indicating that they were arbitrarily included *ex post facto* under the umbrella of the group's loose collective identity as opposed to acting as catalytic statements of a burgeoning cinematic movement. As Anderson explains:

> In 1956, the year of the first Free Cinema programme, Karel Reisz and Tony Richardson were making a little film for the Film Institute called *Momma Don't Allow*, and I had got involved in editing a film for Lorenza Mazzetti called *Together*, which wasn't a documentary at all. We weren't exactly documentarists: we were independent film-makers. We asked ourselves – 'What are we going to do when we've finished these films?'

because we knew nobody would want to see them; there was no way of showing them. I think I got the idea: 'Well, let's make a Movement.' For journalistic reasons as much as anything ... if you put your films together and make a manifesto and call yourself 'Free Cinema' and make a lot of very challenging statements – then of course you write their articles for them, and they're very happy to print them. You do their work for them.[13]

Anderson added his own film *O Dreamland* (made three years earlier) to the line-up and suddenly they had a viable programme. The other five Free Cinema Programmes were put together in a similar piecemeal way. 'It was really our aim only to show those films in one programme', recalls Anderson. 'It wasn't our aim to start a series of programmes, but what happened was that Lionel Rogosin [the American independent film-maker] turned up in London with his film, *On the Bowery* [1955]. We thought a way to help him to try and get a booking for his film was to concoct a second Free Cinema Programme. We got together a programme of, I think, Georges Franju's *Le Sang des Bêtes* [1949] and maybe another film [Norman McLaren's *Neighbours*, 1952], and *On the Bowery*, and we called that Free Cinema 2. That's how the programmes started and we thought we would do some more'.[14]

The programmes thus showed little consistency of content, whether in terms of genre, style or national identity. Of the six programmes of films shown under the Free Cinema banner between February 1956 and March 1959, only three – the first, the third and the last – contained British films. All but one of these (Lorenza Mazzetti's *Together*) were documentaries. Three programmes were New Wave surveys including works from Poland (Roman Polanski's famous early short, *Two Men and a Wardrobe*, 1957), Switzerland (*Nice Time*, 1957, by Claude Goretta and Alain Tanner), and France (Truffaut's *Les Mistons*, 1957 and Claude Chabrol's *Le Beau Serge*, 1958). 'We did have a personal association, but it was not a formal one and there were not very many of us', notes Anderson. 'But we made much more impact than we could possibly have made if we'd worked separately, in isolation'.[15] In that regard there's no denying that the 'Free Cinema' slogan paid obvious dividends, despite its all-encompassing sweep, for 'Without that declamatory title, I honestly believe the Press would have paid us no attention at all ... it was a successful piece of cultural packaging'.[16]

It's also apparent that Reisz and Anderson's intent was not primarily political, at least not at first (their subsequent attachment to the Campaign for Nuclear Disarmament (CND) and the New Left and their deliberate use of the political rallying cry 'Commitment!' dates from late 1956 and early 1957, as we shall see). Implicit in the critical and social attitudes of the early films was a belief in the ideal-istic possibility of *reform* rather than revolution – a 'breaking down of bourgeois restrictions of theme and style', as Anderson put it[17] – the opportunity to circumvent the all-pervasive middle-class parochialism that was suffocating mainstream British cinema. In a 1969 interview with Alexander Walker, Reisz recalled that Free Cinema was 'a reac-tion against the Ealing tradition that films were made in a "school" and the Rank system that they were made in a factory. With the British film industry in bad straits, this kind of power structure was becoming irrelevant, so this was the moment to say, "We shall take things into our own hands and become film authors." And it did give the films we made a very different feel – directors' films, not industry films'.[18] For Reisz at least, the ideological content of specific subject matter was less important than the freedom to choose the kind of film you wanted to make without worrying about commercial viability: 'We were not interested in treating social problems so much as we were in becoming the first generation of British directors who as a group were allowed to work freely on material of their own choosing'.[19] This is, of course, easier said than done, and the group of would-be auteurs were forced to face two intractable elements head on, namely the problem of financing, distribution and exhibition (particularly as their subject matter – stories about deaf-mutes, London jazz and youth clubs, the Covent Garden Market or Margate's Dreamland amusement arcade – fell squarely outside the normal economic framework of the British film industry); and more ambivalently, the legacy and reputation of that doyen of British documentary, John Grierson (1898–1972).

In some respects, Free Cinema's timing in terms of financing couldn't have been better. Richard Barsam has argued that the first half of the 1950s was a relatively healthy period for documentary film-makers in Britain compared to their American counterparts: 'Not only was the British movement better staffed and suited to continue its limited film-making activities, but several major public events gave impetus to expanded production'.[20] The latter included the 'Wealth of the World' series produced by the Pathé Documentary Unit in association with Film Centre; the increasing production role of UNESCO, sponsors of Basil Wright and Paul Rotha's *World Without End* (1953); and most importantly, the creative impetus of the 1951 Festival of Britain which, under the organizational aegis of the BFI, spawned several documentary and experimental film commissions – most notably *The Waters of Time* (Wright and Bill Launder, 1951), *Forward a Century* (Napier Bell, 1951) and *David* (Paul Dickson, 1951). The Festival of Britain was also the cata-lyst for the construction and management of an ultra-modern viewing theatre – the Telekinema (later renamed the National Film Theatre or NFT) – as an intrinsic part of the new South Bank arts complex in London. The NFT became the original venue of all but one of the six official Free Cinema Programmes.

The latter connection was facilitated by Reisz's own affiliation with the BFI, because from 1952 to 1955 he worked as Programmes Officer of the NFT. According to Denis Forman, the British Film Institute's Director at that time (1949–55):[21]

> In arranging the initial programmes for the theatre, the Institute had three objectives in view; first, to present a steady repertory of the acknowledged masterpieces of the screen; second, to concentrate attention on some theme of contemporary interest or importance in the cinema, and thirdly (in keeping with the traditions of the Telekinema), to demonstrate what was new and experimental. Thus two nights every week were devoted to a chronological survey of film history under the general title of *Fifty Years of Film*, four nights in each week were given to a series of studies of the work of outstanding directors, or else to some decisive trend in the cinema, past or present.[22]

As Programmes Officer, Reisz had the opportunity to propagate his own didactic and critical interests through strategic programming with an overtly auteurist bent. He was not only the main instigator of the 1954 Erich von Stroheim season[23] but also oversaw retrospectives of works by Alfred Hitchcock, Vittorio de Sica, Charlie Chaplin, Carol Reed, Humphrey Jennings, Luis Buñuel, George Cukor, Fritz Lang, John Huston and John Ford. The programming also had a strong international and non-western bias, covering Mexican cinema and films from Asia in addition to familiar European fare. (For a complete list of National Film Theatre programmes under Reisz's aegis, see the Appendix.)

More importantly, the position also gave Reisz direct access to the BFI's Experimental Film Production Fund, the financing source for over fifty shorts produced between 1952 and 1965, including five Free Cinema projects. The key instigator behind the Fund was Forman, whose importance to Reisz and Free Cinema cannot be underestimated. During the early stages of his tenure as BFI Director, independent film production was at its lowest ebb. The state-funded documentary movement was in crisis, culminating in the closing of the Crown Film Unit by the Tory Government in March 1952. Britain would no longer sponsor documentaries for home consumption except in the special case of specific propagandist and informational purposes. Needless to say, this created a large vacuum that Free Cinema eventually hoped to fill by finding an alternative sponsorship. Fortunately, Telekinema had been extremely popular at the Festival of Britain and Forman astutely parlayed this success into obtaining two grants to continue the theatre's ties to the BFI and also to create an Experimental Film Production Fund to produce films for exhibition at the new 'experimental cinema'. He then appointed Stanley Reed as the BFI's first 'film appreciation officer'. Forman saw the BFI's new operating subsidy as an opportunity to give the Institute a dynamic, progressive role in fostering a new alternative to mainstream cinema: 'I hope it will be possible too for the British Film Institute to sharpen the experimental edge of the film industry which, in the tradition of Len Lye, [Alberto] Cavalcanti and Norman McLaren, has often been associated with documentary achievements in the past', he noted.[24]

Forman wisely decided to foreclose industry opposition to the Fund by inviting 'the enemy' – i.e. the trade – to sit on the committee in charge of grant allocation. The first chairman was Ealing Studios' Head of Production, Michael Balcon, who fervently believed in the need to foster young talent if the industry were to survive. Balcon's first line-up (1952–56) included film-makers Frank Launder (*Millions Like Us*, 1943, *The Belles of St. Trinians*, 1954), Thorold Dickinson (*Gaslight*, 1940, *Hill 24 Doesn't Answer*, 1955), documentarians Basil Wright, Howard Thomas and Humphrey Swingler, and film technician Baynham Honri. All meetings were held at Balcon's Ealing Studios. Reisz eventually graduated from his position as NFT Programmes Officer and joined the committee in 1957, serving alongside scriptwriter Bridget Boland (*The Prisoner*, 1955, *War and Peace*, 1956), the head of the Shell Film Unit, Sir Arthur Elton, as well as committee regulars, Honri, Swingler and Wright.[25]

The committee itself was unique within the BFI, for it was completely independent with no official status and absolutely no responsibility to the Institute's governors. It also received no money from the BFI and therefore had to seek its finances from private donations. Fortunately, in May 1953 the Fund earned an Eady Levy trade organizations award (derived from a 7 per cent tax on box office receipts). The Institute was awarded £7,000 (the cost of *one* cheap feature film trailer – small potatoes indeed!) with a remaining £5,500 to be granted once the trade saw how the first grant had been allocated. By 1958, the combined £12,500 had been spent on a total of fifteen short films, necessitating the search for yet another sponsor. Eight years later, in July 1966, the Fund was eventually reorganized with a fixed budget under the new Labour government and Jennie Lee's tenure as Minister of Arts. It was now run by the British Film Institute Production Board ('Experimental' was conveniently dropped from the title), once again under Michael Balcon (he eventually retired in 1972). It's a testament to Reisz's dedication to supporting young talent that even though he had now become an

important director in his own right, he continued his BFI tenure, sitting
on the new board from 1966 to 1970 alongside a broad range of arts
luminaries that included film-makers Carl Foreman and Bryan Forbes,
the art critics John Berger and David Sylvester, theatre director William
Gaskill and Walter Lucas of the British Drama League.

Although the Fund's initial focus stressed the catch-all description
'experimental', this was not seen as an end in itself – like Reisz, the
committee eschewed formalist and avant-garde cinema for its own
sake – but as a practice geared towards the *benefit* of the commercial
industry. Early projects thus included animation, 3D film (although its
expense guaranteed that no footage was ever produced), and art documentaries such as *Rowlandson's England* (John Hawkesworth, 1955) and
The Vision of William Blake (Guy Brenton, 1957). The key turning point
for the Fund's artistic credibility was its encounter with the nascent
Free Cinema group in 1954–55. The BFI was already a forum where
Anderson, Reisz, Richardson and cinematographer Walter Lassally
regularly met and shared their views on cinema. All had contributed
to *Sight and Sound* and Reisz obviously knew of the Fund through his
job at the NFT. The committee was looking around for new projects at
that time, and its selection of Lorenza Mazzetti's *Together* (1956) and
Reisz and Richardson's *Momma Don't Allow* (1956) formally initiated the
collaboration between Free Cinema and the Experimental Film Production Fund. Both films were eventually shown in the first Free Cinema
Programme in February 1956.[26] As Christophe Dupin notes,

> By financing five 'official' Free Cinema films between 1956 and 1959, the
> Experimental Film Fund became de facto the movement's main sponsor.
> In return, one can argue that Free Cinema secured the immediate future
> of the Experimental Film Fund by providing its first public successes.
> The identification of the two became so strong that Balcon had to clarify
> the situation in a brochure promoting the films funded by the BFI: '…
> although the link between the British Film Institute and Free Cinema is
> close and friendly, the movement is essentially an independent one. The
> films have not all been financed by the Experimental Fund; nor all the
> productions of the Fund made in the spirit of Free Cinema'.[27]

However, despite Balcon's disclaimer, Free Cinema principles started
to become a guiding rubric in the committee's selection process. Much
of this was financial: the inexpensive use of 16mm, black and white
film stock, small-scale production and the imaginative use of sound and
image juxtaposition not only compensated for the lack of slick production values but also, like Italian neo-realism, generated a certain recognizable style that increasingly became a common standard of excellence.
As Anderson pointed out in the Second Free Cinema Manifesto, 'With a

16mm camera, and minimal resources, you cannot achieve very much – in commercial terms. You cannot make a feature film, and your possibilities of experiment are severely restricted. But you can use your eyes and ears. You can give indications. You can make poetry'.

For the committee, this innately auteurist strategy was not only the best way to guarantee artistic freedom, but also, 'From the Committee's point of view, it is easy to understand why they were so keen to make their own an approach to film-making which, in a way, *justified* their miniscule film-making grants!'[28] Not surprisingly, given his role on the Fund committee, Reisz became one of its most influential and active members, strongly influencing the selection of a considerable number of Free Cinema-style documentaries for future funding. These included Robert Vas's *Refuge England* (1959) and *The Vanishing Street* (1962), Heather Sutton's *Michael, a Mongol Boy* (1960), Michael Grigsby's *Enginemen* (1959) and *Tomorrow's Saturday* (1962), and John Irvin's *Gala Day* (1963).[29] Reisz and Anderson were also important mediators between the film-makers and the Fund when they applied for grants, placing great emphasis on the role of the film-maker as creative artist, thus imbuing the Fund's aesthetic outlook with the basic principles established in *Sequence* four years earlier.

Having effectively 'hi-jacked' the BFI for the bulk of their initial funding, all that remained for Free Cinema's 'Young Turks' was the development of a documentary aesthetic that could do full justice to the *Sequence* agenda. For this they chose the 'poetic realist' style of Humphrey Jennings over the sociological approach of the so-called 'Grierson Legacy'. 'Very often the people who influence you a great deal are people whom you react against', notes Reisz. 'That is to say, because [John] Grierson and [Paul] Rotha and [Edgar] Anstey and all those people started a tradition, a tradition of factual film-making that we didn't like, that in itself was a valuable springboard, because it pointed out the areas of experience that their films don't touch. Jennings is the one we admired. I never met Jennings, but *A Diary for Timothy*, *Fires Were Started*, *Listen to Britain* were beautiful films and we felt we were going on from them ... *Fires Were Started* would be the source film for "Free Cinema"'.[30] Anderson agreed, stating in his 1954 *Sight and Sound* tribute to the director that, 'it might reasonably be contended that Humphrey Jennings is the only real poet the British cinema has yet produced'.[31]

Fundamental to Grierson's philosophy was the notion that documentary cinema – which he defined as 'a creative treatment of actuality'[32] – should be harnessed as a means of mass communication, documentation and education, in short as a social-democratic bulwark against irresponsible escapist entertainment epitomized by Hollywood and the levelling effects of lowbrow mass culture. Thus, as Andrew Higson points out, 'at the heart of the documentary idea is a powerful differentiation between "realism" and "escapism": between a serious, committed, engaged cinema, and mass entertainment'.[33] However, this distinction isn't necessarily the same as a dialectic between 'fact' and 'fiction' for, 'The aesthetic implications of Grierson's maxim, "the creative interpretation of actuality", refuse such a reductionism, which is further complicated by the development of the story documentary form, which employs some of the devices and strategies of the narrative film – that is, the *fiction* film'.[34] The resulting 'constructed realism' was the hybrid aesthetic chosen by the 1930s documentarists as the preferred form and style for propagating a social-democratic approach to British cinema in general. They were primarily *sociologists* before they were artists, their objective essentially didactic. Thus for Grierson, the documentary movement

> was from the beginning an adventure in public observation. It might, in principle, have been a movement in documentary writing, or documentary radio, or documentary painting. The basic force behind it was social, not aesthetic. It was a desire to make drama from the ordinary; a desire to bring the citizen's mind in from the ends of the earth to the story, his own story, of what was happening under his nose. From this came our insistence on the drama of the doorstep. We were, I confess, sociologists, a little worried about the way the world was going ... We were interested in *all* instruments which would crystallize sentiments in a muddled world and create a will towards civic participation.[35]

Although he confessed to no great interest in films *as such* (and certainly not film as art),[36] Grierson felt that it could serve as a form of pedagogical and propaganda 'publication' for a wide variety of audiences. His main intent was to develop ideas of community and promote world peace: 'somehow we had to make peace exciting, if we were to prevent wars. Simple notion that it is – that has been my propaganda ever since – to make peace exciting'.[37]

In Anderson's opinion, however, the Grierson School failed because it was essentially producing social-democratic propaganda that, because of the exigencies of supporting the war effort, became totally identified with the Establishment: 'So after the war the work had no kind of progressive quality; they were simply making rather sentimental, conformist social-democratic pictures'. Grierson was essentially a social theorist, 'and the feeling for human beings in the films he inspired was always rather cold, showing human beings as types'.[38] A more balanced view is that Grierson's lasting legacy lies less in his role as a sociologist or educator than as the creative catalyst for a tradition of film-making which injected British national cinema with a realist imprint. This is epitomized by films of the 1940s where elements of the documentary and the feature film came together to create a truly national cinema, defined by Ealing's cheerful 'backs against the wall, chaps' wartime output. *Sequence* and the Free Cinema group refused to accept the validity of this hybrid genealogy, stubbornly maintaining a clear distinction between sociological reportage (Grierson) and poetry (themselves). Jack C. Ellis rightly sees the quarrel with the Griersonians as a contrived New Left vs Old Left polemic, a form of political generational warfare. Reisz fired a clear warning shot across the bows of the generational divide in 'A Use for Documentary', his provocative 1958 article in *Universities and Left Review*: postwar documentary of the Grierson School, he argued, has lost all contact with contemporary life:

> Where in the thirties they made valuable films about life as it was lived in this country, and tried to lead public opinion towards enlightened legisla-tion, today they make at best the (admittedly valuable) scientific film or, at worst, spend their time 'projecting Britain'. (This means films about the Lake District, Stirling Moss, old trams, and the beauties of spring) ... One of the answers to their arguments is, quite simply, that their facts are wrong. Social problems continue to exist; old age, the colour bar, juvenile crime – take your pick. Another answer is that the human films are not only needed in 'problem' situations. To say that they are, implies a faith in documentary as propaganda but not as art. It implies too, that socialism is a sort of good housekeeping system: when people have houses, work and food, all is well. The socialist humanism which we're all working towards in these pages may not yet be well defined, but it is not *that*.[39]

Anderson and Reisz's chosen stylistic precursor was not the socio-logical approach of Grierson but rather the poetic realism-cum-surre-alism of Jennings. Reisz himself made a clear distinction between 'sociological fact' and 'poetic truth': 'The basic premise of documentary in my view, which is a premise which Humphrey Jennings and certainly Flaherty worked, is that you must make the drama out of *the ordinary*. If you choose "problem" subjects – you know, pathological ones, pros-titution, child crime, that sort of thing – you must be informational or you end up with Kitsch. Ideally, of course, for these subjects, you must use fiction because documentary does not get inside the indi-vidual. It can't. Which is why I feel the ordinary, the everyday, is the proper subject of documentary. But that does not mean you should not interpret it'.[40] Following Jennings, who made poetry out of hundreds of pieces of separate observations rather than the preconceived reconstruc-tion of received ideas, Free Cinema films were thus about discovering the poetic within the ephemera of the everyday world, of 'finding things that interest you and then making the film from things that happen … It was about wanting what you got, rather than going out and getting what you want'.[41]

The term 'poetic realism' was first employed in the literary context of prewar France by Jean Paulhan, editor of *La Nouvelle Revue Française*, to describe the mix of realism and symbolism in the novels of Marcel Aymé, specifically *La Rue sans Nom* (1929), a work about the forgotten homeless on the streets of Paris. Pierre Chenal's 1933 screen adaptation of Aymé's book led to the term entering into film criticism (where it was opposed to 'artificial realism') and it was quickly applied to the late 1930s works of Marcel Carné and Jacques Prévert, notably *Le Quai des Brumes* (1938) and *Le Jour se Lève* (1939). The main characteristics of these films were: 1) The depiction of a fantastic, stylized world; 2) The merger of reality and imagination while at the same time retaining the concrete truth and immediacy of the real; 3) The attention to everyday detail and a heightened concern for subjective mood; and 4) The evocation of atmosphere through charged objects in order to create a reality imbued with a sense of destiny and implacable fate. Carné's biographer, Edward Baron Turk, has linked the style to the surrealism of Vigo and Buñuel:[42]

> Images in these films – like words in Aymé's fiction – take on values independent of their narrative function. Not reproducing reality so much as recreating it, stories in these films are anchored to defined social settings, but aim to convey 'essential' human truths that transcend social realities. Poetic realism undervalues a film's direct links with the material world in order to explore the symbolic resonances which the world – when photographed – is capable of releasing. Through condensation, concentration, and delicate blending, these resonances form fields of evocative, connotative correspondences, resulting in the 'suggestive magic' that Baudelaire believed must characterize modern poetic art.[43]

Reality is thus transfigured into style, which is both dependent on, but also disengaged from, the world depicted, creating a heightened 'realism effect' akin to Freud's dream-work or Walter Benjamin's idea of the image-constellation.

In Jennings's specific case, World War Two was the catalyst for generating this heightened sensibility in films such as *London Can Take It* (1940, co-directed with Harry Watt), *Words for Battle* and *This Is England* (both 1941). As Anderson observes, 'A style, in fact, is being hammered out in these films; a style based on a peculiar intimacy of observation, a fascination with the commonplace thing or person that is significant precisely because it is commonplace, and with the whole pattern that can emerge when such commonplace, significant things and people are fitted together in the right order'.[44] Unfortunately poetic imagination is stifled in these early wartime films – all are accompanied by propagandist commentaries which impede and clog the progress of the picture: 'The images are so justly chosen, and so explicitly assembled, that there is nothing for the commentator to say'.[45] In contrast, the mature war films' inspiration lay less in propaganda than in their quiet pride in the courage and doggedness of ordinary British people – evoking both the spirit of humankind *and* the spirit of England. Jennings thus sought a public imagery and, by extension, a public *poetry*, to fuse idea and affect into an essentially *felt* perception of national identity.

For both Reisz and Anderson, the pinnacle of poetic realism was *A Diary for Timothy*, which was constructed entirely through an endlessly varying pattern of relationships and contrasts (i.e. associative montage) rather than a logical and causal plot. Set during the last year of the war and addressed to Timothy, a new-born baby, the film focuses on four representative characters: an engine driver, a farmer, a Welsh miner and wounded fighter pilot. 'But the story is by no means restricted to scenes involving these', argues Anderson:

> With dazzling virtuosity, linking detail to detail by continuously striking associations of image, sound, music and comment, the film ranges freely over the life of the nation, connecting and connecting ... Not least among the virtues that distinguish Jennings from almost all British filmmakers is his respect for personality, his freedom from the inhibitions of class-consciousness, his inability to patronise or merely to use the people in his films. Jennings' people are ends in themselves.[46]

Much of this effect is generated by Jennings's ability to provide a direct link between the outer world and the inner. For Reisz, the outer world – populism, social critique, class analysis, the intersection of economic and social factors – is usually a function of *mise-en-scène*. The inner world – fatality, affect, emotion – is usually the function of character and acting. Poetic realism is the interaction of these two strains, marked by the tension between the drive towards realism and an impulse to transcend or essentialize reality *as such*.

Reisz's own stress on the affective in Jennings bears out this argument: 'The whole style of a Jennings film is so completely different from, say, a Rotha film. In a Jennings film a character is observed and held on the screen and savoured before he goes on to the next thing. For Rotha a face was an illustration of a predicament ... There is a thesis and the faces illustrate it. It's a different aim. We went from the Jennings view. Jennings's films worked with naturalistic material but organized it in an emotional way'.[47] The latter approach is reflected in

Free Cinema's subject matter. Their films focused less on work – the province of the Grierson group – than on leisure time and its import on social psychology and the collective spirit. For the most part their works are impressionistic and non-didactic, playfully aesthetic rather than directly informative, directed at affect and emotions instead of reason. As a result, as Ellis notes, 'the filmmakers' points are made through their choice and arrangement of sights and sounds. Juxtaposition of symbolic contrasts and counterpoint of the visible and audible abound. Considerable irony and humour result'.[48] *Momma Don't Allow* and *We Are the Lambeth Boys* typify this process, for they attempt to extol the playfully vigorous, iconoclastic and idiosyncratic in one poetic breath.

Co-directed with Tony Richardson (who had been working as a BBC TV director since the early 1950s), the 22 minute *Momma Don't Allow* was shot on nine Saturday evenings at Art and Viv Saunders's Wood Green Jazz Club, based at The Fishmonger's Arms pub in North London, where Chris Barber's jazz combo was the resident house band. As the directors noted in the original 1956 Free Cinema Programme, 'Suburban London jazz clubs are run for and by enthusiasts; their atmosphere is not whipped up by promoters but created by the typists and students, shop-girls and teddy-boys who have evolved their own free styles of dancing and who, on several evenings each week, meet and create their own world. It is the freedom, exuberance and vitality of this world that we set out to capture and to admire'.[49] Filmed with the full co-operation of the club's members, the film utilized the considerable talents of Free Cinema regulars Walter Lassally (camera) and John Fletcher (editing and sound), two men who, according to Reisz, 'were absolutely central to the whole movement of films which developed in the years to follow'.[50] Because of the limited BFI funding – the total grant was a paltry £581/18/– [51] – the film was shot on 16mm stock using non-synch, single-track sound transferred from tape recordings. Lassally used a predominantly hand-held Bolex camera with lights strung up in fixed positions from the pub's rafters.

Offering the barest hint of a story line, the film's use of parallel editing and associative sound-image montage places it squarely in the debt of Jennings's *A Diary for Timothy*. The film opens with Chris Barber and three band members – Pat Halcox on trumpet, drummer Ron Bowden and skiffle legend Lonnie Donegan on banjo – arriving at the empty pub and setting up their instruments on the platform-like stage. As Halcox, Barber and Donegan start an impromptu rehearsal jam, the music track links us to a series of brief vignettes that introduce the film's three main working-class protagonists: a plump young woman cleaning rubbish from the dining car of a British Rail train (who, for want of proper names, we shall call 'Train Cleaner'); a lean young man in his late teens cutting meat in the back room of a butcher's shop ('Butcher Boy'); and an attractive young 'Dental Assistant' attending to a woman patient in the dentist's chair. Segued by the music, the cross-cutting between the workers and the band continues until the teenagers eventually quit work for the day. The Dental Assistant meets briefly with her boyfriend outside the surgery, probably to confirm their date for the evening; the Butcher Boy cleans off his cutting block and unties his apron; the Train Cleaner strips off her work overalls, checks her hair in the locker room mirror, and hurries away across the train tracks towards her waiting girlfriends. The enticing prospect of the evening's entertainment is thus inextricably linked to the immediacy of the workplace through delib- erate cross-cutting between production and consumption. For Reisz, this was less an issue of idle escapism from the drudgery of dead-end jobs than a sense of economic self-empowerment, an example of 'that confidence of the post-war generation, when people in their teens had money for the first time. Making the connections between work and play – that's something that was central to the film – and most of the so-called Free Cinema films that followed'.[52] This social agenda is rein- forced by the teenagers' clothing – most of the boys are smartly dressed in suits, white shirts and narrow ties, the girls in elegant party dresses – an outward signifier of the new working-class affluence (and by exten- sion, ideological inoculation) that will receive more detailed treatment in *We Are the Lambeth Boys* and *Saturday Night and Sunday Morning*.

The next ten minutes of the film is spent injecting the three principal characters into the club environment, where they pair off with regular or impromptu dance partners as the band rips its way through a series of traditional jazz and skiffle numbers. Reisz and Richardson's careful pre-production paid major dividends here, creating an intimacy with the teenagers that is notably lacking in the Griersonians's more objec- tive, sociological approach. According to Reisz, they visited the club 'for several months with still cameras so people got used to our presence. And then we attempted a kind of "fly on the wall" treatment: then cobbled together some sort of continuity'.[53] The unselfconscious abandon of the dancers is ample reward for this preparation as it gives the events an intimate, in-crowd quality, with Lassally's hand-held camera – using mostly short close-ups and medium shots – acting as both casual spec- tator and spontaneous participant in the evening's events. Part of this stylistic technique was the product of limitations in the Bolex camera itself. As Lassally later recalled, 'The main limitation ... was that it was a spring-operated camera and it had the maximum running time of twenty-one seconds or twenty-two seconds. So not only could you not shoot things [with synch] sound because the camera made a noise, but you also had to limit yourself to the maximum length of twenty-two seconds'.[54] Fortunately, such limitations eventually became a virtue in the cutting room because the resultant free-form narrative style opened up a critical space that allowed the viewer to discover for themselves what was natural and vital about 1950s youth without the imposition of patronizing editorializing.

However, it would be a mistake to see *Momma Don't Allow* as a purely impressionistic film: its narrative structure is as much 'realist' as 'poetic'. Reisz and Richardson's lip-service to 'dramatic conflict' occurs with the arrival of two elegantly dressed, upper middle-class couples – Raymond Durgnat colourfully describes them as 'upper-class hoorays' – who pull up in a swank, classic 1930s Bentley. If there were any doubt that they are slumming, the older of the two women ('Older Slummer') hands a toy poodle to a younger, chic woman in her early twenties ('Chic Slummer'), who promptly leaves the dog in the back of the car before joining the two husbands/boyfriends at the front door of the pub. They go in, leaving the Bentley parked outside, but in a telling detail, one of the men re-enters the shot from stage right, unscrews the hood ornament from the car and puts it in his pocket (in 1956, working-class and crime-ridden Islington was far removed from its subsequent gentrification as 'the new Bayswater'!).

Despite the fact that there are no actor credits for the film, what follows is obviously scripted and staged – i.e. *Momma Don't Allow* is a prime example of the 'story documentary' form – in order to set up a series of binary juxtapositions, all the better to contrast but also deconstruct class stereotypes. On entering the pub, the slumming women seem a little diffident, suggesting that their knowledge and appreciation of jazz are the intellectual product of listening to records rather than the visceral somatic experience of attending live gigs in suburban clubs. Reisz and Richardson underline the 'conflict' by immediately cutting to the Train Cleaner, gyrating with abandon, then back to the Older Slummer, who looks on with a mixture of jealous interest and apprehension. As she enters the dance area with her companions, we cut to the Dental Assistant and her boyfriend, swinging to the beat, the Butcher Boy jiving with his regular dance partner, and the Train Cleaner be-bopping alone in the middle of the dance floor. Inspired by the sheer exuberance of the dancers, the Older Slummer tries to get her younger friends to join the dance, but they're either too embarrassed or, more likely, horrified at the prospect of rubbing shoulders with the great unwashed.

Sociologically, this division between working-class bodily participation and middle-class intellectual observation is actually quite spurious.

As Durgnat correctly points out, the film 'creates the impression that the jazz revival was widely popular among working-class teenagers and was a working-class phenomenon. In point of fact the vast majority of working-class teenagers preferred pops, and, later, rock-and-roll ... The jazz revival was at least as much, if not primarily, a middle-class movement. The film reminds us, at least, of the inter-class gulf; the upper-class hoorays who beam patronizingly at everyone don't dance as well as the lower-class lads and lasses'.[55] More serious, however, are the film's aesthetic and stylistic limitations:

> It's badly cut, badly shot, with no feelings for jazz, for dancing, for bodies, for clothes, or for place. The directors have even less feeling for rhythm than the hoorays at whom they laugh so heartily, for at one point all the couples are dancing a slow blues to an up-tempo jazz number. You wouldn't guess from this film that the actual jazz club had a red lamp placed strategically low so that the thighs of unwary girls would be very prettily silhouetted through their dresses. It's not just that *Momma Don't Allow* that sort of joke in here: she just doesn't wish to know that thank you very much.[56]

For Durgnat, not only did the film fail as poetry, documentary *and* sociology, but it actually made jazz appear sexless, thus making the film-makers' claim of raw, on-location authenticity appear meaningless. Gavin Lambert had the same misgivings, noting that the film exuded a curious abstraction from real life: 'Partly this comes from the film's refusal to over-dramatise its material – this jazz club is not on the sex, violence and marijuana fringe, but more like a specialised community centre. Partly, though, it comes from a lack of definition in the makers' attitude'.[57] There is some truth in both these arguments, although many of the lapses in cutting rhythm are probably due to budget and the resultant difficulties of post-synchronization. Thus when the cutting is appropriately choppy, gradually shortening the length of each shot as the film builds towards its musical climax, the Train Cleaner is whirling like a dervish before a bevy of male admirers but the Butcher Boy remains monotonously 'in the zone', oblivious to the changing parameters of beat and rhythm, suggesting that shots of a single dance sequence have been selectively spliced throughout the course of the film.

Part of the film's 'lack of definition' was also due to the difficulties of collaboration: by all accounts Reisz's creative partnership with Richardson was not smooth sailing. 'We had quite a bumpy ride', admits Reisz. 'It's a ridiculous notion, really, to try and co-direct anything. There were six couples in the film, roughly. I did three, and he did three, and since what you get is what you want in this kind of cinema, the thing was really created in the cutting room'.[58] Richardson concurs, recalling in his autobiography that, 'Karel and I were very different personalities. I veered from wanting to expand or hint at dramatic situations involving individuals outside the group to using ideas of montage as abstract as a music video. (Alone of the group, I was a keen Eisenstein fan.) Karel had a much calmer and more straightforward approach, respecting the musicians' wanting to record their achievement without letting an imposed aesthetic get in the way. It's a line he has continued, with insufficient credit'.[59]

However, there are instances of editing and sound-image juxtaposition in the film that underline deeply sexual moments that belie Durgnat and Lambert's main criticisms. In another of the film's prescripted incidents, Ottilie Patterson takes the stage to sing a slow blues. At this juncture, the Dental Assistant's boyfriend starts 'chatting up' another girl, and the film expressively links the Assistant's fit of jealousy with the unfolding lyrics of the song. Thus as the boyfriend and girl stand talking in the foreground, Patterson sings, 'I had a pretty daddy, as sweet as he could be ...' The boyfriend and girl then exit frame right to reveal the Dental Assistant sitting alone in the background, obviously heartbroken. We then cut to the girl and boyfriend dancing, with Ottilie's appropriate lyrical comment: 'He found another woman, but now he don't want me'. Although on the surface such sound-image juxtaposition seems simplistic compared to the aforementioned Hamlet-V2 scene in *A Diary for Timothy*, Reisz and Richardson extend the metonymic ramifications of the sentiment along class lines by cutting to the Older Slummer, who is dancing seductively with her husband/boyfriend. As the latter removes the woman's shawl and gazes searchingly into her eyes, Patterson sings: 'I think I hear him calling, but it's the blues knocking on my door'. Our first reaction is to assume that the lyric refers to the slumming couple, but this doesn't seem to fit. They are obviously deeply in love, because the camera holds on their mutual gaze beyond the needs of narrative diegesis. Why would the blues be knocking on *this* woman's door? We receive our answer as we cut back to the Dental Assistant, clearly 'dying' of jealousy. Thus the first half of the song's line – 'I think I hear him calling' – applies connotatively to the slummers, while the second half encapsulates the feelings of the Dental Assistant. In this way the song is used syntagmatically to underline both the similarities and differences between two women equally smitten with love. This linkage is reinforced by our cutting back to the Older Slummer, who returns her partner's gaze with a sexually charged eroticism. Reisz had obviously learned his poetic realist lessons well, realizing that affect comes from the lingering observation of character *for its own sake*, that a face should be held on the screen and savoured for as long as possible before cutting to the next logical stage of the narrative. Thus despite Durgnat's claims to the contrary, both the song, editing and composition are used to create an affecting intimacy between the different romantic situations of the two couples, as well as bridging the class divide to suggest that sexuality (and its corollary, jealously) transcends clear-cut sociological distinctions.

But the sequence doesn't stop there. After the Dental Assistant's flighty boyfriend returns from his dance, she runs away tearfully from the camera, crosses the crowded dance floor and ducks out into the street clutching her handkerchief. Although the contrite boyfriend emerges from the pub to comfort her, she angrily turns her back on him. At this point, we cut to a close-up of Chris Barber's feet tapping out the beat to start the film's final number, the up-tempo title song, 'Momma Don't Allow', which sets the dance floor gyrating.[60] The Older Slummer seems eager to party but her increasingly uncomfortable friends are ready to leave and they all head for the exit. We then cut to a tight exterior two-shot: the boyfriend and the Dental Assistant are shown in profile, painfully trying to work out their misunderstanding. Suddenly, they're distracted, and look off to the left. From their point-of-view we see that the slummers have returned to their Bentley. As the Older Slummer does one last twirl before climbing into the back seat, we cut back to the two-shot as the boyfriend utters something inaudible to his girl. Finally she laughs, he kisses her hair, and in a wider angle they go back inside the pub, reconciled at last.

It seems highly likely that the Dental Assistant's jealous snit was mollified because of a joke made at the expense of the slummers. The sequence has thus come full circle, but with a key difference. What originally brought the classes together – the common denominator of intimacy and sexual desire – is now used to differentiate them, if not drive them apart. This division is reinforced by the film's dance finale. For all its obvious sense of emotional catharsis – the film ends with wild applause to coincide with the conclusion of the eponymous song – we are left with the overall impression that this hermetically sealed world of insiders (as opposed to the intrusive world of hybridity and difference, represented by the now absent slummers) represents the real communal status quo. As John Ellis comments, 'the film presents its world of the jazz club, and of the young people who spend their evenings in it, as already understood, typical, and integral with the everyday life of its community. Within the film it is the middle-class youth who are "exotic", out of place and requiring explanation'.[61]

Although the vitality of this working-class community is central to the film's message, several critics complained about the film-makers' lack of emotional engagement with the material. Writing in the American avant-garde film journal, *Film Culture*, Lewis Jacob acknowledged that, 'Underlying the jazz enthusiasm which brought the participants together was a significant commentary: the need of the individual to be part of something vital, to be hep, to belong. But because of the general lack of definition, the point seemed overextended and weakened ... the result was objectivity to the point of remoteness'.[62] Gavin Lambert agreed, arguing that the film failed as a uniquely personal statement; that when it set out to interpret it became hampered by reservation and therefore sank into the realm of the commonplace. Lambert also raised a key point in terms of film poetry: just how free and exuberant is the jazz club? How does it function analogously as a symbol for broader class and social issues?

> Folk dance is an affirmation of character – people reveal themselves in it, make an imaginative comment on their lives, part conscious, part unconscious. Here no such revelation is made; the dancing just happens, people are the same at the beginning and the end. Perhaps, if the prologue had been more penetrating, and complemented by an epilogue showing the dancers going home again, returning to their everyday lives, a real perspective would have been gained. As it is, the surface detail is nearly always very good, there is a freshness and affection about it that is genuinely personal, but the final impression is of an activity too isolated, too unrelated to the life from which it springs.[63]

Lambert's critique is well noted, but it is essentially a dialectical materialist analysis and *Momma Don't Allow* is not really a dialectical film. Lambert is, in effect, advocating a causal 'sandwich-effect', whereby the world of play is positioned as a kind of insubstantial filler activity between the more serious cultural lifeblood of work and social context. To return the main protagonists to their places of employment as a tacked-on epilogue would simply establish a cyclical temporality – an eternal return of the same, with pleasure serving as a benign inoculation effect – that reinforces his orthodox Marxist 'Base-Superstructure' model. Lambert wants the film to do our analysis for us – to show that pleasure springs naturally from work (and by extension, class) and then returns inexorably back into the pre-existing mode of production, rather than creating a dialogue or tension between them. By leaving the jazz club on a cathartic high note, a non-dialectical *jouissance*, Reisz and Richardson at least leave the opportunity open for creating a line of flight whereby work and pleasure are no longer seen as the twin jaws of the same economic trap.

Although the fifty-two minute *We Are the Lambeth Boys* represents a major step forward artistically and technically – particularly in its use of faster Ilford film stock and synchronized sound – its incorporation of several of Lambert's dialectical suggestions and the use of an overly didactic commentary also created some serious aesthetic shortcomings. By 1959, Reisz had spent three years as the head of the Ford Motor Company's TV and Films Programme. As Films Officer, he literally produced dozens of commercials and training films about tractors, engines and automobiles. However, he also forged an informal understanding with the company, namely 'that I would make their commercials and films for ball-bearings if they gave us money every year for a Free Film. And the first was Lindsay's *Every Day Except Christmas* [about London's Covent Garden market] and the second was *We Are the Lambeth Boys*'.[64] Both films were released as part of Ford's 'Look at Britain Series', which also included John Fletcher's *The Saturday Men* (1962), a profile of West Bromwich Albion football club.[65] Reisz assured the executives that the production deal would be to their mutual advantage: 'The first film I ever made was called *The Three Graces* and it was about the Ford Zephyr, Zodiac and Consul, and the problem about doing those films was that there was nowhere to show them ... so I said if we make these [Free Cinema] films, get some publicity for them, there will be non-commercial screenings in which we can show our sales films. And they bought it. It worked for about three years ... enough to see three movies through. And I have to say they were very generous sponsors'.[66]

Reunited with Lassally and Fletcher and armed with an evocative Johnny Dankworth jazz score, Reisz followed his usual practice of scrupulous research for the new film, visiting the Alford House Youth Club near the Kennington Oval cricket ground every night for about three months in order to get a feel for the working-class teenagers – their passions, interests and ideas about work, politics, the death penalty, fashion and entertainment.[67] Although a key catalyst for the film, triggered by Reisz's personal experience teaching his Marylebone Secondary Modern students, was 'a sense of how impossible modern society is for young people',[68] the main social ingredients of the project were developed on the spot from what the teenagers themselves wanted to express, not from Reisz's own preconceived notions: 'In that sort of documentary, the premise is that you want the things that *they* can do. And your job is to organize that into meanings, into associations, into statements. It's true of course that when you have, say, six spontaneous shots of a game of cricket and your editor's mind tells you that you absolutely need two reverse angles, then stage that. You have to be a craftsman as well. But the premise is: what they *do* is the script'.[69] Nonetheless, unlike the more free-form narrative of *Momma Don't Allow*, *We Are the Lambeth Boys* still has a clearly discernable structure, breaking down into four rough sections or 'Acts', allowing Reisz to score certain didactic and sociological points through the exploitation of distinct dramatic climaxes.

Part One begins with the introduction of the film's main 'characters' as they make their way to the youth club from the surrounding South London neighbourhood. We meet the boys from the faceless London County Council (LCC) flats off Kennington Lane – Kenny, Brian, Woody, Bobby and John – who always arrive and spend the evening together as a tight-knit group. There's Percy, who may dress and look like a spiv, but is quietly good-natured – he turns out to be the only voice *against* the death penalty – and always seems to have a girl on his arm. The smartly dressed, relatively affluent Adie is a newcomer to the club, having tried several others, but is confident, gregarious and never shies away from expressing an opinion. Chief among the girls is Beryl, a fun-loving platinum blonde who works at a food-processing plant, her seamstress friend Janet, and Frances, a pretty brunette who has a desk job in a London office. Following Free Cinema principles, all are presented as unique individuals with their own subjective stories to tell, *not* as social types.

Unlike *Momma Don't Allow*, Reisz begins the film with a long sequence showing the kids at play rather than individuated at work, in order to stress the benefits of communal activity and to affirm a sense of group belonging. Thus while the boys enjoy some cricket practice in the nets, the girls gossip and giggle about boyfriends, prospective dates and the varying merits of 1950s teen idol, Tommy Steele. As Reisz later recalled, 'I felt it was worthwhile to have a five-minute sequence of the boys horsing around in the yard, knocking a cricket ball around in the nets. I thought it was interesting. We wanted to start from obser-vation of the contemporary world. The traditional idea of documen-tary – of using factual footage to illustrate argument – seemed to us to be as wrong-headed as the reliance of the feature industry on the theatre'.[70] The advantage of Lassally's mobile camera and Reisz's first use of synchronized sound is that, much like *cinéma vérité*, we are able to eavesdrop on these conversations as if we were a privileged member of the group. Unfortunately, this intimacy is undercut by the intrusive presence of Jon Rollason's voice-over commentary, which tells us what to think and often simply reiterates what we are already seeing and hearing for ourselves. Richard Hoggart eloquently voiced the general critical consensus, arguing that, 'I think this sort of essay will do better when it can either dispense with a commentary or find one which works within the same imaginative field as the camera; when it does not stab into the film's evocations, mediating, ordering, conceptualising and relating them to the world of rational assent; but when it lies obliquely to the scenes ... and so creates a richer resonance'.[71] Reisz later admitted that the voice-over was imposed on the film at the insistence of the Ford executives, who presumably wanted greater narrative control over the teenagers' own indigenous discourse: 'I put on a very, very sparse one', says Reisz, 'which is a little bit embarrassing now'.[72]

In contrast, the advantages of the 'direct cinema' approach are borne out in the open discussion scene that follows, where Ron, one of the club's volunteers, leads the group in a spirited debate on fashion. As usual, Adie is not short of input, admitting to spending 'nearly thirty bob a week on clothes' and considering fifteen guineas a decent price for a new suit. However, the suit would only last eight months, because 'after eight months to a year it doesn't look smart any more so you've got to buy a new one'. Reisz allows the content of the discussion itself to make his sociological points, namely that the immediate postwar period had given rise to a new class of affluent teenagers (from 1945 to 1950 the average real wage of teenagers had increased at *twice* the adult rate), so that Teddy-boys and other youth sub-cultures had plenty of money to spend and, because money was often all they had, it became immensely important as an outward signifier of their status and identity. Thus, according to Tony Jefferson, clothes' cultural meaning for the Teds and other sub-groups, 'becomes explicable as both expression of their *social reality* (basically outsiders and forced to live by their wits) and their *social* "aspirations" (basically an attempt to gain high, albeit grudging, status for an ability to live smartly, hedonistically and by their wits in an urban setting)'.[73]

This freedom of expression and status is also acknowledged in the boys' relationship to their parents. Adie admits that, 'My mother didn't know I could smoke, but I had enough money to smoke when I was 14'. When Ron asks Adie what his parents could have done to prevent him from taking up the habit, he says, quite forthrightly, 'Not given me so much money to spend ... I got 10 shillings a week when I was 14'. Still, money is tight for some of the lads, and Ron asks them whether a girl should have to pay for herself when on a date. Beryl feels that the girls should be given a large enough allowance to be able to pay their own way, a position endorsed by Percy: 'I'd say to my girl ... "OK, if you wanna go dancin', you pay." But if I wanna go to the pictures, I pay, like that. Like this Sunday, she wanted to go dancin'. Not me. She didn't 'ave no money so we didn't go. We went to the pictures'. As if to underline the advantages of community (as opposed to 'freelance') entertainment, we then slam cut to a mid-week disco, as the club members have fun as a group, whether it be dancing to the latest singles, arranging dates for the weekend, or just watching from the sidelines, enjoying the spectacle. Although the general abandon of Beryl, Janet, Frances and Kenny evokes many of the dance numbers in *Momma Don't Allow*, rock'n'roll was no longer considered 'forbidden fruit' by 1959, and the choice of Lonnie Donegan's 1957 chart-topping hit, *Puttin' on the Style*, seems strangely arcane. Although Hoggart praised its use as an oblique commentary on the visual action, its lyrics paint a patronizing and objective view of youth from the outsider position of a mature adult (not unlike Reisz himself), thus undercutting the film's insider association with its protagonists as agents of a hybrid working-class culture.[74]

This ambivalent position is reinforced by Part Two – which focuses on school and work as catalysts for leisure – and is immediately underlined by Rollason's opening voice-over: 'Being young in the morning is different from being young at night. For one thing, there's no crowd about'. Stripped of the support network of the club's communal identity, life is very different for the isolated teenagers when forced to face the workaday world in the stark light of day (significantly we never see any of the kids' parents or extended families as an alternative support network). Reisz structures this section through another Jennings-like series of sound-image associations, starting with young, school-age Brian from the council flats. Reisz opens the sequence with a wide-angle shot of the Victorian school assembly hall, with the all-male pupils facing the front in regimented military lines, underscoring the monotony and uniformity of the school day after the be-bopping excitement of the youth club the night before. The headmaster bids them 'good morning', the oppressive sound of the organ fills the air and the opening hymn – 'Jesus Is Your Good Shepherd' – begins. As we hear the lines, 'The King of love my shepherd is, Whose goodness faileth never', Reisz singles out the fair-haired, almost angelic Brian singing sweetly with a high alto voice that rises ethereally above the harmonious chorale of the other boys. As Brian intones the words, 'I nothing lack if I am His, and He is mine forever', the singing continues over a series of cuts which show other members of the youth club at work in their mundane jobs. Bobby, a junior postman, puts mail from the sorting boxes into a mail pouch. He whistles as he works, as if in synch with the hymn's lyrics – 'Where streams of living water flow, my ransomed soul He leadeth/And where the verdant pastures grow, with food celestial feedeth' – but this is obviously an ironic contiguity. There is nothing verdant or celestial about the GPO.

The hymn then continues over Janet sewing at a Mayfair dressmaker's, Woody cutting meat at the butcher's, Frances doing the accounts at her office desk, and Beryl working at a conveyor belt in a food processing factory. We finally cut back to a close-up of Brian as the hymn concludes with the words, 'Good Shepherd, may I sing Thy praise, within Thy house forever'. The return to Brian after the anecdotal insights into the others' workaday worlds is sobering on several fronts. As Georg Gaston notes, 'The hymn, and the boy's imagination, may be full of the finest sentiments. But the future for this youth and those around him, largely because of the existence of the British class system, is no doubt rather dismal'.[75] Although Reisz clearly paints religion as the opiate of the masses, he also seems to suggest that Brian has a slim chance to escape from the shackles of his class and that it is education that holds the key. The extreme formality of the school assembly suggests an old-fashioned, 'crack the whip' approach to academics, and one is led to conjecture that if Brian studies hard and passes his O and A levels, he may become the scholarship boy that Hoggart – himself a Yorkshire-bred, working-class insider who became an eleven-plus boy and eventually left his community to study at Leeds University – lionizes in his seminal 1957 book, *The Uses of Literacy*. Hoggart hoped that a traditional proletarian culture could be upheld by the educated working class against the encroachments of the 'shining barbarism' and 'candy floss' of modern mass culture (a key theme of *Saturday Night and Sunday Morning*, as we shall see in the next chapter). Alexander Walker perceptively noted that the role of education is crucial to Reisz's Free Cinema films, not only for his subjects, but also for the film-maker himself and his eventual embrace of the cultural policies of the New Left: 'Once more one sees the mixed blessings of education, their own and that of others, on the "Free Cinema" film-makers. Jazz-club and youth-club, the milieux of Reisz's two films, were not only the rallying points of boys and girls after school was out: they were places where the social education of the ex-teacher was continued once he himself had quit the classroom for good'.[76]

Although Rollason's commentary acknowledges the benefits of learning a trade and working your way up the apprenticeship ladder – Bobby is keen on cars and may get to drive the post office van one day; Woody's carving skills may ensure a life-long career in the meat trade – unfortunately for Beryl there is little opportunity for escape: 'Beryl sits at her bench, making food in a factory', notes Rollason. 'She has done for three years. Probably will do until she gets married'. Glossing over the patriarchal implications that only the acquisition of a husband can free Beryl from wage slavery, the commentary then adds the patronizing kicker: 'Work is something that has to be done. [We cut from Beryl to Frances at her calculator]. By *everyone*. And it's good to have it. Just the same, the day doesn't go by any too fast'. Although the sequence begins an important theme in Reisz's films, that 'work should be a challenge which ennobles man, not a depersonalising burden',[77] Walker is quick to point out the limitations of this perspective in both of Reisz's Free Cinema films: 'The service element is plugged hard, if unconsciously so. Certainly the films celebrate the escape from work and don't conceal the fact that many of the youngsters are doing dirty, dull or dead-end jobs; but there is no incitement to revolt against the conditions or the society that enforces them – indeed hardly any resentment at all. "The work is there, it's got to be done." That's the attitude'.[78]

Unfortunately this position is further reinforced when the film explores the possible alternatives. 'In the working hours, thoughts about the evening have time to pile up', notes Rollason. 'Pleasant thoughts, maybe. Or ... [We cut to a close-up of Bobby, shuffling papers at a desk, blowing out his cheeks, bored to tears] ... *frightening*'. Reisz punctuates the word by cutting to a close-up of Bobby's hand as it bangs down on a stapler. However, the synchronized sound of the latter is quickly replaced by the subjective soundtrack of a voice-over conversation between Bobby and an unseen friend, superimposed out of synch with the images, as if to express both Bobby's drifting concentration – the dialogue is probably from a day or two earlier – and the disconnection between the tedium of the repetitive routine and the reality of life outside the workplace. Unfortunately, the latter is no less circumscribing, because the conversation is about the tribalism of gang warfare, about how Georgie Ratcliff's mob is going to go out and get a team together and 'do' Smitty's mob. Apparently Smitty is easy meat because he's not 'hard' and may even be 'queer'. The subjective 'interior' conversation ends with one last slam on the stapler, but the scene continues for a few more seconds as Bobby continues stapling his papers without sound. The effect is very powerful, as it allows time not only for the spectator to understand and evaluate the serious ramifications of the conversation, but also to communicate the fragile nature of Bobby's ego and the fact that his spirit may already be irrevocably broken. Although it is obviously extremely tempting for Bobby to join a gang – the recent violence surrounding the Teddy-boy phenomenon would have made this issue all the more relevant for contemporary audiences – Reisz's own position seems clear. The brief silence is immediately followed by Dankworth's perky jazz score and a return to Alford House, where Bobby is shown paying his club dues. The drudgery of work is thus justified *tout court* through a chain of cause and effect that moves inexorably from job (and thus wages) to the payment of membership dues and the resultant possibility of organized entertainment and positive self-identity instead of the dangerous alternative of the London gang world.

With this in mind, the Friday night activities that follow – indoor football in the gym for the boys, sewing and art classes for the girls – create the dialectical 'sandwich effect' that Lambert found lacking in *Momma Don't Allow*, whereby work and play are seen to be part of a mutual Base-Superstructure model where one reflects and justifies the sociological existence of the other. The resulting expression of entrapment and interpellation is, of course, central to Reisz's oeuvre, but unlike the fiction films that follow, *We Are the Lambeth Boys* seems to be unsure whether it is justifying or critiquing it. A good example can be seen in the Death Penalty debate that closes Part Two. Spurred on by Ron, the discussion is heated but the consensus (with the notable exception of Percy) is pro-hanging. Woody even goes so far as to suggest a Biblical 'eye-for-an-eye' punishment: 'I say, not hang 'em. If something like some bloke come up to a woman and stabbed her, I say that he should have the same as what she had, stab *him*'. Reisz cannot resist an editorializing comment of his own, superimposing a high-pitched saxophone squeal over Woody's dialogue as if to simulate both the effect of the proposed stabbing's pain and a dismayed critical commentary on Woody's right-wing proselytizing. Once again, Rollason redundantly over-determines the effect with his commentary, noting that, 'When a good subject like murder comes up, everybody pitches in. The words pour out wild, and they're felt … It's good to have strong feelings, but for living in the world a bit of knowledge is needed too. And a bit of curiosity to look further than the headlines of the morning paper. Who's helping Bobby to find that? And Beryl? And Percy? And all the others'. Once again the film makes a call for continued advanced education, and the scene ends with a series of cuts of the teenagers laughing, leaving us with the positive final impression of the volatile and impassioned but also generous and galvanizing nature of youth.

More problematic, however, is the film's refusal to comment on the general quiet-ism of the kids' response to Ron's provocations, for they are 'doggedly attached to their parents', and even their grandparents', opinions on social issues thrown up in a determinedly "positivist" way by their club leader. But the film-makers show no desire, either, to *provoke* among their subjects reactions that don't correspond to accepted traditions'.[79] To be fair, this ingrained conservatism has less to do with Reisz's analytical shortcomings than with the very nature of sub-cultures in general. In their collection of essays on youth sub-cultures in postwar Britain, Stuart Hall and Tony Jefferson make an extremely useful distinction between a sub-culture's relationship to the 'parent-culture' of which it is a sub-set – e.g. Alford House's position as a working-class youth club in relation to other working-class sub-cultures, such as criminal gangs or rival football fans – and its relation to the dominant culture, i.e. the overall disposition of hegemonic cultural power in society as a whole: 'Thus we may distinguish respectable, "rough", delinquent and the criminal sub-cultures *within* working-class culture: but we may also say that, though they differ amongst themselves, they *all* derive in the first instance from a "working-class parent culture": hence, they are all subordinate sub-cultures, in relation to the dominant middle-class or bourgeois culture'.[80] Thus while Bobby is given the choice between Alford House and joining a gang, as a member of the proletariat he is just as subordinate to the dominant culture as any other member of a working-class group. Thus there is always a double articulation: 1) The relationship to the parent – i.e. working-class – culture; and 2) The relationship to the dominant culture and its ongoing struggle with subordinate groups. For the film to be truly successful, it must explore the Alford House youth culture both within *and* across these boundaries, expressing its inflection *by* class difference, as a class in and of itself, and also within the dialectical relation between teenagers and the broader 'youth market industry' (i.e. their self-identity both *as* a commodity, and in relation to that commodification through clothes, style, music, etc.). In other words, youth culture needs to be deconstructed via the complex relation between the dominant issues of 'everyday life' and the 'sub-cultural life' of different sub-sections of teenage identity.

Unfortunately, Reisz's film limits the bulk of its analysis to the first part of the double articulation – Alford House's relationship to other working-class cultures – *not* its role as part of a larger class divide. As Walker rightly argues, 'Community differences are more implicit than class consciousness; local pride gets the nod, not social deprivation. There is a respect for proletarian traditions and no desire at all to overturn the system that maintains them'.[81] Although Part Three of the film – Alford House's annual cricket match against the public schoolboys of Mill Hill – makes some effort in this regard, it delivers a mixed message at best. 'Old boys from the school have long been connected with the club', says Rollason (the governing body is made up exclusively of Old Millhillians), 'so for one summer afternoon each year, Lambeth comes to Mill Hill for cricket and tea and a swim in the open air'. With its ivy-covered walls, giant classical columns, acres of playing fields and huge swimming pool, Mill Hill couldn't be more starkly contrasted to the makeshift, backyard playground of Alford House.[82] As if to underline the class difference, Reisz inserts some reaction shots of the working-class lads as they lounge on the grass beside the pool, looking uncomfortably out of place and not a little envious. However, he subsumes any hint of class-consciousness and resentment at bourgeois privilege by stressing *community*, not class difference, expressed through the staging of two simultaneous cricket matches. While the First XI play in immaculate whites in front of the main pavilion, the Second XI match is played on a secondary playing field well away from the main action. Here, formal cricket dress is optional and the tactics are a little more unconventional, as if the game were being played by 'street' rules. Reisz underscores the distinction by cutting to an angle behind the Lambeth supporters watching the Second XI game, framing the First XI match and the imposing pavilion in the background, thus composing two parallel sub-sets within the same working-class sub-culture as an artificial discrepancy in group 'privilege'.

A similar ambivalence to class distinction is shown on the ride home. As the boys' truck passes through Westminster on its way south to Lambeth, they strut their stuff with some cocky self-defiance by wolf-whistling and jeering at passers-by and singing their tribal songs, such as the eponymous *We Are the Lambeth Boys*:[83] 'That's how it always goes on a Saturday night when the club gets away from home', comments Rollason. 'When the boys pass through the West End, the West End remembers for a while that they have passed through. And that's how the boys want it'. In other words, the teenagers have a clear-cut sense of a defining social frame or cultural order and, more importantly, of their own fixed place within it. Instead of challenging it head on, like the good soldier Schweik they simply bounce ironically off its confining walls, as seen in the words to another ditty: 'I'll sing you a song, It won't take long, All Coppers are ...' Just as we wait for an appropriate derogatory word, such as 'wankers', the lads instead replace it with an ingratiating 'handsome', thereby reducing class conflict to a lyrical sleight of hand.

However, once back in Lambeth, the cockiness disappears and everyone suddenly goes quiet: 'On this side of the river, people know the boys. And the boys know them. Back in these familiar streets, there's no need to shout so loud any more. There's not so much to shout about'. Reisz reinforces the affect of their return to grim reality by using Dankworth's plaintive jazz to underscore his travelling shots of the local neighbourhood – working-class families of all ages walking on the street or sitting on the stoop, mothers with prams chatting to their neighbours in their doorways – inter-cut with reaction shots of Bobby and Brian, obviously unhappy to be home so soon. Reisz ends Part Three with a familiar Jennings-like trope – complete silence over long travelling shots along the rooftops and chimneys of endless terraced rows, stressing the monotony and homogeneity of working-class life. However, the effect is more poetic than inflammatory, reinforcing Turk's complaint that, 'Poetic realism blunted populism's social edge. Barely acknowledging class differences, the literature of poetic realism focused on the atmosphere in which human dramas unfold. Social milieu was important not for its political implications but for the mood that its representation might effect. Likewise, words were valued more for their evocative power than for the reality to which they purportedly referred'.[84]

However, *We Are the Lambeth Boys* turns out to be a little more subtle than that, and Reisz redeems its political stance in the film's concluding section, the Saturday night dance followed by a closing epilogue at the local fish and chip shop. Once again Reisz uses *Puttin' on the Style* – this time played live by The Mickey Williams Group – as his musical centrepiece, which allows him to bring all his protagonists together for a final communal bonding. Far better edited in terms of tempo and rhythm than the corresponding finale in *Momma Don't Allow*, this time we are really convinced when Rollason says, 'Saturday night's the best night of the week'. But unlike the earlier film, Reisz doesn't end with a musical catharsis. Instead, he follows Lambert's critical advice by including an epilogue, which in many ways is the most effective part of the film because it is used both dialectically *and* associatively. As the kids assemble outside the fish and chip shop the voice-over attempts to universalize their experience by once again stressing community, and in the process tries to bridge the generation gap: 'A good evening for young people is much as it has always been. It's for being together with friends. And dancing, and shouting when you feel like it. Things we'd *all* like to do'. Reisz cements the sentiment by holding on a laughing Peggy, innocently sucking her fingers, as if she represents the youthful vitality in all of us.

However, the film ends on a far more sobering note, effectively combining poetry *and* working-class realism in an understated, but politically affecting conclusion. The teenagers have now broken up and are making their way home in groups of twos and threes. It's almost pitch-black because of the poor street lighting. We see Janet and Beryl, then Percy walking his girlfriend towards the camera down Kennington Lane. They turn into Gasholder Place and walk away from us towards the ghostly skeleton of the Kennington gasometer. We then see Woody, Kenny and their friend Phil saying goodnight and arranging their next date as they make their way past the council flats. Finally, as Phil, the last LCC boy, disappears into the darkness, we pan left to take in the lighted windows of the blocks of flats. Reisz then cuts to a wider angle of the apartment complex from a higher elevation, with the rest of the city spread out beyond like a series of illuminated pinpricks. We now pan right, across a street with accompanying traffic noise, before finally coming to rest on another horizontal block of flats, with its stark

rectangles of lights, the Kennington gasholder and a giant crane to its
left. The film ends with the plaintive sound of a train whistle (invariably a symbol of longing for escape) and a chiming church clock. 'The
mood, contrasting so starkly with the buoyancy of much of the film, is
profoundly mournful', writes Gaston. 'The dark shapes of the last shot,
belonging to the bleak working-class world which faces the youth, grow
in the imagination like phantoms. The film begins with the exuberance of youth, but it appears to end with the despair of lost illusions'.[85]
Although the ending evokes the 'suggestive magic' of Carné's fatalistic
night-time scenes in *Le Quai des Brumes*, we are also reminded of the
plight of the poor at the conclusion of Bertolt Brecht's *The Threepenny
Opera*, where the forgotten workers disappear into the darkness, leaving
the stage completely black as the chorus sings, 'For the ones they are
in darkness, and the others are in light. And you see the ones in bright-
ness ... those in darkness drop from sight'. Poetics and dialectics thus
come together to create a genuinely felt *and* critical response to class
difference.

We Are the Lambeth Boys enjoyed its greatest success on the international festivals circuit, winning a diploma at the 1959 Venice Film
Festival and a Certificate of Merit at the Cork Festival. The film also
carried off the Grand Prix at the 1959 Tours Film Festival, amid great
controversy. Reisz's future wife, Betsy Blair, was on the jury and helped
to promote audience acceptance of the judges' decision – they had
earlier booed the British ambassador who received the award on Reisz's
behalf – by comparing the Lambeth youths to the plight of Marty and
Clara in Delbert Mann's 1955 film, *Marty*.[86] Domestically, however, the
film marked the effective end of Free Cinema as a viable enterprise.
First shown as part of Free Cinema Programme 6 (18–22 March, 1959)
along with Elizabeth Russell's *Food for a Blush*, Robert Vas's *Refuge
England* and Michael Grigsby's *Enginemen*, it was deliberately packaged
as a formal farewell to the 'movement' – indeed the programme note
dramatically proclaimed, 'Free Cinema is dead. Long live Free Cinema!'
As Reisz later recalled, 'I very much regret that we never had the chance,
any of us, to go further with this *Every Day Except Christmas–We Are the
Lambeth Boys* genre ... *But there simply is no money or audience for this
kind of movie in the English cinema* ... Besides, we never found an audience for the pictures. (The booking fee for *We Are the Lambeth Boys*,
in circuit houses where it played as a second feature, was £5!)'.[87] Ultimately Ford withdrew their sponsorship and Reisz's ambition to parlay
his documentary résumé into a career in features was also temporarily
forestalled. His next film, *Saturday Night and Sunday Morning*, was
spawned not as a direct result of Free Cinema but, as we shall see in the

next chapter, through the agency of Tony Richardson and a serpentine detour through the 'Angry Young Men' of the theatre.

Almost from its inception, critical opinion has been equally divided about the aesthetic merits of Free Cinema. Richard Barsam saw it as an important precursor of *cinéma vérité* and a serious attempt to understand working-class youth in non-stereotypical terms: 'What all of these film makers achieved was not so much the films themselves, but rather a spirit of free and uninhibited inquiry. The films are important, especially for their experimental and inventive handling of sound, but even more for their place in the development of the live, direct cinema which was to follow'.[88] Matt McCarthy couldn't have disagreed more, arguing that the films are not even realist – they are fripperies: 'is anyone really convinced by the obviously engineered sequences, and the pseudo realistic plots, that posturing Cockneys are the salt of the earth?'[89] Jeffrey Richards is equally scathing, seeing little but the Emperor's new clothes: 'In fact, in personnel, approach and philosophy, they resembled nothing so much as the "documentary boys" of the 1930s grouped around John Grierson; there was the same middle-class romanticization of the working class, the same commitment to a realist aesthetic, the same belief in location-shooting, the same rejection of studio artifice'.[90] As one might expect, Grierson agreed, dismissing Free Cinema as 'baby stuff', and engaged in a long-running war of words with Anderson in the pages of *Sight and Sound*. He was supported by Ralph Bond, a former member of the Empire Marketing Board film unit in the early 1930s, who reminded his readers that 'Grierson and his group proved the same thing in other fields twenty years ago, often with much keener penetration'.[91] Derrick Knight, a young documentary director, concurred: 'This group of films has, in my opinion, shown us no real innovation in content, technique, style or approach'.[92] More constructively, Knight instead praised Associated Rediffusion's hard-hitting television documentaries which included direct speaking to the camera by the films' subjects as a form of 'documentary with the gloves off'. In December 1957, the National Film Theatre presented a selection of Rediffusion's films under the title 'The Captive Cinema' as a direct answer to 'Free Cinema'.[93] The following year, an attempt was made from within ACTT (Association of Cinematograph, Television and Allied Technicians) to bridge the gap between the warring factions and form a 'social documentary unit', going so far as to elect an official 'Social Documentary Committee' to continue the group's activities. Reisz was chosen as the Free Cinema representative but nothing productive ever came of the association. Alexander Walker gives a more pragmatic verdict on the 'movement', comparing Free Cinema unfavourably with the television work of Tony Garnett and Ken Loach in the late 1960s. He argued that Free Cinema was less important for its influence, which was minimal – the film-makers were non-committed middle-class reformists, not revolutionaries – than for the experience it gave Reisz and his cohorts in the basic principles of film-making: 'If not absolute beginners, they were pretty well sandwich-course learners. They had to make films while they did other jobs. What sustained them, unlike the TV professionals, was scarcely much more than improvisational zeal'.[94]

Such criticisms have their place, but they ignore a political undertow to the 'movement' itself that almost guaranteed its eventual redundancy in face of the changing ideological climate of the second half of the 1950s. As Alan Lovell points out, the intellectual evolution of *Sequence* into Free Cinema and beyond can be viewed as symptomatic of the general crisis of postwar liberalism (and, one could also add, Old Left socialism), so that it was almost inevitable that the artistic efficacy of 'poetic realism' would have been called into question as both Reisz and Anderson moved closer to the political activism of the New Left:

> The liberal principles developed by *Sequence* were challenged in a number of ways at very different levels: at the level of criticism through the obvious dilemmas that reliance on personal response leads to; at the level of film-making through the film-maker's difficulties in trying to express himself in a personal way within the existing commercial system; at the level of politics through the pressures of the cold war. Free Cinema was the result of this conflict, an attempt both to affirm and to adapt liberal principles in an unsympathetic cultural and political climate. For a time a solution seemed to be provided by an alliance with the New Left, hence the use of *Universities and Left Review*; but Free Cinema's suspicion of theories and ideas meant that the alliance could only be a temporary one.[95]

We saw an early inkling of this problem at the end of the last chapter in our discussion of 'Hollywood's Anti-Red Boomerang', Reisz's perceptive analysis of the crisis of political commitment in the context of the Hollywood Cold War film. Although the issue lay dormant for several years, 'Commitment' was quickly resurrected as the new rallying cry as Free Cinema rapidly evolved into a more politically active stance during 1957 and 1958. By that account, *We Are the Lambeth Boys* was probably already obsolete long before it was released.

Gavin Lambert had already begun the critical preparation for this new tack in his seminal *Sight and Sound* article, 'Who Wants True?', in which he proclaimed that, 'If one wants true and moving in the cinema, in a more than lip-service sense, then commitments are vital'.[96] Anderson expanded the sentiment in 'Stand Up! Stand Up!', published in *Sight and Sound* in Autumn 1956 (later reprinted as 'Commitment in Cinema Criticism' in the New Left journal *Universities and Left Review* in Spring of the following year). In addition to restating the earlier *Sequence* rhetoric that cinema is an art with no clear-cut difference between form and content, Anderson introduces a new stress on the need to acknowledge political commitment and be prepared to fight for it. 'In so far as film criticism is being written here and now, and deals with an art intimately related to the society in which we live, it cannot escape its wider commitments', he notes. 'Essentially, in fact, there is no such thing as uncommitted criticism, any more than there is such a thing as insignificant art. It is merely a question of the openness with which our commitments are stated. I do not believe that we should keep quiet about them'.[97] Here commitment is a question of basic human values rather than Lambert's earlier-stated idea of aesthetic *standards*. The latter emerge out of the former and no longer need separate consideration. Anderson continued this strain of thought in a follow-up article entitled 'Get Out and Push' (published in the 1958 anthology, *Declaration*), in which he argued that 'Fighting means commitment, means believing what you say, and saying what you believe. It will also mean being called sentimental, irresponsible, self-righteous, extremist and out-of-date by those who equate maturity with scepticism, art with amusement, and responsibility with romantic excess. And it must mean a new kind of intellectual and artist, who is not frightened or scornful of his fellows; who does not see himself as threatened by, and in natural opposition to, the philistine mass; who is eager to make his contribution, and ready to use the mass-media to do so'.[98]

Reisz quickly followed Anderson's lead. In his own 1958 *Universities and Left Review* article, 'A Use for Documentary', he reiterates his desire to separate sociological fact from poetic truth but introduces a new polemical tone in his writing, suggesting that the film-maker is also responsible for *constructing* society, not just capturing it through poetic representation:

> There is a difference in kind between a sociological fact and poetic truth, and the artist had better remember it if he wants to keep his audience. The fallacy of assuming that you can give the artist a series of facts and conclusions which he then invests with 'feeling' is the fallacy of socialist realism as well as of the British Council film. The artist must not be expected to spread honey on bread which someone else has provided. He must bake his own bread. Of course the artist must see things through the individuals with whom he is directly concerned. The strength and relevance of his commitment and depth of his instinctive response will determine how significant his images will be.[99]

Similar opinions were being delivered from the New Left side of the fence. In a review of *Declaration*, subsequent *New Left Review* editor Stuart Hall wrote: 'The political intellectual is concerned with the institutional life of the society: the creative artist with the attitudes, the manners, the moral and emotional life which the individual consummates within that social framework. It seems to me that the beginning of a common socialist humanism is the realization that these are not two distinct areas of interest, but the complementary parts of a complex, common experience. Our attitudes mirror the realities of power, of status, of success and failure; and these things are both social and personal facts, the very limits of the human condition ... The public and the personal life are deeply interrelated, and we must learn to comprehend them as a totality'.[100] For Hall, like Reisz and Anderson, commitment was seen as much in terms of artistic endeavour as political action, with society now considered in *cultural* rather than political terms.

This symbiosis of art and the new society was spawned in 1956, for as Hall reminds us, 'The "first" New Left was born in "1956", a conjuncture (not just a year) bounded on one side by the suppression of the Hungarian Revolution by Soviet tanks in November and on the other by the British and French invasion of the Suez Canal zone'.[101] Paralleling their attempts to formulate an anti-state socialism lying somewhere between Stalinism and social democracy, the New Left writers and intellectuals rarely adopted clear-cut ideological positions towards either western imperialism or the Soviet Union, opting instead for the alternative, anti-colonial 'Three Worlds Theory' prevalent at the time. In this case, the 'Third World' was lionized as a key player in a military non-alignment 'movement' that also included Tito's Yugoslavia, creating, in effect, a 'Third Way' between the inexorable military madness of the First and Second Worlds. One of the key catalysts for this position in Britain was the CND, which was initiated by largely middle-class, high-profile dissidents such as J. B. Priestley, Bertrand Russell, Michael Foot, A. J. P. Taylor, Benjamin Britten and Barbara Hepworth. As Alan Sinfield has pointed out, the group's philosophy 'was rooted in liberal humanism; Bertrand Russell acknowledged the capacity of "Man" for "cruelty and suffering", but appealed to "potentialities of greatness and splendour." The problem with this humanism is that it disregards the actual structures of power in class and patriarchal society. It takes at face value the "humanism" of capitalist society, accepting the bourgeois universalization of itself as the human, and appeals to the current order to ameliorate "man's inhumanity to man."'[102]

This inevitably circumscribed liberalism underwent a profound change as the CND began to be embraced by a younger generation of writers – Alan Sillitoe (author of *Saturday Night and Sunday Morning*), David Mercer (author of *Morgan, A Suitable Case for Treatment*), Iris Murdoch, John Berger and Robert Bolt – and became instead a focus for ideologically left-wing activity, specifically through the writers' overt connections to the burgeoning New Left. Just as the CND leaders hedged their bets on how far Britain should depend for its security on the American 'nuclear Umbrella', *New Left Review* editors Hall and E. P. Thompson were already promoting the position that Britain might be better off subscribing neither to NATO nor to the Soviet Bloc. Although this non-alignment strategy and tripartite division of the world subsequently proved to be simplistic, the non-dialectical nature of the 'Three Worlds Theory' became a useful jumping-off point for a more multiplicitous reading of Cold War power relations, where difference was now seen as irreducible to a Western historical master narrative.

Reisz and Anderson became directly involved in this developing New Left strategy with *March to Aldermaston* (1959), the documentary record of the CND's first fifty mile Easter March from Trafalgar Square to the atomic weapons factory at Aldermaston, Berkshire in 1958. As we have seen, they had already received overtures to write for *Universities and Left Review* and, as Anderson recalls, 'It was the political (or social) people who wanted to make connections and be friendly. It was surprising and very, very encouraging – because it suddenly seemed as if there could really be a "Popular Front" of political and creative people; and in that popular front, movies and theatre could have a place and enjoy sympathetic support. For just a short time that is what actually happened'.[103] This view is endorsed by a collective statement from the editors in the final issue of *Universities and Left Review*, which opines that, 'Without CND supporters, Anti-Ugly protesters [a protest movement against the banality and conformism of postwar British architecture], African demonstrators, Free Cinema and the Society for the Abolition of The Death Penalty, we would be nowhere'.[104]

For the record, it's important to note that the Aldermaston film was *not* a Free Cinema project, but instead emerged out of the 'Film & TV Committee for Nuclear Disarmament', initiated by ACTT members Derrick Knight and Kurt Lewenhack, the American Allan Forbes, as well as a committee heavily drawn from ACTT that included, in addition to Reisz and Anderson, Charles Cooper, Christopher Brunel, Lewis McLeod, Elizabeth Russell, Eda Segal and Derek York.[105] According to the committee statement, 'The film would have no individual credits, only a single one for the committee [so that] there would be no claims, grumbles and so forth as a result of someone's work not being properly recognised'.[106] In all, thirty unpaid 'technicians' – including Reisz

– were involved in the shoot, with political beliefs running the gamut from Communists to Labour, pacifists to anti-nukes. In another ironic twist of fate, Reisz and Anderson also found themselves working directly alongside representatives of the Grierson School. A total of three hours and twenty minutes of 35mm film was shot over the course of the four day march (although several cameras were used, only one was synched for sound) which Anderson and co-editor Mary Beales trimmed down to a final release print of twenty-two minutes.

As one might expect with such a varied group of participants, the end result is an odd mish-mash of styles and approaches to activist political cinema that helps to explain Reisz and Anderson's eventual move away from both the increasing dogmatism of New Left politics in general and poetic documentary in particular, in favour of a more subjectively incisive, but no less political, *dramatic* realism associated with fiction filmmaking. In this sense, *March to Aldermaston* is extremely instructive in helping to negatively define Reisz's subsequent film-making aesthetic. According to many commentators at the time, the film's main problem lies in its unsuccessful attempt to pool two different influences: television documentary (participants speaking directly to the camera) and Free Cinema (poetic realist *observation*). Writing in *The Tribune*, Derek Hill acknowledged that the film was 'an invaluable record of an occasion which merits that misused word momentous',[107] but he also wondered why it wasn't more emotionally moving: 'I suspect that the fault is at least partly due to the contrasting approaches of the technicians, who were broadly divided between the matter-of-fact techniques of television and the poetic and usually more penetrating Free Cinema style'.[108]

The film focuses more on halts in the march than the linear continuity of the walk itself, thus giving the film-makers a chance to show what the march was *for* rather than merely reiterate an obvious antinuclear party line. This is for the most part very successful, as the direct interviews ('documentary with the gloves off') are often extremely touching, allowing the film to emphasize the eclectic backgrounds and motivations of the people who took part – students, housewives, miners, clerks, artists, etc. Thus one woman says she is marching because she wants to safeguard the future of her children; an elderly Welshman who took part in the hunger marches of the 1920s and 1930s felt compelled to continue the legacy of grass-roots resistance; while a jazz musician participates because he wants to continue playing and hearing good music. 'Throughout, the film-makers show a tremendous respect for people', notes Alan Lovell in *Peace News*. 'There are no gimmicks in the way they are presented. When people come before the camera to say why they are on the march they explain in their own straightforward way; the film-makers have confidence in the people so they feel no urge to dress them up'.[109] Unfortunately, although these TV-style interviews of individual marchers are effective when taken separately, they tend to get repetitive and interrupt the forward momentum of the narrative whole. Also, we get no input from the politicians who took part, which would have widened the discursive scope of the film to include an understanding of the 'Third Way' in the context of Cold War *realpolitik*. Penelope Houston notes that the issues behind the CND march were based on two foundations: 1) The determination to see nuclear warfare outlawed; and 2) That Britain had the duty to lead the way by unilateral disarmament. The film deals only with issue 1) and shirks the question of 2), as if one were implicit in the other. By excluding the politicians' voice, the film sets up an artificial binary opposition between 'us' (i.e. ordinary people) and 'them' (the politicians): 'It implies that "they" must be castigated for failure, while "we" can take political action and keep our hands clean ... The Aldermaston marchers do us all a service by raising political issues in moral terms. But a film like this, with the mistrust and resentment of politicians that it makes so explicit, must still ultimately throw the responsibility back to them. One would have welcomed a little more straight political thinking along with the humanitarianism'.[110] Equally excluded from the direct interviews are the passive onlookers who observe the marchers as they pass through their neighbourhoods. What are they thinking? Why aren't they marching? They are not given the opportunity to speak, so the question is evaded. The film 'attempts no real argument and never begins to explore the widely differing convictions, ethical, political and religious, which led the marchers to take part', bemoans Hill.[111] Instead it presupposes a favourable audience so that its overall stance comes across as both smug and priggish.

While the television documentary component is an ideological and didactic mixed bag, the Free Cinema contributions – i.e. poetic detail – are far more successful insofar as they stress the importance of ordinary, everyday things, personal emblems that are now seen to be all the more precious and self-defining because they are threatened with mass destruction. Thus queuing for a life-sustaining cup of tea, sitting down to rest one's feet after a day's marching, a band playing 'I dreamt that the Bomb had fallen, and a million people were dead' as the marchers pass a cemetery, eating sandwiches at the base of the Albert Memorial, the torrents of rain that threatened to cancel the first day's march, nights spent drying out in improvized dorms, two men playing chess by the wayside – all contribute to a mosaic of detail that, like Jennings's *Listen to Britain*, roots the demonstration in the very fabric of everyday life.

'In this way', states Lovell, 'the film establishes that the march was a demonstration by people, and that it was a demonstration that sprang directly out of the people's lives and not a sudden excitement over something. The marchers not only did not want to die, they also very much wanted to go on living and doing the things that they thought worth while'.[112]

Unfortunately, if two competing styles were not enough, *March to Aldermaston* also has a voice-over commentary, in this case written by Christopher Logue and Lindsay Anderson, and read by the actor Richard Burton.[113] With its odd mix of irony and compassion, sentiment and cynicism, the commentary irrevocably stamps the film with Anderson's more polemical narrative voice rather than Reisz's cooler analytical tone (Reisz always tries to place the viewer in the middle of two incompatible positions and forces us to work through the antinomies ourselves). Although it clearly reflects Reisz and Anderson's new-found attachment to collective 'commitment', chief among the commentary's problems is the over-familiar use of the word 'we', which creates an bogus self-identification with the marchers. The result is an overload of calculated simplicity and emotionalism, for as Derek Hill complains, 'the insistence that "we" are just ordinary folk doing our best becomes a little sanctimonious',[114] thus playing right into the hands of the march's political critics. Moreover, like Rollason's voice-over in *We Are the Lambeth Boys*, Burton often redundantly reiterates what we have been shown through poetic detail, illustrated by his observation that, 'Living's a big word: but it means a million little things, like being with people we like, or people we love, reading the Sunday newspapers, eating, sitting around talking, or making music, being human, in fact'.

Far more effective are the occasions when Anderson and Logue use the commentary to ask a simple question: 'We look at the world, and we see madness. But how can we bear witness to what we see?' Firstly, we bear witness through a knowledge and understanding of an unspeakable history that threatens the very possibility of a viable future: 'We stood for a minute in silence, as we used to stand on Armistice Day', intones Burton. 'But we were standing for Hiroshima and Nagasaki, where 200,000 people were condemned to death in our name. And we weren't only thinking of the past. We were thinking of H-bomb tests, and missile bases, and science used to mutilate and destroy – the radioactive dust in the air we breathe and the food we eat ... the two thousand people a year who are dying now because of strontium 90 in their bones. And how many next year; and the year after that?' The 'madness' of the religious right is specifically singled out for criticism. Although the marchers received welcome succour *en route* from Quakers and

Methodists, who opened their meeting halls so that 'we could sit down for a bit, have a cup of tea and dry off', they quickly encountered opposition on the first day, for as they reached Hyde Park Corner, 'we found some people who were demonstrating for the bomb. They were Christians, too, they read from the Bible, and they prayed against us. And the place they had chosen for their meeting was a memorial to men who had died in a war to end war. But we, the living, remembered the Commandment "Thou shalt not kill," and we went on our way'. Similarly, as the marchers entered Reading late on Easter Sunday, the church bells were ringing 'and we felt they were ringing for us. Now we had to get organized again. We had to find out where we could get something to eat and where we'd meet tomorrow. We had to find our packs and somewhere to sleep. We asked the vicar to stop the bells. But he said – "I do not approve of you. If my bells drown your voices, so much the better!" And we realised again how many people were against us. But we weren't discouraged'. Although it would have been far more convincing to have the vicar speak directly to the cameras instead of having Burton speak for him, the film-makers' didacticism precluded any sense of open discourse. The educator in Reisz must have found this tactic pretty hard to swallow.

Perhaps the most lasting image of the film is towards the end, when the marchers reach the Aldermaston factory gates to the accompaniment of mocking laughter by the local onlookers. 'We didn't arrive in triumph', notes Burton. 'We came in thinking. Thinking of the people who laugh – as perhaps people laughed in Hiroshima the day before a small bomb exploded in the sky. Does an H-bomb have to explode HERE before we can wake up?' This voice-over is accompanied by photographs of Hiroshima victims cross-cut with the images of the resting marchers. We then cut to shots of enormous stockpiles of nuclear arms amassed by the superpowers, thereby placing the responsibility for ending the lunacy squarely on the shoulders of the audience. Alan Lovell, for one, was completely convinced by the gesture, stating that, 'Because we have been made to feel the dignity and importance of people we feel that we *can* end the madness, if we struggle hard enough ... *March to Aldermaston* is not just the record of a historic event. It is a weapon in the campaign for nuclear disarmament. Everybody who wants to get rid of the bomb has a responsibility to see that the film is seen by as many people as possible. There will be no better advertisement for the next Aldermaston march'.[115]

Released by Contemporary Films on 20 February 1959, *March to Aldermaston* ran for several weeks at the Academy Cinema in London on a double bill with Jean Renoir's *La Grande Illusion* (1938). Labour MP

Frank Beswick arranged a special screening in the Grand Committee Room of the House of Commons, while Charles Cooper entered it at the 1959 Moscow Film Festival (it was later released in East Germany with some cuts). Domestic opinion tended to reflect already hardened political beliefs. Peter G. Baker vilified the film in *Films and Filming*, calling it 'a singularly inept piece of documentary. A year late, it falls far short of what a reasonably competent TV team could do in less than a week. "What's Worth Doing is Worth Doing Well" says a poster some-where in the film. When these precious propagandists have digested *that* perhaps they'll realise there's more to filmmaking than having a union ticket or a political affiliation'.[116] Penelope Houston had the most balanced view, noting that the film had less to say about political convic-tion *per se* than about people, neatly capturing the marchers' puzzled, honest, purposeful mood:

> *March to Aldermaston* is humane, journalism given a charge of poetry: in its emphasis on the need for gaiety as well as protest, it is strongly affir-mative. Rather surprisingly, it carries gentleness almost to the point of softness ... When the film sets out to underline its message, by intercut-ting still photographs of Hiroshima victims with shots of the marchers, it generates pity but not horror. Here it avoids the flashier techniques of propaganda, but somehow its method of quiet statement is less telling and powerful than it should be.[117]

In short, echoing Alan Sinfield's earlier comment about the CND, the film was a little too liberal-humanist for its own good.

More importantly for our purposes, the film helped to polarize Reisz and Anderson's relationship to the New Left. It revealed that, following a brief honeymoon where both sides saw politics and culture as significantly interrelated, organized political commitment and art's more poetic reflection of social reality were now irretrievably at odds. 'I don't regret having tried to join a New Left', Anderson later recalled, 'because it would have been very nice if the New Left had ever amounted to anything, if there really had been a radical movement we could have joined together in, both as writers, film-makers and politicians. But it did not take very long for the New Left to degenerate into a new genera-tion of politicians or a new generation of academic theorists. And it did not take very long for us to discover that their interest in the arts was a purely propagandist one. It was only in so far as we made work that seemed to reflect what they thought to be socially acceptable that our work was in any way interesting'.[118]

For their part, the New Left intellectuals were not so naive as to believe that individual artworks could do anything more than influ-ence the general climate of public opinion. While Hall acknowledged the contribution of Reisz and the Free Cinema group to the London New Left clubs as centres of discussion and debate, he also realized that 'the "question of agency" had become deeply problematic'.[119] Writing in the September/October 1959 issue of the theatre magazine *Encore*, Hall wrote that 'it would be reassuring to think that a couple of showings of *O Dreamland* would bring the Rank organization to a dead stop, that *We Are the Lambeth Boys* would prevent race riots in Notting Hill, and that by now every new housing-estate would had its open-air perfor- mance of *Chicken Soup With Barley*. It simply isn't as easy as that'.[120] Commitment's real weakness lay not in the passion of its advocates, but in its lack of clear and practical definition. Unfortunately, its largely subjective nature led to a form of classless neo-romanticism tied to *rive gauche* bohemianism and the American Beats (Allen Ginsberg's *Howl* appeared in Britain in 1956, Jack Kerouac's *On the Road* was published in 1958), which would rapidly metamorphose into the 1960s counter- culture – epitomized by Ken Kesey and the Merry Pranksters – and a radical variation on anti-activist subjectivism (the central subject of Reisz's *Dogs Soldiers*).

By 1963, Anderson was acknowledging that, 'the word "commit- ment" has become a bore, not because the idea behind it is insignificant or unimportant, but because discussion of it, by Rightists and Leftists alike, has been so lazy and so shallow'.[121] The first wave of the New Left was effectively moribund by 1961. Tensions within the core editing group of the *New Left Review* led to Stuart Hall's resignation and Perry Anderson taking over as editor. Among the changes was the abandon- ment of the idea of the New Left as a social movement and its replace- ment by the development and dissemination of a rigorous Marxist *theory*. Extremely wary of practical involvement in politics, the *New Left Review* eventually retreated into an aestheticized, Cultural Studies arena, fighting the class war through articles on a 'textual' as opposed to street-level battleground. Free Cinema's suspicion of theory – a holdover from the *Sequence* days – proved to be crippling in this new context, for as Bert Hogenkamp argues, 'what neither Anderson and Reisz nor the cultural spokespeople of the New Left managed to develop was a systematic, theoretically sustained body of work based on the assump- tions expressed in these articles: the power of the mass media, the posi- tive role of the cinema for the community and the film maker's need to express her/himself personally'.[122] Instead, Reisz's immediate response was to piggyback his career on the 'new wave' of northern working-class provincial writers – specifically Alan Sillitoe and David Storey – who had emerged in the late 1950s on the heels of the 'kitchen sink' realism of the Angry Young Men.

Notes

1 Published as part of the First Free Cinema Programme notes, 5–8 February, 1956.
2 Reisz, quoted in Orbanz, *Journey to a Legend and Back: The British Realistic Film*, p. 62.
3 Lindsay Anderson, 'Get Out and Push!', in Tom Maschler, ed., *Declaration* (New York, E. P. Dutton and Co., 1958), p. 154.
4 Lindsay Anderson, National Film Theatre notes, 15 August 1977, quoted in John Hill, *Sex, Class and Realism: British Cinema 1956–1963* (London, BFI, 1986), p. 129. Also available online through the British Film Institute. Accessed 28 January 2005. www.bfi.org.uk/features/freecinema/archive/anderson-77prognotes.html.
5 Alan Cooke, 'Free Cinema', *Sequence*, No. 13, New Year 1951, p. 13.
6 Lindsay Anderson, quoted in Elizabeth Sussex, *Lindsay Anderson* (London, Studio Vista Ltd, 1969), p. 30.
7 Alan Lovell, 'Free Cinema', in Alan Lovell and Jim Hillier, *Studies in Documentary* (New York, Viking Press, 1972), p. 134.
8 John Caughie and Kevin Rockett, *The Companion to British and Irish Cinema* (London, BFI/Cassell, 1966), p. 38.
9 James M. Welsh and John C. Tibbetts, eds, *The Cinema of Tony Richardson: Essays and Interviews* (Albany, State University of New York Press, 1999), p. 7.
10 For an eloquent argument in favour of the French New Wave's progressive modernism against the 'second rate' realism of the British New Wave, see Wollen, 'The Last New Wave', in Friedman, ed., *Fires Were Started*, pp. 37–8.
11 Lindsay Anderson, interview 25 February 1971, in Walker, *Hollywood, England*, p. 26.
12 Reisz, quoted in Lovell, 'Free Cinema', p. 145.
13 Anderson, quoted in Orbanz, *Journey to a Legend and Back: The British Realistic Film*, pp. 46–7.
14 Anderson, interviewed in McFarlane, *An Autobiography of British Cinema*, pp. 10–11.
15 Anderson, quoted Orbanz, *Journey to a Legend and Back: The British Realistic Film*, p. 47.
16 Anderson, quoted in Walker, *Hollywood, England*, p. 27.
17 Anderson, 20 July 1979, quoted in Allison Graham, *Lindsay Anderson* (Boston, Twayne, 1981), p. 29.
18 Reisz, quoted in Walker, *Hollywood, England*, p. 36.
19 Karel Reisz, interview in Gene D. Phillips, *The Movie Makers: Artists in an Industry* (Chicago, Nelson-Hall Company, 1973), p. 186.
20 Richard Meran Barsam, *Nonfiction Film: A Critical History* (New York, E. P. Dutton, 1973), p. 226.
21 Forman was the chief instigator for bringing *Sequence* critics Gavin Lambert and Penelope Houston to the BFI to modernize their official journal, *Sight and Sound*.
22 Denis Forman, *The Film and the Public*, cited in Ivan Butler, 'To Encourage the Art of the Film': The Story of the British Film Institute* (London, Robert Hale, 1971), p. 98.
23 For Reisz's observations on the director's visit to the NFT, see 'Stroheim in London', *Sight and Sound*, Vol. 23, No. 4, April–June 1954, pp. 172–3.
24 Denis Forman, cited in Christophe Dupin, 'Early Days of Short Film Production at the British Film Institute: Origins and Evolution of the BFI Experimental Film Fund (1952–66)', *Journal of Media Practice*, Vol. 4, No. 2, 2003, p. 81.
25 Reisz was by that time (1956–59) acting as Films Officer for the Ford Motor Company, itself a major underwriter of two Free Cinema projects, including *We Are the Lambeth Boys*.

26 Other Fund-sponsored Free Cinema films included *Nice Time* (Claude Goretta and Alain Tanner – Free Cinema Programme 3, May 1957), *Refuge England* (Robert Vas) and *Enginemen* (Michael Grigsby) – both Free Cinema Programme 6, March 1959.

27 Dupin, 'Early Days of Short Film Production at the British Film Institute', p. 86; Michael Balcon cited from the 'Introduction' to *Experiment in Britain* (London, BFI, 1958).

28 Dupin, 'Early Days of Short Film Production at the British Film Institute', p. 87.

29 *Ibid.*

30 Reisz, quoted in Orbanz, *Journey to a Legend and Back: The British Realistic Film*, pp. 53–4.

31 Lindsay Anderson, 'Only Connect: Some Aspects of the Work of Humphrey Jennings', *Sight and Sound*, Vol. 23, No. 4, April–June 1954, p. 181.

32 John Grierson, *Grierson on Documentary*, Forsyth Hardy, ed. (London, Faber and Faber, 1966), p. 13.

33 Andrew Higson, 'Britain's Outstanding Contribution to the Film: The Documentary-Realist Tradition', in Charles Barr, ed., *All Our Yesterdays: 90 Years of British Cinema* (London, BFI, 1986), p. 74.

34 *Ibid.*, p. 81.

35 Grierson, *Grierson on Documentary*, p. 18.

36 *Ibid.*, pp. 15–16.

37 *Ibid.*, p. 25.

38 Anderson, in Orbanz, *Journey to a Legend and Back: The British Realistic Film*, p. 41.

39 Karel Reisz, 'A Use for Documentary', *Universities and Left Review*, No. 3, Winter 1958, p. 24.

40 Reisz, quoted in Orbanz, *Journey to a Legend and Back: The British Realistic Film*, p. 62.

41 Reisz, quoted in Claude Lichtenstein and Thomas Schregenberger, eds, *As Found: The Discovery of the Ordinary* (Zürich Museum of Design, Lars Müller Publishers, 2001), p. 239.

42 This is highly appropriate given Jennings's links to the movement. As a painter and friend of André Breton he was heavily influenced by Surrealism, helping to organize the London Surrealist exhibition of 1936. Jennings also dabbled in Marxism and played a leading role in Mass Observation, co-editing the *12th May 1937 Survey*.

43 Edward Baron Turk, *Child of Paradise: Marcel Carné and the Golden Age of French Cinema* (Cambridge MA and London, Harvard University Press, 1989), pp. 109–10.

44 Anderson, 'Only Connect: Some Aspects of the Work of Humphrey Jennings', p. 182.

45 *Ibid.*

46 *Ibid.*, p. 186.

47 Reisz, quoted in Orbanz, *Journey to a Legend and Back: The British Realistic Film*, p. 53.

48 Jack C. Ellis, *The Documentary Idea: A Critical History of English Language Documentary Film and Video* (Englewood Cliffs NJ, Prentice Hall, 1989), p. 210.

49 From the original 1956 Free Cinema Programme notes. Accessed 8 October 2004. www.bfi.org.uk/features/freecinema/prog5.html.

50 Reisz, quoted in Welsh and Tibbetts, *The Cinema of Tony Richardson: Essays and Interviews*, p. 28.

51 The film-makers received no personal stipend and the money was only paid on completion of the film to defray production costs.

52 Reisz, quoted in Welsh and Tibbetts, *The Cinema of Tony Richardson: Essays and Interviews*, p. 28.

53 *Ibid.*, p. 27.

54 Walter Lassally, speaking during the post-screening discussion, 'Free Cinema at the NFT', 22 March 2001. British Film Institute. Accessed 28 January 2005. www.bfi.org.uk/showing/nft/interviews/freecinema/03_technique.html.

55 Raymond Durgant, *A Mirror for England: British Movies from Austerity to Affluence* (London, Faber and Faber, 1970), pp. 127–8.

56 *Ibid.*, p. 128.

57 Gavin Lambert, 'Free Cinema', *Sight and Sound*, Vol. 25, No. 4, Spring 1956, p. 176.

58 Reisz, quoted in Welsh and Tibbetts, *The Cinema of Tony Richardson: Essays and Interviews*, p. 28.

59 Richardson, *The Long Distance Runner: An Autobiography*, p. 94.

60 Typical lyrics: 'Mama don't allow no trombone playing around here ... /Mama don't allow no trombone playing around here ... /We don't care what Momma don't allow/We're gonna' keep on playing anyhow/Mama don't allow no trombone playing around here'.

61 John Ellis, ed., *1951–1976: British Film Institute Productions* (London, BFI, 1977), p. 32.

62 Lewis Jacob, 'Free Cinema 1', *Film Culture*, Vol. 4, No. 2, February 1958, p. 10.

63 Lambert, 'Free Cinema', p. 176.

64 Karel Reisz, cited in Tom Vallance, 'Karel Reisz: Director of *Saturday Night and Sunday Morning*', Obituary in *The Independent*, 28 November 2002.

65 All three films are available on the BFI video, *Free Cinema: A Compilation*.

66 Karel Reisz, speaking during the post-screening discussion, 'Free Cinema at the NFT', 22 March, 2001. British Film Institute. Accessed 28 January 2005. www.bfi.org.uk/showing/nft/interviews/freecinema/12_audience.html.

67 In the first week of January 1985, the BBC aired three programmes on consecutive evenings under the title, *The Lambeth Boys*. Reisz's original film was given its first full TV screening, followed by a 'where are they now?' documentary directed by Rob Rohrer that included new interviews with the Alford House teenagers twenty-five years on. The third programme was a look at the club's members in the 1980s. Although there's nary a black face to be seen in Reisz's film, by the 1980s there were more blacks than whites, but a group largely unaffected by colour difference. See Richard Hoggart, 'Lambeth Boys', *Sight and Sound*, Vol. 54, No. 2, Spring 1985, pp. 106–9.

68 Reisz, quoted in Orbanz, *Journey to a Legend and Back: The British Realistic Film*, p. 55.

69 *Ibid.*, p. 61.

70 Reisz, quoted in McFarlane, *An Autobiography of British Cinema*, pp. 476–7.

71 Richard Hoggart, '*We Are the Lambeth Boys*', *Sight and Sound*, Vol. 28, Nos 3 and 4, Summer–Autumn 1959, p. 165.

72 Karel Reisz, speaking during the post-screening discussion, 'Free Cinema at the NFT', 22 March, 2001. British Film Institute. Accessed 28 January 2005. www.bfi.org.uk/showing/nft/interviews/freecinema/12_audience.html.

73 Tony Jefferson, 'Cultural Responses of the Teds', in Stuart Hall and Tony Jefferson, eds, *Resistance through Rituals: Youth Subcultures in Post-War Britain* (London, HarperCollins, 1975), p. 86.

74 The key lyrics are: 'Puttin' on the agony, puttin' on the style/That's what all the young folks are doing all the while/And as I look around me, I sometimes have to smile/seeing all the young folks putting on the style'.

75 Gaston, *Karel Reisz*, p. 26.

76 Walker, *Hollywood, England*, pp. 36–7.
77 Karel Reisz, quoted in Gene D. Phillips, 'An Interview with Karel Reisz, *Cinema* (Beverly Hills), Vol. 4, No. 2, Summer 1968, p. 53.
78 Walker, *Hollywood, England*, pp. 29–30.
79 *Ibid.*, p. 32.
80 John Clarke, Stuart Hall, Tony Jefferson and Brian Roberts, 'Subcultures, Cultures and Class', in Hall and Jefferson, eds, *Resistance through Rituals*, p. 13.
81 Walker, *Hollywood, England*, p. 32.
82 The annual cricket match lapsed over the years but was revived in the 1980s because of interest from Alford House's large West Indian contingent. It's far less uncomfortable an event today.
83 'We are the Lambeth Boys. We are the Lambeth Boys. We know our manners, we spend our tanners, we are respected wherever we go'.
84 Turk, *Child of Paradise: Marcel Carné and the Golden Age of French Cinema*, p. 109.
85 Gaston, *Karel Reisz*, p. 28.
86 Blair, *The Memory of All That*, pp. 303–7.
87 Reisz, letter to Alexander Walker, in Walker, *Hollywood, England*, p. 38.
88 Barsam, *Nonfiction Film: A Critical History*, pp. 234–5.
89 Matt McCarthy, 'Free Cinema – In Chains', *Films & Filming*, Vol. 5, No. 5, February 1959, p. 10.
90 Jeffrey Richards, 'New Waves and Old Myths: British Cinema in the 1960s', in Bart Moore-Gilbert and John Seed, eds, *Cultural Revolution? The Challenge of the Arts in the 1960s* (London and New York, Routledge, 1992), p. 219.
91 Ralph Bond, 'Not So Free Cinema', *Film & TV Technician*, June–July, 1957, p. 92.
92 Cited in Bert Hogenkamp, *Film, Television and the Left in Britain 1950 to 1970* (London, Lawrence and Wishart, 2000), p. 55.
93 *Ibid.*
94 Walker, *Hollywood, England*, pp. 31–2.
95 Alan Lovell, 'Free Cinema', in Lovell and Hillier, *Studies in Documentary*, p. 155.
96 Gavin Lambert, 'Who Wants True?', *Sight and Sound*, Vol. 21, No. 4, April–June 1952, p. 148.
97 Lindsay Anderson, 'Stand Up! Stand Up!', *Sight and Sound*, Vol. 26, No. 2, Autumn 1956, p. 69.
98 Anderson, 'Get Out and Push!', pp. 159–60.
99 Reisz, 'A Use for Documentary', p. 66.
100 Stuart Hall, 'In the No Man's Land', *Universities and Left Review*, No. 3, Winter 1958, p. 87.
101 Stuart Hall, 'The "First" New Left: Life and Times', in Robin Archer, *et al.*, *Out of Apathy: Voices of the New Left Thirty Years On* (London and New York, Verso, 1989), p. 13.
102 Alan Sinfield, *Literature, Politics and Culture in Postwar Britain* (Oxford, Basil Blackwell, 1989), p. 239.
103 Anderson, quoted in Archer, *et al.*, *Out of Apathy*, p. 140.
104 Quoted in Hall, 'The "First" New Left: Life and Times', in Archer, *et al.*, *Out of Apathy*, p. 33.
105 The ACTT Annual General Meeting had adopted a resolution renouncing nuclear weapons, 8–9 March 1958.
106 Statement cited in Hogenkamp, *Film, Television and the Left in Britain 1950 to 1970*, p. 56.
107 Derek Hill, 'Failure on the March' (*March to Aldermaston*), *The Tribune*, 27 February 1959, p. 11.

108 *Ibid.*

109 Alan Lovell, 'March Against Madness', *Peace News*, No. 1182, 20 February 1959, Supplement, p. IV.

110 Penelope Houston, '*March to Aldermaston*', *Sight and Sound*, Vol. 28, No. 2, Spring 1959, p. 89.

111 Hill, 'Failure on the March', p. 11.

112 Lovell, 'March Against Madness', Supplement, p. IV.

113 Christopher Logue and Lindsay Anderson, '*March to Aldermaston* (complete commentary)', *Peace News*, No. 1182, 20 February 1959, Supplement, pp. I–II.

114 Hill, 'Failure on the March', p. 11.

115 Lovell, 'March Against Madness', Supplement, p. IV.

116 Peter G. Baker, 'Re-Presentation (*March to Aldermaston*)', *Films & Filming*, Vol. 5, No. 7, April 1959, p. 25.

117 Houston, '*March to Aldermaston*', p. 89.

118 Anderson, quoted in Lovell, 'Free Cinema', in Lovell and Hillier, *Studies in Documentary*, p. 156.

119 Hall, 'The "First" New Left: Life and Times', in Archer, *et al.*, *Out of Apathy*, pp. 29–31.

120 Quoted in Robert Hewison, *In Anger: Culture in the Cold War, 1945–60* (London, Weidenfeld and Nicolson, 1981), pp. 181–2.

121 Lindsay Anderson, 'Sport, Life and Art', *Films & Filming*, Vol. 9, No. 5, February 1963, p. 18.

122 Hogenkamp, *Film, Television and the Left in Britain 1950 to 1970*, pp. 54–5.

Kitchen sink realism and the birth of the British New Wave: *Saturday Night and Sunday Morning* (1960)

4

There's nothing more elegant than beautifully shot poverty. (Karel Reisz)[1]

The good life is not simply a matter of 'putting up with things', of 'making the best of it', but one with scope for having the 'bit extra' that really makes 'Life'. Most working-class people are not climbing; they do not quarrel with their general level; they only want the little more that allows a few frills ... Where the routine of work is rarely changed and is almost entirely imposed from outside, the attitude towards free and personal acts takes on a special complexion. (Richard Hoggart)[2]

I didn't want Arthur Seaton ... getting transmogrified into a young workman who turns out to be an honest-to-goodness British individualist – that is, one who triumphs in the end against and at the expense of a communist agitator or the trade unions. I didn't want him to become a tough stereotype with, after all, a heart of moral gold which has in it a love of the monarchy and all that old-fashioned muck. (Alan Sillitoe)[3]

'Don't let the bastards grind you down! That's one thing I've learned', soliloquizes bolshie young Arthur Seaton (Albert Finney) as he stands at his capstan lathe, mechanically cranking out components amid the deafening din of Nottingham's Raleigh bicycle factory late one Friday afternoon. 'What I'm out for is a good time. All the rest is propaganda'. Work might be a daily grind for the rest of us, but our Arthur clearly has the mastery of it. You see, he's on 'piecework', i.e. he is paid by the number of components he produces, not by a fixed weekly or monthly rate of labour, and he's learned to manufacture just enough bicycle parts per hour to keep his wages at an optimum level. 'Fourteen pounds three and tuppence for a thousand o' these a day', he muses. 'No wonder I've allus got a bad back'. He stops work for a moment, draws gratefully on a cigarette: 'I could get through in half the time if I went like a bull, but they'd only slash me wages, so they can get stuffed!'

Indeed, £14 a week is a decent wage for the likes of Arthur, especially for a man who still lives in a back-to-back terraced house with his parents and rides a bike to work. He always has plenty of cash left over to stock his wardrobe full of smart suits, keep himself in beer change and sneak around with his girlfriend Brenda (Rachel Roberts) under the unsuspecting nose of her husband, Arthur's earnestly conformist workmate, Jack (Bryan Pringle). Arthur takes his pleasure very seriously, whether it be indulging in drinking contests down at the local (and falling drunkenly down the pub stairs into the bargain), fishing in the local canal while philosophizing about life, love and marriage with his cousin Bert (Norman Rossington), placing dead rats on co-workers' lathes, or terrorizing old Mrs Bull (Edna Morris), the neighbourhood gossip, with an air-rifle. Fancying himself as Nottingham's answer to Don Juan, he is even able to juggle an extra bird on the side in the form of pretty young Doreen Gretton (Shirley Ann Field), who works at the local hairnet factory and lives with her divorced mum on one of the posher new housing estates.

Unfortunately this endless 'Saturday Night' can't last forever and Arthur's hedonistic Eden comes crashing down when Brenda discovers that she's pregnant with his child. Although Arthur suggests that she keep the baby and raise it as Jack's progeny along with her son Tommy, Brenda wants to hide her affair from her husband and get an abortion. In desperation, Arthur turns to his Aunt Ada (Hylda Baker): 'She'll know what to do. She's had fourteen kids of her own and I'm sure she's got rid of as many others'. Alas, the 'three hour hot bath and pint of gin' abortion attempt fails and Brenda is forced to turn to a doctor who will do it illegally for £40.[4] To make matters worse, Arthur is also getting pressure from Doreen, who is starting to drop unsubtle hints about getting married and settling down.

Stalling for time, Arthur invites her to the annual October Goose Fair, where they double date with Bert and Doreen's girlfriend Betty (Louise Dunn). To his horror, Arthur spots Brenda, who is there with her family, as well as Jack's hard-as-nails brother, who is on two weeks' army leave with another squaddy. Slipping away from Doreen, Arthur meets surreptitiously with Brenda behind a sideshow tent and discovers that she's decided to have the baby after all – let's face it, there's nothing much he can do, is there? By now, Brenda is starting to be missed and Jack and the two squaddies split up to look for her. Panicked at being seen together, Brenda and Arthur hide in plain sight on one of the rides but they're quickly spotted by the squaddies. Anticipating their next move, Arthur jumps off in mid-ride and disappears into the fairground throng, leaving Brenda to her fate – a brutal slap in the face from an enraged Jack. However, Arthur gets his final comeuppance as he makes his way home. After a quick pint in the pub he is waylaid onto a patch of waste ground by the squaddies, who exploit their two-against-one advantage by beating him senseless. Saturday night has passed over into one giant hangover of a Sunday morning.

Over the next few days, Arthur takes to his bed to recuperate and lick his wounds. When he is visited by a concerned Doreen, he is finally forced to confess his affair with Brenda, but takes the opportunity to declare his love and propose marriage. Back at work, Arthur runs into Jack and asks after Brenda. The expected fireworks fail to materialize as a surprisingly level-headed Jack explains that he is 'taking care' of his wife and warns Arthur that he will get more trouble from the squaddies if he ever goes near Brenda again. After a final bout of fishing with Bert, where despite being mercilessly ribbed about his engagement Arthur insists that he's still got plenty of fight left in him, the film ends with the young lovebirds sitting on a hill overlooking a new housing estate. Arthur stares at his domesticated future life with Doreen with an ambivalent mixture of resignation and defiance. Suddenly, his mood lightens: 'Come on duck, let's get down'. He pulls her up and together they walk away from the camera towards the city below.

As we noted at the end of the last chapter, the so-called 'British New Wave', of which Reisz's *Saturday Night and Sunday Morning* is exemplary, emerged less out of the documentary roots of Free Cinema than in response to the burgeoning world of proletarian drama and literature. The former included the work of theatrical producers such as Joan Littlewood, whose Theatre Workshop was based in Stratford, East London and spawned Brendan Behan's *The Quare Fellow* (1956) and *The Hostage* (1958) as well as Shelagh Delaney's *A Taste of Honey* (1958); and young working-class actors who, in addition to Finney and Roberts, included Richard Burton, Rita Tushingham, Tom Courtenay, Richard Harris and Ronald Fraser. Of crucial importance for Reisz (and subsequently, Lindsay Anderson, whose first feature was an adaptation of *This Sporting Life*) was the work of younger, second generation kitchen sink novelists such as Alan Sillitoe (b. 1928) and David Storey (b. 1933) who were just starting to emerge as important regional voices from the Midlands and Northern England.[5] 'Though the new realism they offered, and their outspokenness about the social constrictiveness of British life and institutions, have now lost their power to startle, there is no denying how influential they were at the time,' notes Brian McFarlane. 'At no other period in British film-making has there been so close a congruence between contemporary film and literature, and it is a congruence rooted in the representation of a particular class and region. The films that grew out of these novels adhered closely to the narrative lines of the originals; however, they are stamped with a distinctively cinematic look and feel that allow for individual emphases but confer a collective identity on them as a subgenre'.[6] One should also note the continuing impact of the Angry Young Men, most notably the works of John Osborne, John Braine and Kingsley Amis, not so much because they were still topical in avant-garde circles but because the film versions of their works were only just starting to reach local cinema screens (*Saturday Night and Sunday Morning* was published in October 1958, just three months before the film release of Braine's *Room at the Top*).[7]

The key link between Reisz and the new literature was his old cohort, Tony Richardson. After *Momma Don't Allow*, Richardson had failed to find any viable openings in the film industry and moved quickly into theatre, establishing (with George Devine) the English Stage Company at the Royal Court Theatre. His May 1956 production of John Osborne's seminal *Look Back in Anger* was the shock to the system that the British stage desperately needed. Richardson's aim was to use his new-found theatrical fame as a convenient opening to worm himself and his old Free Cinema buddies into the film industry. Joining forces with the American producer Harry Saltzman (who would later be involved in the James Bond franchise), he and Osborne formed Woodfall Productions on the strength of Osborne's theatre royalties. 'Its capital was the film rights of *Look Back in Anger*,' recalls Reisz. 'That's what they had to sell – and they could do it on their own terms'.[8] When Richard Burton became interested in playing the role of Jimmy Porter, Warner Brothers came on board to finance the film version, which was released in May 1959. 'After that, they hung out their shingle and invited projects from kindred spirits,' says Reisz. 'Tony said to me, "If you've got anything you want to make, bring it, and we'll get you the money." And then there was suddenly this golden period of Woodfall, where we were all making films'.[9] For Reisz, one of the key advantages of working for an independent outside the aegis of the majors was that it became, like the auteurist cinema of the French New Wave, primarily a directors' and writers' medium, where the original authors were invariably called in to adapt their own novels and plays directly for the screen. 'The important thing about our company is that we insist on having artistic control,' proclaimed Saltzman at the time. 'We want to make them honestly. In other words, we control the script, the cast, the shooting and the completion of the picture'.[10] Artistic control is all well and good, but Sillitoe had no scriptwriting experience whatsoever, and had to be cajoled by Saltzman into doing the adaptation because of a lack of production funds. With narrative help from an enthusiastic Reisz, the script evolved over twelve months and involved five drafts of synopsis and another five of actual full-length script. 'The greatest difficulty was to simplify, to re-mould the episodic novel into some sort of order; and also to decide what to leave out', recalled Sillitoe.[11]

Despite Reisz's optimism, Richardson's 1958 film version of *Look Back in Anger* was not particularly successful and effectively ended Woodfall's further association with Warner Brothers (who had provided Burton). They turned instead to Michael Balcon's 'Bryanston' consortium of independent producers (formed in 1959) to finance their next project, *The Entertainer*.[12] The latter, starring Laurence Olivier (and featuring Finney in his film debut) was also a critical and commercial disappointment. Probably nervous at Woodfall's rocky financial position, Richardson subsequently delayed directing the film version of Delaney's *A Taste of Honey* and instead opted to produce *Saturday Night and Sunday Morning*, which he had recently optioned from the independent producer, Joseph Janni, for about £2,000. Richardson then promptly moved to Hollywood to direct Twentieth-Century Fox's William Faulkner adaptation, *Sanctuary*, bringing in Reisz to direct the Sillitoe project. If he had any doubts about his friend Karel's abilities as a first-time features director, Richardson certainly didn't show them. 'Tony wasn't around when we were shooting,' remembers Reisz. 'He arrived, I think, during the last week. Nor would he have had any desire to interfere in the sense of wanting to control me. His attitude was, "You have a go." And, actually, it wouldn't have interested him to do more'.[13]

The success of Jack Clayton's version of *Room at the Top* (1959) and the emergence of Bryanston as a potential co-backer had suddenly made *Saturday Night and Sunday Morning* a much less risky proposition. Nevertheless, raising the budget was still tricky because no one would finance even a medium-sized budget for a film starring relative unknowns. The picture was eventually made in six weeks (the fairground sequence was shot in a single night!) for £117,000, with considerable financial help (70 per cent) from Bryanston.[14] The film turned out to be the most commercially successful of all Woodfall films, ending up grossing £100,000 in London alone. It thus made the company financially stable, enabling Richardson to shoot *A Taste of Honey* on location the following year. 'In America, of course, we were only in the art houses,' notes Reisz. 'We were banned by the Legion of Decency, so it didn't go on to the big circuits'.[15]

Production was further hampered by the British cinema industry's diehard conservatism, as well as restrictive film censorship, alleviated only with the appointment of the liberal-minded John Trevelyan as Executive Secretary of the British Board of Film Censors (BBFC) in

1958. As Walker explains, 'The post-Osborne writers, challenging class traditions and sexual *mores*, did not find a cinema prepared to welcome their aggressively individualist values until these self-same values could be demonstrated not to hurt box-office, but actually to augment it'.[16] A good case in point is the attempt by the producer Joseph Janni (*A Town Like Alice* (1956), *The Savage Innocents* (1959)), who held the original option on Sillitoe's novel, to develop a more sexually explicit, class-based British cinema on the same lines as the Italian neo-realists. 'Compared to Rome, England was then like a monastery,' recalls Janni. 'In those days England had forgotten she possessed provinces. She denied that her people even had a sex life: sex was regarded, if it was regarded at all, as an exclusively continental pursuit'.[17] Italian films epitomized this fusion of sex, realism and provincial life and Janni saw a golden opportunity to inject this potent cocktail into the drab neighbourhood Odeons and ABCs when he was able to option *Saturday Night and Sunday Morning* for a mere £1,000. But getting it into production proved to be a night-mare. A typical response came from the film production company and distributor British Lion: 'You've lived in England all these years, he was told, and you haven't understood the English. It was the wildest imag-ining on Sillitoe's part that any factory worker in the Midlands should sleep and have sex with his best pal's wife and that the woman should then have to seek an abortion. Such things were simply not done by the workers, said British Lion'.[18] His option expiring, Janni reluctantly sold it to Woodfall.

Fortunately, Woodfall immediately developed a harmonious rela-tionship with Trevelyan, who was willing to be pragmatic in order to promote British films of quality (i.e. *realist* films with a genuine literary pedigree, as opposed to the modernist plots and fractured narratives of the French New Wave and Nouveau Roman). In fact R. Barton Palmer goes as far as to suggest that far from being a censorious watchdog, Trevelyan actually became an effective shaper of public taste: 'It thus seems fairly clear that the BBFC during the late 1950s and early 1960s was not an enemy of the new "realism" in cinema, but rather a fairly astute and conscientious judge of what in the new "realism" would be generally acceptable to a British audience'.[19] Although almost all the British New Wave films received an 'X' certificate (introduced in 1950) for serious adult themes presented with 'sincerity' as opposed to sensa-tionalism, commercialism and exploitation, Sillitoe's preliminary drafts still met with considerable opposition, especially his use of ripe vernac-ular language. 'Whore', 'bitch' and 'bastard' were eventually deemed acceptable, but 'Christ', 'bogger' and 'bugger' were cut. Not surprisingly, it was Brenda's successful abortion in the original novel that came in for most criticism. In a letter to Harry Saltzman dated 24 November 1959, Trevelyan noted that the script 'shows a rather casual attitude to abortion and suggests to the young that if they get into difficulties all they need is to find a kind-hearted older woman who has had a lot of children. Provided that it is not too obtrusive it would probably be acceptable, but I must ask you to bear in mind that this film is likely to be seen by a considerable number of young people of 16 to 20 years of age, and to recognise that social responsibility is called for'.[20] Brenda's eventual decision to keep the baby – with all the difficulties that entails for the future of her marriage – certainly makes for better drama in the final film, but even here, film censor Audrey Field assumed that the abortion had still taken place: 'her husband later tells Arthur that she is "all right", but we are left to assume that the pregnancy had been terminated without any outside interference'.[21]

Run-ins with the censors were at least constructive and in many ways served to develop and enhance the ambivalences in Sillitoe's original novel, whose rambling, somewhat episodic structure tended to undercut incisive moral and ideological criticism of his characters. Far more serious was the much larger malaise affecting British cinema as a whole, a phenomenon that Walter Lassally dramatically dubbed 'the Dead Hand. The Dead Hand of apathy, of complacency and convention, whose grip is felt on all sides of the industry'.[22] Anglo-American film production had gone into a major decline from 1954 onwards: the British simply couldn't compete with Hollywood wide-screen blockbusters or low-budget horror and teen 'quickies' (for, example, The Blob, 1958, starring Steve McQueen).[23] Apart from the usual quota of high-quality costume dramas and literary and stage adaptations, the bulk of domestic production was a predicable litany of comforting but completely illusory Ealing Comedies featuring bumbling amateurs taking on rigid bureaucrats and authority (Passport to Pimlico, 1949); comedic nostalgic and sentimental views of Britain as a 'living museum' of the past (the vintage cars of Genevieve, 1953, the steam trains of The Titfield Thunderbolt, 1953); the light titillating comedies of Richard Gordon's Doctor series, later superseded by the equally popular Carry On films; or heart-warming stories of endurance (Scott of the Antarctic, 1948), suspense (The Sound Barrier, 1952) and crusading tragedies (White Corridors and Cry the Beloved Country, both 1951). Even more depressing was the endless refighting of World War Two in films such as The Cruel Sea (1953), The Dam Busters (1954), The Battle of the River Plate (1956), The Bridge on the River Kwai (1957), Dunkirk (1958) and Sink the Bismark (1960), each serving as a nostalgic return to the patriotic glories of a simpler era defined by clear-cut middle-class values. George

Stonier (writing under the pseudonym, William Whitebait) put it best in the *New Statesman* in April 1958:

> A dozen years after the Second World War we find ourselves in the really quite desperate situation of being, not sick of war, but hideously in love with it. Not actively fighting, we aren't at peace. The H-Bomb looms ahead, and we daren't look at it; so we creep back to the lacerating comfort of 'last time' ... While we 'adventure' at Suez, in the cinemas we are still thrashing Rommel – and discovering he was a gentleman! – sweeping the Atlantic of submarines, sending the few to scatter Goering's many. The more we lose face in the world's counsels, the grander, in our excessively modest way, we swell in this illusionary mirror held up by the screen. It is less a spur to morale than a salve to wounded pride; and as art or entertainment, dreadfully dull.[24]

The *Spectator*'s Isabel Quigly agreed, admitting that 'for years and years we have known that the British film picture of ourselves was phoney. Everyone in the country knew it, it was one of the big national lies that everyone concurred in'.[25] Part of this phoniness was due to the films' innate reluctance to talk about or even acknowledge sexuality, or, as John Ellis notes, 'to express tenderness in anything but "stiff upper lip" terms. The characters seem locked into their middle-class world: certain values and certain things are left unexpressed: it is for this reason that at the end of the decade the portrayal of the working class is intimately connected with the first frank portrayal of sexuality in feature films'.[26] In this respect, the import of the New Wave films as a presaging of far more explicit themes in 'Swinging Sixties' cinema – e.g. Lewis Gilbert's film version of Bill Naughton's *Alfie* (1966), or Nicolas Roeg and Donald Cammell's *Performance* (1968) – cannot be overstated.

The overall impact of this openly 'naked' sexuality in *Saturday Night and Sunday Morning* had much to do with Reisz's apprenticeship in documentary, particularly his commitment to realistic detail and authentic depiction of locations, which further enhanced his ability to get inside the character of Arthur and discover what made him tick, both as a visceral *and* social animal. The critical impetus for this approach was Richard Hoggart's insightful 1959 *Sight and Sound* review of *We Are the Lambeth Boys*, which was written in the form of an open letter to Reisz. Hoggart wondered how the film-maker could show the combination of resignation, horror, but also spiritual fortitude that lies below the drab outer surface of working-class life. He felt that the answer would be to become much more subjective and to find a way to encompass the characters' *inner* lives with the same success as Chekhov's short stories. Indeed, Reisz himself had acknowledged in his own film criticism that it is this very substance of 'inwardness' that you *can't* and *shouldn't* attempt with documentary. For Hoggart, the most common weakness of Free Cinema was that it tended towards idealization: 'it still has a vaguely "poetic" blur of sensitive commitment and social concern round its own edges. It will only stand out clear and sharp – committed and concerned in the right way – when it faces better the more demanding (and more exciting) problems of the imagination'.[27] This is essentially a cue for *Saturday Night and Sunday Morning*, which is, in effect, Reisz's public reply to Hoggart's critique: 'The hero of the picture is, if you like, one of the Lambeth Boys,' acknowledged the director. 'An attempt is made to make a movie about the sentimental and social education of *one specific* boy: thus the "inner" things which the *Lambeth Boys* type of picture simply cannot apprehend ... was attempted in *Saturday Night and Sunday Morning*. To put it more simply, and risking pretentiousness, the first work attempted a picture of a world, the second a portrait'.[28]

For critics such as Raymond Durgnat and Roy Armes, however, Hoggart's suggestions were the very crux of the problem, for the New Wave directors were essentially creating middle-class views of working-class life that were by their very essence inauthentic.[29] John Hill disagrees: 'The importance of the point ... is less the actual social background of the film-makers, none of whom ever lay claim to be just "one of the lads", than the way this "outsider's view" is inscribed in the films themselves, the way the "poetry", the "marks of the enunciation" themselves articulate a clear distance between observer and observed'.[30] Although by transforming its working-class milieu into poetic art the film runs the risk of transforming its reality into 'comfortable contemplation,' *Saturday Night and Sunday Morning* mitigates this problem by attempting to fill in the interior voices of the characters that were noticeably missing from the Free Cinema documentaries. This is realized through Arthur's interior monologue and subjective point-of-view shots, creating an individualized image of how Arthur sees his fellow workers and lovers, not simply an objective depiction of working-class life. However, there are always scenes that exclude Arthur – e.g. between Jack and Brenda – thereby displacing his subjective authority. Thus unlike in the French New Wave films, this subjectivization never becomes dominant – it's held in check by the authority of the enunciating voice of Reisz himself, and more specifically through his stylistic vocabulary: poetic realism.

Although *Saturday Night and Sunday Morning* is largely a studio film with some location exteriors (despite appearances to the contrary, the bulk of the interiors were shot at Twickenham Studios), Reisz undertook painstaking preliminary research for the film by making a 'dry run' documentary in Nottingham about a miners' welfare centre for the

Central Office of Information. This allowed Reisz to get a true feel for the region – for five weeks he and Sillitoe tramped around Nottingham together, choosing locations and soaking up atmosphere – and thus avoid accusations that *Saturday Night and Sunday Morning* was simply a case of 'Free Cinema goes slumming in the Midlands'. In fact, many of the locations were shot where the author grew up, including his mother's house and workplace. As Sillitoe later recalled, 'It gave me a wonderful emotional shock to see Albert Finney standing at exactly the same place at the bench in the Raleigh factory where I had worked'.[31] This sense of on-the-spot realism is facilitated by cinematographer Freddie Francis's use of lightweight cameras and highly sensitive black and white film stock, which made it possible to film with less equipment and a more mobile camera.

At first glance, Reisz's *mise-en-scène* and editing patterns seem to reinforce this documentary realist perspective. Using predominantly deep focus in order to create strong spatial relief between his characters and their backgrounds, Reisz's self-effacing visual style is largely concerned with recording what goes on in front of the camera, with a minimum of editorial comment. Relying on medium shots and occasional close-ups for emotional emphasis, he keeps his camera at a polite distance, allowing an intimate and yet detached observation. Long shots of Nottingham and the surrounding hills are also used to express a determinist overview of the urban environment and its socio-cultural effect on the characters and the community as a whole. Similarly, Reisz's editing is largely seamless and invisible for the first half of the film as he relies predominantly on long takes. 'That's due in large part to the nature of the story,' notes Gaston. 'Basically, it is episodic, leading in a cause-and-effect way from confusion to a kind of resolution. By linking the various episodes closely together into a logical chain of fate, Reisz mesmerizes us into accepting the course of the story without question'.[32] This modulated rhythm changes in the final thirty minutes of the film, picking up momentum through increasingly truncated cross-cutting as Arthur tries to juggle his conflicting relationships leading up to the Goose Fair.

However, Reisz wouldn't be a disciple of Jennings if he didn't imbue this seemingly neutral mimesis with a more poetic and, by extension, ironic commentary. Although most of the film is shot at eye level except for occasional higher angles looking down – for example, when the workers stream out of the Raleigh factory, or when establishing shots on the terraced houses and the ever-vigilant Mrs Bull on the street corner are employed to express depressing conformity – Reisz uses an occasional baroque angle or camera movement to underline a specific psychological and narrative point. Thus he opts for an extreme low angle up on a drunken but unvanquished Arthur at the top of the pub stairs after the drinking contest, but then immediately cuts to an extreme reverse angle down as he clatters down the flight, creating a premonition of his ultimate 'fall' at the film's end. In contrast, Reisz uses a highly subjective camera (as opposed to an omniscient perspective) during the fairground scene as Arthur and Brenda shake violently on one of the rides – as if the whirlwind excess of Arthur's hedonistic life were passing before him (and us) for one last time before being stifled by domesticity and a life of suburban conformity.

A more subtle example of Reisz's quietly expressive touch is the scene where Brenda tells Arthur that she's pregnant. They enter a park at night and the camera tracks slowly back before them, creating a tight intimate bond between the couple. However, when Brenda tells him the bad news, the camera stops, as if holding them in its grip. Although the composition hasn't changed, the lack of camera movement seems to tighten the frame around them (especially Arthur) as an objective correlative of their mutual entrapment. Reisz underlines the gesture by adding an off-screen train whistle on the soundtrack, as if life were mocking their predicament. He extends this spatial trope still further when Arthur and Brenda visit Aunt Ada to discuss the abortion. As Arthur waits in the narrow alley, he peers in through the window and from his point-of-view we see Brenda listening and talking to Ada, spatially wedged into a tight frame formed by the window pane and curtain. In this way, Reisz underlines the fact that it is Brenda alone who will have to undergo the physical anguish of the abortion, leaving Arthur – himself confined by the bricked-in alley – as a helpless, albeit emotionally invested observer.

Jennings's poetic ability to provide a direct link between the outer and inner worlds of his protagonists is also a vital catalyst for understanding Reisz's use of landscape, which came under considerable criticism at the time of the film's release. V. F. Perkins, for one, felt that the descriptive contextualizing shots of Nottingham were little more than the worst kind of cultural tourism, whose sole purpose was to create environmental ambience as a contrived form of class-consciousness, completely lacking integration with the narrative as a whole: 'Richardson, Reisz, Schlesinger and Clayton are weakest exactly where their ambitions most demand strength: in the integration of character with background. Because of this weakness they are constantly obliged to "establish" place with inserted shots which serve only to strengthen our conviction that the setting, though "real", has no organic connection with the characters'.[33] This is a surprising comment, for as we noted in the previous chapter, Reisz always tends to use *mise-en-scène* and editing to express the objective outer world – i.e. the intersection of economic and social factors – as a forum for class analysis, while character and acting are the main province for exploring the subjective inner world of fatalism and emotion. Poetic realism is the genre that holds these two apparent inconsistencies together as it both represents and *transcends* the ordinariness of everyday reality by eliciting sympathy for the working-class figure as the environment's unwitting victim.

Consequently, despite Perkins's claims to the contrary, landscape isn't just used as a neutral backdrop against which the narrative can unfold on prescribed class or cultural lines, for as Andrew Higson points out, each of the Nottingham location shots in *Saturday Night and Sunday Morning* 'demands also to be read as a real historical *place* which can authenticate the fiction. There remains a tension between the demands of narrative and the demands of realism, however, with the narrative compulsion of film working continually to transform place once more back into space'.[34] This binary between objective place and subjective space is dissolved when the townscape is incorporated as part of the inexorable movement of character narration itself. Place can then act as a signifier or metaphor of character and as an objective correlative for the protagonists' state of mind. The result is a compelling tension between the drabness of Reisz's settings and their poetic quality; between documentary realism and romantic atmosphere; between the representation of class as a social *problem* and its enjoyment as pleasurable *spectacle*. 'This we may call the discourse of poetic realism,' says Higson. 'It involves a more perfect conjunction of surface realism and moral realism, a conjunction which in fact *transcends* ordinariness, which makes the ordinary strange, beautiful – *poetic*'.[35]

A good example of the stock *spectacle* shot as a form of visual pleasure for the film's spectator is what Higson calls 'That Long Shot of Our Town from That Hill' – the industrial city as a form of deterministic urban sublime, equal parts archetypal, awe-inspiring and terrifying. Reisz uses three such shots, establishing Nottingham as both materially specific (in a literal and dialectical sense) but also as an incommensurable space of subjective and psychological import. The first such occasion is towards the beginning of the film where Reisz uses a long shot of the city as a transition between Arthur and Bert enjoying a spot of Sunday afternoon fishing in the neighbourhood canal and the beginning of the subsequent workday as Arthur and his father, Harold (Frank Pettitt), head off for work. The high horizon line and a thin sliver of sky weighs down on this grim picture of industrial England like a deathly pall, reinforced by the insistent sound of the factory whistle calling the city to work. However, Johnny Dankworth's plaintive accordion over the shot imbues the image with a sense of human pathos, of cyclical inevitability, as if pleasure must inevitably give way to work, which in turn makes further pleasure possible (a key feature, as we have seen, of *We Are the Lambeth Boys*).

At first glance the second use of the shot – a wide angle down on the Black Meadows district and the grassy hills beyond the Trent – is very similar, marking the transition between some light-hearted banter between Doreen, Arthur and Bert following the air gun shooting of Mrs Bull and Arthur's subsequent meeting with Brenda on the parapet of Nottingham Castle, where he learns that the abortion attempt has failed. Again the space is used *narratively* as a transition from childish pleasure to adult responsibility (in effect, the metaphorical shift from 'Saturday Night' to 'Sunday Morning') but it is also psychologized as it relates directly to the ensuing diegesis between Arthur and Brenda. During the course of the scene, Arthur comes to identify with the view on two separate levels. Firstly, it metaphorically represents his individualist sense of being outside and above the gritty working-class problems of the city. Secondly, it also draws him inexorably back into those problems as soon as Brenda enters the shot with her bad news, thus allowing us to move from the objective and general back to two different subjective specificities. Finally, Reisz uses the shot again towards the film's end as a transition between Arthur's beating at the hands of the squaddies and his recuperation in bed and Doreen's visit. Although we hear the factory hooters summoning the workers to work, we know full well that Arthur won't be joining them, so the shot's communication of generic place becomes immediately subordinate to space, as the realm of Arthur's psychological subjectivity:

> the initial townscape is on the screen long enough (thirteen seconds) for the spectator to scan this real place, to make some sense of the city as a city, to notice details of movement (a trail of smoke or steam), perhaps to examine the extent to which the landscape has been worked over and transformed by industrial labour under capitalism. It is a place with a history which might possibly be read off the image. But at the same time, the narrative always returns to make a *particular* sense of this multiplication of detail, to psychologize rather than historicize the space, to marshal it into a representation of a state of mind. It is a new day, the sun is shining, the urban-industrial image seems peaceful, stable, there are no immediate signs of work, of struggle: exactly – Arthur Seaton has turned over a new leaf in his life, and the geography, the *mise-en-scène*, is a sign of this change.[36]

The shot thus combines the abstract, metaphorical time of the working class – i.e. the life of Arthur and others like him in industrial Nottingham – and a specific narrative time (Arthur does some soul searching and gets a visit from Doreen) rolled into one. More importantly, the fore-grounding of space over place, psychology over locale, reinforces the film's focus on a moral rather than a historical materialist landscape, on human as opposed to social and economic concerns. For Higson, 'the "kitchen sink" films are less about the conditions of the indus-trial working class and their collective class-consciousness, than they are about the attempts of individuals to escape from those conditions and that consciousness, associated as they are with an older generation irredeemably tainted by mass culture'.[37] In short, *Saturday Night and Sunday Morning* is liberal rather than Marxist in its approach to ideo-logical change.

This dialectic between personal commitment and the evils of the culture industry is a key conflict within the film, represented in equal measure by Arthur's own internal conflicts as well as his generational antagonism towards his parents. Sillitoe originally conceived of Arthur as a well-integrated individualist, a brash, hard-drinking loudmouth who reduces class-consciousness to 'bolshie' rhetoric because he is far too comfortable in his lifestyle to see himself as part of an oppressed class:

> I wanted to write a novel about a working man who, though not neces-sarily typical of the zone of life he lived in, belonged to it with so much flesh and blood that nothing could cause him to leave it – not even his mother ... There was nothing heroic about Arthur Seaton, nor was there meant to be. The hero is always in the eye of the beholder, in any case. He was a man basically without a story, and not even typical, no matter what he may seem. Those individuals who work in factories are only members of a 'class' when they band together to come out on strike for better wages and conditions. In normal circumstances they see each other as unique people, otherwise they would not see each other as human beings at all, and a writer who claims to know something about their life would not be able to write with any aspect of truth whatsoever if he did not do the same.[38]

Arthur is thus an outsider, separated from the rest of his class: the 'poor beggers' around him who have been 'ground down' (epitomized by the cuckolded Jack) or Robboe, the upwardly mobile foreman (Robert Cawdron), 'the enemy's scout'. 'And look where it got Robboe', notes Arthur, with venom: 'A fat gut and lots o' worry'.

However, Arthur's biggest gripe is not so much with his immediate bosses or even the ruling class in general but with those who try to foist on him a personality and set of values against his own better instincts. In this sense, his destructive and anarchic spirit is highly romanticized in the novel, largely because his irresponsibility towards the women in his life is downplayed in favour of his rebellion against authority, pomposity and stupidity.[39] To his credit, Reisz modified this conflict considerably in the film by giving far more screen time to Arthur's 'victims', thereby humanizing them for greater audience empathy. Brenda's persona is greatly enhanced both by the excision of her married, sex-pot sister Winnie (in the book the two sisters are clichéd archetypes and tend to cancel each other out as identifiable personalities) and by Rachel Roberts's wonderfully modulated performance. Reisz paid Roberts the highest compliment by comparing her to the neo-realist icon, Anna Magnani. Similarly, Doreen is only a marginal figure in the novel, introduced in the last quarter as a mechanism through which to see Arthur as a desirable potential husband: 'She created his image: a tall young man of the world, nearly twenty-three and already a long way past his military service, a man who had been a good soldier and who was now a good worker because he was earning fourteen pounds a week on piecework. He would also make a good husband, there being no doubt of this because above all he was kind and attentive. What's more, he was good-looking, was tall, thin, had fair hair. What girl wouldn't be happy with a man like that? Also, she affirmed, he loved her, and, as far as she could tell, she loved him'.[40] By introducing her much earlier as stiff competition for Arthur's affections, Reisz makes her intrinsic to the spirit of the narrative as an alternative drive towards respectability. In this way, Arthur is forced to face up to his own self-identity and value system from within the diegesis rather than from an outwardly imposed *deus ex machina*.

In addition to the power of Finney's own charismatic performance as the quintessential 'winning rogue' (anticipating his similar role in *Tom Jones* by three years), Reisz also expands this self-examination through *mise-en-scène*, specifically the strategic placement of mirrors.[41] Arthur looks into mirrors three times during the course of the film. Firstly, the effect is narcissistic as he checks himself out while putting on his jacket and straightening his tie prior to his first night out with Brenda. In Lacanian terms, this is the equivalent of the over-determination of omnipotent self-identity associated with the Imaginary Mirror Stage, where the individual enters subjecthood by pointing at their own reflection and stating, 'Look, that's me'. It is, like the effects of interpellation, an ideological misrepresentation of self because the image is neither whole nor of their own making – it is presented to them already constructed (i.e. it's an ideological fabrication) by the culture at large. The second mirror image occurs when Arthur and Brenda return home after the drinking contest. As Brenda locks up for the night, Arthur calls her over and they kiss drunkenly prior to going up to bed. Arthur checks himself out in the mirror as he 'performs' but his earlier narcissism has given way to a more quizzical look, as if he cannot quite equate his mirror reflection to his own body because of the intrusive presence of Brenda, who is clearly objectified as an Other, both physically in his arms *and* in the mirror. Arthur is thus beginning to see himself as a 'split subject' for the first time – both self *and* other, subject *and* object, without the possibility of easy reconciliation.

This process is completed with the final mirror shot, which occurs in his bedroom after his beating. It is tied in directly with his second major soliloquy: 'They'd bested me right enough. Still, I'd had me bit of fun. It ain't the first time I've been in a losing fight. Won't be the last either, I don't suppose. [He sits up]. How long have I been lying here though? A week? Can't think. [He holds his head, gets out of bed and starts to walk around the room]. Mum called me barmy when I told her I fell off a gasometer for a bet. But I'm not barmy. I'm a fightin' pit prop that wants a pint of beer, that's me'. At this point he stares into the mirror, creating a doppelgänger effect: 'But if any knowing bastard says that's me, I'll tell 'em I'm a dynamite dealer, waiting to blow the factory to kingdom come. I'm me and nobody else. Whatever people say I am, that's what I'm not, because they don't know a bloody thing about me'. But neither, apparently, does Arthur, because the preceding speech is all bravado, pure self-delusion. Arthur's metaphorical Lacanian mirror has finally cracked into a thousand disconnected pieces because in a reverse angle, in actual rather than reflected space, he suddenly puts his fingers over his mouth and says, 'God knows what I am'. This is a major victory for Arthur because it is the first step to the self-realization that he is not in control of his own subjectivity, that society literally constructs its subjects 'with mirrors' to the point that there is no way to tell will-to-power from interpellation, and vice versa. Arthur's brazen masculinity has thus taken on a more positive, 'feminine' side that has shifted from an earlier narcissism to a greater understanding of the need to identify with and relate to others/the Other. Marriage to Doreen, even with all its conformist drawbacks, will go some way to fulfilling that trajectory.

However, the feminine is also represented in *Saturday Night and Sunday Morning* by a more negative reading that is tied to a more implicit critique of mass culture as a whole. In this respect the film reflects the *Zeitgeist*, for the late 1950s debate on popular cultural standards tended to be set in strict Manichean terms: the Good Angel (the education system) vs the Bad Angel (commercial mass media).[42] It's significant that Reisz – the former schoolmaster – attended a three-day National Union of

Teachers (NUT) Special Conference at Church House, Westminster in October 1960.[43] The conference was titled *Popular Culture and Personal Responsibility* and was subsequently called by the New Left's cultural maven, Raymond Williams, 'the most remarkable event of its kind ever held in this country'.[44] Apart from Reisz, the speakers included 'Rab' Butler (the Home Secretary), the playwrights Arnold Wesker and Colin Morris, an absent Richard Hoggart, whose paper, 'The Quality of Cultural Life in Mass Society' was circulated in advance, and Williams himself ('The Growth of Communications in Modern Society'). The basic assumption of the conference was that British society was largely an affluent one, particularly among the young. Social problems were less the result of poverty than, if anything, of too much materialistic prosperity and consumerism, aided and abetted by mass communications, causing a concomitant deterioration in the standard of *values*. According to Jack Longland, the Director of Education for Derbyshire and radio broadcaster, 'the school seems to sit there in the middle of an adult and workaday environment like an oasis in a wide desert ... the whole clanging and ubiquitous machinery of mass communications in newspaper, film, advertisement and much of broadcasting chants the message of wealth without earning it, success without deserving it, pie in the sky some day soon. The mirage of miraculous affluence flickers in front of our young customers' eyes, the reward not of work but of the lucky flutter on the pools or of Ernie's blind fingers rummaging among the Premium Bonds'.[45] The mass media were thus vilified as the enemy of honest educational values. Hoggart and Williams's wider research – especially the former's *Uses of Literacy*, where everyday life and its community values were integrated with, expressive of, and transforming of its leisure activities and lifestyle – was rarely discussed. More influential in 1960 was Hoggart's less interesting analysis of the new affluence of the late 1950s (whether real or imagined), particularly the negative impact of new housing estates on old communal relations, and the role of mass-produced goods in creating a culture of conspicuous consumption rooted in the triviality of mass media ('candy floss'). The chief culprit was, of course, television, whose natural vice was 'more dangerous to the soul than wickedness'.[46]

Ironically, *Coronation Street*, which began in December 1960, carried the mantle of *Saturday Night and Sunday Morning* and its kitchen sink style to television, just as the exponents of the British New Wave were leaving the genre. It proved to be the main training ground for director Michael Apted and writer Jack Rosenthal, as well as the realist catalyst for the subsequent television and film work of Tony Garnett and Ken Loach as well as actor/writer, Colin Welland. However, it was Hoggart and Williams's anti-TV positions that defined the more subtle aspects of the debate, and give us some insight into the prevailing discourse through which Reisz was thinking and creating his art. Reisz admitted the connection in a 1977 interview, stating that *Saturday Night and Sunday Morning* 'came out of the notion – the *shared* notion – that political action was leading us to better things. That's how we felt in England in the fifties. But even then, the film began to ask the question whether material improvements in people's lives weren't going to be accompanied by a spiritual crisis. In the last moments of the film, the hero, if you remember, begins to conform, to face personal defeat'.[47] In this respect Reisz and the New Left's culture of commitment became inextricably tied to the problem of the working class's spiritual crisis, an issue that came to dominate New Wave films in general: 'The "national community" of the war years has now become the "traditional working-class community", which on the one hand is nostalgically valorised as the site of authentic cultural values and a responsible morality, but on the other hand is constructed as tainted by the encroaching mass culture, the culture of consumerism, affluence, social mobility – the culture of television'.[48]

Saturday Night and Sunday Morning makes no bones about stating its allegiances from the outset. As Arthur arrives home from work he finds his dad entranced in front of the TV as Mrs Seaton (Elsie Wagstaff) takes away his empty tea cup. Harold is oblivious to Arthur's attempt at small talk, so the son tries another tack: 'D'you hear about that accident in the three-speed shop today, dad?' After a minimal response he continues: 'Aye, this feller got his hand caught in a press. He didn't look what he was doing. Cause he's only got one eye. He lost the sight of the other one lookin' at telly day in and day out'. Harold's only comment is 'Oh ah', as the sound of the TV commercials fills the room.[49] Later in the film, during his final chat with Bert by the canal, Arthur relates the issue to a broader generational divide. 'They've got a television set and a packet of fags but they're both dead from the neck up', he says about his parents. 'I'm not saying it's their fault, mind yer. They've had their hash settled for 'em, so's all the bloody gaffers can push 'em around like a lot of sheep ... There's a lot more in life Bert than me mum and dad have got'. This intrinsic conflict (which is, of course, internal to Arthur's own character – he is also an inveterate consumer, as we have seen) is worked out as a dialectic not only between the generations but also between the community of the neighbourhood (metonymically reduced to the family) and their intrusion on the private and sexual life of the individual, who is defined as the anti-hero of the film. Unlike in Jennings, where montage is used to highlight binding communal relations, here 'the function of montage construction has shifted from an articulation of the look of the documentary, the public gaze, to the privatised look of the narrative protagonist – that is, from an "objective" statement of commonality and universality, to a "subjective" impression of experience. It is this establishment of an intensified psychological realism which seems as remarkable in these films as their attempts to foreground working-class protagonists'.[50]

The aforementioned binaries are also reinforced by gender stereo-typing, where women are associated with the problematic side of the equation, namely conspicuous consumption and increased entrapment. It's notable that Arthur's transition from the 'irresponsibility' of pleasur-able sexuality (i.e. sex with Brenda) is punished by an unwanted preg-nancy and a beating at the hands of the squaddies (in effect, a symbolic castration), which leads to a safe retreat into the domain of marital and procreative sexuality with Doreen. Class is thus imbricated with issues of sex so that Arthur, representative of the male working class, is femi-nized within the confines of conventional marriage, with its implica-tions of domestication and, even worse, potential *embourgeoisement*. As John Hill notes, 'With physical pleasure apparently so divorced from marriage and domesticity, it is inevitable that those films which rely on marriage as a means of conclusion tend to imply less a positive endorse-ment than an emphasis on compromise and acceptance of constraint, the eschewal of fantasy'.[51]

However, the film's real target is not so much women, but a much wider target, effeminacy, which is negatively associated with pettiness, superficiality and materialism. Although Arthur already has a lot of these qualities – namely his obsession with clothes and physical appear-ance – Jack is the real prototype here. He is weak, easily deceived, gets others to do his dirty work for him, and his ideal of 'getting on' in life is to get a new television set, the new icon of feminized domesticity. It's significant, however, that these negative traits are far less prevalent in Jack or Arthur's household than in Doreen's posher home on one of the newer working-class estates. 'This interior bears all the marks of Hoggart's new working-class consumerism. The kitchen is a fitted one: the living-room furniture is "fifties modern", with a glass fronted china cabinet. The walls are hung with "contemporary" wallpaper, with wall-mounted lights and flush doors', observes a keen-eyed Terry Lovell.[52] Lovell also notes the illogicality of this set-up – Doreen's father left the family fifteen years earlier, while Arthur's household has two bread-winners, yet the household affluence is completely reversed. One can only surmise that this antinomy is designed to better associate the new consumerism – with the betrayal of class and culture that implies – with

the all-feminine household of Doreen and her mother. It's thus no accident that Mrs Gretton (Irene Richmond) takes an immediate dislike
to Arthur, commenting that, 'He looks a bit rough if you ask me'. 'The
young male protagonist has, then, a relationship to "feminine" domestic
space in these films which is problematic both personally and ideologically,' argues Lovell. 'Sexual encounters are typically initiated outside, in
space which is conventionally regarded as masculine [e.g. the pub], but
consummated inside, in stereotypically feminine space. He must therefore enter inside, but he risks either punishment (the beating of Arthur
by the squaddies) or containment (marriage to Doreen) as a result'.[53]

In light of the above comments, the film's ending thus becomes all
the more problematic. Insisting that Arthur's individualist and masculine spirit remains alive, Sillitoe had originally planned a wedding scene
at the registry office that became a travesty because of Arthur's childish
horseplay. As the Minister utters the line, 'Marriage voluntarily entered
into for life, to the exclusion of all others,' 'Arthur's face shows disappointment at this last clause, as if he wants to begin bargaining about
numbers'.[54] Although undeniably funny, this ending was subsequently
replaced by a third and final soliloquy over a shot of Arthur working at
his lathe following the final confrontation with Jack: 'Jack's not all that
bad. He's a good bloke in some ways. Lets the factory do as it likes with
him though. They've bossed all the guts out of him. If he had any to
begin with. There's thousands like him though: just love to be told what
to do. I'll never get like that. Anybody opens their trap too much to me,
gets it shut for 'em. Me, I was born fighting. Like I told Bert: you've got
to fight in this world. But there's a bit of sweetness sometimes, and I
know that much as well'.[55] For Sillitoe, 'These last scenes stamp Arthur
as having changed from when we first saw him at the beginning of
the film; yet they also show him to be basically the same person, to the
extent that he is still going into the future as someone with a mind of his
own, a mind that can't be so easily got at as most people's seem to be. It
is also obvious that for him, life is just beginning. Monday morning lost
its terrors a long time ago'.[56]

By integrating many of its sentiments into the film's opening soliloquy, this ending was also eventually cut in favour of the final denouement where Arthur meets Doreen on a hill behind the housing estate.
Sitting on the grass, she states her determination to move out from
under her mother once the couple are married and buy a new house,
'with a bathroom and everything'. Clearly alienated, Arthur gets up,
and the camera moves up with him, leaving Doreen out of frame, as
if to underline their separate worldviews. He looks out across the new
construction site and starts to reminisce: 'Me and Bert used to roam all

over these hills when we was kids. Blackberrying. There won't be black-berries or a blade of grass here much longer'. Then he turns and flings a stone at the construction workers' hut in the background, displaying not only his contempt for sprawling suburbia but the very idea of domes-tication and conformity in general. Doreen is appalled: 'What did you do that for?' 'I dunno. Just felt like it, I suppose', says Arthur, less than contrite. 'You shouldn't throw things like that', reprimands Doreen, reminding him that one of the houses might be theirs one day. 'It won't be the last one I'll throw', responds Arthur, defiantly. They then walk down the hill towards the rows of new houses, 'like an octopus waiting to suck them in'.[57]

Sillitoe saw the final ending as upbeat, a restatement of Arthur's rebelliousness, or, as he put it, 'only a temporary lapse from militancy which would revive when things got economically tougher'.[58] Reisz, in contrast, saw it as pessimistic, a forecast of Arthur's inevitable taming by the system, only he doesn't know it yet:

> In a metaphorical way Arthur embodied what was happening in England: he was a sad person, terribly limited in his sensibilities, narrow in his ambitions and a bloody fool into the bargain – by no means a stan-dard-bearer for any ideas of mine. I never work with spokesmen. All my education, my teaching experience warned me off treating people as representatives of their world, rather than giving them the dignity of individuals; and I certainly disagree strongly with the idea that Arthur Seaton embodied my values, my outlook – I am a middle class Jew from Central Europe. The stone-throwing is a symptom of his impotence, a self-conscious bit, telling the audience over the character's shoulder what I think of him. I wanted to continually contrast the extent to which he is an aggressor with the extent to which he is a victim of this world. I wanted the end to have this feeling of frustration, but I'm not too keen on it today.[59]

The film thus sets up a clear tension between Arthur's and Reisz's conflicting points-of-view, the former represented by Finney's brash, physical stature, the latter expressed through formal style, allowing Reisz to foreground his character's perspective while at the same time showing it to be yet another example of 'received wisdom' doing its insidious work.

Notes

1 Reisz, quoted in Hachem, '*Sweet Dreams*', p. 32.
2 Richard Hoggart, *The Uses of Literacy: Aspects of Working-Class Life with Special Reference to Publications and Entertainments* (London, Chatto and Windus/Penguin, 1957), p. 140.
3 Alan Sillitoe, 'What Comes on Monday?', *New Left Review*, Vol. 1, No. 4, July–August 1960, p. 58.
4 In the novel the abortion is successful.
5 The term 'kitchen sink' was originally coined by the British art critic David Sylvester to describe a social realist tendency (some might call a fascination with domestic squalor) in British painting in the 1950s. Paradigmatic artists included John Bratby, Derrick Greaves and Jack Smith.
6 Brian McFarlane, 'A Literary Cinema? British Films and British Novels', in Barr, ed., *All Our Yesterdays*, pp. 139–40.
7 The label Angry Young Men is largely a myth: some of them were not very angry and some were certainly not very young. Most of their 'radicalism' was imposed on them by outraged members of the literary right such as Somerset Maugham who referred to their characters – usually provincial, state-aided iconoclasts – as 'scum.'
8 Reisz, quoted in Welsh and Tibbetts, *The Cinema of Tony Richardson: Essays and Interviews*, p. 26.
9 *Ibid.*
10 Harry Saltzman, 'New Wave Hits British Films', *Films & Filming*, Vol. 6, No. 7, April 1960, p. 11.
11 Sillitoe, 'What Comes on Monday?', p. 58. Key casualties of the deletions axe were Arthur's older brother Fred, younger brother Sam, sister Margaret and another son still living at home; Brenda's younger married sister Winnie, another of Arthur's conquests, as well as Aunt Ada's huge tribe of children.
12 In addition to Balcon, Bryanston also included luminaries such as Charles Frend, Norman Priggen, Ronald Neame, Julian Wintle, Leslie Parkyn and the Shipman Brothers. Originally linked with British Lion, they eventually sold out to Associated Rediffusion.
13 Reisz, quoted in Welsh and Tibbetts, *The Cinema of Tony Richardson: Essays and Interviews*, p. 27.
14 To give some idea of the paltry budget, *Look Back in Anger* cost £250,000, *The Entertainer* £210,000, while Hollywood's then current blockbuster, *Ben Hur*, was budgeted at £3 million.
15 Reisz, quoted in McFarlane, *An Autobiography of British Cinema*, p. 478.
16 Walker, *Hollywood, England*, p. 44.
17 Joseph Janni, interviewed 11 May 1971, in *ibid.*, p. 109.
18 Walker, *Hollywood, England*, pp. 109–10.
19 R. Barton Palmer, 'What Was New in the British New Wave?', *Journal of Popular Film and Television*, Vol. 14, No. 3, p. 128.
20 Quoted in Anthony Aldgate, *Censorship and the Permissive Society: British Cinema and Theatre 1955–1965* (Oxford, Clarendon Press, 1995), p. 94.
21 Quoted in *ibid.*, p. 95.
22 Walter Lassally, 'The Dead Hand', *Sight and Sound*, Vol. 29, No. 3, Summer 1960, p. 114.
23 This was accompanied by a concomitant decline in British cinema attendance: 1,635 million attendances at 4,709 cinemas (1946); 1,396 million (1950), 1,101 million (1956), to an all-time low of 501 million in 1960.
24 William Whitebait (i.e. George Stonier), 'Bombardment', *New Statesman*, Vol. 55, No. 1412, 5 April 1958, p. 452.

25 Isabel Quigly, 'Out of the Bag', *Spectator*, No. 6835, 26 June 1959, p. 911.

26 Ellis, ed., *1951–1976: British Film Institute Productions*, p. 19.

27 Hoggart, '*We Are the Lambeth Boys*', p. 165.

28 Reisz, letter to Alexander Walker, in Walker, *Hollywood, England*, p. 38.

29 See specifically Roy Armes, *A Critical History of the British Cinema* (New York, Oxford University Press, 1978), pp. 264–5.

30 Hill, *Sex, Class and Realism: British Cinema 1956–1963*, p. 133.

31 Alan Sillitoe, interviewed 19 June 1972, in Walker, *Hollywood, England*, p. 82.

32 Gaston, *Karel Reisz*, p. 41.

33 V. F. Perkins, 'The British Cinema', in Ian Cameron, ed., *Movie Reader* (New York and Washington, Praeger Publishers, 1972), p. 9.

34 Andrew Higson, 'Space, Place, Spectacle: Landscape and Townscape in the "Kitchen Sink" Film', in Higson, *Dissolving Views: Key Writings on British Cinema* (London and New York, Cassell, 1996), p. 134.

35 *Ibid.*, pp. 137–8.

36 *Ibid.*, pp. 140–1.

37 *Ibid.*, pp. 146–7.

38 Alan Sillitoe, 'The Long Piece', in *Mountains and Caverns* (London, W. H. Allen, 1975), p. 37.

39 'Sillitoe's political beliefs are difficult to classify on conventional party lines; he said in 1960 that if he were to join a particular party he would choose the Communists, but a more accurate label might be that given to describe Brian Seaton's politics in *Key to the Door* – 'socialist-anarchist'. This category can encompass his inclination to admire the Soviet Union, his support for the anti-Polaris marches in 1961 and, a decade later, his refusal to fill in a government census form'. Harry Ritchie, *Success Stories: Literature and the Media in England 1950–1959* (London, Faber and Faber, 1988), p. 196.

40 Alan Sillitoe, *Saturday Night and Sunday Morning* (New York, Alfred A. Knopf and Plume Books, 1958 and 1992), p. 165.

41 '[Finney] wasn't my idea of Arthur', claimed Sillitoe. 'My Arthur was taller and thinner in the face and the whole film should have been rougher, more brutal, to match him'. Alan Sillitoe, interviewed 19 June 1972, in Walker, *Hollywood, England*, pp. 82–3.

42 See Stuart Laing, *Representations of Working Class Life 1957–1964* (Basingstoke, Macmillan, 1986), pp. 193–217.

43 Reisz's commitment to the NUT was further borne out that same year when he co-produced, with Leon Clore, John Krish's thirty-minute short, *I Want to Go to School*, for the union.

44 Quoted in Laing, *Representations of Working Class Life 1957–1964*, p. 194.

45 Quoted in *ibid.*, p. 203.

46 Quoted in Charles Barr, 'Broadcasting and Cinema 2: Screens within Screens', in Barr, ed., *All Our Yesterdays*, p. 218.

47 Reisz quoted in Orbanz, *Journey to a Legend and Back: The British Realistic Film*, p. 58.

48 Andrew Higson, 'Britain's Outstanding Contribution to the Film', p. 92.

49 Arthur is even more explicit in the novel, railing against television like an early version of Mary Whitehouse: 'They'd go barmy if they had them taken away. I'd love it if big Black Marias came down all the streets and men got out with hatchets to go in every house and smash the tellies. Everybody'd go crackers. They wouldn't know what to do. There'd be a revolution'. Sillitoe, *Saturday Night and Sunday Morning*, pp. 198–9.

50 Higson, 'Britain's Outstanding Contribution to the Film', p. 93.

51 Hill, *Sex, Class and Realism: British Cinema 1956–1963*, p. 161.

52 Terry Lovell, 'Landscapes and Stories in 1960s British Realism', *Screen*, Vol. 31, No. 4, Winter 1990, p. 367.

53 *Ibid.*

54 Quoted in Walker, *Hollywood, England*, p. 85.

55 Sillitoe, 'What Comes on Monday?', p. 59.

56 *Ibid.*

57 Lovell, 'Film Chronicle', p. 53.

58 Walker, *Hollywood, England*, p. 85.

59 Reisz, quoted in *ibid.*

Keeping up with the Truffauts:
Night Must Fall (1964)

5

It was a film made on the rebound. About a week before we started shooting, I said to Albert, 'We could make a very good movie out of this subject, if only Danny didn't have to be a murderer.' It ended up rather uncomfortably between a matinée thriller and a character study. (Karel Reisz)[1]

There are moments in *Night Must Fall* when Susan Hampshire takes on an unnerving look of Monica Vitti, and moments when the thread of a mood snaps so sharply ... that one feels the shade of Truffaut at the director's shoulder. I would not suggest that Karel Reisz consciously copied anyone: merely that he cannot but find himself thinking in a European idiom, however devastating the results may look in a context of old English melodramatics. (Penelope Houston)[2]

Reisz's *Night Must Fall* craves indulgence and points the way to Polanski's *Repulsion*. (Raymond Durgnat)[3]

Saturday Night and Sunday Morning premiered on 26 October 1960 at the Warner Theatre, Leicester Square to an initial hostile reception from the film trade and distributors. However, the film did exceptional business during its first week and subsequent word of mouth and mostly positive critical reviews quickly transformed it into a box-office success, turning an overall profit of £500,000. Eager to piggy back another project onto this commercial breakthrough, Reisz and Finney immediately formed a production company and started research on a film about Ned Kelly, the mythic nineteenth-century Australian outlaw. After commissioning David Storey to write a script, they flew to Australia in October 1962 and spent ten weeks researching the subject and scouting authentic locations. Principal photography was set to begin in March 1963 with Columbia (UK) putting up the financing. However, there were major problems from the outset. Firstly, the studio disliked the screenplay. 'David Storey's script was very good, very dark', recalls Reisz. 'When we delivered it to Columbia, who had commissioned it, I remember Mike

Frankovitch said, "I've commissioned a Western and you're giving me Macbeth. I'm not making this. Goodbye.'"[4] Secondly, because British labour regulations required the use of an exclusively British crew – which would necessitate flying them out to Australia and keeping them on location for several months – the studio abandoned the project when it became obvious that the budget would be prohibitive. Frustrated, but keen to keep their creative momentum alive, Reisz and Finney then accepted an offer from MGM to remake Emlyn Williams's classic 1935 theatrical warhorse, *Night Must Fall.*

Meanwhile, Reisz was also involved in the convoluted process of bringing another Storey project to the screen. Lindsay Anderson 'had read and been impressed by David Storey's novel, *This Sporting Life*', states Reisz. 'He took it to Tony [Richardson] at Woodfall as a project for himself. Tony read the novel and said, "It's very good, of course, but not for you." This was because he decided to make a film of it himself. He made an offer for the rights, but was outbid by Julian Wintle and Leslie Parkyn. Their company had a distribution deal with the Rank Organiza-tion, and they were acting on behalf of Joe Losey [who had worked with them on *Blind Date* in 1959]. Then Wintle fell out with Losey and offered *This Sporting Life* to me. But it was Lindsay's project, and I didn't want to direct it anyway, as the material seemed too close in some ways to *Saturday Night*. So I offered to produce it with Lindsay directing, and Wintle agreed'.[5] Shot in Wakefield, where Anderson had filmed his first non-industrial documentary, *Wakefield Express* in 1952, the production was fraught with difficulty, not least because of Anderson's emotional obsession with the film's star, Richard Harris, but also because of the director's technical inexperience. 'The camera crew was hostile, partic-ularly the very conservative, old-school operator', said Reisz. 'Julian Wintle disliked the early rushes and wanted me to take over. I refused, of course'.[6] Despite the stormy set, Reisz believed the final result was 'the most completely achieved of the "new wave" films, because the most passionately felt and ambitious'.[7]

However, the film turned out to be the last in a very short-lived line rather than the first of a new stylistic breed. Usurped largely by televi-sion – most notably *Coronation Street* and the Merseyside-based *Z Cars* (1962–77), itself an important training ground for up-and-coming real-ists like Ken Loach – the New Wave's regional kitchen sink formula had become prime-time's dramatic bread and dripping. In any case, *Saturday Night and Sunday Morning* was as much 'poetic' as 'realist' and in retrospect it is hardly surprising that, like Tony Richardson's rollicking and cinematically gimmicky adaptation of Henry Fielding's eighteenth-century novel *Tom Jones*, Reisz would veer further away from his roots in documentary towards the lure of powerful continental influences – not only the historic poetic realism of Carné's *Le Jour se Lève* and Vigo's *L'Atalante* (Reisz's favourites since his *Sequence* days), but also its more self-conscious and playful contemporary manifestation in the French New Wave cinema of Truffaut, Resnais and Godard.

Although at first glance *Night Must Fall* seems to be an odd choice of material for a director eager to break the kitchen sink stranglehold, in retrospect it proves to be an extremely adaptable vehicle for experimental risk-taking and is arguably one of Reisz's most underrated films, fusing elements of poetic realism and Resnais-like elliptical disjuncture into a penetrating psychological hybrid. Emlyn Williams, the Welsh playwright and actor, wrote the original play – a classic drawing-room suspense thriller set in a rural Essex bungalow – as a bravura acting and directing vehicle to further his own career.[8] After an extremely successful stage run in London and New York, it was adapted for the screen by John Van Druten and released by MGM in 1937 with Robert Montgomery, Dame May Whitty and Rosalind Russell in the leads. Although disowned by Louis B. Meyer, Richard Thorpe's film received excellent notices and was named as 1937's best picture by the National Board of Review. Both Montgomery and Whitty earned Academy Award nominations as Best Actor and Best Supporting Actress respectively.

Updated to the 1960s by screenwriter Clive Exton (subsequently the co-writer of *Isadora*, which shares several of *Night Must Fall*'s themes), Reisz's version was shot on location in a bucolic, almost primordial lakeside setting. The film opens to the sound of Ron Grainer's thundering dramatic chords as a shirtless young man savagely hatchets a human body in the middle of a dense wood. He then dumps the headless corpse and murder weapon into the lake before jumping into the water for a spiritually cleansing swim. This is our horrifying introduction to Danny (Albert Finney), a charmingly handsome waiter with slick-backed hair and a soft Welsh brogue, who works at a local resort hotel. It turns out that he is also the father of the unborn child of Dora (Sheila Hancock), the careworn housekeeper for the wheelchair-bound hypochondriac, Mrs Bramson (Mona Washbourne), who lives close to the lake with her blonde ex-actress daughter, Olivia (Susan Hampshire).[9] On the dubious pretext of reassuring Mrs Bramson that he will do his paternal duty by marrying Dora, Danny ingratiates himself with the elderly lady and starts working as a live-in handyman/gofer in her home, redecorating the house and becoming indispensable to her creature comforts in the process. Among countless other lies and fabrications, he claims to be an orphan who lost both parents at an early age and panders to Mrs Bramson's maternal instincts by playing the role of a dutiful but prankishly 'naughty' son, wheeling her around the garden with gay abandon and pampering the 'invalid' by plying her with chocolates and other niceties. The play-acting works like a charm and before long he is calling the old woman 'mother', much to Mrs Bramson's delight. More conveniently, his new employment also enables him to keep a watchful eye on the search for a missing local woman – Mrs Chalfont – which is being conducted by the local police in the nearby wood and lake.

Meanwhile, the bored and restless Olivia is herself in an unsatisfactory relationship with the pompous and needy Derek (Michael Medwin), who makes unreasonable demands on her time and hides his own sexual insecurities behind a veneer of aristocratic disdain for his class inferiors and flaunts his flashy sports car in over-determined compensation for his obvious lack of sexual charisma. Threatened to the point of catatonia by Derek's constant intrusion into his exclusive ménage with the three women – significantly, one of the film's musical leitmotifs is *Three Blind Mice* – the class-conscious Danny takes an immediate dislike to the would-be suitor, for if catering to Mrs Bramson's every whim were not castrating enough, Derek rubs salt into the wound by publicly questioning his masculinity. 'You'll make someone a wonderful wife', he sneers, as Danny serves them lunch in the dining room. 'Very kind of you to say so, sir', he replies, his Schweik-like restraint barely concealing his hatred. However, it doesn't take long for Danny to realize that the effete and whiney Derek is no real competition and that the deeply frustrated Olivia is ripe for seduction. Before long she has fallen irresistibly in love with him. Eager to find out more about this enigmatic Welshman, Olivia searches his room and suitcase but fails to examine an ominous-looking leather hatbox – the perfect size for concealing a severed head! – sitting tantalizingly atop his cupboard. A furious Danny catches her in the act, but the showdown leads not to Olivia's estrangement but even greater desire and sex.

The plot takes its first dramatic turn when police divers eventually discover Mrs Chalfont's headless body in the lake, along with the hatchet. The local papers have a field day with the news and Mrs Bramson is morbidly excited by the whole affair, especially when she learns that 'The search for the head continues'. The police begin questioning the local villagers and their suspicions are immediately aroused when they discover that the promiscuous Mrs Chalfont used to pick up eligible young men at the hotel bar where Danny worked prior to joining the Bramson household. Danny responds that he kept well away from her, everyone did – 'She had a bit of a reputation'. Inspector Willett (Martin Wyldeck) asks to look through Danny's belongings – just routine, of course – but a protective Olivia steps in on Danny's behalf, demanding that Willett obtain a search warrant.

Although Danny is off the hook for the moment, the showdown with Willett exacerbates the jealous antagonism between mother and daughter that has been simmering since his arrival: 'Danny doesn't belong to you, you know', complains Mrs Bramson, who is fully aware of their sexual relationship, 'Who do you think pays his wages every week?' Attempting to drive a wedge between mother and 'son' and forge her own conspiratorial bond, Olivia tells Danny that Mrs Bramson knows everything. But Danny protects his privacy, forcing Olivia to keep her emotional distance. In fact, he goes out of his way to alienate Olivia still further by playfully rough-housing with Dora and making lewd sexual advances right under her nose. Rejected and humiliated, a hysterical Olivia realizes that she has to get away and drives off to town in her Mini convertible, leaving Danny abandoned and distraught. Is this yet another replay of his mother's desertion? He takes refuge in Olivia's room, as if to relive his earlier sexual conquest, where he is found lying on the bed by a horrified Dora. His fiancée knows immediately what has been going on: 'She knows you come in here'. Danny torments Dora by turning the episode into yet another childish game, jumping up and down on the bed and stalking her half-menacingly around the room. Disgusted by such lewd exhibitionism, Dora slaps his face, calling his behaviour 'filthy'. That evening, the two rivals for Danny's affections run across each other in town and their mutual class antagonism results in a nasty cat fight that ends with Olivia running off and finding sanctuary in a local cinema (ironically, the feature attraction is John Sturges's *The Great Escape*).

Night has finally fallen and it's raining cats and dogs as Danny and Mrs Bramson play out their final charade of mother and son through a suspenseful game of hide and seek. Unfortunately it's no longer a harmless game for Danny. His repeated, almost desperate cries of 'Chase me!' suggest that he is sinking deeper into infantile regression to the point where he can no longer resurface from the depths of the masquerade. When an exhausted Mrs Bramson tells him to stop and chides him for his childish antics, he walks off petulantly to the kitchen for some water. When he fails to return or answer her repeated calls, Mrs Bramson becomes so alarmed that she forgets her 'disability', rises from her wheelchair for the first time, and after knocking over a vase discovers him soaking wet in the conservatory clutching a huge curved knife. Where on earth is Olivia? Unfortunately, the daughter has been unavoidably delayed in the rain by a flat tyre and Danny takes advantage of her absence by savagely hacking Mrs Bramson to death. Reisz then cuts to a Buñuel-ian close-up of Danny's orgasmic expression, implying that he is either having sex with his surrogate mother or ejaculating onto her corpse. Olivia eventually returns home to find her mother dead. After calling the police, she confronts Danny, who is taking another spiritually cleansing bath, but by now her lover has completely metamorphosed into his petulant 'naughty boy' persona and he desires nothing more than to be punished. His infantile regression is finally complete.

Night Must Fall premiered in May 1964 to almost universal derision from the public and critics alike. Despite the sensational allure of the MGM's publicity campaign – 'The lusty, brawling star of *Tom Jones* goes psycho in *Night Must Fall*' – Finney's loyal fans boycotted the film in droves. 'All the wives at M.G.M. who had seen the star as Tom Jones, adoring him, rounded on me like avenging Furies screaming, "What have you done to this beautiful boy?"' recalled Reisz.[10] Nor did it help that the dashingly handsome Finney was heavily made-up to give his face a waxen, spectral look akin to a serial killer in Madame Tussaud's Chamber of Horrors. Although Alan Lovell, a loyal advocate of *Saturday Night and Sunday Morning*, praised Reisz for making 'a genuine experiment', he also felt that it was a mistake to use Willliams's play and Danny the charming sex-killer as a dramatic starting point: 'Since Emlyn Williams simply used the character as a pretext for a "shocker," anybody who wanted to do something more with the subject would have to forget the play completely. So completely that you might as well write an original script about the subject. Karel Reisz and his writer, Clive Exton, haven't left the play far enough behind'.[11] This is particularly apparent in the film's anachronistically mismatched time frames. While Mrs Bramson and her country house seem to come from the 1930s and 1940s, filtered through the prism of a West End 'cosy' mystery setting – one almost expects Margaret Rutherford's Miss Marple to come blustering onto the set and solve the case in the middle of afternoon tea and crumpets – the policemen and their investigation, as well as Derek's sports car and Danny's Lambretta, are modishly contemporary. In contrast, John Cutts in *Films & Filming* argued that the film might have done better to stick closer to the dynamics of the original play, which can only work if played as an out-and-out shocker. As soon as you start to justify and analyse its psychological substance the drama collapses: 'And once you try, as Reisz has done, to broaden the scale of the thing ("We are trying," he has said, "to look at the boy alone, to divide the audience's sympa-thies between the madman and his victims"), then you immediately lose its curious dark strength'. In short, it's 'a sure misfire and a sad disappointment'.[12]

In retrospect, Reisz couldn't help but agree. His original plan was to update the original by using Danny's murders as a mechanism to reveal society's cultural prejudices, thereby making the story more of a class-based sociological character study than a melodrama. Left largely unexplained in Williams's play, Danny's urge to kill now comes from a life of increasing despair – all his relationships have failed, he has drifted from one humiliatingly menial job to another – and murder is the only way to get the power and respect he craves. Unfortunately, the film became inextricably caught between the two genre extremes: 'We didn't get the balance right. I remember Clive Exton, who wrote the script, said to me two or three weeks before we were due to shoot, "We could make a very good movie about this man if only he didn't have to commit the murders." So we were in a considerable state of confusion. And I think the mixture of melodrama and psychological study is a little immature in that movie. But it was my first attempt at real narrative film-making. And not a terribly good one'.[13]

More serious were criticisms of Reisz's elliptical, self-reflexive style, which was compared unfavourably to the French New Wave. Tom Milne, for one, noted that 'there are numerous hints in *Night Must Fall* that [Reisz] has been radically influenced by the new cinema in general, and by Godard in particular. Like *A Bout de Souffle*, each sequence in *Night Must Fall* has its beginning and end lopped off, giving a choppy, staccato rhythm; and as in *Vivre sa Vie* there seems to be a Brechtian influence in the constant attempts at distanciation ... Reisz distanciates – or attempts to – by making sharp cuts: for instance, from Danny in a pathological rage with Olivia after he has found her searching his room, to him happily encouraging her as she learns to ride his scooter on the lawn'.[14] Milne believed that this awkwardness in absorbing influences was due to Reisz (and British film-makers in general) not making enough films compared to the prolific output of Hollywood journeymen such as John Frankenheimer: 'One learns one's metier by exercising it'.[15] Nonetheless, he praised the director for at least attempting to throw off the limitations of kitchen sink realism: 'One can only applaud Reisz's courage in making such a complete breakaway – more so than anyone else – from the brand of social realism which has ended by strangling the British cinema, and regret that his leap into darkness only landed him in a quagmire'.[16]

Penelope Houston, Reisz's old *Sequence* colleague, was less generous. In an insightful overview of the British New Wave's clumsy attempts to 'keep up with the Antonionis', she observed that,

> Recent British film-making has assimilated a good deal from across the Channel; and when the influences actually seem to work, as in the exuberant introduction to Julie Christie in *Billy Liar*, they can refresh and lighten the whole tempo of a picture. This, however, is merely a glancing

reference, a sudden shift of idiom for a particular purpose. It is different with a film like *Night Must Fall*, where one feels that a great deal of theoretical rather than practical intelligence went into the problem of how to reconstruct an old warhorse of a stage melodrama to make it work in the modern anti-narrative medium. And one can only wish that in fact it did work; that Emlyn Williams' play did not keep obstinately pushing its way to the surface, calling out for attention as relentlessly and obstreperously as the head in the hatbox itself.[17]

This is not to say that the antinomy between hackneyed source material and personal style is necessarily a problem *tout court*, because directors such as Truffaut and Godard often chose pulp fiction as their jumping off point for expressing a more auteurist vision – e.g. Truffaut's adaptations of David Goodis's *Shoot the Piano Player* (1960) and Cornell Woolrich's *The Bride Wore Black* (1968); or Godard's appropriation of Dolores Hitchens's *Fool's Gold*, the *policier* source for *Bande à Part* (1964). More importantly, one can also argue that Reisz's fusion of poetic realism and narrative disjuncture in *Night Must Fall* is the perfect stylistic expression of Danny's interior psychological state, a paradigmatic example of Reisz-the-critic's ongoing dictum that style should always be tailored to fit content.

Reisz and Exton's most significant change from Williams's play and Thorpe's subsequent film is the shift in focalization from Olivia to Danny. The term focalization derives from the structuralist literary theorist Gerard Genette, who distinguished between the role of the narrator recounting the events of the fiction – the enunciating voice of the agent who 'speaks' – and the activity of the diegetic character through whose perspective those events are perceived or focalized – the agent who 'sees'. This is a far more useful term than simple 'point-of-view' because it allows the film-maker to incorporate individual characters as subjective centres of consciousness within the *mise-en-scène*, which can itself act as an objective correlative of their inner psychology – a crucial combination in poetic realism where commonplace objects are imbued with symbolic resonances and evocative, subjective correspondences. In the 1937 version, the whole film is essentially Olivia's sexual fantasy, with Danny, for all his psychoses, taking on the passive role of catalyst or emotional trigger. Rosalind Russell's Olivia is a repressed, bespectacled bluestocking who resists the insistent overtures of her aunt's straight-laced, cricket-playing lawyer, Justin, and despises Mrs Bramson, a mean old harridan who viciously exploits and bullies her. Like Madame Bovary, she is a depressed, unfulfilled romantic (she secretly writes earnest love poems), yearning for excitement and adventure. She is attracted to Danny, even though she suspects he might be a murderer, because he flatters her vanity and more importantly because he fuels her gothic imagination, allowing her to mould him in terms of her own sexual desires and fabricated self-image. Thus at the end of the film she returns to the house not to save her detested aunt or, as she claims, to 'find him out', but because she needs to confirm for herself that Danny really is mad, horrible and loathsome, incapable of loving anyone but himself or living up to the role of bold adventurer that she has constructed for him. In contrast, Susan Hampshire's Olivia is merely a pampered rich girl. She seems to be genuinely oblivious to Danny's psychopathic tendencies and their relationship is clearly a love-hate mismatch across class lines, designed more to alienate Derek and her mother than to further her own emotional needs. Moreover, their 'affair' is also shown so elliptically that little or none of their developing bond is shown on-screen. This would be a major defect if Reisz's film were primarily a character study of Olivia, but because the story's focalization has shifted directly to Danny as a form of psychic 'contagion' it's possible to argue that the film's elliptical structure is crucial to expressing his psychology. In short, the bulk of their relationship has to exist off-screen because, as we shall see, its psychological essence cannot be accurately represented.

In this respect, poetic realism is the perfect medium for Reisz's needs. In her extremely insightful study of psychoanalytical operations in Carné's poetic realist masterpiece *Le Jour se Lève*, Maureen Turim notes that the film 'prefigures the psychoanalytic narrative economy of the 1940s melodrama and *film noir* in its configuration of a compulsive desire forcing repetitions that can only be stopped with death'.[18] However, unlike the expressionist side of *film noir*, with its Manichean reinforcement of binary oppositions such as hero/villain, self/other, good/bad and conscious/unconscious, poetic realism produces an incommensurable weave of internally conflicting meanings rather than a reduction of the filmic text to one prevailing diagnosis or clear-cut stylistic expression. In other words, it tends to flatten out the usual hierarchy of psychic and visual language by stressing metonymic and syntagmatic connections *between* images and objects, whereby all are treated equally and interchangeably (much like Freud's 'displacement'), rather than closing down meaning through metaphoric or paradigmatic consolidation (Freud's 'condensation'). Consequently, character focalization is necessarily far more diffuse in poetic realism, undercutting clear-cut distinctions between separate individuals on the one hand, and between subjects and objects on the other. Thus, describing Jean Gabin's string of working-class characters in the late 1930s (who seem uncannily to anticipate many of Danny's psychological traits in *Night*

Must Fall), Turim notes that, 'this hero tends to represent the troubled aspect of a subject whose desires are poetically magnified as outside of control or compromise. The death act then takes a structural place in the narrative as a refusal of suffering and the danger of being further misunderstood or manipulated, as well as presenting psychic volatility as marking the construction of this hero'.[19]

This over-determination of the death drive as untrammelled desire explains poetic realism's tendency – again typified by *Night Must Fall* – to start with the crime itself and then spend the rest of the film trying (and failing) to explain its cause or motivation. Instead of becoming the key to unlocking the repressed past – as in, for example, Alfred Hitchcock's *Marnie* (1964) – memory becomes a series of repetitive gestures which the style of poetic realism reinforces through associative memory-links and objective/symbolic over-determination. In French, the word *souvenir* means both memory *and* memento – objects and memories are effectively inseparable – but in poetic realism they fail to conjure up a fixed or definitive psychic source of behaviour. Thus Danny's infantile regression to birth/oblivion simply *happens*, it doesn't disclose the cause of his psychosis (although Danny's clenching of his hands in a strangling posture when he refers to his mother suggests acute separation anxiety that may have led to matricide – to put an end to her persistent absences once and for all). Similarly, the severed head in the hatbox is not just a simple Freudian castration symbol – an over-compensated fetish to ward off Danny's obvious castration anxiety at the hands of the punishing father (which is at the same time a constant *reminder* of castration, reinforced by the homosocial nature of the all-female household) – but a singular element of over-determined memory that cannot be reduced to a meaningful structure. This slippage is reinforced by the wide difference of signification that the fetish possessed in the past – i.e. as Mrs Chalfont's functioning head – compared to its objective role in the present: as Danny's portable trophy. Thus, while objects become a metaphorical expression of the unconscious in relation to death (Thanatos), they also work metonymically as part of the Eros complex – as triggers for endless chains of desire: 'Each of the objects represents in microcosm this difference between two states of being, one in which there are restrictions, but also dreams and hope for change, and one in which hope is lost and death is inevitable'.[20]

The endless recurrences and repetitions of these object relations produces a structure of repetition and return in which death is the fold that links them but also acts as a catalyst for difference (a major motif of *Isadora*, as we shall see in Chapter 7). This cyclical double bind also supersedes class difference, for 'Pleasure ... is always deferred and unattainable; identifying with bourgeois dreams will certainly not bring happiness, but neither, apparently, will acceptance of one's proletarian being'.[21] It's clear then that the film offers not so much causes and explanations of Danny's madness but circular, non-linear forces associated with objects, and therefore memories, which have no outlet to dissipate or to become cathected as socially useful drives. Metaphors thus become reconstituted as metonyms and vice versa, with little or no possibility of emotional closure: 'In Poetic Realism, then, the accent is on poesis, on the trope deployed strategically, framed in a manner that sparkles with a simultaneous sense of design and imaginative play of thought and language ... It is a response that sees fiction and the reality that is its context as completely interactive'.[22]

In *Night Must Fall*, this fluid interactivity between subject and Other, Imaginary and Real, is played out both performatively – through Finney's deliberately mannered acting – and through *mise-en-scène* and elliptical editing. Because he is caught in the limbo between Eros and Thanatos, where the object of his desire (the plenitude of the mother) is at the same time manifested through regression and oblivion, Danny finds it extremely difficult to distil his identity into a specific outward persona that is anything other than Imaginary. Like Arthur Seaton's misconceived relationship to his own 'omnipotent' self-image in *Saturday Night and Sunday Morning*, Danny can only know himself as a mirror image of other people's desire, in effect reflecting back what others project onto him. Thus each time he meets one of the different women in the film, his performance shifts into a different emotive register. With Dora, he plays the violent buffoon, suggesting that she enjoys a spot of rough sex and wilfully feeds her own desire off Danny's psychological abuse. For Olivia he is the envious and brutal lover, flattering her sufficiently to aid and abet her need for sexual adventure but also her unacknowledged desire to leave her mother and break off with Derek. As a former actress, it's highly likely that she is also giving a theatrical performance in her scenes with Danny, thus strengthening their psychic masquerade for each other's mutual benefit. Finally, for Mrs Bramson, he adopts the role of the dutiful loving son. 'Danny adapts his image to people's expectations of him', acknowledged Alexander Walker, 'but where Finney himself felt he went wrong was in never satisfactorily finding a way of getting to grips with Danny when alone'.[23] But surely this is exactly when the character is at his most real, a perfect rendering of a dissociated personality who has no grip on the difference between self and Other, subject and object. When left to his own devices, Danny simply doesn't know who he is and thus has no way to be natural inside his own skin and, by extension, to appear outwardly 'authentic' to the film's audience. The fact that we are far too conscious of Finney acting in most of the scenes with his conquests is completely appropriate, because Danny has to project himself into the role of another (an Other) as his own mirror double in order to retain a grip on reality in the first place. Even the scene where he peeks into the hatbox and murmurs a quiet 'hello' to Mrs Chalfont's head is mostly shot in a mirror, suggesting that he can only address his own crimes by constructing multiple personae. These endlessly reverberating mirror images thus act as both a threat (in the form of a multiple splitting) and a comfort – 'that is me, I am whole' – that can never be resolved except through extreme psychic regression.

Reisz establishes this crystalline dynamic in the film's brilliant opening sequence, which seems to have been heavily influenced by the murder scene in George Stevens's *A Place in the Sun* (1951). Writing in *Sight and Sound* in 1952, Reisz noted in the earlier film that, 'The scene of the murder on the lake develops in a series of slow, isolated impressions taken in different settings at different times of day and evening, in which the changing quality of the images rather than any continuous dramatic development creates the powerful effect of hysteria: it is a most daringly conceived piece of cinema'.[24] *Night Must Fall* establishes its psychological mood in much the same way. We begin with an early morning establishing shot of the Bramsons' country house, surrounded by trees and flowering shrubs. However, dramatic chords indicate that this seemingly innocent pastoral scene is the site of much darker forces. We then cut to the conservatory at the rear of the house and begin a slow pan and simultaneous zoom in as Olivia comes out of the house in her dressing gown and walks aimlessly across the garden. She seems restless and unsure of herself, as if she had something weighing on her mind. After following her circuitous movements for a few seconds, Reisz cuts to a tighter shot as she sits facing the camera on a garden swing. Suddenly, she looks up and we cut to a static shot of tree tops in the nearby woods. It's unclear at first whether this is Olivia's literal point-of-view or, more suggestively, her subjectivity linked to other, more primordial forces in the undergrowth. The latter seems more likely as we pan down the trees to the sound of yet another dramatic chord. The camera zooms in on the thicket and tracks left as we hear a piercing animal cry. However, just as we are thinking that the forest is acting as an objective correlative of Olivia's animal desires and unsettled state of mind, we suddenly zoom in on Danny as he hacks away at Mrs Chalfont's body before carrying it off to the nearby lake. We then hear similarly shrill bird noises as he runs towards the camera and flings the hatchet into another part of the water. Olivia has thus been linked to Danny by the common association of the untamed environment, locking them inextricably together through both spatial contiguity and an interchangeable psychic displacement. As if to underline this metonymic connection, Reisz cuts to a close-up of the hatchet soaring through the air, thus mimicking Olivia's earlier upward gaze. We then cut back to Olivia on the garden swing and she promptly turns her back to the camera, as if we were intruding on her most private thoughts. Is she mentally 'seeing' the murder in her mind's eye, or fate-fully connected to it through a form of psychological contagion? As the film unfolds, such clear-cut distinctions become irretrievably blurred as Reisz exploits the relationship between Danny and Olivia through a fluid economy of psychic exchange. One libido literally cannot exist without the catalytic Imaginary of the other, so that the characters no longer desire each other, but the chain of desire itself.

However, Olivia is only one of the Three Blind Mice. Reisz follows this opening episode by immediately cutting to Mrs Bramson as she spies on Olivia through the bay window of her bedroom. The thick leafy pattern of her wallpaper creates an almost camouflage-like effect, echoing the foliage of the forest and thus linking the widow with Danny (and now, by extension, Olivia). She then turns to look out of the opposite window just in time to see Dora arriving for work on her bike. Mrs Bramson is thus placed at the fulcrum of a spatial triangle, which 'not only implies a female triangle of 'blind mice', but it also suggests that, because the widow is at its upended apex, she is the most vulnerable'.[25] The psychological and dramatic dynamics of the film are thus laid out formally and spatially without a word having been spoken, so that Danny and his victims form a metonymic connection of mutual desire long before he actually moves into the Bramson household. Danny is then shown bathing blissfully in the lake, thereby reinforcing his earlier symbolic connection with water. Up to now Reisz has associated the lake symbolically with murder and death, but in Freudian (or more accurately, Lacanian) terms water is also symbolic of a desire for plenitude with the lost mother – i.e. a return to the amniotic fluid of the womb – evoking libidinal drives towards rebirth, baptism, the life force and the erotics of play (*jouissance*). Lacking a real or symbolic Father (and thus unable to enter into a 'healthy' Oedipal relation with the linguistic Name of the Father), Danny attempts instead to recapture his lost plenitude with his mother by surrounding himself with mother substitutes (thus the need to exclude Derek from the homo-social household) and to symbolically 'kill her' again and again (in the form of Mrs Chalfont and Mrs Bramson), all the better to transform lack into incommensurable oblivion.

Danny's ambivalence towards water is reinforced later in the film when the frogmen discover Mrs Chalfont's body and the hatchet. Reisz opens the sequence with an establishing shot of the divers on the lake, before cutting to a close-up of the submerged frogman's air bubbles on the surface of the water. Using a very long dissolve, the bubbles are then superimposed on the lampshade in Olivia's bedroom, before we pan down to Danny stretched out alongside Olivia on her bed. During the intimate conversation that follows, Danny opens up to Olivia for the first time, telling her picturesque childhood stories of going to chapel and observing the 'smelly old women with their black coats and fat behinds ... I didn't fancy the idea of going to hell with that lot', he says. However, when Olivia finally admits that she loves him, he can't look her in the eye. 'This is where I live', he says, pointing to his forehead. 'Private'. Reisz then cuts back to the frogmen in the lake just as a hand breaks the surface clutching the hatchet. Danny's earlier *jouissance* and the tender scene with Olivia is thus bracketed by its syntagmatic linkage to the Symbolic Order (the rule of Law) and punishment (castration).

However, as we have seen, such fears are also desires: death as oblivion and physical termination is associated with water just as plenitude and non-individuated bliss are associated with the oblivion of the womb. Reisz plays out this psychic ambivalence in the film's conclusion, where Danny gargles happily while taking a cleansing shower after murdering Mrs Bramson. Having removed this latest in what is probably a long line of mother substitutes, he then immerses his body in the 'baptismal', womb-like bathtub with just his head peeking out of the water, as if to envelop his body and thus deny its physicality. However, Reisz's use of a sharp, frontal angle down on Finney makes it look as if his head has been decapitated and is floating on the surface of the water, thus reconnecting him to Mrs Chalfont and the castration anxiety that he can never completely sublimate. Meanwhile, although Olivia is equally associated with water – she gets soaked to the skin while changing her tyre – thus reinforcing the primordial psychic connection with Danny that was forged in the film's opening sequence, she is now also representative of the rule of Law and the Symbolic Order. After she calls the police and tells Danny to get dressed in preparation for his inevitable arrest, he shows a final bit of bravado – 'I'm getting dressed and then we'll see what's what. I can handle myself in a punch-up, remember that!' – but unfortunately it's nothing but empty rhetoric. He collapses and cowers by the bathroom sink, pawing the air like a punch-drunk boxer. Far from getting physically aggressive with either Olivia or his captors, Danny's true desire is less to reassert his somatic power than to dissolve his physical self into a sublimating oblivion.

Cinematographer Freddie Francis fulfils Danny's desire pictorially by shifting the tonal qualities of the *mise-en-scène* to a starker black and white contrast, outlining Danny from his white tiled surroundings like a poorly fashioned matte shot. The film ends with progressively increasing over-exposure, so that just as Danny is at his most vulnerable – psychically and emotionally – the more he melts into the dazzling white ground and finds his true resting place, dematerialized into pure light. In Lacanian terms, this psychic and somatic regression is a Phallic phase determined by the desire for plenitude and is a male *phantasy* of maternity rather than an actual, lived experience of it. In this sense it is an accurate description of Danny's contradictory desire for annihilation and *jouissance*, but more important is the fact that because it is unrepresentable *as such*, it can only be alluded to through ellipses and absences.[26] This is why the choppy montage of *Night Must Fall* is less a faddish appropriation of Resnais and Godard than an absolutely appropriate objective correlative for Danny's contagious desire, because what goes on off-screen in the interstices of the shots is just as important as what we see onscreen.

The most overt narrative ellipses in *Night Must Fall* directly connect Danny's past crimes to the seduction of Olivia, thereby consolidating their mutual psychic bond. The first instance follows a fight between Olivia and Derek after they arrive home after a date. Danny gets a 'grandstand view' as he watches them from his room and when she enters the house he invites her for a warming cup of tea in the kitchen. Although she chides him for eavesdropping and accuses him of spying on her private life, they repair to the conservatory where Danny accuses her of being too sentimental and advises her to cut off the relationship with Derek. 'You're really a swine, aren't you?' says Olivia, bluntly, but he's unfazed by the insult. 'Nice car he's got, too', adds Danny. 'Powerful'. He then caresses her cheek very gently. She closes her eyes for a split second as the sexual tension builds, but before we can see Olivia's reaction Reisz slam cuts to the following morning as the couple enjoy a playful bit of 'jousting' in their respective vehicles on the estate lawns. Olivia is happy for the first time in the film, throwing out her arms as if she were flying. 'Not bad for a girl', says Danny, admiringly. Derek's Oedipal and phallic sports car has thus been displaced by the more modest, 'feminine' qualities of the Mini and the Lambretta and we quickly assume that the earlier ellipse concealed a probable sexual interlude.

The second occasion expands the sexual inference by tying Olivia and Danny's desire directly to the annihilating effects of the unrepresentable itself. While Olivia rifles through his things in an inquisitive attempt to understand something about his secret past, Reisz uses crosscutting from Olivia in the box-room to Danny wheeling Mrs Bramson around the garden as a conventional means of building up dramatic suspense. Will Olivia be caught in the act and, if so, how will Danny react? Will his true colours as a psychotic be uncovered at last? Firstly, Olivia pulls Danny's suitcase from under the unmade bed and opens it to reveal a wooden glove-maker's hand, a mirror and some newspapers. She picks up the hand and examines it. Psychologically, one can easily read the object as a displaced phallus/fetish akin to Mrs Chalfont's missing head (i.e. as a compensation for Danny's castration anxiety), but it is also directly associated with his mother who, if Danny is to be believed, was herself a glove-maker. More importantly, the hand's fingers can be dismantled and reconfigured to suit the desired shape of the glove, and in this sense it resembles the psychic mechanism of Freud's famous 'Fort-Da' game described in *Beyond the Pleasure Principle* (1920). In this famous incident the psychologist's eighteen-month-old nephew was observed tossing a reel of cotton over the rail of his cot, thus making the object disappear ('Fort', meaning 'gone' or 'away' in German) and then reeling it back into his field of vision ('Da' or 'there') as a self-empowering objective substitute for the painful experience of dealing with the routine of his mother's absence and subsequent reappearance. For Freud, the incident marked the birth of language and its effective autonomy from actual reality, allowing the individual to distance himself (and by extension empower himself) from the painful lived experience of the real. The glove-maker's hand would thus allow Danny symbolically to dismantle and reconstitute his mother at will. Interestingly, Olivia accidentally breaks the hand apart and panics when she is unable to put it back together again, generating a symbolic threat to Danny's psychic and linguistic control over maternal lack. It is at this point that Danny enters the room and discovers her intrusion. He quickly looks up to see if the hatbox (itself constitutive of a giant narrative ellipse) has been moved – thankfully it hasn't – and then looks at her accusingly: 'Well, well, well. Having a bit of a poke around, eh? Did you find anything interesting?' He quickly puts the hand back together again (thereby restoring the precarious equilibrium of the Symbolic Order), but then grabs her roughly and violently thrusts his underwear and socks into her face before flinging her brutally against the door. He sarcastically invites her to go through his jacket, and then forcefully presses her head down to his bed: 'Have a look at this. See? Do you like it?!' The symbiosis of Olivia's desire to understand Danny's past, and Danny's desire for plenitude with his mother (who is in turn displaced back onto Olivia and her own desire for Danny) creates such an overdetermination of psychic jamming that the film's narrative, in effect, short-circuits. Desire has become so hyperbolic that its literal representation has become impossible.

Instead of a renewed primal scene we slam cut to Olivia joyfully riding Danny's Lambretta on the back lawn. What happened during the ellipse? Did this rough foreplay lead to sex? We cannot be entirely sure of the answer, but Reisz gives us enough *symbolic* clues to allow us to fill in the gaps. Olivia is uneasy on the bike because she is driving too slowly: 'I can't steer it', she cries. Wielding a chair like a circus lion-tamer, Danny urges her to speed up, to increase the power if she wants to 'stay in the saddle'. Finally she stops beside him and he revs the engine loudly, creating a cloud of exhaust fumes, metaphorically evoking the 'heat' of their new, sexually charged relationship. This implies that Olivia did indeed 'like the bed' in the previous scene and it led to extremely gratifying sex. However, the playful interlude is brief because we then cut from exhaust to water, as the police pull the headless Mrs Chalfont from the lake. The metonymic skidding of substitutions has once again come full circle as the contagion of Danny's psychosis spreads to yet another surrogate, yet another ephemeral articulation of unquenchable desire. Night, inevitably, has fallen once again.

Notes

1 Reisz, quoted in McFarlane, *An Autobiography of British Cinema*, p. 478.
2 Penelope Houston, 'Keeping Up with the Antonionis', *Sight and Sound*, Vol. 33, No. 4, Autumn 1964, p. 167.
3 Durgnat, *A Mirror for England: British Movies from Austerity to Affluence*, p. 220.
4 Reisz, quoted in McFarlane, *An Autobiography of British Cinema*, p. 478.
5 Reisz, quoted in Lambert, *Mainly About Lindsay Anderson*, p. 110.
6 Reisz, quoted in *ibid.*, p. 117.
7 Reisz, quoted in Walker, *Hollywood, England*, p. 175.
8 Williams was later renowned for *Beyond Belief*, his searing 1968 account of the infamous 'Moors Murders'.
9 Olivia is her niece in the original play.
10 Reisz, quoted in Walker, *Hollywood, England*, p. 149.
11 Alan Lovell, 'Karel Reisz's Experiment', *Peace News*, 5 June 1964, p. 8.
12 John Cutts, '*Night Must Fall*', *Films & Filming*, Vol. 10, June 1964, p. 22.
13 Reisz, quoted in Gow, 'Outsiders: Karel Reisz in an Interview with Gordon Gow', p. 15.
14 Tom Milne, '*Night Must Fall*', *Sight and Sound*, Vol. 33, No. 3, Summer 1964, p. 144.
15 *Ibid.*
16 *Ibid.*
17 Houston, 'Keeping Up with the Antonionis', p. 167.
18 Maureen Turim, 'Poetic Realism as Psychoanalytical and Ideological Operation: Marcel Carné's *Le Jour se Lève*', in Susan Hayward and Ginette Vincendeau, eds, *French Film: Texts and Contexts* (London and New York, Routledge, 1990), p. 103.
19 *Ibid.*, p. 104.
20 *Ibid.*, p. 108.
21 *Ibid.*, p. 112.
22 *Ibid.*, p. 114.

23 Walker, *Hollywood, England*, p. 149.

24 Karel Reisz, 'A Place in the Sun', *Sight and Sound*, Vol. 21, No. 3, January–March 1952, p. 121.

25 Gaston, *Karel Reisz*, p. 53.

26 Lacan draws a clear distinction between the Phallus – an imaginary plenitude representing the primal lack of unity with the primordial mother, a condition shared by both sexes – and the phallus/penis, the defining signifier of the patriarchal Symbolic Order, which is possessed only by the male.

Gorilla war: *Morgan: A Suitable Case for Treatment* (1966)

6

The diagnosis schizophrenia is a political act. (R. D. Laing)[1]

I am concerned with paying attention to the person who struggles to act consistently with himself, independently of whether his actions are socially acceptable or not. (David Mercer)[2]

Then raise the scarlet standard high! Within its shade we'll live or die. Though cowards flinch and traitors sneer, we'll keep the red flag flying here. (Jim Connel, lyrics to 'The Red Flag', 1889)

I've become all furry! (Morgan Delt)

By 1964 the so-called British New Wave was a spent force, its realist aspirations having been channelled into regional television drama. Mainstream cinema now took up a fashionable popular current – Swinging London – fuelled by the instant obsolescence of the new consumerism and exemplified by the King's Road and Carnaby Street, mini skirts and Mini Coopers, discotheques and dolly birds, *Ready Steady Go* and *Juke Box Jury*, Veruschka and Jean Shrimpton. Looking back from the vantage point of the late 1990s, Anthony Aldgate and Jeffrey Richards evoked the period in almost apocalyptic tones:

> With the backing of the Hollywood giants, British film-makers set out to capture the glitter and the glamour. Sober realism and earnest social comment gave way to fantasy, extravaganza and escapism; black and white photography and Northern locations to colour and the lure of the metropolis; Puritanical self-discipline to hedonistic self-indulgence; plain, truthful settings to flamboyant, unrealistic decorativeness. Films became locked in a heady spiral of mounting extravagance, febrile excitement and faddish innovation. Seen from the depressed and sober vantage point of succeeding generations, these films seem akin to highly coloured ephemera from the last days of the Roman Empire, a madcap efflorescence preceding extinction.[3]

Decadent or not, the chief socio-political catalyst for this dramatic shift in cultural consciousness was the 1964 victory of Harold Wilson's Labour government which, after 'thirteen years of Tory misrule' emphasized a new broom approach to both social legislation and popular culture by stressing youth and innovation and the concomitant development of Swinging London as the economic and fashion centre of the new Europe. Issues of class, race, religion and gender now began to take second place to the fetishization of a classless and consumerist national and personal identity. Peter Wollen has correctly noted the new era's debt to earlier counter-currents rooted in the Independent Group – most notably Eduardo Paolozzi and Richard Hamilton (subsequently the designer of The Beatles' *White Album*) – with their embracing of American Pop consumer culture, comic books and science fiction; Peter Blake (the originator of the cover montage for The Beatles' *Sgt. Pepper's Lonely Hearts Club Band*); as well as the critical influence of Lawrence Alloway, the leading contributor to the early 1960s auteurist film magazine, *Movie*.[4] 'Pop broke through to a wider cultural audience with the 1961 appearance of a new phalanx of artists, the Young Contemporaries [who included David Hockney], encouraged by Alloway, and then Ken Russell's benchmark television show, *Pop Goes the Easel*, the following year', notes Wollen. 'In retrospect, we see that the nonexistent British "New Wave" of the time would have been much more closely linked to pop than to the Angry Young Men. Pop prefigured the sixties transformation of British culture'.[5]

Although Wollen's analysis is valid on a broader, arts-related basis, his genealogy of 1960s popular culture is partly belied by the key filmic example of Tony Richardson whose career, as we noted in Chapter 4, evolved out of Free Cinema and the landmark staging of John Osborne's *Look Back in Anger*. Most critics acknowledge that it was Richardson's Oscar winning *Tom Jones* which almost single-handedly killed off kitchen sink realism overnight, for 'Where the emphasis had been on the dark side of the self – discontent, repression and deprivation – it switched to the bright side, to self-assertion, personal fulfilment and the good life'.[6] One can also point to a key transitional film such as John Schlesinger's *Billy Liar* (also 1963), based on Keith Waterhouse and Willis Hall's popular play, which juxtaposes Manchester's Billy Fisher (Tom Courtenay) enduring a dull job, boring girlfriend and nagging working-class parents with his fantasy daydreams of Julie Christie as a liberated figure of escape who eventually moves to Swinging London. These early cues were quickly taken up by Dick Lester in *The Knack* (1965) and his Beatles films, *A Hard Day's Night* (1964) and *Help!* (1965), with their obvious debt to the fast-motion, rapid cutting and visual non sequiturs of TV commercials, comic strips, the Theatre of the Absurd and the inspired lunacy of *The Goon Show*. One should also note the films of Michael Winner (*The Girl Getters/The System*, 1964; *You Must Be Joking*, 1965; *I'll Never Forget What's'isname* and *The Jokers*, both 1967) and Clive Donner (*What's New Pussycat*, 1965 and *Here We Go Round the Mulberry Bush*, 1967). However, by 1966 the surface glitz and glamour of the Swinging Sixties had already started to tarnish into the psychedelic, drug-addled 'alternative lifestyles' of the second half of the decade (epitomized by Roeg and Cammell's *Performance* (1970) and Richard Hamilton's aptly named 1968 screenprint, 'Swingeing London', depicting Mick Jagger and art dealer Robert Fraser's infamous drug bust), with Losey's *Modesty Blaise* (1966) and Antonioni's *Blow-Up* (1966) offering more sharply satirical critiques of the Pop/Mod *Zeitgeist*.

It's in this latter context that Reisz's *Morgan: A Suitable Case for Treatment* can perhaps be viewed as an appropriate formal hybrid. It seems at first to be stylistically similar to Dick Lester's madcap, Mack Sennett approach to social satire,[7] but under the comedic veneer lies a serious study of an individual's descent into madness and, as we have seen, a broader metaphor for the intrinsic failures of both the Old and New Left's ideological response to the burgeoning counter-culture. Reisz, for one, refused to see his desertion of classic realism for the new cinematic trickery as a capitulation to fad: 'It was sometimes bracketed with "swinging London" and Dick Lester and all that. I don't see that at all, because I think *Morgan* has a certain substance; it's not pure *jeu d'esprit*, which is what the Beatles films and the swinging London thing were. Morgan was a one-off'.[8] As we saw in the case of *Night Must Fall*, Reisz refused to separate style from content and was more than capable of using different, almost radically opposed techniques for the sake of a heightened poetic realism: 'I take my cue from the scriptwriter, since, unlike Fellini, I don't conceive my own plots. I look for a technique that will do justice and inform the material I am working with. The "stream-of-consciousness" technique would never have worked for *We Are the Lambeth Boys*, but it was perfect for *Morgan*'.[9]

The film reunited Reisz with two former colleagues: Leon Clore, his co-producer on John Krish's *I Want to Go to School*, a thirty–minute short made for the National Union of Teachers in 1960; and the ubiquitous Richardson. According to Reisz, 'The Bryanston people had gone out of business and British Lion had been sold to six producing units. One of these units was Tony Richardson's and mine, and we had an agreement that each group could make its own films. When we put *Morgan* on the table, the other five groups all said, "Please don't! This is an experimental highbrow picture!" I thought it was a comedy – about serious things'.[10] *Morgan* was originally designed to be one part of a three-episode film – the other two shorts were Lindsay Anderson's *The White Bus* and Richardson's *Red and Blue* – produced by Oscar Loewenstein and eventually released as *Red, White and Zero* (1967). Ultimately Mercer's script turned out to be too long for the project and Reisz's sequence was eventually replaced by a short, *The Ride of the Valkyrie*, directed by Peter Brook and starring Zero Mostel. It's fortunate that Reisz's involvement in the episodic project was abortive because *Morgan* turned out to be one of his most successful and popular films, earning an Oscar nomination for Vanessa Redgrave and six British Academy Award nominations, including Best Actor, Best Actress and Best Film. It has remained something of a cult classic to this day.

As we noted in our earlier discussion of the film, Morgan Delt (David Warner) is a young working-class artist with Trotskyist tendencies who is irrevocably alienated from the two women he loves most: his staunchly Stalinist mother (Irene Handl), who runs a London café and cruelly denigrates her wayward son as a class traitor; and his beautiful upper middle-class ex-wife Leonie Henderson (Vanessa Redgrave), who has just been granted a *decree nisi*. Unable to find meaningful solace in his art, organized politics or unconditional love, Morgan instead withdraws into the world of primordial nature. In short, he is obsessed with gorillas, not as a harmless hobby or artistic project but to the point of complete and utter identification. Indeed, as the film opens, we find him at the London Zoo gorilla house listening to the recorded commentary on the living and mating habits of these gentle primates. As Reisz cross-cuts between the simian-looking Morgan and Guy, the great ape – there seems to be some mutual understanding – the voice-over becomes uncannily prescient of Morgan's own subsequent behaviour: 'Gorillas have no natural enemies, and they are enemy to no one. Young gorillas stay with their mother for several years, remaining safe even from the attacks of the predatory leopard. An angry adult male gorilla however is a formidable sight. Surprised by an intruder, he will tear down great branches, roar his anger and beat his chest'. In effect, we have been forewarned!

On the day of the divorce, Morgan takes advantage of Leonie's presence in court to return to their town house and 'liberate' his assorted Marxist and gorilla bric-à-brac from his old attic studio. As if to reassert his continued symbolic and emotional role in Leonie's life, he removes the dust sheets from his canvases and restores his atelier to its former glory, paints a hammer and sickle on the mirror, and conceals a skeleton in Leonie's bed as a practical joke. Although she still loves him and indulges these childish excesses with bemused good-humour, Leonie craves some domestic normalcy in her life and proceeds to take out a court injunction barring Morgan from the house. Far from taking the hint, he instead shacks up in her car on the street outside, bedecking the Ford station wagon with pictures of Trotsky and Stalin as ideological symbols of his own personal dilemma and passes the time discussing the historical import of Trotsky's exile and assassination with a dim-witted, hop-scotch playing local constable (Bernard Bresslaw). Mean-while, Leonie has a new fiancé, Charles Napier (Robert Stephens), who happens also to be Morgan's art dealer. Armed with an assortment of weapons, Morgan pays an unscheduled visit to Charles at his West End gallery and tells him to stay away from his wife. But the nonchalant dealer is unperturbed, disarms his bellicose client and urges Morgan to concentrate on his career instead of worrying about his irretrievably wrecked marriage: 'I wish you wouldn't be so aggressive. It's quite out of character and prevents me from taking you seriously'. Mindful of the gorilla's tendencies, Morgan protests: 'Where's love got me? Where's gentleness got me? You know, violence has a kind of dignity in a loving man, and I'm full of love. I shall punish you with love'. Morgan then threatens Charles with a pair of knuckledusters: 'Now where would you like love, in between your eyes or in your teeth?' After Morgan attacks Napier, the visit comes to a premature end with a humorous fast-motion sequence as the dealer and his staff pursue a crazed Morgan around the gallery before throwing him out onto the street.

Morgan, however, remains undaunted. He sneaks back into Leonie's house and rigs up a tape machine in the hall closet, which plays a deaf-ening recording of a Cape Canaveral rocket launch as Charles takes Leonie to bed. Later, once again hoping to sabotage Napier and Leonie's connubial bliss, Morgan plants a bomb under their bed but only manages to blow up his snobbish mother-in-law (Nan Munro), much to Leonie's devilish amusement. Although Leonie relishes Morgan and Charles's territorial battle for her affections, she eventually grows tired of her ex-husband's pranks and has the car towed away. Morgan moves back in with his mother – a temporary retreat to plot his next insurrec-tionary move – and informs Mrs Delt that he has visited a psychiatrist, who considers him 'a suitable case for treatment'. Then, in a moment of weakness, Leonie sleeps with Morgan, who fantasizes that they are wild zebra, mating on the Zerengeti Plain. He wants her to have his baby – the thought of her producing 'little Napiers' defies all rational thought – but Leonie is set on a bourgeois marriage to Charles and proceeds to make her wedding plans. Drastic circumstances demand drastic actions, so with the help of his mother's friend Wally (Arthur Mullard), a professional wrestler who performs under the name of 'Wally the

Gorilla', Morgan kidnaps Leonie from her bed and drives her to Wales, where they bivouac by a picturesque lake. After building a raft, Morgan fantasizes that he and Leonie are Tarzan and Jane and (as Johnny Weissmuller) 'rescues' her from a savage crocodile. But Leonie is unmoved and tells Morgan that this time he might be facing a prison sentence. 'You wouldn't let me go in the nick, would you?' asks a genuinely frightened Morgan. 'I could marry Charles before you come out', she replies. As Leonie tries to comfort him, Morgan starts to cry: 'Nothing in this world seems to live up to me best fantasies. Except you!' Tipped off by Wally, Leonie's father (Newton Blick) rescues her and an unrepentant Morgan is sent to prison.

The jail sentence is a life-changing, soul-shattering experience for a holy innocent such as Morgan, a 'Prince Mishkin at the dawn of Swinging London' as Harlan Kennedy aptly described him.[11] No longer the symbolic and allegorical catalyst for prankish fun-and-games, Morgan's gorilla persona is now symptomatic of a complete 'becoming-animal'. As it happens, Morgan's release from prison coincides with Leonie's wedding day. After seeing *King Kong* at the local cinema he dons a gorilla suit and gatecrashes the reception, scaling the hotel walls like Kong ascending the Empire State Building (Reisz inter-cuts the two episodes, suggesting that Morgan is acting out a filmic persona as much as an animalistic regression). Morgan literally crashes down onto the wedding party just as Charles and Leonie are cutting the cake. In the ensuing chaos, the gorilla suit accidentally catches fire and Morgan hurriedly exits the building. Spewing smoke, he steals a motorbike and weaves through the traffic towards the Battersea docks before careening into the river. He is eventually washed up next to a Thames-side junk yard and struggles to remove the gorilla head as he writhes agonizingly amid the tin cans and assorted scrap metal. Panicking, he starts to hallucinate that everything he loves (Leonie, his mother, Trotsky) has conspired with his mortal enemies (Napier, his mother-in-law, Stalin) to destroy him. He dreams that he is straitjacketed by the local constable and shot by a firing squad, with Leonie applying the *coup de grace*. After he wakes up, Morgan is wheeled into an ambulance and taken to hospital. The film ends as a pregnant Leonie walks through the neatly trimmed grounds of Morgan's new residence – an insane asylum. He enquires if the baby is his and she laughs uncontrollably. Relieved at the guarantee of another generation of Delts incubating and prepared to take their future place in the class struggle, Morgan seems happy at last. The camera cranes up to reveal that 'The People's Gardener' has made a flowerbed in the shape of a hammer and sickle.

Although their class backgrounds couldn't have been more different

– the Wakefield-born Mercer (1928–80) was the son of an engine-driver father and a mother who had been 'in service' as a maid – Reisz and his screenwriter had much in common politically and ideologically, not least their mutual connection to Czechoslovakia. Like Reisz, Mercer studied chemistry (at Durham University) before transferring to study Fine Art at King's College, Newcastle. An accomplished painter, he also started to read widely in politics, psychiatry, philosophy and history. Mercer's political awakening occurred when he married a Czech girl from a wealthy, upper-class family, whose father had been murdered by the Nazi Gestapo. Also echoing Reisz, who had become alienated from the Moscow party line following the Stalinist coup in Czechoslovakia in 1947, Mercer's first encounter with Marxism (c. 1949–53) was extremely ambivalent: 'I grew up simultaneously with a feeling that Marxism-Leninism was the basis for a coherent political philosophy, and at the same time with a horrified awareness of what had happened to the Bolshevik Revolution, and what Stalinism meant. Like most people of my age I was deeply influenced by people like [George] Orwell and [Arthur] Koestler and [Alexander] Weissberg. I never had any illusions about Stalinism, which meant that I never considered joining the Communist Party'.[12] Ultimately, like Reisz and his Free Cinema colleagues, Mercer became involved with the New Left through the CND, but this too failed to generate any lasting loyalty to a party-based ideology: 'I think it became a focus and to some extent a mystification. Because to concentrate on the issue of nuclear weapons was an undialectical thing to do. I perhaps still hadn't properly understood the dialectical approach to history, and so I was a bit impressionistic in my politics, the communist-without-a-party-idea. I couldn't see any development of communism to which I could give my allegiance'.[13]

Instead Mercer moved to Paris during the mid-1950s and eventually turned to novel-writing, soaking up the influences of Franz Kafka and Dylan Thomas. Unfortunately, this burgeoning literary career was temporarily short-circuited in 1957 when Mercer suffered a nervous breakdown following the collapse of his marriage. He immediately went into analysis at the British Institute of Psychoanalysis and it was this therapeutic experience that became the creative catalyst for his first television plays, including the original idea for *Morgan*. Like the British New Wave, Mercer's first teleplay, *Where the Difference Begins* (broadcast by the BBC, 15 December 1961) was inspired by kitchen sink realism – specifically Shelagh Delaney's *A Taste of Honey*. The play was concerned with the younger generation's break with the traditional socialist values represented by the Old Left, a theme which Mercer explored further in two more TV plays, *A Climate of Fear* (1962) and *The Birth of a Private*

Man (1963), which dealt with characters struggling to sustain a viable left-wing political vision in the new 'affluent' society (a major theme of *Saturday Night and Sunday Morning*, as we have seen). Mercer was also instrumental in challenging the prevailing 'realism' of television drama by replacing the usual combination of objectively rendered industrial locations and local argot with subjective and allegorical flights of fancy. This anti-mimetic style was recognized at the time as an imaginative use of the television medium, but alienated critics of all political persuasions:

> Conservatives objected to Mercer's self-professed Marxist position, liberals found the plays too explicit and lacking in subtlety, while orthodox left-wing critics questioned the emphasis on the problems of Socialism: the compromises of the British post-war Labour governments, the revelations about Stalin's atrocities, and the failures of communism in Eastern Europe. The plays may be Marxist in their stress on the need for a political revolution, but the revolutionary impulse is usually blocked and becomes internalized as psychological breakdown.[14]

This impasse is the chief impetus for Morgan's behaviour in Mercer's original 1962 television play, *A Suitable Case for Treatment*, starring Ian Hendry as Morgan and Moira Redmond as Leonie, which differs considerably from Reisz's subsequent film.[15] In this case, Morgan is a novelist, not a painter, and Napier is his best friend and literary agent. His separation from Leonie leads to an existential crisis, mild schizophrenia and frequent sessions on the psychiatrist's couch, which he refuses to take seriously. There is no kidnapping, no prison sentence or disruption of Leonie's wedding and thus no subsequent confinement in a mental institution. Instead, the teleplay refocuses much of Morgan's ideological and psychological angst through his ongoing troubled relationship with his working-class girlfriend, Jean Skelton, a socialist who forces him to choose between herself and Leonie. Although, as in the film, Morgan refuses to recognize the reality of the divorce and spends much of the play attempting to win Leonie back, the story ends with his romantic and ideological commitment to Jean as he finally decides to move into her flat. Thus unlike in the film, where he goes defiantly insane, Morgan's life comes full circle. He returns to the bosom of the working class, surrounded by the ideological security blanket of his Marxist revolutionary trappings but at the same time schizophrenically loyal to his 'becoming-gorilla' persona as an imaginary line of flight. As Mercer argued in a 1973 interview, 'I think that if you are intellectually and emotionally committed to a particular ideology, as I was and am to theoretical Communism, and yet find no way of becoming active in the world which is consistent with your beliefs, this does create just the kind of split that is dramatized in *A Suitable Case for Treatment*. Morgan, remember, was the son of a Communist working-class family, and perhaps turning the whole thing into a joke and resorting to fantasy was his only way of coping with the situation'.[16]

However, between 1962 and 1966 Mercer's response and solution to Morgan's dilemma underwent a radical change, largely due to his introduction in 1963 to the revolutionary psychiatry of R. D. Laing (1927–89), specifically his seminal early works, *The Divided Self* (1960) and *The Self and Others* (1961). These texts gave Mercer a theoretical methodology for dealing with the problems of the disaffected individual in society and helped to spawn his radically revised screenplay for *Morgan* as well as his subsequent TV play, *In Two Minds* (1967), on which Laing was the official (albeit disaffected) consultant.[17] Laing was also an important link to the beliefs of the emergent British counter-culture which eschewed the vulgar Marxist class dialectic of historical materialism in favour of a more Gramscian (and by extension, Althusserian) analysis of hegemonic state power. Stuart Hall makes the crucial point that, 'The counter-culture did not arise from the experience of repression, but rather from the "repressive tolerance" of the liberal-capitalist state. It redefined this liberalism, this tolerance, this pluralism, this consensus as repressive. It renamed "consensus" as "coercive"; it called "freedom" "domination"; it redefined its own relative affluence as a kind of alienated, spiritual poverty'.[18] For the counter-culture, true revolutionary change lay at the non-intellectual level of the personality rather than in class or ideology (i.e. it was seen as a post-Freudian rather than conventionally Marxist issue). Theodore Roszak, one of the most influential theorists of the movement, traced its roots to the romantic tradition of Blake, Shelley, Wordsworth and Goethe: to escape the one-dimensional wasteland of technocracy we must cease to censor our dreams, 'annihilate the stopwatch', and 'open the doors of perception'. According to Roszak, advocates of the counter-culture believed 'that building the good society is not primarily a social, but a psychic task. What makes the youthful disaffiliation of our time a cultural phenomenon, rather than merely a political movement, is the fact that it strikes beyond ideology to the level of consciousness, seeking to transform our deepest sense of the self, the other, the environment'.[19]

Laing provided the groundwork for this exploration by making a clear distinction between theory and experience, calling into question analytical and intellectual clarity for its own sake as the sole basis of knowledge or political conviction. Instead Laing redefined 'true sanity' *per se* as being, 'in one way or another, the dissolution of the normal ego, the false self competently adjusted to our alienated social reality'.

Instead he called for 'the emergence of the "inner" archetypal mediators of divine power, and through this death a rebirth, and the eventual re-establishment of a new kind of ego-functioning, the ego now
being the servant of the divine, no longer its betrayer'.[20] Far from
being an 'illness', schizophrenia is actually a rational response to the
intolerable pressures imposed on non-conformists by the rigid structures of the Oedipal family and patriarchal society. These pressures are
compounded in Morgan's case because his parents also represent the
corrupted idealism of the Old Left, which has destroyed his faith in the
efficacy of organized politics. 'The frontiers between what society calls
"sane" or "insane" are blurred and obscure', argues Mercer. 'In these
border territories, there are people who live trapped in a struggle to
face both ways at the same time – to be "sane" for the external world,
yet not wholly able to deny the validity of an "insanity" which demands
expression and enactment'.[21] Given the impossibility of resolving this
Janus-faced dilemma, Morgan's only recourse is to withdraw into his
imaginary and act out his 'furry' fantasies as a disjunctive series of
schizoid situations. It's not surprising that these ideas struck a strong
chord with Mercer, who was already using Morgan's schizophrenia as a
political rallying cry and exploiting his madness as an act of reclamation
for psychic forces denied or repressed by the broader society. Thus for
Mercer, Morgan's descent into madness in Reisz's film should be read
as a necessary Laingian *affirmation* of his condition that is a far more
healthy response to his social and political dislocation than his passive
return to the symbolic trappings of the working class at the end of the
original teleplay. In this respect, the world of the imagination is lionized
as a form of salvation from normalizing forces, a precursor to much of
the Situationist rhetoric that shaped the discourse of the events of May
'68 in Paris. Thus *Morgan*'s Laingian ideology is firmly in line with
Situationist slogans such as 'All Power to the Imagination' and 'Long
Live the Ephemeral'. In effect, Morgan had already said as much two
years earlier.

But what of Reisz himself? Does he share this Laingian counter-
cultural perspective or does he use the stylistics of his film to foreground its shortcomings? The short answer is that he does a little
of both. Unlike in *Night Must Fall*, where Reisz's use of ellipses and
jump-cuts perfectly complimented Clive Exton's script by focalizing
Danny's singular search for unrepresentable plenitude, in this case the
choppy editing style and resort to Benny Hill-like fast motion serves two
parallel, but at the same time *contradictory* purposes. Firstly, it allows
Reisz to create a subjective correlative for Morgan's increasing descent
into schizophrenia – his literal 'becoming-gorilla' – and thus reinforce

Mercer's obvious sympathy for his character's ill-fated attempts to act consistently with his own anti-social desires. Secondly, the jarring cuts are also used as an objective correlative to *distance* the viewer from Morgan's solipsism and critique his behavioural self-indulgence as ideologically misconceived and politically counter-productive. In other words, despite Mercer's authorial intentions, Morgan is no more Reisz's mouthpiece than Arthur Seaton and is used instead to hold up a mirror to other, more complex hegemonic forces.

Reisz plays out this double trajectory in two main areas: the shifting role of gender relations and the ideological import of fantasy and art as both poison and cure for the film's own ambivalent political position. In her provocative essay on femininity and national identity in the Swinging London films, Moya Luckett has noted a marked transition from the New Wave's masculine-oriented dismissal of mass culture's false pleasures (epitomized by Arthur Seaton's hatred of television), to the new genre's pro-feminine perspective of a more liberated sexual expression and self-identity attached to the restructuring and positively enabling role of commercialization and the glamour industry. Despite their often conservative and marginalizing endings, the positive focus on guilt-free hedonism in films such as *Darling* (John Schlesinger, 1965), *The Knack* (Richard Lester, 1965), *Smashing Time* (Desmond Davis, 1967), *Georgy Girl* (Silvio Narizzano, 1966) and *Joanna* (Mike Sarne, 1968) underscores the genre's confluence of pleasure, star attraction, sexuality and locale. More importantly, London is associated not with stasis and entrapment, like Arthur's Nottingham, but with mobility and social diversity. Moreover, this shift is also reinforced by a distinct gender divide, for the films 'contrast young women's mobility to the stasis of young men, suggesting that travel and mobility play a pivotal role in the period's discourse on sexuality, power and gender'.[22] Former north versus south rivalry is now relegated to an outmoded, male-controlled past with London now celebrated as the new seat of feminine power. This sense of movement is reinforced stylistically by rapid cutting and a constantly tracking camera, thus creating a visual analogy to the new milieu's protean creative energy. On one level, Morgan could thus be seen as an obsolescent New Wave man (in that regard it's highly appropriate that David Warner himself was born in Manchester) lost in a Swinging London environment, an intransigent Marxist male in an increasingly mobile, feminized (and by extension ideologically *hegemonic*) milieu. As Robert Murphy rightly points out, 'Morgan carries his masculinity as a vulnerable, battered banner: a natural man unfit to live in the urban jungle. He dreams constantly of a return to the real jungle where man, gorilla-like, can swing through the trees, scare off rivals with a show of bravado, and physically carry off the mate of his choice'.[23] In this sense, Reisz's use of Resnais-like ellipses and Godardian jump-cuts is not just a correlative of Morgan's increasingly creative and schizophrenic state of mind but also a focalization of his ideological alienation from the spiritual poverty and coercive consensus of London's permissive new pluralism, as if one were the mirror of the other. In other words, while Mercer celebrates Morgan's schizophrenia as a necessary and 'reasonable' response to a world gone awry, Reisz also suggests that it may beg the larger question of whether this too is yet another inoculation, another example of hegemony's 'repressive tolerance' at work.

However, it's also important to acknowledge that Morgan is an artist, a dreamer, a man whose schizoid shifts from one reality to another also mark him as symbolically 'feminine'. As Reisz reminds us,

> The fact that we can laugh at Morgan does not mean that we do not sympathize with him. It means that we have made contact with him as a person. He doesn't become a mere object or case study, but remains a human being that we care about and can react to in a human way. Often in films dealing with neurotic people the director treats them as specimens to be analysed rather than fellow human beings with problems we must try to understand ... The way a director distributes the sympathy he wants to arouse from the audience for the characters in his film will indicate his point of view toward them. In illuminating Morgan's feelings of frustration, the film also illumines your feelings and mine. Morgan was crazy, we say, but there was something special about him, something that makes us want to understand and sympathize with him.[24]

Reisz's 'distribution of sympathy' for Morgan is directly related to the shifting pattern and psychological tenor of his fantasies. The first third of the film is restless and unsure in tone – as if this were an expression of Morgan's agitated state of mind as Leonie is awarded her *decree nisi*. In this context, the gorilla fantasies act as a balancing force for wounded innocence, with Morgan relating to Trotsky as the defeated, murdered visionary and Napier standing in for Stalin, the iron dictator who can control reality (and, in his role as a commercial art dealer, pictorial fantasy). The early gorilla sequences are thus funny and charming, particularly Morgan's opening identification with Guy in London Zoo, and the following scene which shows Morgan approaching Leonie's house, where he spots painters hard at work on a scaffolding redecorating the exterior. Reisz cuts to a monkey swinging from limb to limb, illustrating how Morgan's mind creates playful metonymic connections between urban and jungle reality.

However, there is an early clue to the sad and disturbing fantasies to come and their increasing impotence in the face of Oedipal societal pressures. While camped out in the car outside Leonie's house, Morgan dreams of a gorilla happily and gracefully swinging through the trees, his loud snores overlapping the shot as if to fuse the primate with his own subjective line of flight. Following a close-up of a blissful-looking Morgan, his alarm clock rings and the ape's grip suddenly slips from a branch. The monkey falls from the tree, dropping off the bottom of the screen as if into an abyss. We return to a close-up of Morgan, reluctantly stirring to face a hostile world, his substitute persona now equally endangered by a cruel 'nine-to-five' reality. It's significant that this sequence is followed by Morgan's first meeting with the constable, where he playfully daubs the bobby's nose with some shaving cream, recklessly expanding his anarchic fantasy world into the dangerous realm of the superego. The policeman later argues that Morgan's gesture, however innocent, was an assault, 'technically speaking'. 'Is there anything which isn't an assault, technically speaking?' replies Morgan philosophically: 'Birth, sex, work, life, *death*'. The constable is taken aback by the word 'death', uttering that great cliché of all cinema coppers: 'You wanna watch it!' As he exits the frame, the camera holds on Morgan: 'Yeah I know. But where is *it*?'

This is, of course, a good question, ontologically and psychologically. Morgan doesn't know and evades the issue by blurring the distinction between fantasy and reality. But society, fuelled by the modernizing forces of one-dimensional conformity, holds itself up to a very different standard. Thus when Morgan lounges dreamily in court after being charged with kidnapping Leonie, he imagines giraffes being hunted down by two men on horseback. The shot is directly superimposed on Morgan, underlining the fact that for him the borderline between Freud's pleasure and reality principles has now completely dissolved. Morgan smiles as the giraffes escape, galloping free across the screen, but it's a freedom confined exclusively to his imaginary. He might refuse in principle to recognize the validity of the court but he will still do jail time that will ultimately break his spirit. 'Morgan's predicament becomes increasingly unfunny as soon as his behaviour causes society to intervene in his life – i.e. by sending him to prison', notes Mercer. 'We did not assume Morgan to be a paranoiac. How could we, since the main intention of the film is to challenge prevailing assumptions about sanity? ... Our film is about a human being under stress and about the manner in which he ultimately preserves his integrity against society'.[25] The severity of this stress is borne out by Morgan's regressive identification not with the gentle nature of gorillas *per se*, but with *the* Gorilla, King Kong, the ultimate avenging monster, the crazed symbol of unrequited love savagely cut down by an atavistic society's avenging bullets.

Warner is at his most heart-wrenchingly appealing in this sequence for, as Michael Kustow notes, 'The eloquent close-up of Morgan's tired eyes through the gorilla mask is powerful cinema. In a single image it shows us the character trying to assume an impossible invulnerability by adopting a mask'.[26] Morgan's final fantasy – his surrealistic death vision set in a factory scrap yard – is a nightmare of everything Morgan fears most: industrial capitalism and its corollary, wasteful consumer society, gone wildly out of control. At this point the 'real' Morgan is dead, leaving only the outward trappings of the gorilla. 'I've become all furry', he says, having finally attained his true ontological state. Unfortunately, modernism's 'repressively tolerant' society will never allow him to act it out.

As in *Night Must Fall*, it is this contradiction between the societal impossibility of Morgan's regressive desires and the difficulty of representing them except through familiar ideological and cinematic tropes that lies at the core of Reisz's film. How do you visualize pure unabashed schizophrenic instinct (and gain audience sympathy in the process) within the context of an objective and cautionary political tale? Reisz's narrative solution is twofold. Firstly, he illustrates the impasse between Morgan's ideological baggage and his protean imagination by using his mother as a political and psychological foil. According to critic David Paletz, Morgan 'lacks the class-consciousness vital to make his ideology matter (even if it could matter in 1966). All he has is self-consciousness. Whereas ideology depersonalizes, he personalizes. His mother, a much simpler person, can still make this distinction: she can like Leonie as a person and ask her to come and visit, but she still detests the upper-class and, gentle and kind as she is, wants to do away with them en masse'.[27] Thus for all her ingrained Stalinism, Mrs Delt is able to juggle two contradictory positions without the need to synthesize or overcome the difference. In contrast, Morgan is incapable of accepting difference except by resorting to a subjective line of flight. Secondly, Reisz treats Morgan and Leonie as mirror images of the same dilemma of identity through a shared crisis of agency. As Vanessa Redgrave perceptively recognized about her character, 'She has no clearly worked-out ideas, no worked-out principles and this is what enchanted me about her. This movie was the first time I'd ever played a part purely on instinct'.[28] In other words, both the masculine *and* feminine sides of the Swinging London equation are equally adrift and unable to find a coherent ideology to surmount the hegemonic forces of late capitalism. Both Morgan and Leonie are overwhelmed by representations, from the former's dependence upon ideological and cinematic symbology to the latter's flirtation with the ephemera of romance (is she attracted to Morgan and Charles for who they are or what they represent?) and consumerism. For both Morgan and Leonie, clear-cut difference slips over into an endless deferral of possible meanings where semantic slippage becomes an end in and of itself.

However, much the same can be said of the film's audience – we too are saturated with cinematic trickery and floating signifiers to the point that we share the protagonists' difficulty in finding a viable semiotic ground zero. This is a perfectly valid response in films such as *A Hard Day's Night* and *Help!*, where the semantic indecision is part of the films' audio-visual *jeu d'esprit*, but it is far more problematic in a film with serious ideological intent. In a hostile review in *Films & Filming*, Raymond Durgnat noted that the film was 'an agreeable mish-mash of various kitchen sink formulae; there's a prole whose lawless virility fascinates the rich girl (ex-Osborne), he half-lives in a fantasy world (ex-*Billy Liar*), and tenaciously clings to all that's best in Communism (ex-Wesker) ... Reisz has been content to churn up all the New Left issues ... and then ducked the job of re-thinking them, hoping we'll be dazzled by quick cutting, zooming, tracking and panning galore, actors and actresses hurling themselves around the screen image, and innumerable changes of location and subject'.[29] Pauline Kael agreed in principle, but felt that it was this very refusal to rethink the film's main ideological points that helped Morgan strike a recognizable chord with young audiences in particular: 'Those who made *Morgan!* probably not only share in the confusion of the material but also, like the college audience, *accept* the confusion. This indifference to artistic control is new. I think *Morgan!* is so appealing to college students because it shares their self-view: they accept this mess of cute infantilism and obsessions and aberrations without expecting the writer and director to straighten it out or resolve it and without themselves feeling a necessity to sort it out'.[30]

Obviously these interpretations run directly counter to our general Althusserian reading of Reisz's films. For Althusser, art (which, as a practice, does not itself rank among the ideologies) was supposed to play the key role of deconstructing these conflicting mechanisms and reveal the constructed nature of ideology itself by transforming its confusing raw material and producing a *felt* response to interpellating representations. Moreover, Reisz the former schoolteacher was too conscientious an educator to leave his audience thrashing about in a quagmire of semantic indecision. A more accurate reading of *Morgan* is that, contrary to Durgnat and Kael, Reisz rescues the audience from mass confusion by setting up a revealing discrepancy between his protagonist Morgan – who is a *failure* as an artist – and the film *Morgan*, which exploits its role as serious art to set up a defamiliarizing commentary on Morgan's creative impotence, which is rooted in self-pitying solipsism. Although Morgan complains about being kicked out of Leonie's attic – 'I did all me best work up there' – his ex-wife quickly reminds him that he hasn't finished a painting in eighteen months, a fact that Napier reaffirms when Morgan visits the gallery. The problem is that the love-sick Morgan is so locked into his fantasy world that his imaginary no longer finds an outlet in concrete bodies of *work*. In other words, unlike the film we're watching, Morgan no longer challenges the world of representations by holding up a mirror to their hegemonic excesses, but simply retreats into ephemeral self-indulgence. In fact, the only visual evidence of Morgan's artistic activity in the film is his Situationist-like graffiti – 'Charles Napier Go Home' – scrawled across the back of one of Leonie's paintings. Similarly the film's ironically comical ending, where Morgan transforms one of the asylum's flower beds into a hammer and sickle, while it has been commonly read as symptomatic of Morgan's continuing revolutionary spirit, can also be dismissed, like the anti-Napier graffiti, as pure sloganeering, as effective as shouting 'Up the workers!' in the middle of a performance of *Madame Butterfly* or pinning a poster of Che Guevara on one's suburban bedroom wall. For Reisz, Morgan's art remains locked in a solipsistic vacuum while hegemonic society busily goes about its consensus-building work around him. All that remains is to wait for the next generation of Morgans to reach maturity under the dubious nurture of Leonie and Charles. If our maths is at all accurate, Morgan's progeny will reach college age in 1984, the apogee of Reagan–Thatcher conservatism and Generation X apathy. The Orwellian ironies are obvious and would certainly not have been lost on Reisz.

Notes

1 R. D. Laing, quoted in Anonymous, 'David Mercer on Why He Writes the Plays He Does', p. 6.
2 David Mercer, quoted in *ibid.*
3 Anthony Aldgate and Jeffrey Richards, *Best of British: Cinema and Society from 1930 to the Present* (London and New York, I. B. Tauris, 1999), p. 217.
4 See in particular David Robbins, ed., *Independent Group: Postwar Britain and the Aesthetics of Plenty* (Cambridge MA, The MIT Press, 1990).
5 Wollen, 'The Last New Wave', p. 42.
6 Jeffrey Richards, 'New Waves and Old Myths: British Cinema in the 1960s', p. 228.
7 Mack Sennett was the silent film era's creator of the madcap Keystone Kops and original producer of Charlie Chaplin's first shorts. His name is synonymous with Keystone anarchy.
8 Reisz, quoted in McFarlane, *An Autobiography of British Cinema*, p. 478.

9 Reisz, quoted in Phillips, 'An Interview with Karel Reisz', p. 54.
10 Reisz, quoted in McFarlane, *An Autobiography of British Cinema*, p. 478.
11 Harlan Kennedy, 'Minute Reisz: Six Earlier Films', *Film Comment*, Vol. 17, No. 5, September–October 1981, p. 29.
12 David Mercer, quoted in Francis Jarman, 'Birth of a Playwriting Man', *Theatre Quarterly*, Vol. 3, No. 9, January–March 1973, p. 45.
13 *Ibid.*
14 Jim Leach, 'David Mercer: British Writer', The Museum of Broadcast Communications. Accessed 26 February 2005. www.museum.tv/archives/etv/M/htmlM/mercerdavid/mercerdavid.htm.
15 Transmitted by the BBC, 21 October 1962, and directed by Don Taylor, the TV play was wiped within a few weeks of its original broadcast, so there is no chance to see the original.
16 Mercer, quoted in Jarman, 'Birth of a Playwriting Man', p. 48.
17 *In Two Minds* was directed by Ken Loach, who also directed the film version, retitled *Family Life* (1971).
18 Stuart Hall, quoted in David Caute, *The Year of the Barricades: A Journey Through 1968* (New York, Harper and Row, 1988), p. 64.
19 Theodore Roszak, *The Making of a Counter Culture: Reflections of the Technocratic Society and Its Youthful Opposition* (Garden City NY, Doubleday and Company, Inc., 1969), p. 49.
20 R. D. Laing, *The Politics of Experience and The Bird of Paradise* (London, Penguin Books, 1967), p. 119.
21 Mercer, quoted in Anonymous, 'David Mercer on Why He Writes the Plays He Does', p. 6.
22 Moya Luckett, 'Travel and Mobility: Femininity and National Identity in Swinging London Films', in Justine Ashby and Andrew Higson, *British Cinema, Past and Present* (London and New York, Routledge, 2000), p. 234.
23 Robert Murphy, *Sixties British Cinema* (London, BFI, 1992), p. 74.
24 Reisz, quoted in Phillips, 'An Interview with Karel Reisz', p. 54.
25 David Mercer, quoted in *The Guardian*, 22 September 1966.
26 Michael Kustow, '*Morgan, a Suitable Case for Treatment*', *Sight and Sound*, Vol. 35, No. 3, Summer 1966, p. 144.
27 David Paletz, '*Morgan*', *Film Quarterly*, Vol. 20, No. 1, Fall 1966, p. 52.
28 *Morgan: A Suitable Case for Treatment*, DVD biographical notes.
29 Raymond Durgnat, '*Morgan – A Suitable Case for Treatment*', *Films & Filming*, No. 12, June 1966, p. 6.
30 Pauline Kael, 'So Off-Beat We Lost the Beat', in *Kiss Kiss, Bang Bang* (Boston, Little, Brown and Co., 1968), p. 21.

Life into art – Reisz and the biopic: *Isadora* (1968) and *Sweet Dreams* (1985)

7

We have our highest dignity in our significance as works of art – for it is only as an *aesthetic phenomenon* that existence and the world are eternally *justified*. (Friedrich Nietzsche)[1]

Why is it that the Artist's hope is almost always an unfulfilled dream? (Isadora Duncan)[2]

Why can't I forget you and start my life anew / Instead of having sweet dreams about you? (Don Gibson)

Morgan is an important film in the Reisz canon, not only because it reinforced his continued move away from the last vestiges of social realism associated with the first British New Wave, but also because it was his first truly self-reflexive film. Reisz's negative critical assessment of Morgan's artistic and ideological shortcomings allowed him to take stock of his own relevance as an artist and political activist and present his own film as a necessary antidote to Morgan's self-defeating solipsism. Such self-examination was particularly timely given the anachronistic relationship between the gender and class mobility spawned by the highly commercialized Swinging London phenomenon and the darker, more concrete political realities of Vietnam, the Civil Rights Movement, Britain's ongoing struggle with decolonization and immigration, and the watershed events of May '68. Although cinema was in many ways the perfect medium for exploring such contradictions (epitomized ten years later by *Dog Soldiers*), Reisz had by now lost the organizational and philosophical safety net of the CND and New Left which had fuelled his earlier Free Cinema work. The New Left movement as originally formulated by Stuart Hall and E. P. Thompson had collapsed in favour of a more hermetically sealed theoretical discourse – mostly influenced by Antonio Gramsci, Laingian psychoanalysis and Continental theory – centred on a radically revised *New Left Review*.

Given such unsupportive political circumstances it is perhaps

REISZ AND THE BIOPIC **159**

unsurprising that Reisz would make a parallel withdrawal into examining the nature of the committed artist, particularly an art that comes into inevitable conflict with its necessary psychological corollaries – love and death, Eros and Thanatos. In this respect Isadora Duncan (1877–1927) and Patsy Cline (1932–63) are perfect, if unlikely, soul mates, for both biographies are haunted by their tragically premature deaths, one killed by accidental strangulation, the other in a plane crash.[3] Both women successfully fought to revolutionize extremely traditionalist (not to say, sexist) artistic fields – i.e. modern dance and country music – and both struggled in vain to find an equitable balance between career, family and healthy sexual desire. As Isadora observed in her memoirs: 'My life has known but two motives – Love and Art – and often Love destroyed Art, and often the imperious call of Art put a tragic end to Love. For these two have no accord, but only constant battle'.[4] Finally, following Nietzsche's famous description of the world as 'a work of art that gives birth to itself', the two films' protean use of mind-screen and fantasy continues an aestheticizing, dream-like trend in Reisz's approach to realism linking *Morgan* (where 'the ego is the servant of the divine, no longer its betrayer') to Angela Crispini's logic-defying multiple personalities in *Everybody Wins*.

Reisz was originally approached to direct *Isadora* by producer Robert Hakim at the 1966 Cannes Film Festival, where *Morgan* was the official British entry. Working in tandem with his brother Raymond, Hakim was already planning to cast Vanessa Redgrave to play the title role on the strength of her Best Actress award as Leonie.[5] Funding, however, was another matter, particularly in the face of British cinema's deep economic crisis, a combination of spiralling production costs (low-budget feature film-making had become almost impossible by mid-decade) and the increasing dependence on foreign (especially American) markets for production, exhibition, profits and casting.[6] *Isadora* was paradigmatic of the latter trend when, in 1967, Universal Pictures (at that time under the aegis of MCA) sent their vice-president, Jay Kantner, to Britain to organize an ambitious slate of over a dozen films to take advantage of lower labour costs, home-grown British talent and the still-trendy ambience of 1960s Swinging London. These star-studded films included Joseph Losey's ill-fated Tennessee Williams project, *Boom!* (1968, featuring Elizabeth Taylor and Richard Burton) and *Secret Ceremony* (1968, with Taylor and Mia Farrow), François Truffaut's Ray Bradbury adaptation, *Fahrenheit 451* (1966), and Peter Watkins's *Privilege* (1967), starring Manfred Mann vocalist, Paul Jones. Budgeted at a generous $1,700,000 and with over a year allocated to scouting locations, *Isadora* seemed destined for substantial studio support and a strong likelihood of critical and commercial success.

Written by Melvyn Bragg and *Night Must Fall*'s Clive Exton, with additional dialogue by novelist Margaret Drabble, the film was adapted from Isadora's autobiography, *My Life* (composed shortly before her death), and Sewell Stokes's *Isadora Duncan: An Intimate Portrait*, a first-hand account of the dancer's last year by her secretary and amanuensis. Eschewing strict linear chronology, Reisz unfolds his subject's life through an elaborate series of flashbacks from the vantage point of September 1927, as a cranky, self-absorbed forty-nine-year-old Isadora dictates her memoirs to Stokes (here renamed Roger Thornton and sympathetically played by John Fraser) while staying at the lavishly expensive Hotel Negresco in Nice. Now in semi-retirement and hard up for cash, Isadora is writing largely to pay off her creditors until she can sell off her assets, which include her greatly prized collection of love letters. Accompanied by her friend and business manager, Mary Desti (Cynthia Harris), the cantankerous recluse spends her time hiding from her overbearing admirers, railing against the abominations of the jazz age – 'Jazz is America laughing at Isadora Duncan', she proclaims – insulting her literary acquaintances Archer (Wallas Eaton) and Bedford (Nicholas Pennell), and indulging her superstitious dread of death by reading (and shamelessly rigging) tarot cards with her handsome companion Pim (John Quentin). However, the driving force of Isadora's 'golden years' is her unabashed love for younger men, in this case a dashing but elusive black-shirted young Bugatti driver (Vladimir Leskova), who almost runs her down as she crosses the street with Roger.

The flashback structure allows Reisz selectively to edit and condense Isadora's long and colourful career in order to stress the main theme of the film, namely the antinomous weave of art, love and death that encapsulates the driving force of her desires. Reisz's director's cut divides her life into four rough sections, the first encompassing the Duncan family's successful arrival in European art circles, with the three subsequent parts devoted to each of Isadora's lovers: Edward Gordon Craig, Paris Singer and Sergei Essenin. The film opens in San Francisco as a twelve-year-old Isadora ceremonially burns her parents' marriage certificate, dedicating herself 'to the pursuit of art and beauty and to the single life'. Reisz then unfolds Isadora's early career through a series of short but effective vignettes: her brief flirtation with Chicago vaudeville as a means of subsidizing her family's move to England; the aesthetic and spiritual revelation of Greek antiquities and Hellenic culture during visits to the British Museum and the Parthenon; performances with her mother (Bessie Love) and brother Raymond (Tony Vogel) before the cream of London society; and her life-long commitment to build a string of dance schools for underprivileged children, starting in Grünewald, Germany in 1904. By eschewing the staple biopic strategy of tracing the precocious young Isadora's hard-earned rise to fame (the main narrative trope of *Sweet Dreams*), Reisz makes these sequences seem effortlessly preordained, just as they would appear in the older Isadora's memory. In addition, as Stephen Farber rightly points out, 'Reisz clearly wants a wide *range* of responses to Isadora, so that we begin to define an impression of her only gradually, after looking at her from a startling variety of perspectives. Reisz shows us more and more of Isadora, but he never "explains" her with flat psychological or moral labels. We may dislike Isadora or find her maddening at moments, but we can never condescend to her'.[7]

From these early scenes, not least through Redgrave's extraordinary recreation of Isadora's revolutionary choreography, we also gain a keen insight into Isadora's vision of the dance.[8] This was rooted in her avid hatred of ballet, which she dubbed 'inane coquetry', outside the pale of all art, 'whose every movement shocked my sense of beauty, and whose expression seemed to me mechanical and vulgar'.[9] Instead of subscribing to the prevailing ballet dogma that the central spring of all movement lies in the centre of the back at the base of the spine, Isadora discovered the 'crater of motor power' in the solar plexus, as if art were a biological function of a universal endowment.[10] Following the tenets of Henri Bergson, she felt that the spontaneous movement of the body is a fundamental reaction to sensory or emotional stimuli, and for Isadora this intuitive wellspring derives directly from nature. 'My first idea of movement, of the dance, came from the rhythm of the waves, and my first understanding of music from the sighing of the winds in the giant redwoods', declares the mature Isadora, dictating her theories to Roger. 'For I was born by the sea, and all the great events of my life have taken place by a sea. I was born under the star of Aphrodite, goddess of love'. Inspired by the primordial, atavistic poses of the Dionysaic figures depicted on Attic pottery, Isadora threw off the corsets of conventional ballet attire, dancing bare-legged under diaphanous veils or a tunic of silk chiffon, the latter tucked under her breasts like one of the Graces in Botticelli's *Primavera* (1477–78). 'I will dance this picture and give to others this message of love, spring, procreation of life which had been given to me with such anguish', she wrote. 'I will give to them, through the dance, such ecstasy'.[11]

However, for Isadora such purely sublime and spiritual *ex stasis* cannot exist in an aesthetic vacuum and it quickly comes into conflict with its carnal counterpart in the form of Edward Gordon Craig (1872–1966), the English scene designer, producer, actor and son of the renowned actress, Ellen Terry. Craig (played against type by a dashingly Byronic James Fox) may have been dubbed 'the vile seducer' by Isadora's disapproving mother but he was clearly the love of the dancer's life: 'Here, at last, was my mate; my love; my self – for we were not two, but one, that one amazing being of whom Plato tells us in the *Phaedrus*, two halves of the same soul'.[12] But Craig turns out to be far from being the ideal lover. Extremely vain and full of his own self-importance, he places his career before his relationship and deserts Isadora for an experimental Moscow production of *Hamlet* while she is still pregnant with their daughter, Deirdre (born 1906), never to reappear.

By 1910, Craig had been succeeded in Isadora's affections by Paris Singer (Jason Robards), the millionaire heir to the sewing machine fortune, a man with 'the psychology of a spoilt child'[13] whom Isadora subsequently dubbed her 'Lohengrin'. Handsome but obsessively married to his business – 'Suddenly I realised that *his* vision of America was that of the dozens of factories which made his fortune for him', she recalled with disdain[14] – and prone to violent fits of jealousy, Singer is less Isadora's sexual Adonis than a useful source of money and blueblood sperm. He buys and subsidizes her latest dance school in Bellevue, outside Paris, and also sires a son, Patrick (born 1910). However, Isadora's unabashed joy in her art and family is heartbreakingly short-lived, for in 1913 both children are drowned along with their English nanny when their car crashes into the Seine while returning to Versailles from Neuilly. Although not featured in the film, the tragedy is compounded shortly afterwards when a third child is born dead. Reisz correctly focuses considerable attention on the agony of Isadora's birth pains and the subsequent death of the children as the defining moments of Isadora's life, for the two events motivated most of the dancer's creative and spiritual endeavours in the years to follow. As she describes the experience in her autobiography: 'Only twice comes that cry of the mother which one hears as without one's self – at birth and at death. For when I felt in mine those little cold hands that would never again press mine in return, I heard my cries – the same cries as I had heard at their birth. Why the same? Since one is the cry of supreme joy and the other of Sorrow. I do not know why, but I know they are the same. Is it that in all the Universe there is but one great cry containing Sorrow, Joy, Ecstasy, Agony – the Mother Cry of Creation?'[15]

The bulk of the last quarter of the film takes place in the Soviet Union. In the Spring of 1921, Isadora received a telegram: 'The Russian Government alone can understand you. STOP. Come to us. STOP. *We* will build your school'. Reisz opens the episode with a long sequence which cross-cuts between an inspired Isadora winning over the Soviet workers with a dizzying performance to the Russian folk ballad *Kalinka*, and the establishment of her dance school in a freezing palace stripped of hot water pipes, mattresses and furniture. Less convincing, because of its resort to almost parodic cliché, is Reisz's subsequent evocation of the burgeoning Soviet art scene, where Isadora meets Bolshevik writers, Constructivist artists and designers, including the childishly hot-tempered and alcoholic poet, Essenin (Ivan Tchenko). Estelle Changas, for one, took great issue with these scenes, noting that they seem to have been 'thrown in for those who couldn't care less about motivation or credibility, but who do like their stereotypes of the artist confirmed'.[16] Dubbed 'The Gentle Hooligan', Essenin was the only man that Isadora would ever marry. Although neither could speak the other's language, their attraction is immediate, electric and, as one might expect, mutu-ally self-destructive: 'He was a great poet, even if he did knock me about', she noted in an aside to Sewell Stokes.[17] Eventually, the newly-weds returned to the United States in order to raise money for Isadora's Moscow school but, fuelled by rabid anti-Communist sentiment, her Boston concert – an impassioned 'Dance of Liberation' to Tchaikovsky's *Marche Slave* – is a scandalous disaster, culminating in Isadora dancing topless to a chorus of outraged boos. Reisz ends the film by returning to the 'present' and playing out what we have anticipated (and dreaded) all along: Isadora's final and fateful meeting with 'Bugatti' at a sea-front dance party. As the couple drive away from the dock towards the town, Isadora's scarf gets caught in the rear wheel of the sports car and she is instantly strangled to death.

Stated baldly without the flashback structure, it's easy to dismiss the film's plot as a banal historical soap opera. Moreover, diligent biog-raphers and historians would be acutely aware of what Reisz and his screenwriters have omitted from the story. Apart from diminishing the number and role of her countless lovers – as critic Vincent Canby noted at the time of the film's release, it 'reduces men to the status of consorts to a slightly eccentric queen bee'[18] – the film makes only passing refer-ence to the dancer's relationship with her long-time friend and idol, the Italian actress Eleanora Duse (1958–24) and Duse's lover, the fascist poet and soldier Gabriele D'Annunzio (1863–1938). 'Mitri', Isadora's Russian pianist and a key figure in her life in Nice, is also excluded, his role collapsed into the characters of both Roger and Mary. There is no reference to the Duncans's failed attempt to build a temple at Kopanos in Greece and fashion their lives on the tenets of Plato's *Republic*, or to Isadora's attempted suicide, when she was dragged half-drowned from the Mediterranean by an English captain. Also cut is the abortive 1905 revolution in Russia, where Isadora witnessed at first hand the funeral procession of workers savagely shot down by Tsarist troops before the Winter Palace. By Isadora's own account, the impact was profound, in effect the main catalyst for her radicalization: 'If I had never seen it, all my life would have been different. There, before this seemingly endless procession, this tragedy, I vowed myself and my forces to the service of the people and the down-trodden. Ah, how small and useless now seemed all my personal love desires and sufferings! How useless even my Art, unless it could help this'.[19] Similarly, the impact of the World War One is omitted altogether, an odd decision given that her Bellevue dance school was requisitioned as a hospital and then, irony of ironies, as a factory for the production of poison gas: 'I felt that Dionysus had been completely defeated', bemoaned the dancer. 'This was the reign of Christ after the Crucifixion ... My Temple of Art was turned into a Calvary of Martyrdom and, in the end, into a charnel-house of bloody wounds and death. Where I had thought of strains of heavenly music, there were only raucous cries of pain'.[20]

Perhaps more serious is the writers' over-dependence upon Isadora's autobiography and Stokes's memoir as their main primary sources, rather than the more objective overview of a scholarly biography. Even Margaret Drabble admitted that *My Life* is extremely unreliable, 'dictated through emotional and financial stress, doctored, inaccurate, it does her less than justice'.[21] Similarly, Stokes knew Isadora for less than eighteen months, so his account is obviously limited, often relying on hearsay and Isadora's own distorted memory. However, it's also clear that Reisz never intended *Isadora* to be an accurate historical rendition of the dancer's life. By filtering the film's flashback structure exclusively through Isadora's focalization, the film presents her life as a self-constructed fiction from the perspective of 1927, not as it really happened. This is reinforced by Vanessa Redgrave's deliberately self-parodic, self-deprecating tone and exaggerated body language in the modern sequences, as if she were a theatrical 'grand dame' constantly aware of the need to fabricate and consolidate her artistic legacy for posterity. The film is less a vehicle for objective fact than a subjective Proustian apprenticeship in which Isadora tries to recapture lost time through the contrived artifice of her memoir in an attempt to transform her disappointments and tragedies – specifically the tragic death of her children – into a transcending and spiritually healing Art. This accounts for the fact that most of her recollections, like Proust's use of the madeleine, are involuntarily triggered by specific events or details in the Riviera sequences. For example, during a restaurant discussion of Archer's latest book project, Isadora accuses the writer of false modesty: 'It comes in like a lamb. Will it go out like a lion?' When Bedford defends his friend, complaining, 'Oh

Miss Duncan, do we all have to be lions?' her quick reply, 'Of course, because I adore a lion!', becomes an instant trigger for an extended flashback to her first meeting with that ultimate lion, Edward Gordon Craig. Similarly, when a tarot reading with Pim turns up The King of Pentacles – 'The Dark Man' – the descriptive association causes Isadora's immediate mind-screen of the black-bearded Singer, observing her through opera glasses from his theatre box seventeen years earlier. The non-linear Proustian temporal structure also exacerbates – almost like a contagion – the film's motifs of death and dread that pervade both her memories and the fateful events leading up to her meeting with 'Bugatti'. Art, life and love are thus inextricably woven together from the vantage point of a death always already foretold.

The subjectivity of the flashbacks also helps to explain the stylistic and dramatic contrast between the present-day scenes and Isadora's past. The former are largely autumnal in tone, as if to create an objective correlative of Isadora's state of mind: a combination of tired resignation and exasperation in regard to her career and finances, but also girlish anticipation at the prospect of meeting the beautiful 'Bugatti'. Isadora's appearance is dominated by her flaming red hair and pale, puffy features badly touched up with rouge. Her wardrobe is accented by a large straw hat and her bright orange shawl, which doubles as a turban and scarf (and which will, of course, be the instrument of her ultimate demise). Her hotel room, with its Orientalist, seraglio-like draperies, seems to have been duplicated directly from Stokes's own vivid description: 'An immense green room which immediately reminded me of an imagined temple at the bottom of the sea. The curtains, hung all around in long folds from the ceiling, gave it the appearance of a gigantic green tent. The carpet was also green, and the huge space of the place was dimly lit by lights fashioned to resemble torches set in braziers. There was a grand piano which looked minute in the great room; a gramophone on a tiny stool, an oil stove, a screen, and an immense pile of deep orange cushions'.[22] In contrast, the dominant colour scheme of the subjective flashbacks is white – her dancing costume and those of her pupils, the doves in Singer's indoor swimming pool and the millionaire's Rolls Royce, Essenin's proletarian tunic – as if Isadora were struggling to reconstitute visually the spiritual purity of her art and life from the deathly pall of her children's demise.

In addition, one can't help wondering whether Isadora's selective recall of certain events – particularly the scenes with Essenin and the resultant Boston fiasco – are not exaggerated by hyperbole and a self-pitying martyr complex. Certainly the film makes no reference to her numerous successful visits to America following her move to Europe in 1900 (her stunning performance to Beethoven's Symphony No. 7, for example, although given no specific location in the film, almost certainly took place on Broadway in 1908), as if Isadora were determined to foster the myth that she had been deserted by her homeland, particularly a philistine bourgeois public grown complacent and antipathetic to Modernist innovation. 'I will never come back to America again', she cries at the end of the Boston concert. 'I wanted to dance for you the liberation of the Russian people, the greatest event in this century. Because I thought America would understand. Have you forgotten our own great revolution? Or we were wild once? Don't let them *tame* you!!' This sounds like retroactive special pleading from an artist who has herself been tamed by a combination of excess and hubris and is now a creative spent force, frittering away what remains of her life in pursuit of 'Bugatti' and her lost youth.

This double articulation of Isadora's life, whereby the creative life force is folded into involuntary memory and becoming-toward-death, requires sophisticated embedded motifs – aural *and* visual – as well as expressive linkages and transition devices so that the film's narrative and temporal disjuncture, far from undermining semantic clarity, is actually responsible for generating a broader thematic and ontological continuity. In this respect, the placement and matching of the cross-cutting between past and present is crucial to a proper understanding of the film. Let us examine these motifs in more detail. One of the key themes of the film is Isadora's sense of her own artistic destiny, a motif which spans the decades to link time past with time regained but through a widely varying circuit of difference. For example, in an early scene Isadora performs a vaudeville routine as 'Peppy Dora' before Sullivan (David Healy), the Chicago theatre's penny-pinching impresario. With a future contract dependent on her 'attractability' to the largely working-class audience, Isadora is a raging success and manages to browbeat Sullivan into paying her $300 for three weeks' work. The manager wants to make the deal permanent but Isadora quickly puts him straight: 'Mr Sullivan you don't realize you just paid for the whole sea passage for me and my entire family to Europe. You are an agent of my fate'. 'But honey, $300 is only the beginning. You've got attractability. You'll make your fortune here', he protests. But Isadora has bigger plans: 'It's not my fortune I'm after. It's my destiny'. Of course Isadora is referring to her *artistic* destiny, but Reisz immediately cuts to the Hotel Negresco in 1927 as the washed-up, forty-nine-year-old Isadora stands on her balcony, lost in reverie, looking out to the seafront below. Significantly, we hear the strains of 'Bye Bye Blackbird' from the gramophone inside, the song that will be playing at the film's end at the exact moment of her death. For the spectator, Isadora's destiny has now become an inextricable weave of art and tragedy. However, Reisz expands the metonymic connections still further by a reverse angle zoom from Isadora's point-of-view down to the terrace below, where 'Bugatti' – the agent of both her desire and her demise – sits at one of the tables. Destiny thus takes on multiple meanings, linking artistic creativity, time, memory, desire and death in a crystalline circuit of eternal return – in other words as a creative and affirmative *force*, in Nietzsche's sense – rather than a strictly teleological cause and effect.

Reisz expands the film's protean ontology still further in a subsequent series of complex temporal leaps following Isadora's success in London society. As she holds court at an extravagant soirée, a portly older woman asks Isadora where she first learned to dance. 'Oh, I never learned at all', replies the dancer. 'I danced in my mother's womb ... You see, my father had just left us. He was a remarkable man but unreliable. And that increased my mother's agony. All she could eat was oysters and champagne – the food of Aphrodite. And so naturally I danced right from my conception'. The woman laughs nervously: 'You're speaking metaphorically of course?' 'No', says Isadora, 'I'm speaking of my destiny'. There is hushed silence as she looks at her audience with deadly seriousness. Now, either Isadora was the most pretentious person who ever lived or this is a giant put-on, as if she were constantly giving birth to herself as a work of art as she went along, unable or unwilling to discern the difference between fact and fiction. As this is a memory flashback from 1927, the scene is obviously infused with the self-deprecating irony of the older Isadora, retrospectively recalling her younger self as either an impossibly earnest aesthete or a playfully wicked satyr – in effect living the Nietzschean lie for the sake of constructing a higher Dionysian truth. Farber, however, makes a good case for seeing the strategy in more defensive terms: 'The film astutely perceives the way in which an iconoclastic figure who has outlived the revolution that she began will deliberately exaggerate her own eccentricities, start to *camp*, and parody herself to escape the humiliation of seeing others parody her'.[23] The forty-nine-year-old Isadora could thus be seen as fighting a rearguard action to defy time by grasping at what was bold and beautiful in her youth and exaggerating it to the point of over-determination. Rather than creating an ontological whole, Reisz's contrast between the two time frames instead unpicks the seams of the aestheticized 'real', as if Isadora the Nietzschean high priestess had become the object of a Brechtian *V-Effekt* – all form and no substance.

By 1927, Isadora had clearly lived past the moment when art and life were perfectly compatible and mutually enriching, when a revolution in one corresponded to a concomitant revolution in the other. Reisz expands this antinomy by once again linking Isadora's conception of artistic destiny to the reality of a darker fate. He immediately cuts from the soirée to the narrow village street where Isadora and Roger are almost run down by 'Bugatti'. Roger is rightly outraged: 'Bloody nearly killed us'. 'Oh, one never dies before one's time', responds Isadora. 'Didn't you know?' 'I don't find that much of a comfort, thank you very much', replies Roger, unconvinced. 'Oh but it is, it is. After all, he missed us, didn't he? Perhaps it's an omen. He's a messenger from the gods'. Left without further exposition, this connection would be simply a duplication of the earlier ironic jump from Chicago to 'Bugatti', from art to ill-fated death, but in this case Reisz continues his string of associations with far more complex results. Spurred by her near brush with death, a visibly haunted Isadora recalls the funeral of her children. To the strains of the allegretto from Beethoven's Symphony No. 7, two horse-drawn hearses move past the camera towards the front gates of the cemetery. Suddenly, the music changes to the symphony's riotous first movement (the 'apotheosis of the dance', according to Wagner) as we return to the essence of the life force – Isadora's brilliant performance to a packed house in New York. Reisz ends the syntagmatic chain of temporal leaps by cutting back to the older Isadora lost in thought as she recalls her younger free spirit. Isadora then turns to Mary and wilfully transcends these antinomies of art, love and death by sublimating their differences through her own artistic call to arms: 'I have the gift of beauty in me, and I've always known that my only duty was to express it to the world. All I've ever done is try to express the truth of my being in gesture and movement'.

That Isadora's artistic sublimations were hard won is more than expressed in her heart-wrenching relationship with Craig. Following their first meeting, as Isadora and her new lover lie together in bed, she mutters blissfully to herself, 'Can one die of love?' Craig doesn't reply and, half asleep, turns away from her. Reisz zooms tighter on Isadora as if to reinforce the emotional power of this intimate confession, but it is immediately undercut by her croaky voice-over from 1927: 'I wonder if my baby does ...' Before she can finish the sentence we cut to the outdoor restaurant where Isadora lunches with Archer and Bedford. The 'baby' in question turns out not to be Craig, or even their daughter Deirdre, but the opening line of the song, 'I wonder if my baby does the Charleston', a dance that Isadora absolutely detests. Her passion for Craig is thus indirectly associated with the potential 'death' of both her own art and popular taste in general. Despite her higher artistic calling, it's clear that Isadora is still compromised by fear of abandonment, as

Craig leaves for Russia, and her need for emotional warmth and dependence on a sexual relationship, whether it be Craig or 'Bugatti'. Her artistic success will come only at the expense of such security, as if her inevitable loneliness must be a punishment for her artistic ambitions.

Indeed, the ghost of the absent Craig haunts the entire restaurant sequence that follows. Firstly, Mary returns to the café to inform Isadora that 'Bugatti' dines there nearly every evening. Amorous thoughts of the Italian cause Isadora to reminisce again about Craig, for we instantly flash back to Nordwyck, Holland, as a heavily pregnant Isadora prances along the beach, playing 'tag' with the waves. A final parting scene with Craig follows, as he announces his plans to stage *Hamlet* in Moscow. Just before he leaves, Isadora pulls him into a passionate kiss. Suddenly we hear the older Isadora's voice-over: 'He came straight for me and he tried to kill me'. Again, there is a disconnect between what we are seeing and hearing, until we then cut back to the restaurant as Isadora continues her account of her near accident: 'We've never even spoken and he came straight for me in his beautiful Bugatti'. The literal close call at the hands of 'Bugatti' is thus linked to Isadora's emotional 'death' at the hands of Craig, a connotation reinforced by a subsequent mind-screen. After Isadora tactlessly insults Bedford, the young man puts on his boater and decides to leave. As he moves away from the camera towards the background of the shot, the *mise-en-scène* conjures a similar image of Craig on the beach, moving away from Isadora towards the top of the shingle. The expectant mother turns to watch him go, just as he stops and waves a final farewell: 'If it's a girl, call her Deirdre will you?' Although Isadora refuses to admit the devastating consequences of Craig's departure at the time, the flashback structure makes its psychological ramifications all too clear. If there were any doubt, Reisz repeats the earlier confrontation with Bedford, only this time with Archer. Isadora accuses her friend of bottling up his feelings: 'How can you be an artist when you're all buttoned up? I am an artist, and I'm a woman, and that's hard'. After an entire evening of Isadora's baiting Archer has heard enough and, like Bedford, walks away from the table. Isadora begs him to come back: 'You *can't* walk away'. However, in her mind's eye she's speaking not to Archer but to Craig, because we suddenly hear the voice-over of the young Isadora crying, 'Help me, help me ...' We cut sharply back to September 1906 and a close-up of Isadora undergoing agonizing labour pains, as if all the burden of her life, her love for Craig, her loneliness and the birth/loss of her first child had become condensed into that one combined moment of joy and anguish.

However, it's also important to note that despite her emotional shortcomings, Isadora is first and foremost an artist who utilizes and transforms the raw experience of life – however painful – into the form and rhythm of the dance. Although Craig uses art to seduce her – stripping away her chemise he proclaims her body 'magnificent', thus using an aesthetic evaluation rather than a forthright sexual response – Isadora repays the compliment in kind by using their sexual congress as a catalyst for affirming her own beauty as a form of artistic narcissism:

> As the two make love in Craig's barren studio, Isadora fantasizes in a flash-forward, envisioning herself alone, performing a new dance which epitomizes her fulfilment (dancing to Isadora is primarily the expression of her sexuality), and is more dramatically erotic than the couple's physical passion. Ironically, the love-making excites her creativity (quite a departure from the typical feminine blackout depicted during sexual intercourse), as the cross-cutting makes clear. In her most intimate moments Isadora sees herself as more artist than woman.[24]

This sequence – again to the music of Beethoven – is typical of the artist's creative responsiveness to ordinary experience (as we saw, it is a staple of poetic realism), and also of Isadora's instinctive tendency to transform the details of everyday life through the protean prism of her imagination. She is enraptured by her own artistic sensitivity, exploiting and appropriating experience – even the shared intimacy of the sexual act – to construct a private, narcissistic vision of herself as a committed, aesthetic revolutionary.

This narcissism even extends to the tragic death of her children. Although the incident overwhelms her with grief, her mind-screen recall turns the events into a compelling aesthetic vision. Instigated yet again by a tarot reading – Pim turns up both the Moon and Death cards, which signify 'death by water' – Isadora is propelled into an involuntary memory of events as she struggles to get them down on paper for her memoir. The string of images – a team of horses dragging the death car from the Seine; the funeral procession; Deirdre and Patrick in the back of the car, their noses pressed against the glass of the rear window; a final meeting with Singer; Isadora waving goodbye to her children; the car careening through the bridge balustrade into the river below – are strangely disconnected and non-chronological, as if Isadora were slowly inching her way back into this painful memory with extreme difficulty, revealing a little more detail each time. The result is a Cubistic spatio-temporal montage rather than a coherent narrative continuum. She concludes the sequence with the words: 'There are some sorrows that kill. That tragedy was to end all hope of a natural, joyous life for me. Ever since then I have had but one desire to fly ... to fly from the horror of it. My life has been but a series of flights. I've been but a phantom ship on a phantom ocean'. All the agony is plainly visible in her ravaged face, a horrifying memory seemingly unredeemable by art. Or is it? Changas perceptively notes that through their overt stylization, limpid grey-green colours and surreal, dream-like qualities, 'what is interesting about the death sequences is their poignant beauty. Isadora has transformed an ugly horror into an artistic vision – impressionistic stills, shot through with light, touched with muted pastels, capturing the grace of move-ments of immeasurable meaning to her: a mother's final kiss, a child's upturned face. It is the artist, almost in spite of herself, working upon the experiences of her life, even the most deeply painful, dignifying death with the eloquence of beauty'.[25] Obviously Isadora didn't desire her children's death, but like her narcissistic response to sex with Craig, she has the artistic ability to transform emotional chaos into formal order as a means of remaking herself as a brilliant creator of artistic visions.

Given this overwhelming aestheticizing trajectory, how then should one treat the film's tragic finale? The prelude to Isadora's death shrouds the film from the outset, heightened by the flashback structure. Every time we return to the present it is with increasing apprehension. We know from the outset how Isadora dies, so the combination of fore-shadowing (the flowing scarf) and postponement (the slippery elusive-ness of 'Bugatti') makes the actual event all the more jarring: 'This brutal moment shocks us out of any sentimentality we cultivate about the artist's life. It is the final comment on Isadora's vulnerability; the harsh rebuttal to her creativity, her dedication to life; a mocking of her attempt to clarify reality through art; it is death, the ultimate absurdity art cannot answer'.[26] Because we are forced to confront Isadora's vital youth and imminent death as conjoined temporalities, we are unable to enjoy fully the carefree scenes of her early career – so they too will have their inevitable price to pay. Moreover, Isadora's final tango with 'Bugatti' also underlines the final anachronism of her life in creative retirement: 'their style and expertise are in sharp contrast to the world around them. Isadora and her Grecian ideals of simplicity, beauty, feeling have given way to the gyrations of an indistinguishable mass of jerky, peppy jazz babies – vapid, bob-haired, bow-tied automatons, whose dance is passionless frenzy'.[27]

Yet, despite Changas's valid protestations, one can also argue that Reisz mitigates this degeneration by returning to the elemental visions of birth and art that mark Isadora's connection to the life force. Follow-ing the dancer's death, Reisz zooms in past the Bugatti and the partying dancers on the waterfront to the Mediterranean beyond, so that the shim-mering expanse fills the screen. The banal strains of 'Bye Bye Blackbird' fade out, leaving just the sounds of lapping water on the soundtrack, as if to return us full circle to Isadora's love for the sea, the source of her artistic inspiration. The immanence of life is thus inextricably linked to the image of death as part of a circuit of eternal return, whereby the lasting beauty of the cinematic image – reflecting, in a sense, Reisz's own aesthetic narcissism – transforms the ephemerality of his all-too-human subject. Isadora's revolutionary art of the dance has thus been effectively memorialized by the more lasting art of Reisz's film.

In 1979, eleven years after the release of *Isadora*, Reisz sat down with film critic Gordon Gow and discussed the inherent difficulties of filming a biopic. 'I think making a biography in the movies is a very uncomfortable kind of task', he noted, 'because very often you find that the drama demands that you have a certain scene, or that you go to a certain emotion, and you can't do that because in real life it didn't happen. And, of course, you are making a fiction. You're not doing some kind of research project. So you're always being pulled by what actually happened and by what you think will be dramatic. It's a very uncomfortable mixture, movie biography. I'm not going to try it again'.[28] The latter turned out to be a classic case of 'famous last words', because within five years the director was back on the set, this time filming the Patsy Cline story, *Sweet Dreams*. The original catalyst for the project was Universal Studios' President, Ned Tanen, who had been impressed by *Coal Miner's Daughter*, Michael Apted's acclaimed 1980 film biography of another country music legend, Loretta Lynn, starring Oscar winner Sissy Spacek. Tanen contacted the film's producer, Bernard Schwartz, about doing a follow-up feature on Cline who, seductively portrayed by Beverly D'Angelo, had featured prominently in the Lynn story. Schwartz immediately set about exploring Patsy's working-class roots in Winchester, Virginia, and her recording career in Nashville, interviewing countless people who knew and had worked with her. He then turned over 800 pages of notes to screenwriter Bob Getchell – Oscar nominated for the Woody Guthrie biopic, *Bound for Glory* (Hal Ashby, 1976) and Martin Scorsese's *Alice Doesn't Live Here Anymore* (1974) – to develop a workable script.

At first glance, Reisz's involvement in the project seems entirely misplaced and anachronistic. Up to that point he had never heard of Cline and had little feeling for country music, although listening to her records quickly changed that. One doesn't have to be from the American South to enjoy and understand the working-class pathos of the genre and one can argue that Michael Apted's undeniably English roots in Aylesbury, Buckinghamshire, hardly tempered his sensitive feel for rural Appalachia in *Coal Miner's Daughter*. More problematic for Reisz, however, was the film's casting. Although Meryl Streep was keen to do the film, Reisz and his producers favoured Jessica Lange, fresh from completing Richard Pearce's farm repossession drama *Country* (1984). Unfortunately, unlike Sissy Spacek who performed all her own vocals, the actress couldn't sing a lick. As Reisz recalled to Samir Hachem, 'This was our only worry. I met Jessica and we talked. She's a great mime. She'd trained in mime in Paris, and she has very good rhythm. We decided she would learn to lip-synch the songs and we would go ahead and use Patsy Cline's original vocals on the soundtrack. Still, my only doubt about the project, and hers, was whether she would make the singing stick'.[29] Another problem was that most of Patsy's well-known hit recordings – slicked up by her producer, Owen Bradley (Jerry Haynes) – come from late in her career, when she was being marketed as a cross-over artist, so the backing tracks for her early performances had to be made truer to the raw, mid-1950s barroom sound: 'We took the recordings and stripped the voice, and we put in older, primitive bands and arrangements on them, and used them in the early parts of our movie, to give the effect of that local, unsophisticated colour that they must have sounded like in real life when she sang in honky tonks'.[30] This scrupulous attention to subtle detail is a key facet of the film, for unlike *Isadora*, where the real is largely filtered (and thus aesthetically homogenized) through the dancer's theatrically over-determined subjectivity, the entire purpose of *Sweet Dreams* is to create a clearly discernible dialectic between the realistic context of Patsy's proletarian roots – her raw sexuality and abusive marriage to Charlie Dick, her unspoiled, amateur status as 'one of the guys' – and the increasingly contrived and polished artifice of her professional star persona as an enshrined Nashville icon.

In their extremely insightful research on the Hollywood musical, both Jane Feuer and Cynthia Hanson have noted a strong tendency in biopics to regress the star power of the featured performer – the very intoxicating glamour that attracts the audience to them (and, by extension, the film we are watching) – back to the realm of their unaffected, preprofessional beginnings:

> The Hollywood musical as a genre perceives the gap between producer and consumer, the breakdown of community designated by the very distinction between performer and audience, as a form of cinematic original sin. The musical seeks to bridge the gap by putting up 'community' as an ideal concept. In basing its value system on community, the producing and consuming functions severed by the passage of musical entertainment from folk to popular to mass status are rejoined through the genre's rhetoric ... Through such a rhetorical exchange, the creation of folk relations *in* the films cancels the mass entertainment substance *of* the films.[31]

The main objective of this backwards shift of emphasis is to hide the exploitative and condescending nature of the relationship between the professional entertainer and the audience at large in order to create a sense of shared participation: 'Since stardom is – by definition – distanced from the average, these films pull their characters back toward the mean by exalting their amateur performances'.[32] However, therein lies a major problem, for how can the film biography preserve the illusion of audience identification and empathy given the impersonal nature of the star-making machinery in the creation of mass entertainment (and the necessary distancing that it entails), especially given most spectators' collective desire to both place the star on a pedestal while at the same time claim them as one of their own? One obvious method is to remind the viewer that success always has its price – i.e. by focusing on the artist's private struggles with drugs, hubris, broken marriages and jealousy in films such as *A Star Is Born* (George Cukor, 1954), *Amadeus* (Milos Forman, 1984) and *Sid and Nancy* (Alex Cox, 1986) – or alternatively one can blunt the entertainer's success and restore contact with the average grass-roots community via a regressive 'severance-death syndrome' (i.e. premature accidental demise), typified by *The Buddy Holly Story* (Steve Rash, 1978), *La Bamba* (Luis Valdez, 1987), and, of course, *Isadora* and *Sweet Dreams*.

The latter regression becomes all the more powerful as collective memory if the film, like *Saturday Night and Sunday Morning*, draws the viewer into the character's world through an initial identification with an authentic, grass-roots and class-based reality. In the case of *Sweet Dreams*, this sense of the local vernacular extends to both Patsy herself – particularly her foul mouth and unabashed lust for life and sexual pleasure – as well as the down-home, careworn qualities of her remarkably supportive mother, Hilda Hensley (Ann Wedgeworth), who married at sixteen and raised three children as a single parent (Patsy's abusive father deserted the family when she was a teenager) exclusively through her home sewing business. As Andrew Kopkind noted in his review in the *Nation*, 'Cline was *really* country when country wasn't cool. She was dumpy, frowzy, chubby and down-to-earth in a housewifely or waitressy way. Her mother made her clothes and costumes, which would fit somewhere between the top line of Kresge's and the bottom of Penney's, circa 1953'.[33] Lange agreed with this assessment, admitting that 'I've never played anyone so natural, so uncomplicated before. I've played so many parts where everything has been hidden or rumbling underneath, but Patsy had a way of hitting life head on, nothing neurotic about her'.[34] As Patsy tells Charlie early on in their courtship, 'Since I've been about eleven or twelve years old I've had my life mapped out ... I'm gonna make some money, have some kids, and then I'm gonna stop singin' and raise those kids right. Have a big house with yellow roses all around it'. It doesn't get much more uncomplicated and authentic than that.

Audience identification with the raw and unsophisticated qualities of Patsy as both a character and performer is motivated and filtered through our diegetic stand-in, Charlie Dick. The film opens with Charlie (Ed Harris) and his date Wanda (P. J. Soles) horsing around in the former's convertible as they pull up with a squeal of tyres outside the local high school for the Saturday night jamboree and dance. After letting down the top, Charlie and Wanda enter the gym and mingle with the sock-hoppers. Then, as Patsy emerges in a bright orange cowgirl outfit to sing Bob Wills's classic 'San Antonio Rose', a title sets the historical stage – 'Winchester, Virginia 1956'. Hanson rightly points out that 'the caption is almost unnecessary. The film already has identified its setting through the use of wardrobe, music and, especially, the automobile. Model aside, the use of cars in the opening scene suggests the wildness, speed, and furtive-yet-aggressive sexuality associated with the rebel of the 1950s (the rising convertible top, in particular, is a sly sexual metaphor which reappears in the film)'.[35] Right from the start the film grounds Patsy's early career in an instantly recognizable aesthetic milieu – small-scale, hometown venues, her semi-professional 'Kountry Kracker' band, her authentic square dance outfit – reinforced by the inspired casting of Harris, who, as one critic has noted, 'is naturally retro all the time'.[36]

Estranged and eventually divorced from her boringly introverted, model-building husband, Gerald (James Staley), Patsy seems ripe for sexual conquest, but whether from genuine contempt for men and their constant 'pawin' and snortin' around', or a simple 'love for the chase', she initially resists Charlie's aggressive come-on: 'You want a lot don't ya?' she smirks as he corners her in the high school hallway after the show. 'Well, people in hell want ice water. That don't mean they get it'. Far from cooling his ardour, this brash rejection spurs Charlie to pursue Patsy to her regular weekend gig at Winchester's Rainbow Road Club where she performs another hillbilly country standard, Bill Monroe's 'Blue Moon of Kentucky'. By now it's clear that Charlie not only has sex on his mind but also possesses an uncanny, intuitive knack for understanding and appreciating the true potential of Patsy's talent. 'When he listens to her sing', notes Jack Kroll, 'this six-pack visionary goes into a kind of ecstasy. Watching his rapt face we see his private love and the public love that makes a star'.[37] However, when Charlie lip-synchs the lyrics and indulges in some slow-hand 'air guitar' right in front of the stage, Patsy is momentarily distracted and berates him after

the performance: 'I don't like the way yer listen. Take a walk'. This is
the first sign of separation of the artist from her grass-roots fan base,
where the performer's sense of her own special genius lies beyond the
understanding of average Joes like Charlie: 'Charlie is not allowed to
participate', notes Hanson. 'As the performer matures and begins to
separate from the community, the words of people around them are
unable to penetrate the newly mystified talent'.[38] Ironically, for all his
brash macho and subsequent infidelities and wife abuse, Charlie knows
Patsy's talents better than herself, for even at this early stage he can
see her vocal shortcomings as well as her pluses: 'I don't care if you
have sung on some half-assed television programme, you don't sing that
good. You ever listen to a Kitty Wells record real close? You'd go home
and slit your goddamn throat'. Even though Patsy detests Kitty's insuf-
ferable whine, her Nashville-based manager, Randy Hughes (David
Clennon) will confirm Charlie's advice when he persuades her to switch
from western swing and honky-tonk to slow, heart wrenching ballads
later in the film: 'You've got a voice that was made to sing love songs,
and if I work with you we take advantage of that fact!'

Although Patsy eventually succumbs to Charlie's perseverance and
charm – a romantic slow dance to Sam Cooke's silky smooth 'You
Send Me' in the neon-lit Rainbow Road parking lot quickly transitions
to sweaty sex in the front seat of the convertible – and assents to his
marriage proposal, this is the last time her suitor seems completely at
peace with himself: 'When he and Patsy dance together, it points up the
marriage of opposites', writes Pauline Kael: 'the mysteriously quiet man
who's suspended in the middle of nowhere, who never finds himself,
and the woman who has it all, who knows her gifts almost from childhood. It's Patsy's singing – the sureness of it – that attracts him. As
Charlie is presented, he's sure he knows how to have a good time, and
he's sure of his sexual prowess, but of not much else'.[39] Charlie's growing
alienation from Patsy's increasing professional polish is further exacerbated by unavoidable social and economic circumstances, not least his
inability to earn a living wage (he works as a linotype operator at the
Winchester Star newspaper); his subsequent enforced separation from
his wife due to army service in Fort Bragg, North Carolina; and the ines-
capable macho lure of beer and floozies when he is thrown back on the
company of his wayward buddies, Woodhouse (Gary Basaraba) and Otis
(John Goodman) during his wife's pregnancy or her long absences on
the road. Indeed, Charlie is having sex with his old flame Wanda at the
exact moment that Patsy is giving birth to their first child, Julie.

Charlie's personal and psychological dislocation from Patsy as both
wife and performer is an important factor in the film because it paral-

lels (and in part expresses) the increasing distancing of the filmic audience as a whole. This is particularly evident when Patsy persuades her mother to masquerade as her talent scout and sponsor her 21 January 1957 appearance on television's Arthur Godfrey Talent Scout Show. Although clad in a home-made powder blue and white cowgirl outfit,[40] Patsy's image as a homespun Winchester 'gal' is immediately circumscribed by the slick, commercial trappings of the programme, from the prominent Lipton Tea sponsorship placements to the single-camera framing of the performance in front of a live audience. Moreover, while the prerehearsed Hilda is present for the broadcast, nervously introducing her daughter to the avuncular Godfrey (Bruce Kirby), Charlie, Woodhouse and Patsy's teenage siblings, Sylvia (Caitlin Kelch) and John (Robert L. Dasch) are at home, watching the show on television. As Patsy sings her early signature song, Don Hecht's 'Walking After Midnight', Reisz opens the sequence by mediating the performance through the frame-within-a-frame of the TV screen, cutting back to the family's proud reaction as if the singer were no longer their private property but was already beginning to slip inexorably into the public domain. Even though Reisz then switches his show coverage to colour – allowing us an unmediated relationship to *our* Patsy – when she sings the line, 'I'm always walking after midnight, searching for you', we cut back to Charlie, blissfully playing 'air guitar'. However, as our diegetic surrogate he is no longer standing in front of her at the Rainbow Road, making direct eye and body contact, but is countless miles away in his living room watching his wife on a 16–inch monitor in monochrome. This spatial and psychological displacement is reinforced at the song's end as we see Arthur Godfrey and Hilda, followed by the studio audience applauding, as condensed television images. The subsequent black and white shots of the applause meter – it shoots meteorically into the 'red', giving Patsy the grand prize – underline the fact that at the very moment that Patsy forges an indelible bond with the diegetic studio audience, the exclusive relationship with both Patsy's family and Reisz's filmic audience is suddenly and irrevocably broken, creating empathetic distance. As Hanson notes, 'When the audience in the film is "won over" by the entertainer, he or she ceases to be the private experience of the viewer and becomes a professional performer'.[41]

This widening gap between the former amateur and the burgeoning professional is exacerbated by an immediate cut to a recording studio where Patsy lays down the master for 'Walking After Midnight'. Instead of filling the frame, as she did on the Arthur Godfrey Show, she is now squeezed tightly into a tiny window in the top right-hand corner of the composition, spot-lit and cropped from the neck up. Her band fills a much larger, sound-proofed window to the left, while the session producer and engineer dominate the immediate foreground. Patsy finishes the take and although the producer shouts, 'Bullseye', she is dissatisfied and wants to do it again: 'That was draggy to me that time, real draggy'. The producer disagrees, predicting that the song is going to make everyone a lot of money and denies her request for a retake, underlining the fact that she no longer controls the quality or judgement of her own talent and is literally being shoehorned into Nashville's prepackaged commercial box.

Ironically, of course, the more Patsy loses the rights to her own creative authenticity, the bigger star she becomes. Conversely, the world of Charlie – the true, heartfelt appreciator of her genius – now starts to shrink in inverse proportion to her growing success. Just prior to his being drafted, he soaks in the bathtub drinking bourbon as Patsy gets a phone call from Decca Records: 'Walking After Midnight' is number sixteen on the charts. Reisz frames the excited Patsy on the telephone, dominating the immediate foreground of the shot in an exact mirroring of the placement of the producer in the previous scene, only it is now Charlie who is squeezed into a tight box in the upper right, framed by the bathroom door, bathtub and staircase. In their very different ways, both husband and wife may be 'feeling the pinch' of Patsy's rising star but it is Charlie's psychological horizons that are narrowing beyond hope of repair.

However, before Patsy is completely eaten up by the Nashville music machine, Reisz spends considerable time keeping it real in terms of both her career and personal life. The singer spends most of 1958 trying to exploit the chart success of 'Walking After Midnight' by undertaking a gruelling road schedule with her touring band, playing various honky-tonks with a broad repertoire ranging from the Bakersfield sound of Harlan Howard and Buck Owens's 'Foolin' Around' (which actually dates from 1961) and Hughie Cannon's 'Bill Bailey, Won't You Please Come Home'. However, the high point of the film, musically and dramatically, is a magical rendering of the traditional folk ballad, 'Roll in My Sweet Baby's Arms', sung by an exhausted band in sweet harmony to a lone guitar accompaniment while slumped around in their motel room. Few scenes in cinema have communicated the hardship of being on the road while at the same time celebrating the unique communal camaraderie of being a travelling musician and the authentic power of song to strike a universal chord of soulful purity. Alas, the feeling is short lived because Patsy discovers that she's pregnant and is forced to take an extended hiatus from touring and recording until after Julie is born. As a result, all of her new-found career momentum is dissipated. Instead, the film focuses on her ongoing battles with Charlie: the conjugal visits to Fort Bragg, fuelled by turns with tender love-making and fisticuffs; his pathological infidelities and lies; his unctuous begging for forgiveness. Just as their marriage seems to be heading for the rocks, Charlie goes AWOL from Fort Bragg and drives his motorcycle north to Winchester. He then takes Patsy back to the Rainbow Road parking lot, the scene of their first date and a symbol of their mutual love and desire, only this time they slow dance in the cleansing rain to Acker Bilk's 'Stranger on the Shore' (five years before its actual release!). Charlie makes a desperate plea for forgiveness: 'I need something from you. I need you to look me in the face and say, "You screw up a lot, but I still love you Charlie. And always will."' Patsy says the words – twice in fact – but one wonders if their marriage can ever survive the psychological damage promulgated by two warring egos, particularly when both parties have struggled to overcome the Oedipal fracture induced by broken homes and absent fathers.

These regressive, vernacular scenes with Patsy's band and her husband are reinforced by Reisz's meticulous use of *mise-en-scène*, particularly his commitment to an authentic, class-based psychological realism rooted in the power of significant detail. Thus the couple's cramped, dingy apartment at Fort Bragg includes a row of plates on the wall typical of déclassé 1950s décor, but instead of saying 'Home Sweet Home' or 'God Bless this House' one cynically states 'God Bless this Lousy Apartment', giving us far more insight into Patsy and Charlie's warped sense of humour than any specific line of dialogue. Similarly, in a later scene when Patsy is busy baking pies and frying chicken on the stove for her sister's belated high school graduation party, Charlie enters the kitchen and immediately starts fooling around, pulling her to the linoleum floor for some spontaneous sex. As they disappear out of frame to the bottom right, 'the camera stays on the chicken, and then her hand comes up and turns the stove off. It's the way they would've shot it in the fifties',[42] notes the film's cinematographer Robbie Greenberg. Comparing this detail with, say, the kitchen sex scene in Bob Rafelson's 1981 remake of *The Postman Always Rings Twice*, where Lange and Jack Nicholson are explicitly erotic, we can appreciate how Reisz not only amusingly suggests a 'modern' woman who can simultaneously juggle sexuality and domesticity, but also is able to meta-communicate the cinematic prudery typical of the period, as if we were watching an early episode of *I Love Lucy*. As Reisz reminds us, 'Detail is very important to me, how the potatoes look, and how the pies she's baking look, how she picks up the children. What you choose to see is what expresses your feelings. The way a director expresses his feelings is by what he chooses to show on the screen ... It's very important, for example, that the audience believe Patsy was a good cook. It's part of her character'.[43]

However, this realist authenticity starts to transform into a far more contrived persona as Patsy's professional career is revitalized following the birth of her daughter. When, in 1959, the singer finds herself in the embarrassing position of singing 'Blue Christmas' at a drive-in theatre while being interrupted by the mocking laugh of Woody Woodpecker on the movie screen behind her, she realizes that its time she put herself under the aegis of some serious talent management.[44] Enter Nashville's Randy Hughes and his sage advice that she start to focus exclusively on singing love songs. We now jump ahead two years to 1961 where we find Patsy – once again a new mother – struggling to reconcile her own innate musical instincts with the Nashville formula. Reisz cuts to a recording studio where Patsy reluctantly enters her glassed-in cubicle to start recording Hank Cochran and Harlan Howard's 'I Fall to Pieces', but instead of her regular touring band she is now accompanied by faceless session players and the somewhat over-intrusive Jordanaires as syrupy backing singers. Significantly, just as we hear the opening bars of the song, we slam-cut immediately to Stonewall Jackson introducing Patsy to wild applause at the Grand Ol' Opry. The latter – with its giant PET Milk Family Foods advertisement behind the stage – is the ultimate in Nashville commercial endorsement. Moreover, Patsy herself has been radically transformed. Her hair has been cut and neatly bobbed, her mother's homemade cowgirl outfits have been replaced by a pale green gown, and her one last concession to her country girl roots – her lapel corsage – is quickly removed by an overly fastidious Randy just as she takes the stage, much to Patsy's disgust. More importantly, Charlie is now part of the diegetic audience, but he is forced to sit quietly along with the other fans – no more 'air guitar' in front of the stage – so that he not only shares their distance from the prepackaged performance, but also is caught up in the overriding power of Patsy's professionalism. She is on the verge of becoming an untouchable star.

To fit Feuer and Hanson's biopic model, Patsy's rapid career ascendancy must be temporarily forestalled, lest she lose all empathetic connection with Charlie and the filmic audience. In that respect her serious car accident following her sister's graduation party on 14 June 1961, from which she incurred severe facial scarring and required months of physical rehabilitation, acts as a necessary regression to mortality, a dress rehearsal for the later 'severance-death syndrome' that ultimately claims her life. Once again Patsy is emotionally dependent on her immediate family for her recovery, and thus temporarily returns to the bosom of her vernacular fan base. Yet this regression is also short-lived, because although her injuries might preclude her from public appearances, they don't prevent her from recording. In a telling scene, Reisz shows a still-scarred Patsy reluctantly listening to a demo tape of Willie Nelson singing his now-classic song, 'Crazy'. Patsy is adamant that the up-tempo number is not for her: 'I don't care how many times you play that, I can't sing this man's songs. I don't know how to sing like that'. 'Nobody wants you to', replies her producer, Owen Bradley, patiently. 'You can take it away from him'. 'Yeah, the hell with the demo', adds Randy Hughes. 'Steal the son of a bitch'. Although, of course, Patsy ends up slowing the song down and 'making it her own', it's clear from Reisz's dislocated spatio-temporal montage that the performer is making a commercial *product* and that it is the producer and the label that owns the recording's public legacy, *not* the filmic audience. Thus, for example, Patsy starts to sing the composition in her sound-proofed booth but quickly stops to ask someone for a beer. Only then does she continue and finish the song. Throughout the film, the recording sessions have become increasingly chopped up into discontinuous parts (much like making a film out of narrative sequence). They are no longer presented as heartfelt continuous performances but instead lack spontaneity, a feeling reinforced by Reisz's constant cutting away from the artist herself to the technical personnel in the studio – the producer, the manager and the engineers. Moreover, Patsy's voice is no longer presented live, but processed by playbacks or disembodied, echo-filled feeds into the producer's booth, an artificial effect reinforced by Lange's slightly out of synch miming. Patsy's creativity has, in effect, become Taylorized, as personal and hands-on as an alienated assembly worker on the Ford production line.

This well-guarded sanctity of the commercial process is underlined towards the end of the film when Patsy and Charlie have their final violent argument. Jealous of Patsy's success – she is now able to buy her 'big house with yellow roses all around it', but with her own money, not his – and increasingly sensitive to his inability to keep pace with what he perceives as her pretentious airs and upward social mobility, Charlie eventually snaps and beats Patsy to a pulp, landing himself in jail for wife battery. Harris is at his brilliant best in these scenes, bringing out what Pauline Kael calls Charlie's 'tragic, pitiable sweetness': 'This husband, who's in awe of his wife's talent, wants a stable marriage more than he wants anything else in the world, yet he has never known how to live on an even keel. Charlie comes on at first bristling with sexual confidence, but the essence of Harris's acting style is the intensity he brings to quietness. Gradually, Charlie loses his bravado, and becomes quieter, more bewildered, and his big scene – a jailhouse monologue about the death of his father – is perhaps the most hushed, most introspective moment he has'.[45] Charlie's attempts to reconcile by walking in on Patsy's recording session of Hank Cochran's *She's Got You* are rebuffed by the angry singer. 'That this interruption is so startling testifies to the professionalizing of the performance', notes Hanson. 'Personal problems have no place in the studio'.[46]

Patsy's tragically short life concludes with a final irrevocable switch in focus from the personal to the professional as she performs her last concert in Kansas City on Sunday, 3 March 1963 – a benefit for the family of the disc jockey, 'Cactus' Jack Call, who had recently been killed in a car accident. This culminating performance of Don Gibson's 'Sweet Dreams' is both the peak of Patsy's career to date and the zenith of the film's distancing of the entertainer from both her diegetic and filmic audience. Its contrast to the early Rainbow Road concerts couldn't be more extreme. Firstly, Charlie is entirely absent from the audience: he is out getting drunk with Woodhouse and Otis, thus reasserting his connection to the film's working-class roots, which Patsy has largely abandoned. Instead of her cowgirl outfits the singer is dressed in a glamorous, tight-fitting, sequinned white evening gown. In lieu of the Kountry Kracker band she is backed by a full string orchestra bathed in a glowing red light. Eschewing reaction shots to the diegetic audience, Reisz now focuses exclusively on the performer, so that even the standing ovation at the end of the song is shot as a darkened silhouette, precluding spectator individuation. The setting is thus more like a high-class resort ballroom than an authentic country music venue and the film's spectator is positioned by Reisz's camera to see only the *professional* performance, with no hint of its amateur origins, as if Patsy had been born full blown as a pop culture phenomenon, like Aphrodite's adult birth from the ocean. Moreover the song's lyrics – 'Sweet dreams of you/Things I know can't come true/Why can't I forget the past, start loving someone new/Instead of having sweet dreams about you' – speak to the viewer's *memories* of the performer, our collective inability to forget the vernacular past, but also, by implication, our inability to live authentically in the real of the present except through the imagination, thus bringing us back into Reisz's dream-like motifs in *Isadora*. In short, Patsy's life and our relationship to the singer as a star exist only as a fabrication, a simulacrum. Thus, for Hanson, the 'film features a final, climactic performance that emphasizes the distance between performer and audience and renders the subsequent death of the performer less disturbing. With death, regression is complete. The outstanding talent is blunted, the average community is restored, and the viewer may carve out a relationship with the performer that *seems* participatory: that of keeping the memory alive'.[47]

Two days after the Kansas City concert, Patsy's plane, piloted by Randy Hughes and accompanied by country stars Cowboy Copas (Charlie Walker) and Hawkshaw Hawkins (Frank Knapp Jr.) crashed near a mountain top near Camden, Tennessee, killing everyone on board. Even though, as in the case of Isadora, we know the inevitable is coming, the suddenness of the crash is all the more jarring, especially after Randy manages to restart the aircraft's stalled engines and the blanketing clouds clear for one brief moment. However, unlike the end of *Isadora*, where Reisz transcends the materiality of death and moves into an image of immanence through his symbolic focus on the dancer's identification with water, in this case he regresses the narrative back from the distanced professionalism of the Kansas City concert and Patsy's very public death to a direct and sensual link with Charlie. After the funeral, the heartbroken husband listens to Patsy's records and weeps quietly in their living room, as if attempting to make his own private connection through her public voice. Then as he starts dancing and playing a last round of 'air guitar' to 'Crazy', he mimes the gesture of slow dancing with Patsy and in a sudden mind-screen we flash back to the couple dancing in the neon-lit parking lot of the Rainbow Road, reconnecting us once again to their first date. Only this time the accompanying music is not Sam Cooke, or even Acker Bilk, but Patsy Cline herself, thereby fusing the past and the present, the personal and the professional, life and art, into one culminating regressive filmic image. Once again Patsy belongs to her Charlie and, by extension, to us.

Notes

1 Friedrich Nietzsche, *The Birth of Tragedy*, trans. Walter Kaufmann (New York, Vintage Books, 1967), p. 52.

2 Isadora Duncan, *My Life* (New York, Liveright, 1927 and 1995), p. 196.

3 Several biographies cite Isadora's birth year as 1878.

4 Duncan, *My Life*, p. 171.

5 The Hakims's career dates back to the 1930s, when they produced Julien Divivier's *Pépé le Moko* (1936) and Jean Renoir's *La Bête Humaine* (1938) for Paramount (Paris). After a spell in the US during the 1940s, whose fruits included Renoir's *The Southerner* (1945), they returned to Europe in time for the French New Wave and Claude Chabrol's *A Double Tour* (1959). Their most prestigious projects were with Antonioni – *L'Avventura* (1959) and *L'Eclisse* (1962) – as well as Losey's ill-fated *Eve* (1962).

6 Continuing the general trend beginning in 1949, cinema attendance had dropped from 501 million (1960) to 215 million (1969). The number of cinemas had also declined, from 3,034 (1960) to 1,581 (1969). Box-office takings, however, remained relatively constant due to a large increase in seat prices: £58 million (1960) to £55 million (1970).

7 Stephen Farber, 'Artists in Love and War', *Hudson Review*, Vol. 22, No. 2, Summer 1969, p. 297.

8 Some measure of the technical and 'spiritual' accuracy of Redgrave's interpretations can be found by comparing her performance to those of Isadora schools alumnae, Lori Belilove and Madeleine Lytton, in the 1989 film *Isadora Duncan: Movement from the Soul*, directed by Dayna Goldfine and Daniel Geller.

9 Duncan, *My Life*, p. 105.

10 See *ibid.*, pp. 58–9.

11 *Ibid.*, p. 84.

12 *Ibid.*, p. 133.

13 *Ibid.*, p. 167.

14 *Ibid.*, p. 168.

15 *Ibid.*, p. 197.

16 Estelle Changas, '*Isadora*', *Film Quarterly*, Summer 1969, p. 47.

17 Isadora Duncan, quoted in Sewell Stokes, *Isadora Duncan: An Intimate Portrait* (London, Brentano's, 1928), p. 173. In 1925, without divorcing Isadora, Essenin married Tolstoy's granddaughter and then committed suicide less than four months later.

18 Vincent Canby, '*The Loves of Isadora*', *New York Times*, 28 April 1969, p. 33:1.

19 Duncan, *My Life*, p. 119.

20 *Ibid.*, p. 221.

21 Margaret Drabble, 'Isadora the Good' (Review of Francis Steegmuller, ed., *Your Isadora: The Love Story of Isadora Duncan and Gordon Craig*), *The Listener*, Vol. 93, No. 2392, 6 February 1975, p. 185.

22 Stokes, *Isadora Duncan: An Intimate Portrait*, p. 48.

23 Farber, 'Artists in Love and War', pp. 297–8.

24 Changas, '*Isadora*', pp. 45–6.

25 *Ibid.*, p. 46.

26 *Ibid.*, p. 48.

27 *Ibid.*

28 Reisz, quoted in Gow, 'Outsiders: Karel Reisz in an Interview with Gordon Gow', p. 16.

29 Reisz, quoted in Hachem, '*Sweet Dreams*', p. 31.

30 *Ibid.*

31 Jane Feuer, *The Hollywood Musical* (Bloomington and Indianapolis, Indiana University Press, Second Edition, 1993), p. 3.

32 Cynthia Hanson, 'The Hollywood Musical Biopic and the Regressive Performer', *Wide Angle*, Vol. 10, No. 2, 1988, p. 15.

33 Andrew Kopkind, '*Sweet Dreams*', *Nation*, Vol. 241, No. 16, 16 November 1985, p. 532.

34 Jessica Lange, interviewed in Hachem, '*Sweet Dreams*', p. 31.

35 Hanson, 'The Hollywood Musical Biopic and the Regressive Performer', p. 16.

36 Kopkind, '*Sweet Dreams*', p. 533.

37 Jack Kroll, 'Lusty Queen of Country, *Newsweek*, Vol. 106, 7 October 1985, p. 88.

38 Hanson, 'The Hollywood Musical Biopic and the Regressive Performer', p. 19.

39 Pauline Kael, 'The Current Cinema: Heroines', *New Yorker*, 21 October 1985, p. 123. Charlie's lack of vocation is largely fictional. In reality, he briefly acted as Patsy's road manger and following her death worked successfully for eight years as a record promoter for Starday Records and then as an independent promoter. In the mid-1980s he became part owner with two Canadian brothers of a video company that focused on the production of country star profiles. He ultimately sold his portion of the business and began handling Patsy's estate with the company Legacy Inc.

40 In fact, the cowgirl outfit was replaced by a cocktail dress at the last minute.
41 Hanson, 'The Hollywood Musical Biopic and the Regressive Performer', p. 18.
42 Robbie Greenberg, interviewed in Hachem, '*Sweet Dreams*', p. 32.
43 Reisz, quoted in *ibid*.
44 In a strange irony, 'Blue Christmas' is actually sung by the real Charlie Dick's second wife, Jamey Ryan.
45 Kael, 'The Current Cinema: Heroines', p. 122.
46 Hanson, 'The Hollywood Musical Biopic and the Regressive Performer', pp. 17–18.
47 *Ibid.*, pp. 22–3.

Reisz in Hollywood: deconstructing existentialism and the counterculture in *The Gambler* (1974) and *Dog Soldiers* / *Who'll Stop the Rain* (1978)

8

Man would rather will *nothingness* than *not* will. (Friedrich Nietzsche)[1]

But I still say that not only too much lucidity, but any amount of it at all is a disease. (Fyodor Dostoyevsky)[2]

In growing used to danger, a man cannot allow it to become part of him. He gets used to evil. (*The I Ching*)

Universal Pictures issued a 177–minute version of *Isadora* in a limited Los Angeles release on 18 December 1968 to qualify for that year's Oscars. The film received universally negative audience response. Understandably alarmed at the prospect of distributing a high-budget commercial 'turkey', Universal re-edited the film twice and a few months later, cut to 131 minutes with Reisz's 'unwilling help', a butchered version of the picture was released with a racy new title: *The Loves of Isadora*. Unfortunately, the studio's radical pruning failed to convince either the paying public or the critics. As Vincent Canby wrote in the *New York Times*, 'I can't quite believe that the movie we are now seeing, with its odd lapses in continuity and its inability to make up its mind whether it is flashing forward or backward in time, is exactly the movie that Reisz originally had in mind'.[3] Many pundits also attributed the film's box-office failure to negative political reaction against Vanessa Redgrave for her vocal anti-war stance (Middle America was still predominantly in favour of the Vietnam War in 1969). Despite her undeniably brilliant performance, which earned Redgrave a Best Actress Oscar nomination (she eventually lost to joint-winners, Barbra Streisand in *Funny Girl* and Katherine Hepburn in *The Lion in Winter*), conservative public opinion declared its antipathy from the start, proclaiming, 'A Vote for Vanessa Redgrave Is a Vote for the Viet Cong!' More importantly, *Isadora*'s commercial failure proved to be the final nail in the coffin of Jay Kantner's slate of Universal-financed British productions. By February 1969, Kantner had resigned and the programme terminated.

Deeply hurt by the enforced recutting of *Isadora*, Reisz retreated from the film business for more than a year in order to lick his wounds. Then, as various projects fell through, for the next five years he chose to keep his hand in by making commercials. Although confessing 'to a slight feeling of shame',[4] Reisz always argued that directing commercials subsidized his independence, allowing him to 'cherry pick' his feature projects. It also accelerated his directorial learning curve, forcing him 'to create images which are so highly condensed and disciplined that they are not only functional but also highly charged with suggestive meaning'.[5] Nonetheless, commercials were no compensation for the lost artistic cachet of directing high-profile features, particularly when Reisz's abortive assignments included prestigious adaptations of John Le Carré's *The Naïve and Sentimental Lover* (eventually abandoned for lack of a workable script), and André Malraux's 1934 classic, *La Condition Humaine* (*Man's Fate*), to which Carlo Ponti held the film rights. Focusing on the 1927 Shanghai revolution, *Man's Fate* was supposed to have the guaranteed support and sanction of the Beijing government, but the political climate in China changed in preproduction and initial favourable interest turned to deep suspicion and distrust. Ultimately, it would be 1973 before Reisz would again direct a legitimate script, a forty-seven-minute television version of *On the High Road* for Melvyn Bragg's BBC Chekhov series.[6]

Reisz's difficulties were symptomatic of a broader malaise affecting the British film industry throughout the 1970s. This was partly due to economic factors, for as Alexander Walker notes, 'United States investment in British films amounted to only £17.5m. in 1970, as against £31.2m. the previous year. The down-turn became a crisis in 1971 when it fell to £8.3m'.[7] EMI exemplified this negative trend: their income crashed from £10,515,000 in June 1970 to £5,427,000 a year later, largely because of huge American investment losses. Theatre admissions were also down by 7 per cent during the same period, although exhibition receipts rose due to increased ticket prices and an expansion of multiplex theatres. More seriously, however, artists' fees had escalated through the roof, exacerbated by Chancellor of the Exchequer Denis Healey's November 1974 Finance Bill that proposed changes to tax laws affecting the highest earners in Britain. This negatively affected American film-makers working in Britain, as well as the highest paid British artists and technicians. For Association of Cinematographic Television and Allied Technicians' General Secretary Alan Sapper, Healey's bill was the proverbial last straw, 'all that is needed to break the industry's back'. Kip Herren, Pinewood Studio's managing director, summed up the general reaction: 'Instead of producing revenue, the new taxes will only exclude talent. Not only will the Americans disappear; there will be every incentive for our own home-grown talent to follow them'.[8] Herren's prediction proved prescient, for by 1975 Joseph Losey was living in France as a tax exile, only returning to the UK for his last film, *Steaming* (1984), while John Schlesinger moved to Hollywood to direct his next two features, *Day of the Locust* (1975) and *Marathon Man* (1976). Even Carl Foreman – a loyal British resident since his blacklisting in 1952 – reluctantly returned to the US:

> There is an even greater danger to the industry, I think, than the large number of people leaving, and that is the lack of money here, the almost complete drying up of finance for real *British* films – that is to say, films of purely British content – or for international co-productions. You have only to look around and see how pitifully bare the cupboard is, nothing in the studios, practically nothing outside the studios, and the only things going are the crumbs from the Hollywood table. I think that conditions are worse this year than in any of the twenty-three years I have been over here.[9]

Although kitchen sink veterans such as Reisz, Richardson and Clayton worked in America during this period, it would be a mistake to read this exodus as tantamount to a sudden British cinematic 'brain drain'. As John Russell Taylor was quick to point out, 'True enough that, for instance, John Schlesinger, Karel Reisz, Mike Hodges, Peter Yates (and for that matter Michael Winner) have been making films in America, while Anthony Harvey, Jack Clayton and Tony Richardson have been making "American" films (i.e. set in America and with largely American casts) in Britain. But that is not exactly a new development. Though all the directors mentioned are British in nationality and training, they have nearly all been flirting with American, or at least international, production for years'.[10] Reisz concurred, defiantly informing Taylor that, 'I don't believe any of us feel that we are betraying anything by making larger-scale, "international" productions, because our beginnings were not made on any national, let alone nationalistic, principle'.[11] For Reisz, the real issue was economic rather than chauvinistic: by the mid-1970s, there seemed to be little alternative to international co-productions, for with the rapid decline of the Swinging London phenomenon, small-scale vernacular British films were widely considered box-office poison. Raymond Durgnat quite rightly posed the problem in broader philosophical terms: 'What has a specifically British culture to contribute? Briefly, perhaps, it's the assertion of a mainstream between American violence and Parisian rationality – both of which tend to schematism, from Douglas Sirk's chromium-plated humanoids through Godard's gray zombies to Sam Peckinpah's Valhalla Bunch'.[12] For Durgnat,

British cinema's only hope was to play to its strengths, cultivating a fertile 'mucky realism' nourished by the working-class novel.

As one might expect, the ever-irascible Lindsay Anderson blamed the directors themselves. 'I think it is the *artists* who are not interested', he complained. 'I don't see any indication that my colleagues are bursting with ideas about Britain and not getting them financed. I think that what they do – out of some vague feeling of guilt – is use this argument about not being able to get finance, in order to justify themselves in not attempting. I think it would be better if they were honest and said, "I find that Britain is boring and not pleasant to work in and I would prefer to work somewhere else."'[13] However, although Anderson 'put his money where his mouth is' and continued to film in Britain, his explicitly Brechtian epic, *O Lucky Man!* (1973) also failed at the box office and became symptomatic of a broader ideological rift with leftist British film critics, exemplified by the director's stubborn commitment to the seemingly outmoded New Left socialism of the 1950s compared to the more Althusserian Marxism manifested in the intellectual film journal, *Screen*.[14] Alexander Walker also blamed the directors, less for their dislike of working in Britain than for their lengthy gaps between films, for it 'underlines one of the worst vices of British film-makers: their relative paucity of output. By temperament, as well as the proximity of the London theatre, British directors have means of waiting until the right film comes along that are denied to their Hollywood counterparts: it may help them keep their artistic integrity, but I doubt if it has benefited the film industry. A Michael Winner will always be working, but more fastidious talents have been simply too choosy about what they did – even allowing for an artist's preferences and unforeseen reverses in setting up subjects'.[15] Walker's protest is especially true of Reisz, who spent most of his career eschewing potboiler projects and opting to work largely outside the commercial studio system. The result, as we have seen, was a mere nine features spanning forty-two years.

Ironically, although British films may have been commercial poison in the American marketplace during the 1970s, British *directors* were never 'hotter' in Hollywood – especially at Paramount, where Reisz was finally able to direct his next feature project, *The Gambler*. Reisz signed on with the studio through the successful independent producers, Robert Chartoff and Irwin Winkler, who approached the director with an idea for a film on gambling.[16] According to Winkler, 'The genesis of that film is that an agent brought us a very early draft of a screenplay that had a very good idea but wasn't well written. We gave it to the director Karel Reisz in London, whom we've always admired, and he was interested in developing it. Over the course of about a year the script was reshaped and rewritten until it was in final form. We then gave it to Jimmy Caan and he said he wanted to do it, and we proceeded under the umbrella of Paramount Pictures'.[17] The semi-autobiographical script was written by a then unknown Harvard and Columbia University graduate, New York sportswriter and City College New York literature professor, James Toback (b. 1944). Toback subsequently wrote the screenplay for Barry Levinson's *Bugsy* (1991) and has since directed a series of provocative independent films, including *Fingers* (1978), *Love and Money* (1982), *Two Girls and a Guy* (1997), *Harvard Man* (2001) and *When Will I Be Loved?* (2004).[18] Although it was a tentative offer with no assurance of realization, Reisz accepted Chartoff and Winkler's proposal because he was eager to work – it had been six years since the release of *Isadora* – and saw a great deal of potential in James Toback's rough screenplay: 'It was a kind of documentary about gambling. I really liked the dialogue, but I said to the writer, "Let's not make a documentary about gambling, let's dramatise it through the story of a passionate gambler," and we invented a kind of "Hero of our Time", a sort of Byronic loser, to put through this story. It ended up being a rather harsh vision. But Paramount were amazingly loyal about it'.[19] Certainly Chartoff was willing to take the risk, although he acknowledged that the producers 'were concerned about the fact that the picture was very depressing and wondered how an audience would respond, and to soothe our own feelings in anticipation of the release, this is the kind of thing we said to ourselves: "Well, *Midnight Cowboy* was a very depressing film."'[20] Of course, John Schlesinger's gritty depiction of New York street hustlers went on to win the Best Picture Oscar for 1969 and grossed $44,785,053 in the United States alone.

Like its literary inspiration, Dostoyevsky's autobiographical 1866 novella *The Gambler*, Reisz's uncompromising character study takes us to the heart of gambling addiction, shifting the action from aristocratic nineteenth-century European spas and gambling resorts such as Wiesbaden and Baden-Baden to the illegal, mob-run gambling dens of 1970s Manhattan. 'I always try and find a manner for a film that will express the chief character', notes Reisz. 'And the character of the gambler is very New York – very jagged, very dark, very quick, very melodramatic, very exciting, rather unhappy. And it seems to me that the New York landscape is a perfect mirror for that character. The story could not have been set elsewhere'.[21] The novel's Aleksey Ivanovich is now Axel Freed (James Caan) who, like Toback, is a Harvard graduate and an English Professor at a New York City College. Axel lectures on Dostoyevsky's nascent existentialism and will-to-power as a philosophical explanation (and justification) for his own obsession with risk and chance, what

REISZ IN HOLLYWOOD **191**

Nietzsche called *amor fati* or affirmation of the luck of the dice throw. Unfortunately, Axel's craving for the visceral 'juice' of uncertainty leads to a disastrous run of luck while playing baccarat and roulette. After a single night's gambling he finds himself in debt to the mob to the tune of $44,000, much to the concern of his regular bookie, Hips (Paul Sorvino), who has to vouch for his client to the unseen 'wise guys' who run the gambling consortium. Desperate for immediate funds, Axel takes the advice of sardonic fellow-gambler 'Monkey' (London Lee) and turns to Bernie (Allen Rich), a notorious loan shark, who sends his enforcer, Carmine (Burt Young) to chauffeur the would-be client to a bar-room rendezvous. On the way, Carmine makes a point of stopping off at the apartment of a defaulting client, and beats him up in front of his hysterical wife, as if to demonstrate to a bemused Axel the serious-ness of Bernie's operation. However, when the latter balks at the size of the loan – $20,000 – Axel arrogantly refuses the deal, dismissing Bernie as a smalltime 'clerk'.

As a last resort, Axel leans on his mother Naomi (Jacqueline Brookes), a hospital doctor, who withdraws her life's savings to bail out her reckless son. However, instead of immediately reimbursing Hips, Axel attends the eightieth birthday party of his wealthy grandfather, the furniture store magnate, A. R. Lowenthal (Morris Carnovsky). During his celebra-tory speech, Axel reminds his audience that 'We are living in an age that subverts the breeding of men like A. R. Lowenthal'. He recalls how at the age of thirteen his grandfather, a Lithuanian Jew living under the oppression of Tsarist Russia, had 'stuck a knife in the back of a cossack pig who had knocked his mother to the ground. At fifteen, he prowled New York as a bandit until he had the cash to feed a family of five. At twenty he opened a furniture store which he built into two, then fifteen, then fifty, then a hundred until finally he had the largest chain America had ever seen'. Axel ends by acknowledging his own personal debt to his illustrious forebear, 'Because every time I think my reach has stretched too far, I remember the moves that he has dared'. Axel toasts 'this man that seized what he wanted. Wanted with nothing there to back him up but wit, and balls and will: this killer, this king!'

This reconnection with his immigrant family roots – in many ways Lowenthal epitomizes 'The American Way' – spurs Axel to indulge his own need for risk and prove himself worthy of his grandfather's legacy. Circumventing Hips, he contacts another bookie, Jimmy (Carmine Caridi) and parlays his mother's $44,000 on a string of three 'can't lose' college basketball games. He then flies to Las Vegas with his girlfriend Billie (Lauren Hutton) in an attempt to double his assets. Playing 'The Strip' like a gambling gadfly, Axel is seemingly 'blessed by the gods' as he racks up huge wins at craps, baccarat and roulette. This culminates in a game of blackjack ('twenty-one') at Caesar's Palace, where he tests both his resolve and fate by calling for a third card even though he holds an extremely strong hand of 'eighteen'. Then, as if by divine will, he draws the trey for the winning twenty-one. However, what the gods giveth, the gods also taketh away and Axel ends up losing half of his overall winnings on the basketball games.[22] Back in New York and eager to recoup his losses, he persuades Jimmy to place the remaining $50,000 of his Vegas winnings on that night's NBA game between the Los Angeles Lakers and the Seattle Supersonics. As Axel soaks in the bathtub listening to Chick Hearn's commentary on the radio, his Lakers lose to a last second bucket and the gambler is suddenly back at square one, minus his mother's $44,000.

Ostracized by Billie, who fails to understand and refuses to indulge his addiction, and pressured by Hips, who has the mob breathing down his neck, Axel has no recourse but to buy more time. However, he is abducted from the Central Park amphitheatre and manhandled to an industrial warehouse where he is confronted by a senior mob captain, 'One' (the ever-menacing Vic Tayback). 'One' wants his money and inquires about Axel's assets. Of course, his teacher's salary is laughable, he owns no property, no boats, and his baby blue Ford Mustang has clearly seen better days. Axel plays his trump card, his grandfather's wealth – 'What's his is mine' – but to his shock and dismay 'One' tells him that he has known Lowenthal for over thirty years and the old man refused to come through: 'He's no schmuck. He's a businessman'. Axel's only alternative is to recruit one of his students, Spencer (Carl W. Crudup), a junior college basketball star, to shave points in that evening's game in order to square his debt once and for all. The film ends not with Axel's reprieve and a well-earned sigh of relief for the audience, but yet another search for existential 'juice'. Eschewing Hips' invitation to dinner and some late night 'pussy', Axel instead sets out on foot into one of the most dangerous neighbourhoods in Harlem. He wanders into a bar where he picks up a prostitute and takes her to a run-down hotel room. Whether through egoism, excitement, self-contempt at forcing Spencer to throw the game, or the need for another adrenalin fix following his narrow escape, Axel picks a fight with the whore and then sets upon her pimp (Antonio Fargas), kicking him in the kidneys as he lies helpless on the floor. Hysterical, the prostitute slashes Axel across the cheek with a knife. Staunching the streaming blood with a scarf, he staggers downstairs to the hotel lobby where he examines the gaping wound in a hallway mirror. With an enigmatic look – is it a smile, a grimace or a momentary state of grace? – he stares at his reflection as

REISZ IN HOLLYWOOD **193**

Reisz freeze-frames. Roll credits.

Along with *Dog Soldiers* and *The French Lieutenant's Woman*, *The Gambler* is the first of three critical meditations on existentialism in which Reisz deconstructs the seeming free will of unfettered individualism as a form of culturally circumscribed interpellation. As Harlan Kennedy correctly points out, 'The fascination of gambling is pure existentialism – an *acte gratuit* with no moral referents, no social or spiritual endorsement beyond the destiny-deciding thrill of a moment – and it seems the best form of self-expression Reisz has yet found for one of his loner-heroes'.[23] However, for Reisz, the popular philosophy (at least in its Sartrean guise) is less a manifestation of creative will-to-power than a potentially dangerous, self-deluding solipsistic construction that can easily lead to nihilism and degradation if it lacks a broader sense of moral and collective responsibility. Which is not to say that Reisz was completely unsympathetic to Axel's 'compulsion', for as he admitted to Gordon Gow:

> I love to gamble, but I'm not a sick gambler. To call it a compulsion is to take a medical, analytical point of view. I felt much more that I wanted to show that for this character this kind of risk-taking was an ideal, an attempt to live a little bit less squalidly, less corruptly than the rest of us do. For him there was some kind of heroism in it. In other words, I tried to see the thing not altogether uncritically but, in the main, *with* him: this continual desire to put question marks around the next half-hour of his life, as an attempt to remain alive, not to go under in the modern morass. I prefer not to think of it in medical terms as a compulsion, but rather as a romantic folly.[24]

As in the case of that other compulsive, Morgan Delt, Reisz begins his film with the central character and defines the film's narrative shape, tone and ambience through his subjectivity, which partially explains why the film is both ambiguous and critically speculative. As Georg Gaston observes, 'Reisz attempts to create a kind of double vision in this as in his previous work. That is, he purposely establishes a style in *The Gambler* which allows us to imagine the interior of the characters while encouraging us to retain at the same time an objective understanding of the surface truths'.[25] These parallel interior and exterior views may create confusion and contradiction, but the narrative is ultimately held together by a unified sensibility developed from the overriding consistency of Axel's manically driven personality. In this respect, Reisz's *mise-en-scène* is crucial, for as he explained to Gow, 'I was extremely anxious not to have long-shots of New York, not to have tourist views – to see New York through that man ... One must make the audience feel the sense of the place through detail, through temperament, not through a city's identifying postcards ... over and above that we were going for the temperament of the city'.[26] The result is an ambivalent portrait of an obsessive-compulsive disorder that strikes at the heart of American individualism and the very fabric of western urbanism.

For Toback, however, given the film's autobiographical origins, Axel is less a mechanism for empathetic analysis than the writer's fictional alter ego, a more idealized extrapolation of his own youthful gambling experiences whereby addiction is at least partly justified on philosophical as well as psychological grounds. Axel's career as a college professor is thus all too convenient insofar as his lectures on Dostoyevsky's *Notes from the Underground* (1864) and William Carlos Williams' *In the American Grain* (1925) afford him (as well as Toback) an ideal stage on which to glamorize his own selfish actions by filtering them through the ethos of a misconceived Nietzscheanism. Thus, as Axel explains to his students, when Dostoyevky's unnamed protagonist detests the fact that two and two make four, and that he reserves his sacred right to insist that two and two make five, he is riding on sheer will. Using the analogy of a basketball player who intuitively shoots from beyond his normal range, convinced that the ball *must* go in the hoop, Axel suggests that an idea is true because he wants it to be true, because he *says* it is true. The issue is not whether he is right or wrong, but whether he has the *will* to believe he is right no matter how many proofs there are to the contrary. 'Reason only satisfies man's rational requirements', cites Axel. 'Desire, on the other hand, encompasses everything. Desire is life'. Axel is obviously talking as much about himself as about Dostoyevsky, and if we had any doubts about Toback's admiration for Axel's irrational creed then they are quickly dispelled by a subsequent lecture on Williams' *In the American Grain*. Here, Axel supports the author's indictment of President George Washington – '90% of the force which made the American revolution...and a supreme symbol of America' – as a man so inherently afraid of losing and terrified of failure that he refuses to take risks. 'There are certain questions Washington just won't ask', asserts Axel. 'Certain borders he'd rather die than cross. D. H. Lawrence says, "Americans fear new experience more than they fear anything. They are the world's greatest dodges because they dodge their own very selves."'

On the other hand, it is this very consciousness of the thinking, rational 'self' that impedes the unbridled actions of a pure will-to-power. Both Nietzsche and Dostoyevsky advocated an 'emptying out' of the intellectual ego so that humans can confront nothingness square in the face and affirm their own being through sheer force of will (in effect, a triumph of raw Dionysian desire over mediated Apollinian reason). In this sense, the film's ending is far less ambiguous for Toback than it might be for Reisz or the cinema audience. Discussing the creative impetus for his 2001 film, *Harvard Man*, which relates Toback's experiences under the influence of LSD while studying at Harvard in the 1960s, the writer recalled undergoing a cataclysmic erasure of the self for a period of eight days:

> Which is to say that the 'I' – which I, like most people functioning in the world, had assumed exists in some absolute way – is in fact a sham, an artificial construct. [In] Heidegger, Kierkegaard and Wittgenstein ... there's a whole tradition of the self as an imposed structure over a void that is the natural state of consciousness. It's one thing to understand that analytically and to be able to get an 'A' on a test in which one is writing about it, and it's another to be viscerally aware that that's the truth and not to have a self. You can't function in the so-called 'real world' and not have one. Maybe for an hour or two, certainly not for a day ... I wanted to continue to function in this mundane world and all of a sudden I found I couldn't for eight days. It remained an experience that I knew that if I ever found an art in which I was sufficiently skillful, it would have to be the subject of my work. And when it turned out to be film about seven or eight years later, it was what I was really writing about and making movies about all along: it's what's at the heart of *The Gambler*, and that last image of *The Gambler* I think conveys that.[27]

As Axel examines the gaping wound on his face in the hotel lobby mirror, he ceases to be a self-reflexive, rational individual and stares at the very core of his being as pure untrammeled desire – as close to living in the absolute 'now' of the moment as any human can attain. The subsequent freeze-frame is completely appropriate because linear, causal time has literally come to a standstill. In that instant Axel is truly alive, beyond consciousness, at one with his visceral being, a sole witness to the fact that he exists, that *something is happening*. In short he has become a manifestation of the pure sublime.

However, there's also something fundamentally suspect with this picture, for Axel's actions seem driven less by pure emotional will than a fundamental need to live up to someone else's expectations, whether they be literary, philosophical or personal in origin. Reviewing the film in the *New York Times*, Vincent Canby attributed this to the inherent failings of Toback's screenplay, noting that 'Mr. Toback writes as if he were a literature groupie, snatching at bits and pieces of other men's ideas for the loose-leaf album that eventually became his screenplay'.[28] Indeed many critics noted the similarities between Axel's obsessive drive towards self-abnegation and that of Norman Mailer's semi-autobiographical character, Stephen Rojack in his 1966 novel *An American Dream*. Perhaps a more accurate assessment is that Toback made a smart decision to construct

Axel as a form of literary pastiche, because this mish-mash of influences meta-communicates a fundamental flaw in the film's character: namely Axel's tendency to displace his own shortcomings as a writer and his eschewal of artistic and intellectual risk onto a bookish romanticization of the anti-hero and his tendency to frame that risk in extremely limited *physical* (read: macho) terms. Thus while Axel might quote the keen existential insights of Dostoyevsky's narrator in *Notes from the Underground*, he conveniently overlooks the character's mean, often spiteful pettiness (the book's opening line is 'I'm a sick man ... a mean man. There's nothing attractive about me') as well as his tendency, like Emma Bovary and Sarah Woodruff in *The French Lieutenant's Woman*, to live his life as a form of received wisdom obtained as much from reading as from direct lived experience. Thus, referring to an awkward conversation with the prostitute Liza, Dostoyevsky's narrator admits that 'I knew that what I was saying was contrived, even "literary" stuff, but then, that was the only way I knew how to speak – "like a book," as she had put it. But that didn't worry me as long as I was sure I was getting my point across. In fact, my artificial style may have made the message more effective as far as she was concerned'.[29] The underground man lives in a world almost solely derived from books (and books about books) to the extent that, as he later admits, 'we've reached a point where we consider real life as work – almost as painful labor – and we are secretly agreed that the way it is presented in literature is much better'.[30]

This literary and philosophical contrivance also extends to Axel's macho sense of his own manliness. As Michael Dempsey perceptively points out, 'When Axel compares the poet to the athlete, we can sense his uneasiness, his guilty, insecure American intellectual's hopeless envy for the man of action ... He tries to counter it by making star turns of his lectures and existential statements of his reckless bets'.[31] Axel longs to resurrect the obsolete heroes of a long-vanished frontier world, whether in the form of Dostoyevsky's underground man, E. E. Cummings' Buffalo Bill or, most pertinently, the existential legacy of his grandfather, A. R. Lowenthal, whose photograph is proudly displayed on Axel's mantle alongside the plaster bust of an ancient Greek hero. Axel genuinely admires his forebear's heroic rise from the gutter and his willingness to use violence to protect his family and his assets, but there is a huge difference between a will-to-power built on need and necessity and one predicated on demand and desire. When Axel berates Lowenthal for refusing to pay off his debt with 'One', proudly stating that he took care of the problem '*your* way – I *fixed* it', the old man enlightens his would-be protégé on the real meaning of acting 'beyond good and evil': 'My way? How would you know how I did things? I was as honest as any man with great responsibility ever could be. I dealt with those vipers because I *had* to. Not because I wanted to'.

The use of the blacklisted Carnovsky as Lowenthal is inspired casting here, as it imbues the scene with a much larger extra-filmic subtext, encompassing the implications of HUAC (House Committee on Un-American Activities), the McCarthy years and the actor's true commitment to his political beliefs against the life-destroying pressures of ideological conformity.[32] Axel's academic equivalent, acting out theatrically before his college students, seems small beer in comparison, especially as his own contribution to the field, his future 'immortal books' as Lowenthal calls them, show no signs of ever being researched, much less completed. In short, Axel shirks the risk of truly creative endeavour – the writer's horror before the blank page, itself a form of abyss that demands a willed overcoming – and that is why his brand of existentialism can never be truly Nietzschean. Instead, Axel opts for the non-creative, non-affirmative alternative, an artificially trumped up possibility of physical violence: the real wellspring of his 'juice'. Thus in a key scene he contradicts Hips' claim that all gamblers secretly want to lose by correctly affirming that he always wants to win; but only when the odds (and reason) dictate that by all rights he should lose. 'Putting himself in peril, then triumphing over it and his fear of it makes him feel rapturously alive, even godlike; it juices him up', notes Dempsey.[33] Juice is for Axel what fear is for John Converse in *Dog Soldiers*. It gives purpose to a meaningless world. The film's conclusion logically brings all of these disparate elements together, for it allows Axel to displace and extend his fascination for gambling onto the world of black athletic prowess through the rigged basketball game, and finally, by extension, to the extreme physical risk of his reckless sojourn into Harlem. Axel has thereby become a 'player' in more ways than one.

This interwoven connection between risk and violence is underscored through Jerry Fielding's eerily expressive soundtrack, most specifically his appropriation of the slow introduction from Mahler's *First Symphony* (1889).[34] As originally conceived, the work evokes the natural world waking after the long hibernation of winter. Low, shimmering strings are gradually punctuated by the sounds of distant hunting horns, while the clarinet imitates the call of a vociferous cuckoo. Then Mahler introduces the principal theme, derived from the second of his *Songs of a Wayfarer*, which expresses a country lad's simple enjoyment of a fine spring morning in the forest. However, Reisz undercuts any sense of youthful innocence or the disinterestedness of unspoiled nature by layering the theme over three catalytic scenes, seemingly unrelated on the surface but inextricably linked by Axel's subjectivity. These are:

1) Axel's opening series of flashbacks as he recalls the details of his devastating losses while driving to school from the gambling den; 2) his sensational run in Vegas, culminating in his huge win at blackjack; and 3) the concluding scene in the Harlem hotel lobby. Thus through strategic use of a recurring leitmotif, positive *and* negative experiences, high-stakes games of chance and Axel's irresponsible deathwish, are homogenized as equivalent parts of the same existential 'high'. It is some measure of the sustained brilliance of Caan's carefully measured performance that he is able to maintain the outward façade of Axel's calm demeanour through the emotional rollercoaster of these events without breaking a sweat, underlining the fact that for Axel they are all grist for the same mill. Caan's skills did not escape the notice of Pauline Kael, who recognized that, 'the actor has to stay clenched, the bit in his teeth: an uncalculated move and the picture's tension would collapse. It's an impregnable performance; even in the near-ludicrous Harlem scenes at the end, Caan commands the screen by his hammer-and-tongs concentration'.[35]

Unfortunately, such concentration does little to help Caan's character in the long term. Because Axel's will-to-power is based on desire rather than necessity – a desire predicated on a lack, which is itself spawned by endless other desires – it means that it can never be completely fulfilled. As a result, as Daniel Read and Peter Roelofsma note in their study of addictive behaviour:

> the quantity of addictive substance or experience needed to achieve or maintain a given level of happiness increases with repeated consumption. Gamblers, for example, need increasingly large and risky propositions to maintain the 'thrill', as do habitual users of cocaine or caffeine. Second, the pleasure to be gained from other parts of the addict's life decreases over time, so that even though the addictive good is losing its power, it always remains more attractive than its alternatives. The gambler spends all of his time at the track or casino, and loses all interest in home or work.[36]

For Read and Roelofsma, Axel's character in *The Gambler* is paradigmatic of this tendency: 'A gambling addict, for instance, may reach a point where constant gambling is necessary merely to maintain a minimum level of well being'.[37] In other words, far from being *progressively* life altering, Axel's existentialism is cyclical, an eternal return of the same.

Reisz expresses this spatio-temporal impasse through both editing and *mise-en-scène*. At the beginning of the film, the director shoots Caan in a series of frontal windscreen shots as he drives away from the gambling joint. Gradually, we enter Axel's state of mind through a series of subjective flashbacks as he recalls what has just transpired, indicating that he is more disturbed than he would like to admit. Thus the character and Caan's acting tell one thing – the dead-pan, poker 'face' of the gambler, itself an essential 'tool of the trade' – the editing another, namely the rush of fear/will/juice that underlies and feeds the performance. Reisz uses a similar tactic to undercut Axel's 'high' during his win at blackjack. He alternates between low angles down on the green baize of the table as the croupier shuffles and deals the cards, to sharp angles up on Caan so that his head is encircled by the radiating lights of a huge chandelier on the ceiling behind him. This creates a penumbra effect, as if Axel were communing with the gods of *amor fati*. However, just as Axel calls for the winning third card, Reisz flashes back to the gambler dancing with his mother at Lowenthal's birthday party. Only then does he return to Axel and the halo of lights as the gambler intones, 'I am blessed', thus linking his will-to-power with his mother's loan, but more importantly the genealogical legacy of his grandfather. Then, with Billie looking on with a mixture of awe and unabashed desire, Reisz zooms in on Axel to hold the moment, as if to sustain his god-like status for eternity. But the banal, cuckoo-like clarinet from Mahler's *First Symphony* breaks the spell and Axel reluctantly turns to Billie: 'That's it, it's over'. We then flash back one last time to Axel hugging his mother, as if to say: 'Debt repaid'. However, the gratifying emotional effects of this culminating shot are quickly dissipated as we slam cut to Axel's hotel room and see him lying in bed, unable to sleep. All traces of the 'high' have been dispelled: Reisz's gambling Icarus has fallen to earth with a crash. As Dempsey notes, 'Technically and emotionally, the scene has two dimensions: while the images capture the "blessed" state which Axel seeks, the editing expresses its transience, which he cannot accept. The passing of his ecstasy so shatters him that he must gamble more and more, as though he could abolish time by winning as often as possible'.[38]

Reisz expresses the impossibility of this desire through his use of mirrors – both real and metaphorical – establishing an entrapping, crystalline space that captures Axel within a hermetically sealed circuit of repetition. For example, Axel is constantly posing in front of mirrors, whether sparring like Muhummad Ali or Joe Frazier to impress Billie with his athletic prowess, or carefully grooming himself prior to going out or giving a lecture. Reisz links this narcissistic self-identity with his gambling by shooting the entire bathtub scene, where Axel listens to the ill-fated Lakers game, into the bathroom mirror, thereby isolating Axel with his obsession as a form of 'virtual' world beyond human reason. Significantly, when Axel wakes up the next morning, Billie has left him for good. 'It's actually a reverse reflection of what we saw just before the scene of Axel's listening to the game begins', says Gaston. 'At that point he left Billie alone in bed because of his obsession. Now she has left him because of it. That this irony depends on reflective imagery is characteristic of this film. It is a film which is filled with images, parallels, and contrasts which mirror important points. Indeed, it is literally filled with mirrors'.[39] In that sense, the film's final freeze frame – itself shot into a mirror as Axel examines his wound – would be less a moment of existential liberation, of eradicating the self in Toback's sense, than a reiteration of entrapment, a brief pause before releasing Axel once again to the inexorable circuit of the dice throw and his next 'high'.

It is also important to note that this constant but impossible need for 'juice' comes at a great moral price. Toback and Reisz take considerable pains to set up Axel's mother Naomi as a sympathetic ethical foil, reinforced by Jacqueline Brookes' superb performance. After an enervating dip in the ocean following Lowenthal's birthday party, she returns to a waiting Axel where she finally discovers exactly how much he owes the mob: 'Forty four ... thousand ... dollars!' Axel seems resigned, even glib, but Naomi refuses to let him off the hook: 'Are you so naive you don't know what those monsters do with the money you give them? They shoot it right in the arms of ten year-old schoolchildren. I see them every day at the clinic. My God, Axel. Have I been such a failure, that I raised a son to have the morals of a snail?' Reisz cuts to a close-up of Axel: 'Are you gonna help me or not?' Outraged by his lack of ethical proportion, Naomi slaps him hard on the cheek. The message here is obvious: that there is no existentialism without moral awareness and that the lack of a wider social commitment inevitably leads to its dark flipside: nihilism.

Axel's continued blindness to this broader ethic is underlined when he drags the otherwise innocent Spencer into his face-saving scheme. This is eerily foretold in yet another mirror scene early in the film when Axel, running late after his all-night gambling binge, meets Spencer on his way to class. They stop off in the men's room and as the basketball player exits the stall, he passes in front of Axel who is 'doubled' as he stands in front of the mirror while washing his hands. Spencer thus walks between Caan's real and virtual images, between the professor and the gambler, between the mentor and the manipulator, presaging his own future entrapment in Axel's points shaving scheme. Axel may be blind to the import of Spencer's potential moral decline, but Hips is quick to see a useful opportunity. As the bookie points out after the game, not only is Axel in the clear with the mob, but 'As a matter of fact, the way I see it, you've even got a favour coming your way ... D'you think they're just gonna let this guy slip out of their hands? He's got another year of college and then maybe even the pros'. 'He did it for me', says

Axel dismissively. 'He won't do it again'. 'Don't kid yourself', replies Hips. 'Once you ain't a virgin no more you're a whore. Besides, what the hell do you care? You're in the clear'.

Reisz reinforces this tainting of the everyday, workaday world by the insider subculture of gambling and corruption through his symbolic use of colour, particularly the predominant use of green, red and black. Green is, of course, the colour of gaming and pool tables (also, meta-phorically, 'the colour of money') but it is also the colour of Central Park's bucolic landscape and the rooftop tennis court where Axel propo-sitions Naomi for a loan, once again tainting 'healthy' recreation with the mark of vice. Red is the colour of desire and violence, epitomized by Carmine the enforcer's name and convertible, as well as the red dress of the prostitute who slashes Axel's face. However, it is also the colour of Naomi's beach robe as she reads Axel the riot act and the outdoor umbrella at Lowenthal's birthday party, under which Axel pays homage to his grandfather's great deeds, indicating that given the genealogy of Axel's family roots, the worlds of vice and virtue are not only connected but mutually interchangeable. Finally, black is the colour of corrup-tion, personified by the noirish shadows of the mob underworld, Vic Tayback's black business suit and 'Monkey' the sleazy drug addict's outfits. However, by the film's end corruption no longer has to conceal its secrets behind the innocent fronts of illegal gambling dens or dark suburban warehouses: it is literally 'hiding in plain sight', under the garish lights of a college gymnasium as a young black athlete sells his soul to the mob for a quick $5,000. Little wonder that Axel must seek atonement on the mean streets of Harlem.

Dog Soldiers, Reisz's ambitious follow-up to Toback's more intimate character study, expands *The Gambler*'s mutual corruption between 'internal' and 'external' milieux to the broader historical and psycho-logical trauma of the Vietnam War and its counter-cultural corollary, the CIA-controlled South-East Asian heroin trade, which flooded Amer-ican inner cities with addictive drugs throughout the 1960s and 1970s. Based on the National Book Award-winning novel by Robert Stone, the narrative is rooted in the author's first-hand experiences of Saigon's gold and heroin black market – an underworld permeated by the CIA, South Vietnamese army officers, foreign diplomats and journalists – while working as a war correspondent for the British bi-weekly, *INK*. Although the magazine quickly folded, Stone stayed on in Vietnam for six weeks, eventually filing his reports for the *Manchester Guardian*. After his brief stint in Saigon, Stone returned to the United States and became a writer-in-residence at Princeton University, where he began work on the manuscript that would eventually become *Dog Soldiers* and, retitled *Who'll Stop the Rain* for the American market, the basis for Reisz's second Hollywood release.

In the film, thirty-five-year-old John Converse (Michael Moriarty) is an embittered former marine and aspiring playwright/novelist who has spent the last eighteen months working as a freelance journalist in Saigon during the Vietnam War. Traumatized by a murderous attack of 'friendly fire' in Red Field near Krek during the covert invasion of Cambodia, Converse decides, whether through an oblique act of political protest or absurdist self-assertion in the face of a world gone mad, to ship two keys of heroin back to the US, damn the consequences! Converse contacts his local friend Charmian (Gail Strickland), a moneyed American with 'connections' at both the Vietnamese and Washington ends of the drug trade. For $25,000, all John has to do is transport the skag back to Berkeley where her unnamed contacts will collect it from Converse's attractive blonde wife, Marge (Tuesday Weld), a dilaudin addict who works with her father, Bender (David Opatoshu) at Cody's Bookstore on Telegraph Avenue.

Converse is hardly the quintessential 'man of action', so for $2,000 he enlists the help of his ex-marine buddy, Ray Hicks (Nick Nolte), a would-be professional soldier of fortune, 'Samurai Zen Warrior' and small-time marijuana smuggler who is now working as a merchant seaman, shipping military supplies between Saigon and the Bay Area. On arrival in Oakland, Hicks dutifully makes the delivery to Marge's Berkeley home but immediately discovers not only that John has failed to inform her of the drug deal but also that she has no money to pay him. To make matters worse, it turns out that the whole deal has been a frame-up from the beginning. Enlisting John and Marge as easy marks, Charmian has tipped off her old establishment friend Antheil (Anthony Zerbe), a corrupt drug enforcement agent, and the Washington man has unofficially sent two of his goons, Danskin (Richard Masur) and Smitty (Ray Sharkey), to shake down Marge for the skag, thereby purloining the drugs free of shipment charges. However, Charmian and Antheil failed to anticipate that Hicks would act as a courier, and when Danskin and Smitty break into the house, Hicks brutally overpowers them while Marge tries desperately to comfort her hysterical daughter Janey (Shelby Balik). Marge pleads with Hicks to give them the dope, but he knows that make-up deals are impossible when it comes to hard drugs: if they return the skag, Danskin will simply kill them. Alternatively, as Hicks bluntly puts it, 'If you call the cops they'll nail you, they'll nail John, they'll take your kid away. It's YOUR dope'.

After making impromptu arrangements for Janey to stay at her uncle's farm in Canada, Hicks and Marge drive south to Los Angeles and hide out in Hicks's run-down Nissen hut in Topanga Canyon until they can find a suitable buyer for the heroin. Meanwhile, Converse has returned home to Berkeley and discovers from Bender that the deal has already gone bad and that Hicks and Marge have high-tailed it to LA. Returning from Cody's, Converse is abducted by Danskin and Smitty, who torture him in order to learn Marge's whereabouts. Fortunately Antheil intervenes, attempting a more systematic approach by threatening to release Converse to the local Oakland drug syndicates unless he co-operates. However, Converse can't tell him what he doesn't know. Antheil will have to wait for Hicks to make the next move. Back in LA, Marge is undergoing severe withdrawals from the dilaudin and Hicks encourages her to snort some of the heroin in order to keep her afloat. It doesn't take long before she is completely addicted.

Desperate to unload the skag, Hicks contacts Eddie Peace (Charles Haid), an old acquaintance who deals drugs to Hollywood insiders. After some initial sparring, Eddie finally arranges for Hicks to meet an English writer Gerald (James Cranna) and his wife Jody (Timothy Blake) at their Beverly Hills mansion. Gerald is researching a book on drugs and wants to experience the 'hard stuff' at first hand to give his work added authenticity. However, Eddie intends to use Gerald and Jody as his own mark: to inflict Hicks on the unsuspecting couple and exploit their fear for financial gain. Alienated by Gerald's bourgeois pretensions and outraged by Peace's vain, self-indulgent machinations, Hicks springs a surprise of his own. After Eddie and Jody have both shot up, he 'mainlines' Gerald, putting his life in extreme danger. Hicks grabs Marge and the heroin, leaving a wasted Eddie to clean up the 'mess'.

The couple hit the road in a stolen Land Rover and head west towards El Ojo Grande (The Big Eye), a mountain in southern New Mexico, where they hide out in a former Jesuit settlement and latter-day hippy colony, currently owned by Hicks's roshi-cum-mentor, a German Buddhist named Dieter. The foot of the mountain is adorned by a large painted peace sign, which serves as a backdrop to a makeshift stage-cum-amphitheatre. The latter is still wired for sound, and includes a psychedelic light show, triggered from Dieter's house on the summit above. Meanwhile, Eddie exacts a measure of revenge by tipping off Antheil as to Hicks's whereabouts and, with Converse as a co-operative hostage, they all converge on the mountain where they are greeted by Angel (Joaquin Martinez), an equally corrupt Mexican cop from across the adjacent border. With a narrow twenty-four hour grace period before the bust becomes an official FBI raid, their plan is to force Hicks to exchange the heroin for Converse's life and keep the skag for themselves. Unfortunately for Antheil, Dieter's estate manager Galindez

(Jose Carlos Ruiz) deliberately leads Danskin and Smitty up the wrong trail to an impassable ravine that blocks all access to the house. The resulting 'Mexican stand off' buys Hicks valuable time. He switches the heroin with harmless cooking flour and sends an unsuspecting Marge down the mountain to make the exchange.

When Antheil discovers the ruse, Hicks opens fire with an M-70 grenade launcher and all hell breaks loose as the amphitheatre explodes into hallucinatory violence. Galindez triggers the psychedelic light show, and to an ear-splitting combination of feedback and Hank Snow's *Golden Rocket* Hicks provides cover as Marge and Converse make their escape. The 'Zen Warrior' plans to meet them by the railroad tracks the following day. Although Hicks manages to kill Danskin and Smitty, he is shot and severely wounded in the exchange of fire. Nonetheless, he staggers across the desert to the tracks, marching like a good marine along the cross ties before collapsing by the side of the rails where he is discovered dead by John and an extremely distraught Marge. After burying Hicks with suitable military honours, Converse scatters the heroin on the ground and drives off, seconds ahead of the pursuing Antheil and Angel. As Antheil kneels over the skag, desperately scooping its remains into his cupped hands, we hear the sound of Angel's cocked rifle offscreen. The film ends as Marge and John drive away from the camera into the shimmering haze of the desert to face an uncertain future, both for their marriage and their country.

Optioned on the strength of a favourable review in the Paris *Herald-Tribune*, the rights to *Dog Soldiers* were owned by the independent producer, Herb Jaffe (*The Wind and the Lion*, 1975, *Demon Seed*, 1977). Jaffe approached United Artists, who expressed interest only if the producer would agree to Reisz as director. Jaffe immediately balked at the idea: 'We thought of Hal Ashby, Bob Rafelson – there were a lot of directors who interested us', recalled Jaffe. 'But U.A. was very keen on Karel because of what he had done with *The Gambler* – even though the movie didn't work. So it was more Karel's acceptability to U.A. than our desire to have him, because we knew U.A. wanted him … One of our fears with Karel was the seeming death-wish quality of *The Gambler* – Karel's whole idea in the film of rejecting any kind of commercial pandering'.[40] The incompatibility extended to problems of adaptation, as Jaffe and Reisz also argued vehemently over the choice of screenwriter: Reisz was determined that Stone should adapt his own novel, while Jaffe was just as adamantly opposed to the idea. Ultimately, Jaffe was right, for although Reisz and Stone worked for two years on shaping the script, the novelist refused to tamper with either the story or the characters. According to Reisz:

Bob found it very difficult to reduce the novel to the dimensions of a film. The screenplay he wrote would have run very, very long. It would have run for hours, and I actually don't think this is a four-hour story. Bob also had enormous problems of translation – *Dog Soldiers* is an extremely daring mixture of interior and exterior narration. A very large part of the novel is the speculation of the characters about their predicament – a kind of free association between what is happening and their past and the political scene. That's something that's almost completely inaccessible in a film.[41]

They also quarrelled over the film's proposed title. 'Dog Soldiers' refers to the elite Cheyenne Warriors who worked outside the tribe's traditional martial conventions. Each year they took suicide vows to protect the collective nation from their enemies, much like Hicks's self-appointed role as the lone Samurai who heroically ensures John and Marge's escape from Antheil at the end of the film. Eventually the title was changed to *Who'll Stop the Rain*, a reference to the Creedence Clearwater Revival song that provides a telling soundtrack commentary of lost innocence throughout the film. According to Reisz, 'The name "Dog Soldiers" implied it was about fighting, and this is not a war film. I also felt that there might be confusion with the more popular novel, "The Dogs of War."'[42] Although he ultimately came to respect the final film, particularly the actors' performances, Stone always hated the title: 'Never use a Swedish diphthong to begin a movie title with – like "Who'll." I mean it's a ridiculous title, an absurd, moronic title. God knows what moron came up with it'.[43]

Eventually, Reisz brought in Stone's writer friend, Judith Rascoe, on the strength of an unrealized script that she had written for Nicolas Roeg: 'We made some changes of course. You see, my thing about adapting a novel is that the way to do it is to very carefully take out whole lumps and treat the bit you keep in detail rather than doing a précis of the plot. A lot of events were dropped. We dropped the character of Dieter [the guru] entirely – that was a great surgical excision'.[44] In addition, Rascoe and Stone made considerable changes to Marge's character. In the book, she is a junkie, works at a seedy San Francisco porn theatre and is sexually promiscuous, so that her relationship with Hicks is rooted in her dependency for sex, drugs and survival rather than the mutual affection that develops over the course of the film. She already knows of John's scheme to smuggle the heroin and gets a phone call from Hicks the night before to set up the deal. In the film, she is more of an innocent victim, which adds considerable tension and confusion to the scene when Hicks first arrives at the Berkeley house. 'There's a technical reason for that', notes Reisz. 'The character works in the novel because Stone is able to take time out and give you a whole chapter about her present life, her history, and her state of mind. You believe that she would conspire in such an enterprise because Stone was able to create a state of mind for the character. But in the screenplay there is more progression to the Marge character – the dope is a new element in her life rather than something she accepts from the beginning. The arc of her character now seems more cinematic than novelistic'.[45] The film also makes more of a concession to an upbeat ending: 'We are left with rather more hope than in the novel [where Antheil and Angel recover the skag and continue their partnership]. Marge and Converse survive', affirms Reisz, 'and I want the audience to wish them well. I want the audience to be happy that they survive. This is a paradoxical story: The people who are involved in sending the heroin are the people we are rooting for. It's really a picture about people caught up in an evil time. I think of Marge and Hicks and Converse as all being decent and moral people who are blown by the winds of time. I want the audience to be with them, to think [of] them as fallible and weak like the rest of us'.[46] For once Jaffe concurred, observing that, 'We've got to have some kind of hope for the audience because otherwise we are in the toilet'.[47]

However, it would be a mistake to say that the film condones the characters' misguided existentialism. As in the case of Axel Freed, Reisz undercuts the subjective indulgence of both Converse and Hicks to draw attention to the dangers of an immoral individualism by portraying both the war and its seeming antidote, the escapism of the drug culture, as twin jaws of the same trap. Both men turn to Nietzsche's *amor fati* from a helpless sense of the absurdity of war, but they apply its tenets in very different ways. Firstly, John's existentialism is fuelled by fear, for as Stone tells us in the book, 'Fear was extremely important to Converse; morally speaking it was the basis of his life. It was the medium through which he perceived his own soul, the formula through which he could confirm his own existence. I am afraid, Converse reasoned, therefore I am'.[48] Fear lies at the root of Converse's reaction to the 'friendly fire' episode in Cambodia, and it plays an important role in his decision to deal the heroin. Reisz outlines this reasoning in an important early scene where John is shown in the half-light, writing a letter to Marge in which he recounts an almost surreal episode: 'Military command has decided that elephants are enemy agents because they carry supplies for the Viet Cong. So now, we're stampeding the elephants and gunning them down from the air. Of course, I filed a suitably outraged story about it. But that was my last one'. John and his voice-over are cross-cut with flashbacks to the Cambodia attack in which the journalist stands helplessly on the battlefield, clutching his camera and staring at the carnage, his hand shaking as he tries to hold onto something tangible. It is at this point that John becomes fully aware of his own impotence, for as he tells Marge, 'I have no more cheap moral to draw from all this death'. Instead, he has taken a specific action of his own. He tells Marge to expect Hicks's arrival and to pay him $1,000: 'I've started something here that I can't stop. And it's the right thing, I know'. Then, as Converse approaches Charmian's house to broker the deal, he continues his voice-over as if to explain his reasoning: 'You see, in a world where elephants are pursued by flying men, people are just naturally going to want to get high'.

This is John's Vietnam epiphany, in which drugs and violence make natural bedfellows. Yet it is also a purely *intellectual* justification of his actions – in a way he knows his plan can never succeed – induced by loss of selfhood and his emotional and moral inability to digest the horror that surrounds him. Thus, he confronts his own irrelevance through the prank of the drug deal, but he really has no idea what game he is playing, by what rules, or how it will turn out. In effect, it's a prank for the sake of playing pranks, detached from the ramifications of its own actions. That is why Michael Moriarty's understated, almost 'lazy' performance is absolutely appropriate, because it perfectly captures Converse's refusal of further agency once he has set his plan in motion. Like Axel at the gaming tables, John has given himself up to the random luck of the dice throw. Indeed, after his capture by Antheil's men, he seems to bask in his helplessness, embracing a stoic fatalism that precludes his need to act, as if to say, 'All you need is fear'. Unfortunately, John is deluding himself. He pays lip service to moral objections against the war and to exacerbating drug habits back home by seeing himself as a victim of an inevitable, almost mythic apocalyptic history. 'In this view', observes Frank Shelton, 'Vietnam does not change people; rather it is the crucible in which their natures are revealed. What Converse learns about himself is his own emptiness: he realizes that there will be no novel. In addition he has never really embraced any moral principles upon which he was willing to act'.[49] The film refuses to give him such an easy out by instead show-casing the devastating effects of his solipsism, both on his innocent wife and child and on the colonized 'other'. In a key exchange of dialogue, as John cements the heroin deal with Hicks, he states, 'I feel that this is the first real thing I've ever done in my life. I don't know what the other stuff was about. Don't they say that this is where everybody finds out who they are?' 'Yeah', replies Hicks. 'What a bummer for the gooks'. What a bummer indeed.

Where Converse is passive and intellectual, Hicks acts first and ratio-nalizes afterwards. In other words, he is a pure sociopath. Also, as Ed

Roginski points out, 'He possesses two other things of vital importance: the knowledge that he cannot internalize a sense of social conscience because none exists – we are a country, a nation, a world of psychopaths; more importantly, he has the knowledge and the desire to treat not the world's condition, but his own'.[50] Like Converse, Hicks's existentialism in the novel is born of a traumatic episode in Vietnam, in his case 'The Battle of Bob Hope', where Ray and his fellow marines were sent on an unnecessary patrol and massacred by the Viet Cong as punishment for sneaking off to see comedian Bob Hope at a United Services Organizations concert. Since then Hicks has adopted Nietzsche's idea of will-to-power through a Zen-like faith in the Samurai code (a poster for Akira Kurosawa's *Yojimbo* hangs by the door of his Topanga Canyon hut). As Dieter explains Hicks's character in the book, 'There was absolutely no difference between thought and action for him … It was exactly the same. An enormous self-respect. Whatever he believed in he had to embody absolutely … He's trapped in a samurai fantasy – an American one. He has to be the Lone Ranger, the great desperado – he has to win all the epic battles single-handed … It may not be a very original conception but he's quite good at it'.[51] This is, of course, not unlike Axel's similar respect for obsolescent rugged individualists like Buffalo Bill and A. R. Lowenthal, but Hicks's existentialism is completely amoral. Like the Cheyenne Dog Soldiers, he internalizes the danger from Antheil and his goons, makes it part of himself, and thus moves beyond Converse's existential terror into a Zen-like tranquillity. This allows him to see events less in terms of right and wrong but, like Nietzsche, as 'beyond good and evil', as a question of pure Machiavellian power. The heroin for Hicks, as he explains to Marge, is simply another object, which belongs to whoever controls it, and he follows its grail logically and unquestioningly to the bitter end.

Both Stone's novel and Reisz's film subscribe to the New Left's received wisdom of the period, namely that the contagious seeds of the war's atavistic madness lay not in the uncivilized 'horror' of the colonial societies themselves – a racist, Orientalist perspective epitomized by Joseph Conrad's *Heart of Darkness* (1899) and subsequently mythologized by Marlon Brando's 'insane' Colonel Kurtz in Francis Ford Coppola's 1980 Vietnam epic, *Apocalypse Now!* – but at home, at the heart of the American Dream. As Clancy Sigal points out, 'During the Vietnam period, a radical shibboleth was "the war at home," meaning that the South-East Asia bloodbath had its moral and political equivalents in the USA which had to be confronted in order to stop the shooting war. Reisz not only illustrates this idea intelligently, but by subtle use of colour and sets also manages to suggest that perhaps the Vietnam War was an extension of an unresolved conflict that originated in the United States itself'.[52]

For Stone, the source of this corruption lay less with clear-cut socio-logical issues of class or inherent racism than with the growing apolitical nature of the counter-culture itself. This was particularly true on the West Coast, where the lure of alternative communal lifestyles, 'free love', and affordable LSD and heroin were already attracting droves of hippies and 'flower children' to Berkeley and San Francisco's Haight-Ashbury district by mid-decade. Perhaps the most notorious of these counter-cultural manifestations were Ken Kesey's famed 'Acid Tests', which began in 1965 in the woods of La Honda, the spiritual home of the Merry Pranksters, whose journeys across America in their psyche-delically painted bus 'Furthur', driven by former Beat Generation icon Neal Cassady, were immortalized in Tom Wolfe's *The Electric Kool-Aid Acid Test*. It was here that invited guests, including the Hells Angels, imbibed LSD-spiked Kool Aid and danced to the ear-deafening music of the nascent Grateful Dead while the local police stood watchful guard between the surrounding trees.[53]

More importantly, not only were Stone and Kesey lifelong friends but the writer was also the co-driver of 'Further' when Kesey was hiding as a fugitive from the FBI in Manzanillo, Mexico, following his mari-juana bust. Stone thus knew from first hand that the counter-cultural guru's first introduction to LSD was in 1959, when Kesey, at that time a graduate student in creative writing at Stanford University, volun-teered to take part in a government drug research programme at Menlo Park Veterans Hospital. The programme tested a variety of psychoac-tive drugs such as LSD (which was still legal at the time), psilocybin, mescaline, and amphetamine IT-290. Over a period of several weeks, Kesey ingested these hallucinogens and wrote of his drug-induced expe-riences for government researchers, thus planting the beginnings of the West Coast counter-culture in the military establishment, which would haunt it throughout its existence.[54] As a result, the war machine controlled the drug culture on the domestic front long before the CIA's more publicized involvement with heroin trafficking through their Air America operation in Laos and Vietnam.

One of the advantages of making *Dog Soldiers* from the hindsight of 1978 was that it afforded Reisz the opportunity to observe these connec-tions with a much more dispassionate and objective eye. Recalling the counter-culture's idealism towards drugs in the mid-1960s, Reisz explained that,

> the drug dream – that Californian dream of enlightenment – was in its inception a very clean dream, a moral one. People thought that they

could purify themselves through joining the movement. And of course that dream collapsed with a horrible thump. Now, looking at that period from the vantage point of history, it seems very different. At the time the hippie culture and the drug culture seemed so diametrically opposed to the people who were going to Vietnam, and of course the protest movement was very much associated with it. Now it begins to look like one thing, and the moral choices that the protest movement made were often rather dubious. Many Americans in their thirties look back on that period rather ruefully. So those people have on the whole responded to the film very well. Older Americans have responded to it very badly. They didn't want to be reminded of that cold wind that was blowing.[55]

As in the case of *The Gambler*, Reisz expresses this chilly undercurrent through careful attention to *mise-en-scène* and editing, collapsing the clear-cut difference between the war and domestic fronts. For example, when we first meet Marge in her Berkeley home, the living room is half-lit in red, yellow and orange hues that evoke the exact same colours of the opening Cambodia sequence. This metonymic connection between domesticity and modern warfare suggests that the violence of the Vietnam battlefields existed as part of the 'California Dream' long before it was exported to South-East Asia, a point reinforced by the subsequent break-in of the film's nominal psychopaths, Danskin and Smitty. As Stephen H. Knox aptly puts it, 'The movement is from orient to occident but also from West to East. Violence is reflexive; it ricochets from Vietnam back to the testing grounds of its origins'.[56]

Reisz extends the point further by tying this violence directly to the counter-culture itself, through Hicks's involvement with Dieter. Although he is physically absent from the film, Dieter's philosophical influence haunts Hicks's specific brand of existentialism, and if there were any doubts that the guru were modelled directly on Kesey himself, they are dispelled by the obvious similarities between the psychedelic light show at El Ojo Grande and the Acid Tests at La Honda. In addition, Hicks's death by the railroad tracks is a direct homage to that of Neal Cassady, who died under similar circumstances in Mexico in 1968, metaphorically reinforcing Kesey's famous dictum that, 'Either you're on the bus or off the bus'. However, Stone makes it clear in the novel that the commune and its accompanying ideals of peace, love and contemplation were corrupted from within by Dieter himself, because of his succumbing to the seductions of the American Dream. As the guru explains to Marge,

'Then it occurred to me that if I applied the American style – which I didn't really understand – if I pushed a little, speeded things up a little, we might break into something really cosmic. The secular world was falling apart. Nobody knew what they were doing or what they wanted. There was a great ear open. Waiting for something ... I was sitting up here hearing it! What they wanted' – with a thrust of his chin he indicated the world below – 'I had. I knew! So I thought, a little push, a little shove, a little something extra to shake it loose. And I ended up as Doctor Dope'.[57]

For his part, Hicks is pragmatic enough to know that the commune ideal is dead: he has already transferred his allegiance to another, more individualistic code. Moreover, Dieter's amphitheatre, the temple of the new culture, is a shadow of its former self, a symbol of the hippie dream gone sour, and it is no accident that its resuscitation in the film is connected less to the liberating psychic effects of free love and mind-expanding hallucinogens than a violent shoot-out between warring drug factions. Moreover, the light show itself, with its shuddering, strobe-like effects, is once again reminiscent of the opening Cambodia sequence, further cementing the connection between the war, drugs and a counter-culture gone horribly bad.

Dog Soldiers is a watershed film in Reisz's career because it marks the culmination of his long relationship to the New Left, beginning with his involvement with the CND and *March to Aldermaston* and his theoretical writings on the social role of documentary for *Universities and Left Review* in the late 1950s. His collaboration with Stone reflects his growing acknowledgement of an irreparable rift between organized politics, rooted in party discipline and commitment to external social change, and the counter-cultural idea of living in and for oneself as a community of enlightened individuals. The former idea was rooted in Marx – a question of changing the world through direct action – the latter in visionary, utopian thinkers such as Emerson, Thoreau and Rimbaud, whereby a change in consciousness will necessitate a concomitant change in life itself. However, as Todd Gitlin acknowledges, the two positions were never mutually exclusive:

> Despite these tensions, there was a direct line from the expressive politics of the New Left to the counterculture's let-it-all-hang-out way of life. Some of the SNCC [Student Nonviolent Coordinating Committee] 'floaters' followed it, in fact, when they shifted to LSD; SDS's prairie power generation of 1965 saw no barrier between radical politics and drug culture. The New Left's founding impulse said from the start: Create the future in the present; sit in right now at the lunch counter, as if race didn't count. Historically the traditions were tangled, intertwined.[58]

Yet *Dog Soldiers* eschews this possibility of hybridity. Instead, like many members of the American New Left of the late 1960s, it draws a clear line in the sand between (counter) culture and politics, with a view to preventing the inevitable tainting of one by the other. The efficacy of this position was borne out by Tom Wolfe. Writing in *The Electric Kool-Aid Acid Test* in 1968, he noted long before the overt visible decline of the counter-culture that acid was destroying the viability and integrity of left-wing political activism in California. By October 1966, for example, the so-called 'heads' were, like John Converse, absorbed in pranks rather than organized politics. Instead of supporting the oppressors by playing their kind of ineffectual political games and simply copying their underhand tactics, the 'heads', with the help of psychedelic chemicals, were exploring the 'infinite regions of human consciousness'.[59]

Kesey, as one might expect, was at the forefront of this new tactic, epitomized in autumn 1965 when he accepted an invitation from Paul Krassner of the Vietnam Day Committee to speak at a huge anti-war rally at UC Berkeley. Kesey's speech was shockingly anti-activist: 'You know, you're not gonna stop this war with this rally, by marching', he proclaimed. 'That's what *they* do ... They hold rallies and they march ... They've been having wars for ten thousand years and you're not gonna stop it this way ... Ten thousand years, and this is the game they play to do it ... holding rallies and having marches ... and that's the game you're playing ... their game'.[60] 'There's only one thing to do', he continued, 'and that's everybody just look at it, look at the war, and turn your backs and say ... Fuck it ...'[61] By October 1966, even the fervent civil rights activist Paul Hawken was cynically referring to the Berkeley anti-war activists as 'A bunch of fraternity men in their Mustangs!' Needless to say, Kesey's anti-activist view was endorsed by the great acid guru himself, Timothy Leary. 'Leary pitched his tent within the non-political counterculture, although he liked to be friendly with anybody who was anybody', writes David Caute. 'He contemptuously dismissed conventional political action; the Free Speech Movement at Berkeley, for example, was "playing right onto the game boards of the administration and police." Indeed, any social action, "unless it's based on expanded consciousness," was simply "robot behaviour." Why attempt to create a better university? The only way was to "turn on, tune in and drop out."'[62] Leary described the New Left as 'young men with menopausal minds'. He urged: 'Don't vote. Don't politic. Don't petition. You can't do *anything* about America politically'.[63]

It is extremely significant that Leary fully endorsed R. D. Laing, the radical psychoanalytic force behind David Mercer's conception of Morgan: 'He weaves science-religion-art-experience into the slickest board game of our time'.[64] However, while Reisz's sceptical indictment of Morgan's madcap, symbolic lip-service to Marxist icons seemed both prescient and justified in 1966, when the British New Left were mired knee-deep in theoretical debate, *Dog Soldiers* seems to be fighting a rearguard action in a factional war that has already been lost. If there were any doubt, then *Everybody Wins*, Reisz's final entry into the political stakes (in which Nick Nolte once again plays a compromised seeker of truth), is clear proof that only an absurdist cynicism can prevail when conventional moral values have lost all meaning. Maybe Axel Freed and John Converse were right to roll the dice after all.

Notes

1 Friedrich Nietzsche, *On the Genealogy of Morals*, trans. Walter Kaufmann and R. J. Hollingdale (New York, Vintage Books, 1989), p. 163.
2 Fyodor Dostoyevsky, *Notes from Underground*, trans. Andrew R. MacAndrew (New York, Signet Classics, 1961), p. 87.
3 Canby, 'The Loves of Isadora', p. 33:1.
4 Oakes, 'New Reputations: Karel Reisz, Break for Commercial', p. 858.
5 Gaston, *Karel Reisz*, p. 149.
6 Alas, like Mercer's *A Suitable Case for Treatment*, the teleplay has been lost.
7 Alexander Walker, *National Heroes: British Cinema in the Seventies and Eighties* (London, Harrap, 1985), p. 115.
8 Quoted in *ibid.*, p. 132.
9 Carl Foreman, quoted in *ibid.*, p. 134.
10 Taylor, 'Tomorrow the World: Some Reflections on the Un-Englishness of English Films', p. 81.
11 Reisz, quoted in *ibid.*, p. 82.
12 Raymond Durgnat, 'Britannia Waives the Rules: The Angry Young Cinema Grows Out', *Film Comment*, Vol. 12, No. 4, July–August 1976, p. 51.
13 Lindsay Anderson, interview with Dennis Barker, *The Guardian*, 28 August 1974, quoted in Walker, *National Heroes: British Cinema in the Seventies and Eighties*, p. 135
14 See Colin MacCabe's 'Realism and the Cinema: Notes on Some Brechtian Theses' in *Screen*, Vol. 15, No. 2, Summer 1974 for a particularly negative assessment of Anderson.
15 Walker, *Hollywood, England*, p. 454.
16 Chartoff and Winkler's impressive credits include *Point Blank* (John Boorman, 1967), *They Shoot Horses, Don't They?* (Sydney Pollack, 1969), *Rocky* (John G. Avildsen, 1976), Martin Scorsese's *New York, New York* (1977) and *Raging Bull* (1980) and *The Right Stuff* (Philip Kaufman, 1983).
17 Irwin Winkler, quoted in Robert Chartoff and Irwin Winkler, 'Dialogue on Film', *American Film*, Vol. 2, No. 3, December–January 1977, p. 40.
18 For more on Toback see Jennifer M. Wood, 'Invitation to a Head Fracture: Straight Talk from Maverick *Harvard Man* James Toback', *Moviemaker*, Vol. 2, No. 7, 2002, www.moviemaker.com/hop/15/directing.html, and Peter Biskind, 'Muscular Contractions', *Sight and Sound*, Vol. 15, No. 2, February 2005, pp. 24–6.
19 Reisz, quoted in McFarlane, *An Autobiography of British Cinema*, p. 479.
20 Robert Chartoff, quoted in Chartoff and Winkler, 'Dialogue on Film', p. 40.
21 Reisz, quoted in Gow, 'Outsiders: Karel Reisz in an Interview with Gordon Gow', p. 16.
22 In an oblique reference to a real life shocker, the impossible had happened: one

of Axel's picks, UCLA, lost 61–57 to Oregon State, snapping the Bruins' record 50-game, Pacific 8 Conference win streak.

23 Kennedy, 'Minute Reisz: Six Earlier Films', p. 29.
24 Reisz, quoted in Gow, 'Outsiders: Karel Reisz in an Interview with Gordon Gow', p. 17.
25 Gaston, *Karel Reisz*, p. 113.
26 Reisz, quoted in Gow, 'Outsiders: Karel Reisz in an Interview with Gordon Gow', p. 16.
27 Quoted in Wood, 'Invitation to a Head Fracture'.
28 Vincent Canby, '*The Gambler*', *New York Times*, 3 October 1974, p. 50:1.
29 Dostoyevsky, *Notes from Underground*, pp. 171–2.
30 *Ibid.*, p. 195.
31 Michael Dempsey, '*The Gambler*', *Film Quarterly*, Vol. 28, No. 3, Spring 1975, p. 50.
32 Carnovsky was blacklisted in 1950 because he refused to 'name names' before HUAC. His career was resurrected by theatrical producer John Houseman, who cast Carnovsky in a New York stage production of Ibsen's *An Enemy of the People*, where he appropriately played a character whose refusal to compromise his ideals ends in persecution and exile.
33 Dempsey, '*The Gambler*', p. 50.
34 Fielding's credits include *Advise and Consent* (1962) for Otto Preminger; *The Wild Bunch* (1969) for Sam Peckinpah, for which he received an Academy Award nomination; and *Straw Dogs* (1971).
35 Pauline Kael, 'The Current Cinema: The Actor and the Star', *New Yorker*, 14 October 1974, p. 174.
36 Daniel Read and Peter Roelofsma, 'Hard Choices and Weak Wills: The Theory of Intrapersonal Dilemmas', *Philosophical Psychology*, Vol. 12, No. 3, September 1999, p. 348.
37 *Ibid.*, p. 349.
38 Dempsey, '*The Gambler*', p. 51.
39 Gaston, *Karel Reisz*, p. 116–17.
40 Herb Jaffe, quoted in Stephen Zito, '*Dog Soldiers*: Novel into Film', *American Film*, September 1977, p. 10.
41 Reisz, quoted in *ibid.*, p. 12.
42 Reisz, quoted in Betty Jeffries Demby, 'Festivals: Cannes 1978', *Filmmakers Newsletter*, Vol. 11, No. 11, September 1978, p. 64.
43 Robert Stone, quoted in interview with Dwight Garner, 'The Apostle of the Strung-Out: The *Salon* Interview, Robert Stone', 14 April 1997. Accessed 5 July 2005. www.salon.com/april97/stone970414.html.
44 Reisz, quoted in Zito, '*Dog Soldiers*: Novel into Film', p. 13.
45 *Ibid.*
46 *Ibid.*
47 Herb Jaffe, quoted in *ibid.*, p. 10.
48 Robert Stone, *Dog Soldiers* (Boston and New York, Houghton Mifflin Company, 1973), p. 42.
49 Frank W. Shelton, 'Robert Stone's *Dog Soldiers*: Vietnam Comes Home to America', *Critique: Studies in Modern Fiction*, Vol. 24, No. 2, Winter 1983, p. 75.
50 Ed Roginski, '*Who'll Stop the Rain*', *Film Quarterly*, Vol. 32, No. 2, Winter 1978–79, p. 59.
51 Stone, *Dog Soldiers*, pp. 271–2.
52 Clancy Sigal, 'Vietnam Wound', *The Listener*, Vol. 112, No. 2870, 9 August 1984, p. 33.
53 Kesey eventually moved the Acid Tests into public places such as the Longshore-

man's Hall, Muir Beach, or musical events at Bill Graham's Fillmore West in San Francisco.

54 Todd Gitlin, *The Sixties: Years of Hope, Days of Rage* (New York, Bantam Books, 1987), p. 206. Kesey subsequently wrote *One Flew Over the Cuckoo's Nest*, which was successfully filmed by Milos Forman in 1975, winning all of the top five Oscars.

55 Reisz, quoted in Gow, 'Outsiders: Karel Reisz in an Interview with Gordon Gow', p. 13.

56 Stephen H. Knox, 'A Cup of Salt for an O.D.: *Dog Soldiers* as Anti-Apocalypse', *The Journal of General Education*, Vol. 34, No. 1, Spring 1982, p. 61.

57 Stone, *Dog Soldiers*, p. 272.

58 Gitlin, *The Sixties: Years of Hope, Days of Rage*, p. 213.

59 Not all 'heads' shared this view *tout court*. Yippie spokesman, Jerry Rubin, advocated the use of marijuana, LSD and mescaline but drew the line at heroin, which was 'the government's most powerful counter revolutionary agent, a form of germ warfare. Since they can't get us back into their system, they try to destroy us through heroin', he said. Quoted in Caute, *The Year of the Barricades: A Journey Through 1968*, p. 60.

60 Tom Wolfe, *The Electric Kool-Aid Acid Test* (New York, Farrar, Straus and Giroux and Bantam Books, 1968), p. 222.

61 *Ibid.*, pp. 223–4.

62 Caute, *The Year of the Barricades: A Journey Through 1968*, pp. 57–8.

63 Quoted in Martin A. Lee and Bruce Shlain, *Acid Dreams: The CIA, LSD and the Sixties Rebellion* (New York, Grove Press, 1985), p. 166.

64 Quoted in Caute, *The Year of the Barricades: A Journey Through 1968*, p. 58.

A sentimental education:
The French Lieutenant's Woman (1981)

9

But the more these conscious illusions of the ruling classes are shown to be false and the less they satisfy common sense, the more dogmatically they are asserted and the more deceitful, moralizing and spiritual becomes the language of established society. (Karl Marx, *German Ideology*, 1845–46)

I'm interested in the side of existentialism which deals with freedom: the business of whether we do have freedom, whether we do have free will, to what extent you can change your life, choose yourself, and all the rest of it. Most of my major characters have been involved in this Sartrian concept of authenticity and inauthenticity. (John Fowles)[1]

The desire for verification is understandable but cannot always be satisfied. There are no hard distinctions between what is real and what is unreal, nor between what is true and what is false. The thing is not necessarily either true or false; it can be both true and false. (Harold Pinter)[2]

Almost thirty years before the release of *The French Lieutenant's Woman*, Reisz published 'Substance into Shadow', an essay on filmic adaptations of novels, in Roger Manvell's annual Pelican review, *The Cinema 1952*. After surveying the 1940s Hollywood screen versions of William Faulkner's *Intruder in the Dust* (1948), Dashiell Hammett's *The Maltese Falcon* (1930), Ernest Hemingway's *To Have and Have Not* (1937) and Harry Brown's *A Walk in the Sun* (1944), Reisz concluded that, 'The relative success and failure of these adaptations show how limited are the kinds of novel which lend themselves to film treatment … Indeed, the more fully the novelist avails himself of the freedoms of his medium, the less likely is his novel to be adaptable into a film'.[3] According to Reisz, the most successful of these adaptations tended to derive from predominantly realist novels (such as *The Maltese Falcon*) where largely mimetic descriptions and verbal dialogue could be translated directly into theatre and film language with a minimum amount of formal or structural change. In contrast, a large number of twentieth-century works notable for more experimental modernist strategies such as self-reflexivity, Brechtian alienation (*V-Effekt*), subjective fantasy or interior stream-of-consciousness monologue in the vein of Faulkner, James Joyce or Virginia Woolf, precluded a realist approach and often forced screenwriters and directors into a clumsy use of voice-over narration or contrived visual metaphor and analogy. This is particularly problematic in the case of Clarence Brown's 1949 adaptation of *Intruder in the Dust*, because at the novel's core lies the moral awakening of a sixteen-year-old white boy, 'Chick' Mallison, and his painful coming to terms with the local community's determination to lynch an innocent black man, Lucas Beauchamp. For long stretches of the text, Faulkner forsakes linear plot in favour of chronicling Chick's internal conflicts. According to Reisz, the film does little to convey this interior struggle, instead opting to heighten the didactic parts of the novel, producing a distorted oversimplification of Faulkner's moral views: 'For all its striving for accuracy, *Intruder in the Dust* captures only small elements of Faulkner's novel without giving it anything in compensation'.[4]

Instead of strict mimesis, Reisz called for a *creative* dialogue between novel and film in an attempt to formulate a workable cinematic strategy that would allow the filmmaker to push the parameters of his art without undermining the essence and narrative content of his literary source. The article thus gives us an early clue to Reisz's eventual approach to adapting John Fowles's bestseller, *The French Lieutenant's Woman*, for as he notes, 'Adapting another man's novel does not absolve the adaptor from the necessity of creating an integrated work within his own medium, nor from the need of starting from a consistent, clearly defined conception. His conception may take the form of wishing to reproduce the balance and emphasis of the original. Or it may be new: the adaptor may treat the novelist's subject as more or less raw material and interpret it afresh in the light of his own creative personality. Though the two forms are different, both are legitimate'.[5] While the adaptation of *Dog Soldiers* clearly takes the former approach, the complex narrative weave of Fowles's book necessitated a far more radical strategy. As Reisz explained to Harlan Kennedy: 'You don't have to be faithful to anything, you have to make a variation on the themes of the novel which, a., is a film, not a filmed novel, and b., is a film in which you can put your feelings and your associations ... The whole business of being faithful is a nonsensical aim'.[6]

This creative approach is particularly necessary for *The French Lieutenant's Woman* because the novel, first published in 1969, unfolds in dual, often contradictory registers, what Fowles calls a 'stereoscopic vision'. Firstly, there is an overt tension between the historical context of the Victorian story itself and the retrospective knowledge of the mid-twentieth century narrator who is telling it (a narrator who is not neces-sarily synonymous with Fowles himself, even though he would like to trick us into thinking so). Secondly, there is also a philosophical dialectic between the artist and the product of his creation, which contrasts the role of the author as an autocratic fabricator of fictions with broader underlying issues of freedom of choice, both from the perspective of the characters within the novel – can they have free will independent of authorial intent? – as well as the productive, interpretative role of the reader to creatively defy and transcend the omniscience of narration. The novel's overall thesis is that we can only express ourselves through the language and cultural artefacts of our own age, that what we might call our 'will-to-power' is necessarily limited by the choices and orthodoxies offered to us by our respective epochs. Fowles expresses this impasse or *aporia* by using the Victorians' struggle towards a nascent existentialism (with all of its understandable fears and self-loathing, as we saw in the case of Dostoyevsky's 'underground man') as a prism through which to understand the difficulties of living authentically through free will in our own modern world.

So, an obvious question arises: why not write a contemporary British equivalent of Camus's *L'Etranger* (1942) or Sartre's *La Nausée* (1938)? 'The sort of novel that Camus and Sartre wrote – it's like the *nouveau roman* – I don't think you can do it in English', argues Fowles. 'It's something that's grown out of the texture of the language; it's dependent upon being able to write in a very metaphorical way and having that tradi-tion behind you. I don't think the English tradition, which is inherently pragmatic and realistic, can do it'.[7] Instead, Fowles turned to the very same novelistic form favoured by the Victorians themselves, namely Thomas Hardy's richly plotted, multi-chaptered provincial novel along the lines of *A Pair of Blue Eyes* (1873) and *The Return of the Native* (1878). Fowles even goes so far as to emulate another great Victorian novelist, Thackeray, by using a self-reflexive narrator as the extra-diegetic 'stage manager' of events: 'Thackeray was a great one for saying, dear reader I am now going to do this, or dear reader you're quite wrong, this isn't what really happened. My book is very much like that'.[8] However, there is also a major difference from the nineteenth-century tradition because Fowles's narrator is the product of a much later age – the late 1960s – when, under the radical influence of structuralism and post-structur-alism, the omniscience of both authorship and narration was seen as a contingent, and therefore highly questionable, *device*. The narrator's function, as Neil Sinyard rightly points out, is much closer to being a

'Brechtian alienation device designed insistently to draw attention to the novel as a contrived fiction rather than a mirror of life'.[9] As the narrator admits early in the book, 'If I have pretended until now to know my characters' minds and innermost thoughts, it is because I am writing in (just as I have assumed some of the vocabulary and "voice" of) a convention universally accepted at the time of my story: that the novelist stands next to God. He may not know all, yet he tries to pretend that he does. But I live in the age of Alain Robbe-Grillet and Roland Barthes; if this is a novel, it cannot be a novel in the modern sense of the word'.[10] Instead, following Barthes, it would be more advantageous to read the book and its advocacy of existentialism as a hybrid *text* that must be produced in the very act of reading (and, more importantly, re-reading), so that the Victorian and modern eras can effectively deconstruct each other, opening up a deeper insight into their basic historical assumptions.

The Victorian story, with its melodramatic love triangle and 'Upstairs–Downstairs' domestic class structure, is typical of its time and would have provided the perfect source for a lavish BBC costume drama. The novel is set in March 1867 in the picturesque Dorset seaside town of Lyme Regis. The date is significant, as it marks a period of eight years since the publication of Charles Darwin's *The Origin of the Species* (1859) and four years since the release of geologist Sir Charles Lyell's *The Antiquity of Man* (1863), groundbreaking scientific works that shook the prevailing creationist orthodoxy to its foundations. Even more ominously, six months later, in September 1867, Volume 1 of Karl Marx's *Das Kapital* appeared in Hamburg, imbuing the age with the spectre of communism. Closer to home, the British parliament passed Benjamin Disraeli's Second Reform Bill, which expanded the franchise by 1,500,000 male householders.[11] Thus, although the bourgeois Victorian world, with its outward façade of class and economic stability and the absoluteness of religious and moral duty, appeared to be at its zenith, it contained the seeds of new energies and ideas, which would ultimately drag it, kicking and screaming, into the modernist era.

In the 'Upstairs' context, Fowles's chief protagonist is thirty-two-year-old Charles Smithson (played by Jeremy Irons in the film), an amateur palaeontologist, geologist and enthusiastic Darwinian. The sole heir to the baronetcy and wealth of his aging but childless Uncle Robert, Charles is currently living off his late father's diminished fortune. Widely travelled, liberal, a 'healthy agnostic' and 'intelligent idler', Charles has come to Lyme because of his interest in the echinoderm, a petrified sea urchin commonly found along the flint beds of the rugged Undercliff that overlooks the town. Accompanied by his cockney servant, Sam (Hilton McRae), Charles is also in Lyme for more sentimental reasons: he is about to propose marriage to twenty-one-year-old Ernestina Freeman (Lynsey Baxter), the pretty but thoroughly pampered and conventional daughter of a London draper and department store magnate.[12] Ernestina is making her annual visit to Dorset to see her maternal aunt, Mrs Tranter (Charlotte Mitchell). Meanwhile, 'Downstairs', the ambitious Sam also has designs of his own, romantic – in the case of Mrs Tranter's sexually active maid, Mary (Emily Morgan) – as well as professional. Sam plans to leave Charles's employ, open a draper's shop of his own and rise into the petit bourgeoisie, working his way up the class ladder like his role model, Ernestina's father, Mr Freeman (Peter Vaughan).

These best-laid plans are shattered when, while out walking with his new fiancée, Charles spots Sarah Woodruff (Meryl Streep), also known as 'Poor Tragedy' or 'The French Lieutenant's Woman', staring out to sea from the precarious edge of Lyme's famous sea wall, the Cobb. Concerned for her safety, Charles offers to escort her back to the inner harbour, but she silently turns away and remains rooted to the quay. However, for one brief moment their eyes meet and Charles, an unadulterated romantic despite his predilection for hard science, is immediately smitten by her penetrating gaze. After making casual enquiries with Ernestina and Dr Grogan, Lyme's resident Darwinist (Leo McKern), Charles learns that after the death of her father – a local tenant farmer who died bankrupt and insane in Dorchester Asylum – the well-educated Sarah returned from boarding school to become a governess to Captain John Talbot's family at nearby Charmouth. It was here that she was subsequently seduced by Lieutenant Varguennes, a badly injured French ship's officer who was taken in by the Talbots after being shipwrecked off the Dorset coast. After Varguennes recovered from his wounds, Sarah followed him to a hotel in Weymouth, only to discover that he was already married. Ostracized and marginalized by polite society, she now spends her time suffering from a profound, self-induced melancholy, willing her lover's return by gazing out to sea from the Cobb and secluded parts of the Undercliff. To add insult to injury, Sarah is also working as a live-in companion to Mrs Poulteney (Patience Collier), a puritan battleaxe of strict Victorian morals, who has forbidden her to engage in such unseemly acts and, recruiting her housekeeper Mrs Fairley (Liz Smith) as a willing informant, has declared the Undercliff strictly off-limits.

However, much like Charmian's exploitation of Converse in *Dog Soldiers*, the import of the whole Varguennes 'affair' is a put-up job: after their initial meeting on the Cobb, Sarah recruits Charles as an easy mark and, through carefully pre-arranged 'accidental' meetings on the

Undercliff, uses his naive pity to seduce him and exacerbate her own sense of rebelliousness. Revelling in her own degradation, Sarah is less in love with Varguennes than enamoured with being a victim of fate. She is exploiting her outsider status to break with conventional nineteenth-century mores, all the better to forge her own existential freedom beyond the shackles of Victorian Duty, literally to force herself into living the radical ideals of a future, as yet undefined, age. As she later explains to Charles, 'I knew it was ordained that I should never marry an equal, so I married shame. It is my shame that has kept me alive, my knowing that I am truly not like other women. I shall never, like them, have children, a husband, and the pleasures of a home. Sometimes I pity them. I have a freedom they cannot understand. No insult, no blame, can touch me. I have set myself beyond the pale. I am nothing. I am hardly human anymore. I am the French Lieutenant's *Whore*'.

Wilfully defying Mrs Poulteney, Sarah throws caution to the winds by brazenly walking on the Undercliff under the watchful eyes of Mrs Fairley, which leads to her inevitable dismissal. With nowhere else to go and threatened with institutionalization by a well-meaning Dr Grogan, she throws herself on Charles's mercy, arranging to meet him at a secluded barn on Ware Commons, a primordial, untamed forest on the edge of the Undercliff. As one might expect, their illicit rendezvous and Charles's concerned solicitations lead to a passionate kiss, a liaison witnessed by Sam and Mary, who are on their way to a sexual rendezvous of their own. After forcing Sam into his strictest confidence, Charles contacts his London lawyer, Montague (Michael Elwyn), and makes financial arrangements for Sarah to stay at Endicott's Family Hotel in Exeter. Back in the city, Charles does some soul searching after a debauched night on the town with some old Cambridge friends before taking the train back to Lyme to confront his future.

So far, our account has held up remarkably well to realist conventions, suggesting that a filmic adaptation would pose few problems. However, it is at this point that Fowles's narrator intercedes directly into the narrative by extending his characters' existential choice to that of the exegetical reader. This takes the form of three separate endings, each of which represent the three very different methods through which Charles can survive and overcome his nauseous angst. The first ending represents his cowardly withdrawal from the new reality – the 'terrible freedom' from convention offered by Sarah – and his preference instead to play the role of 'one of life's victims, one more ammonite caught in the vast movements of history ... a potential turned to a fossil'. In this ending, Charles refuses Sarah's invitation to join her in Exeter and instead returns directly to Lyme where Ernestina sits embroidering a sentimental watch pocket – 'Each time thy watch thou wind, Of love may I thee remind', it reads – and coyly plays the role of the annoyed lover, complaining about his absences. He mollifies her with the gift of a Swiss brooch before confessing to his secret meetings with Sarah. Far from being angry, Ernestina is simply amused. 'And so ends the story', writes Fowles. 'What happened to Sarah, I do not know – whatever it was, she never troubled Charles again in person, however long she may have lingered in his memory. This is what most often happens. People sink out of sight, drown in the shadows of closer things'.[13] Although Charles and Ernestina failed to live 'happily ever after', they did at least live together, producing seven children. Sir Robert, Charles's uncle, married late in life and sired twins, thus depriving Charles of his inheritance and forcing him into business with the Freemans. Mrs Poulteney dies within two months of Charles's return. In spite of her severe piety, she is barred entrance into heaven and instead goes straight to hell.

This is obviously a conservative, backward-looking denouement, whereby Charles imagines that he and Ernestina emerge from the chaos of their present choices to become protagonists of an eighteenth-century novel where Sarah (the signifier of confusion) can be safely 'tamed' as a stock figure of such fiction and dismissed as an annoying malcontent. This is a plausible ending for Fowles's mid-Victorian time frame, as it reflects the residue of arcane eighteenth-century values of civilized intimacy, typified by Jane Austen's *Persuasion* (1818). Here genteel behaviour is rooted in the art of playful conversation – especially the ironical mode of raillery and badinage – that gives the participants the belief of mutual understanding and shared class and social values, causing them to lead inauthentic lives that merely imitate a contrived social artifice. The secret to happiness is to be content 'to be what one was' and always has been – something that Sarah is unable to do as she has renounced 'sentiment' for a developing 'sensibility'. Not surprisingly, Fowles contemptuously dismisses this solution as a 'thoroughly traditional ending'. Fortunately, for Charles and the reader, it also never really happened – Charles dreamed the events while dozing on the train from London to Exeter, as if he were unconsciously constructing his own autobiography in much the same way that Sarah has consciously contrived her own life choices throughout the novel. This would explain his vindictive, albeit appropriate, punishment of the detestable Mrs Poulteney. Fowles obviously rejects the ending because 'a planned world (a world that fully reveals its planning) is a dead world'.[14]

The narrator's proffered second and third endings have far more serious ramifications as they are both existential in outcome and thus, in theory at least, equally valid. However, reader choice will obviously be compromised by the fact that whichever ending is placed second will necessarily appear to be the 'real' ending. The narrator therefore tosses a coin to determine their linear placement and turns back the temporal clock of the narrative by fifteen minutes to make the endings appear to occur simultaneously. In this way, he gives the illusion that neither ending has authorial preference. Both endings must appear to be authentic insofar as they reflect a fictional universe tied to a specific historical period and the characters' relationship to it. They must also make sense in the context of the novel as a whole. For Charles Scruggs, 'They are mirrors that, taken together, continually shift our perspective, forcing us to admit that no single aesthetic reality will ever be truly mimetic, truly representative of the complexity of human life ... Like a picture of two cups that turns into a human profile before our eyes, the two final endings taken together are Fowles's way of saying that reality itself is mysterious, that no single ending can reconcile all the disparate facts'.[15] However, as we noted earlier, the narrator of the text is *not* synonymous with Fowles himself. The actual writer of the fiction *does* have artistic freedom of choice and, as we shall see, has clearly selected the third ending as his preferred denouement.

Fowles's penultimate ending is dictated by Sarah's specific will-to-power. In this case, Charles decides to stay the night in Exeter instead of returning to Ernestina. Under the watchful surveillance of Sam, he visits Sarah at the Endicott Hotel, where she has stage-managed a severe ankle injury in order to seduce him. They have (very brief) sex for the first time and he discovers that, despite her 'relationship' with Varguennes, she has remained a virgin all along. Instead of being angry at this deception, Charles tenderly proclaims his love, largely because, as Barry Olshen rightfully argues, 'He manages to rationalize Sarah's stratagems as devices to "unblind him", to bring him to the full realization of a "new Vision" of personal freedom'.[16] Before returning to Lyme to break his engagement with Ernestina, he sends Sarah a letter and the Swiss brooch via Sam, planning to take her abroad as his mistress. However, the servant, fearful of losing Mr Freeman's patronage for his own professional ambitions, turns traitor and fails to deliver the package. Thus, after an ugly showdown with Ernestina, Charles returns to Exeter to discover that Sarah has already fled. To make matters worse, Mr Freeman forces him to sign a *confession delicti* for breaking the engagement, dragging his reputation through the mud.

After two years of searching for Sarah in America, Charles receives a telegram in New Orleans notifying him of her whereabouts. He finds her in the Chelsea house of Dante Gabriel Rossetti's Pre-Raphaelite Circle, where she lives as the painter/poet's amanuensis and model – a rough composite of the real historical figures, Elizabeth Siddall, Alexa Wilding and Jane Burden. Sarah explains that her flight had nothing to do with Sam's betrayal but everything to do with a 'madness' in her: 'I have seen artists destroy work that might to the amateur seem perfectly good … I was told that if an artist is not his own sternest judge he is not fit to be an artist. I believe that is right. I believe I was right to destroy what had begun between us. There was a falsehood in it'.[17] She declares her right to her own free will and her reluctance to marry: 'I do not want to share my life. I wish to be what I am, not what a husband, however kind, however indulgent, must expect me to become in marriage'.[18] Charles gains a growing respect for this proto-feminist 'heresy', realizing that Sarah has transcended her past and shed her contrived role as the 'scarlet woman of Lyme'. More importantly, she no longer seems to need him. Charles, to his credit, has no desire to deny her this hard-won freedom, but merely, through his love, wishes to enlarge and nurture her present happiness. Sarah, however, sees an immediate conflict between love and personal integrity: 'It is not you I fear. It is your love for me. I know only too well that nothing remains sacrosanct there'. She then admits that she knew all along of his search for her whereabouts, as well as the break-up of his engagement, but she did nothing to contact him. Furious, he feels victimized, accusing her of revelling in his despair: 'You have not only ruined my life, you have taken pleasure in doing so'. He heads for the front door, but Sarah pleads with him to stay before playing her trump card: a two-year-old daughter, Lalage, has resulted from their act of consummation. It turns out that the entire episode has been a test of Charles's love. When Lalage enters, we witness the triumph of the romantic side of Charles's personality – he embraces both his daughter and Sarah's emancipation as if it were his own. It's significant that, like their first meeting on the Cobb, the main catalyst for this mutual transformation is Sarah's scopic power, for Charles opts to rebuild his life by abandoning himself to Sarah's inter-subjective *gaze*. 'At last she looked up at him', writes Fowles. 'Her eyes were full of tears, and her look unbearably naked. Such looks we have all once or twice in our lives received and shared; they are those in which worlds melt, pasts dissolve, moments when we know, in the resolution of profoundest need, that the rock of ages can never be anything else but love, here, now, in these two hands' joining, in this blind silence in which one head comes to rest beneath another; and which Charles, after a compressed eternity, breaks'.[19] This is treacly stuff indeed. That the narrator finds this ending 'unbearably romantic' is borne out by the chapter's closing words: 'a thousand violins cloy very rapidly without percussion'.[20]

The third and final ending, which returns us to the Rossetti House but omits Lalage and the binding import of family duty, is focalized exclusively through Charles. It represents *his* entry into a modern individualism by rejecting Sarah's offer of Platonic friendship without shared commitment in favour of being completely alone in a meaningless world; alone but at the same time truly free. In effect, as Fowles puts it, Charles discovers 'an existentialist awareness before it was chronologically possible'. Refusing to be the Rossetti House's 'pet donkey', he at last sees his true superiority to Sarah, which was based not on class, education or intelligence, but on an ability to give that was also an inability to compromise. In contrast, Sarah could give only to possess, because possession was so imperative in her that it had to be constantly renewed: simply possessing Charles would never be enough. After leaving the house, Charles stares at the grey surface of the Thames and realizes that he has no idea where to go or what to do next. Yet, despite this lack of direction and self-identity, 'he has at last found an atom of faith in himself, a true uniqueness, on which to build; has already begun, though he would still bitterly deny it, though there are tears in his eyes to support his denial, to realize that life, however advantageously Sarah may in some ways seem to fit the role of Sphinx, is not a symbol, is not one riddle and one failure to guess it, is not to inhabit one face alone or to be given up after one losing throw of the dice; but is to be, however inadequately, emptily, hopelessly into the city's iron heart, endured'.[21] And then, in the words of the last line of Matthew Arnold's poem 'To Marguerite' – a work that both Charles and the narrator agree is 'the noblest short poem of the whole Victorian era ' – he looks out again, 'upon the unplumb'd, salt, estranging sea'. The reference is appropriate, for as Scruggs argues, 'in the poem itself there is a tension between centrifugal and centripetal forces (modern currents push us apart, but ancient desires make us want to close ranks), and in *The French Lieutenant's Woman* the emphasis that we place on those respective forces depends upon the ending we accept'.[22]

However, it is obvious that the final, Thames-side denouement is the novel's 'real' ending, because it is the only conclusion that isn't undercut by the rest of the narrative. As Elizabeth Rankin convincingly points out, 'It is absolutely essential that the novel end with Charles's existential rebirth, so that the novel can offer a model of existential freedom which will serve as a "moral norm." It is obvious that the narrator espouses this norm, but without this ending … there would be no perfect exemplar of existential freedom in the novel and hence that concept would remain hazy throughout'.[23] Sarah, like the narrator, is too much of a manipulator and liar to be trusted as that exemplar. Her selfish refusal to resume the relationship on equal terms is vital to the philosophical logic of the story. The novel is thus about the evolution of an existentialist, with Sarah as the necessary sexual catalyst (the stages in Charles's intellectual development are marked by the evolutionary shifts in his relationship with Sarah, suggesting that the lifting of repressed sexuality must go hand-in-glove with the alleviation of repressed individuality) as he learns to recognize the essential absurdity of existence. Only by experiencing the anxiety of freedom can Charles realize that free will is inextricably bound to his ability to choose to act. Only then can he take on and weather the vicissitudes of evolution and Darwinism.

As if three different endings were not enough to challenge Reisz's adaptive skills, Fowles's narrator self-reflexively interjects comments on both the act of narrating, as well as the essential interconnectedness of his parallel temporal discourses. Indeed, Seymour Chatman avers that, 'The novel is unimaginable without the wide-ranging narrator's commentary. Since Charles is largely unconscious of his historical situation, the narrator must be there to explain it to us in the fullest possible detail'.[24] Apart from asides on the gradual maturation of his characters and the problematic nature of authorship in a post-structural era, the narrator also cites a number of recent epigraphs ranging from E. Royston Pike's *Human Documents of the Victorian Golden Age* (1967) to Martin Gardner's *The Ambidextrous Universe* (1967). In addition, the book is replete with modernist references to historical personages such as Freud, Brecht, Hitler, Henry Moore, Marshall McLuhan, Marcel Proust and Stanislavski, as well as modern developments like television, radar and the jet engine. Fowles also connects his fictional Victorian characters to 'real life' twentieth-century references, noting for example that, 'Mary's great-great-granddaughter, who is twenty-two years old this month I write in, much resembles her ancestor; and her face is known over the entire world, for she is one of the more celebrated younger English film actresses'.[25] Similarly, on the subject of Mrs Poulteney, he amusingly observes that, 'There would have been a place in the Gestapo for the lady; she had a way of interrogation that could reduce the sturdiest girls to tears in the first five minutes'.[26] How can one possibly incorporate such resonant literary asides into an analogous filmic language without resort to some form of Brechtian *V-Effekt*? Reisz clearly had his hands full.

Unlike the case of *Dog Soldiers*, Reisz was the preferred director of *The French Lieutenant's Woman* from the start. Aided and abetted by his publisher, Tom Maschler, Fowles had the power to veto any director that might compromise the project: 'We had no argument over the director we should approach first. It was Karel Reisz. In 1969 we therefore took the book, still only in proof, to him. Karel was sympathetic – and we had a devoted ally in his wife, the actress Betsy Blair – but it was a singularly bad moment to try to tempt him. He had only recently finished a difficult period picture, *Isadora*, and the thought of yet another was too much (as Karel himself has remarked, the trouble with the genre is that one can find oneself spending as much time on period as on picture)'.[27] Reisz's initial refusal led to the consideration of several other directors, and at various times the names of Lindsay Anderson (with David Storey scripting), Mike Nichols, Franklin Schaffner, Sydney Pollack, Ken Russell, Dick Lester, Michael Cacoyannis and Sidney Lumet were associated with the adaptation. The only version that came close to production was Paramount's 1975 project under the aegis of Fred Zinnemann with a screenplay by Dennis Potter. Various actresses were considered to play Sarah, including Gemma Jones, Charlotte Rampling, Francesca Annis, Kate Nelligan, Helen Mirren and Vanessa Redgrave; while Robert Redford and Richard Chamberlain were short-listed for Charles.[28] However, by the late 1970s, the project seemed doomed to failure, with even as accomplished a screenwriter as Robert Bolt lamenting that the book was 'un-filmable'. A resigned Fowles was ready to give up the project to television and turned his attentions to completing his novel *Daniel Martin*. Eventually, he acknowledged that the project needed to be reconceived and recast from the bottom up and both he and Maschler agreed that playwright Harold Pinter was the perfect man for the job. After an initial development deal fell through, in 1978 Maschler made another attempt to lure Reisz, fresh from directing *Dog Soldiers*, back into the project and this time he said 'yes', with the strict proviso that Pinter write the script. 'I did have a try with David Mercer', recalled Reisz. 'We talked and talked but never got to writing. And then Harold took to it like a duck to water'.[29] Eventually the project gelled – despite an array of pre-production problems – and filming began in Lyme on 27 May 1980. Although Fowles gave Reisz and Pinter a completely free hand, he did make one exception: Sarah's character must remain 'inexplicable'.[30]

Pinter's script – one-sixth the length of the original novel – is a model of condensation. Apart from a few obvious deletions – Uncle Robert and the sub-plot of Charles's inheritance, Sam's betrayal, Charles's trip to America, the imagined 'first ending' on the Exeter train – the basic shape of the story remains the same. As one might expect, the novel's meta-narrative structure proved to be Reisz and Pinter's main concern. They initially toyed with an idea first suggested by Peter Ustinov, namely to create a character who was the tacit author of the fiction, commenting on the action from without, but who would also play a role in the Victorian story as one of the protagonists, much like Anton Walbrook's on-screen narrator in Max Ophuls's film, *La Ronde*. This idea was discarded when Reisz hit upon a far more daring alternative: that the Victorian story should be a 'film within a film', whereby contemporary actors and lovers, Anna and Mike (Streep and Irons) would play the roles of Sarah and Charles in a feature adaptation of Fowles's book. By cutting sharply back and forth between the two time frames, the modern adulterous romance – Mike is cheating on his stay-at-home wife, Sonia (Penelope Wilton); Anna is casually betraying her French boyfriend, David (Gerald Falconetti) – could be used as a parallel love story to its period counterpart. This would allow a dialectical exchange as fact and fiction, modern and Victorian mores, gradually begin to converge and overlap as Mike falls increasingly, and alas unrequitedly, in love with Anna-as-Sarah. Anna and Mike thus represent the contemporary half of the story's 'stereoscopic vision', meta-communicating the fact that we are watching a film while at the same time, through the power of performance, drawing us into the deceits and antinomies of both romantic dramas. Fowles approved of the strategy, stating that, 'I do not think of the present script as a mere "version" of my novel; but as the blueprint ... of a brilliant metaphor for it'.[31]

However, a closer reading of the film discloses a different story altogether. Firstly, the 'film within a film' structure is *not* directly analogous to Fowles's self-reflexive fiction. Although Anna and Mike spend an occasional scene discussing character motivation in their hotel room – for example, the statistical likelihood of Sarah drifting into prostitution at a time when one out of every sixty houses was a brothel – and Reisz gives us one seamless match cut from modern rehearsal to period action, there are few behind-the-scenes glimpses of extra-filmic activity that might correspond to Fowles's wilful baring of the literary device. Thus there is no looking at dailies, no alternate takes, discussions with the director, forgetting of lines, playful ad libbing, on-set tantrums, elements that are central to, for example, Truffaut's *Day for Night* (1973). Secondly, not only does the film pay mere lip service to Fowles's central theme of existentialism, it actually, like *The Gambler* and *Dog Soldiers*, circumscribes the issue as another form of self-delusion. Instead of tracing the evolution – in the Darwinian sense – of a man who discovers a nascent existentialism ahead of his time, the film is essentially a double love story, 'the sentimental education of a decent Victorian chap',[32] closer to Flaubert than to his biographer, Sartre. In fact, Pinter laid greater stress on the modern affair, admitting that, 'In our first discussions ... there was much more of the Victorian background, the Victorian *facts*. But gradually, we found that those were novelistic considerations, and we refined it to what we finally found to be a love story ... although of a rather bizarre kind'.[33] Indeed, Pinter's initial motivation for the adaptation was the relationship between Anna and Mike: 'Suppose we had a modern relationship that *started* in bed and went from there?'[34]

Another key difference between the film and the novel is that the former is a *performative* medium, so that the audience cannot ignore the fact that identity – existential or otherwise – can only be outwardly expressed through a form of acting, by literally 'playing games', a staple component of Pinter's expressive use of language. Although very few critics have stressed the Althusserian side of Pinter's work, Marc Silverstein has made a convincing case for situating the playwright's work within a post-structural paradigm. Although Silverstein makes no claim for the *direct* influence of Althusser or Lacan on Pinter's oeuvre, he nonetheless argues that they provide a 'conceptual lens' through which to rethink the role of language in the playwright's work. According to Silverstein, Pinter examines the gap between the speaking subject and the structure of language that makes subjectivity possible in the first place, a language that is itself inextricably marked by Otherness. In this respect, *The Birthday Party* (1958) is the quintessential Pinter play, and its lessons reverberate throughout *The French Lieutenant's Woman*. The former is largely concerned with the cultural construction of subjectivity, where the 'I' that speaks – in this case the character, Stanley – is only made possible in the discursive field of the Other and its cultural codes and orthodoxies. 'Pinter dramatizes this process most forcefully in the second-act "interrogation" scene and the third-act "brainwashing" scene', notes Silverstein, 'sequences containing some of the most powerful examples of verbal violence in the Pinter canon – in which Goldberg and McCann expropriate Stanley from "his" language, transforming him into an empty vessel waiting to be filled with the cultural codes that will allow him to speak with the Other's voice, embrace the Other's values, desire the Other's desire'.[35] For Pinter, personal power is an effect of, and vehicle for, a broader cultural power exercised within ideological apparatuses such as the patriarchal family. Thus relationships such as husband and wife, master and servant, friend and lover, are discursive subject positions, formed in and through the performative inflections of language, not just specific subjectivities ruled by specific egos.

Silverstein's compelling argument thus becomes particularly pertinent in the case of *The French Lieutenant's Woman* where we have a 'film within a film', because the performative itself takes place in a double, stereoscopic register. Here, the expropriating characteristics of language games and preconceived role-playing tend to override any claim to authenticity on the part of either the main protagonists or the ostensible author of the work as a whole. As Chatman explains, the 'film's self-consciousness ... rests on the fact that the medium permits a given signifier – an actor – to signify more than one character ... the use of a real British actor, Jeremy Irons, to represent ("Stand for, signify") a fictional British actor named Mike, who in turn plays the Victorian gentleman Charles, is literally possible in cinema (and theatre). This power enables the film to deal self-consciously with the actor's dilemma: falling in love not with the actress but with the character the actress is playing'.[36] This is even more powerful when one considers that 'Sarah', the object of Charles/Mike's attentions, is also playing a number of roles within the diegesis in order to seduce Charles, so that the manipulative power of art and the concomitant control of the gaze that results makes any claim to authenticity almost impossible. Moreover, the Brechtian aspects of the performance make us constantly aware that we are watching Streep in a wig, playing Anna, playing Sarah, who is in turn playing the French Lieutenant's 'Whore' for the benefit of Irons, playing Mike, playing Charles.

The slippery nature of such role-playing is brilliantly staged in one of Pinter's trademark garden party scenes. Desperate to see Anna after she has returned to London, Mike throws a party at his suburban home and for the first time we see the rest of the cast out of costume. Thus, Patience Collier is no longer the self-righteous Mrs Poulteney, but now plays a kindly, grey-haired actress who draws on a cigarette as she admires Mike's young daughter, Lizzie (Joanna Joseph) and comments on Sonia's calm serenity to a distracted Anna. Similarly, Hilton McRae has shed the working-class role of Sam and expertly plays some Bach on Mike's piano as Lynsey Baxter turns the pages. Thus, through a performative sleight of hand, Pinter contrasts Sam and Ernestina's rigid class division in the fictional Victorian story with the fluid mobility of class today and the necessary social upheaval that has taken place to achieve social parity – all nicely condensed in one shot. At the same time, we're also fully aware that McRae is still acting, that he is almost certainly 'miming' to another performer's more expert pianism, setting up a 'deceit within the deceit' that folds back on itself like a Moebius strip. This strategy – clearly inspired by Pinter – is an important new addition to Reisz's cinematic arsenal, because hitherto he had invariably used editing – particularly ellipses and cross-cutting – to open up a space for critical evaluation against the more assertive, subjective register of performance. Now, in *The French Lieutenant's Woman* (and, as we shall see in the next chapter, in *Everybody Wins*) acting *combines* with montage to deconstruct authentic identity, while at the same time returning it to the protean, transformative power of art. In that sense, the film belies Fowles's existentialism in favour of a triumphant return to the Nietzschean aestheticism of *Isadora* and *Sweet Dreams*, as well as the affirmation of art as a critical buffer state between science and ideology.

This power of performance is a running theme throughout both novel and film. It is used both conservatively – as a survivalist tactic to protect one's territory within the fixed conventions of society – and rebelliously, as a means of 'acting out' or stereotyping preconceived roles all the better to deconstruct their prevailing assumptions. Smithson is the personification of the first, chameleon-like strategy: 'Charles, as you will have noticed, had more than one vocabulary', writes Fowles, describing his hero's first liaison with Sarah on the Undercliff. 'With Sam in the morning, with Ernestina across a gay lunch, and here in the role of Alarmed Propriety ... he was almost three different men; and there will be others of him before we are finished. We may explain it biologically by Darwin's phrase: *cryptic coloration*, survival by learning to blend with one's surroundings – with the unquestioned assumptions of one's age or social caste'.[37] In short, 'cryptic coloration' is a type of mimicry or camouflage through which the protagonist can conceal himself and 'fit in' by adapting and 'changing his spots' as the situation demands.

Homi Bhabha has written extensively on the subject of mimicry, noting that it is one of the most elusive but effective strategies of power and knowledge, particularly in the context of nineteenth-century colonialism. It creates an ironic compromise between, on the one hand, the demand for stasis and panoptic domination – Mrs Poulteney's surveillance of Sarah, for example; or Charles's and Dr Grogan's firm belief in the empirical 'certainties' of the new sciences, epitomized by their use of the magnifying glass and the telescope – and, on the other, the counterforce of continuous historical change and difference. As Bhabha explains, 'mimicry is the desire for a reformed, recognizable Other, *as a subject of difference that is almost the same, but not quite*. Which is to say, that the discourse of mimicry is constructed around an ambivalence; in order to be effective, mimicry must continually produce its slippage, its excess, its difference'.[38] Mimicry is thus simultaneously a strategy of *inclusion* – an acceptance of the 'good native' in the form of, say, the obedient servant or live-in 'companion' – and exclusion: denouncing the majority of 'bad natives', represented by Sam and Mary overstepping their designated place 'Downstairs', or Sarah's self-determined role as a brazen sexual and social outcast. 'However', as Peter Childs and Patrick Williams have pointed out in the colonial context, 'mimicry also produces a disturbing effect on colonial rule. Like the stereotype, mimicry results in fantasies of menace; but this is a menace produced by (or forced upon) the colonized. With mimicry, the authoritative discourse becomes displaced as the colonizer sees traces of *himself* in the colonized: as sameness slides into otherness'.[39] Mimicry is thus a double-edged sword – one of reform, regulation and discipline which appropriates the 'other' into its representational economy (almost the same but not quite) – but also one of transgression and difference that refuses to cohere into the dominant episteme of orthodox power (a case, in racial terms, of *almost* the same but not *white*). Mimicry thus becomes the potentially subversive agency of inauthenticity within the domain of the dominant authority through a form of role-playing and theatre akin to mockery or parody. It is within this performative gap between mimicry and mockery, where the ideological mission of authority is threatened by the displacing gaze of its disciplinary double, that Reisz and Pinter transform the existential self into a contingent identity, forever incomplete.

This creative shift from mimicry to mockery is a staple feature in Pinter's work, particularly his strategy of using polite, almost banal dialogue to mask what the characters are really thinking and feeling. We see this at work once again during the modern garden party sequence, where Anna makes friendly small talk with Sonia, claiming to envy her gardening skills while she is at that very moment having an affair with her husband. Similarly, Mike, forever the good host, solicitously ensures that David has enough to drink while he is yearning to be alone with Anna. Within the Victorian story, the mocking use of language is personified, of course, by Sarah, whose theatrical performance as 'Poor Tragedy' holds up a distorting mirror to an otherwise unsuspecting Charles and reveals his own persona as so much conformist camouflage. The key instigating scene takes place on Ware Commons, where Sarah spins her (fabricated) tale of her seduction by Varguennes to an unsuspecting Charles in order to use the details of the earlier 'affair' as a means of cementing (as well as defamiliarizing) their own burgeoning relationship. Reisz carefully uses *mise-en-scène* and camera movement to underline the theatrical and ensnaring objective of the monologue. Firstly, Charles is 'framed' in medium-to-long shot amid a tangle of tree branches and limbs, as if he were already an innocent fly caught in nature's seductive primordial web. Secondly, the camera tracks back and forth, following Sarah's linear movements as she spins her yarn in the foreground, culminating in the mannered, over-theatrical sweep of her body around an all-too-convenient tree trunk. Finally, in case there were any doubt that this is a performance rather than a confession, Sarah unpins her long red hair and lets it fall seductively to her shoulders. We cannot help but think of Rossetti's model, Elizabeth Siddall, and countless moralizing Pre-Raphaelite paintings depicting fallen women, particularly William Holman Hunt's *The Awakening Conscience* (1853–54) or Frederick Sandys' *Mary Magdalene* (1862), as if they were perhaps the visual inspiration for the learned Sarah's 'romantic' imagination.[40] This process of fabrication is reinforced in turn by Pinter's trademark dialogic pauses, as if Sarah were constantly checking the logic of her fevered imagination before trying it out on her 'victim', Charles. Subsequent viewings enrich the power of this scene immeasurably because we become fully aware that we are watching not only a mockery of the confessional, but also a form of epistemic discourse formation, whereby a series of language games are played out for the purposes of reconstructing both the self and the Other.

The 'film within a film' format extends the ramifications of Sarah's mocking charade to greater levels of complexity because we are also subtly aware of Anna/Streep's own performance that lies behind the outward surface of the characterization. Anna and Streep perform the monologue as if their mutual character, Sarah, had initially rehearsed it as a fiction, then restated it to herself so many times that she has actually come to believe it, and consequently acts it out as a true badge of honour. Indeed, as a self-conscious performance it is full of mistruths, designed, as we have seen, not to inform but to seduce, to construct the image of an enigmatic 'fallen' woman so that the genteel Victorian gentleman cannot help but sympathize. The performative aspect also links Sarah more directly to the woman actually playing her – Anna – and the latter's own seductive, off-screen 'performance' with Mike, given that she too has a French lover, David. This raises an important question. Is Mike, who is himself prone to fits of jealousy, playing Charles with added conviction given the overlap of the filmic fiction with this external 'reality'?

This possibility is, of course, central to the filmic deceit and this interweaving of different levels of performance makes any existentialist reading of the film difficult, if not impossible. The fact that Anna – with her 'modern' preference for 'no strings', casual relationships – is not the passionate, fictional Sarah, and that Mike's romantic confusion of one with the other will doom him to disappointment, is established from the opening shot of the film. Reisz begins the picture with a close-up on the black-hooded Anna/Sarah as she makes some last minute adjustments with her make-up assistant. Her face is partially reflected in a hand mirror placed between the back of her head and the assistant's face, thus evoking the virtual world of fiction between artist and apparatus, but also foreshadowing the use of mirrors throughout the film as signifiers of mimicry and masking. It also underlines the fact that Sarah is a *created* character (i.e. by Reisz and the film we are watching, as well as by the 'film within the film'), which will spill over into her diegetic role as a self-created persona. As she turns to face the camera, we pull back quickly to reveal her standing among a film production crew on the beach at Lyme. As an off-screen voice yells, 'OK, first positions, every-body', a clapperboard is placed in front of the camera to slate the scene for a first take.[41] According to Reisz, this meta-communicative device came late in the filming process: 'We had decided that if we started with a Victorian story which then suddenly cut to a modern one, the audience would be very confused. If, on the other hand, we just have some little quotation mark hovering at the beginning of the Victorian story, then the transitions would later become more acceptable. The use of the clapperboard is the only place in the film where we use an illu-sion-and-reality contrast. The intercutting device isn't about film and life or illusion and reality. It's simply a way of showing two parallel love stories'.[42]

However, despite Reisz's claim, the clapperboard is still an important indicator of the art/reality confusion that will follow because it introduces us to Anna outside of her diegetical character from the start, suggesting that she at least is able to keep their identities distinctly separate. Mike, in contrast, is first introduced in character, as Charles chips away at a fossil in his Lyme hotel room. He is only revealed as Mike when Reisz, making his first temporal leap to the modern sequences, shows us the actor lying naked in bed next to Anna prior to her early morning wake-up call. In this way, Reisz and Pinter metonymically connect Mike with Charles's myopic interest in fossils and his misconceived engagement to Ernestina, followed by a contiguous cut to his adulterous affair with Anna, suggesting a potential collapsing of the two time frames and iden-tities that can only be resolved through the intermediary intervention of Anna's fictional persona, Sarah. Unlike Anna, Mike has a much harder time in keeping the two worlds – and their concomitant personae – in separate compartments.

Glen A. Mazis sees *The French Lieutenant's Woman* as a film specifi-cally concerned with this very problem, namely our relationship to the past and our ability to make it real for ourselves in the present, as well as the cinema's unique power to alleviate that process. In this respect, Mike's performative dilemma, what Mazis calls 'commemorative rite', is not theoretically a bad thing, because it is only in the form of cele-bratory rites, via the embodiment typical of acting and performance, that we can actualize distinctive possibilities of memory. The period film or costume drama, as a specific appeal to embodiment, gives us a unique access to past worlds, literally an immersion in a lost historical environment. It is important to note that commemoration does not simply mean a return to, or a recollection of, a past event, but instead allows one to embody its celebratory quality through the re-enactment of play and bring it alive in the present. Thus, Anna re-enacts Sarah's story in 1981 and commemorates it in order to represent its elements of courage, determination and self-assertion against oppressive Victorian mores; actions that ultimately paved the way for the sexual freedoms enjoyed by modern women like Anna herself. This performative effect is particularly powerful for the actual filmic audience, for as Mazis explains: 'Unlike the reader of the novel, the viewer of the film is never able to retreat to his or her detached modern consciousness, but rather is continually forced beyond normal boundaries of individuation to live the past as presented on the screen – to live it carnally, emotionally, imaginatively, sensually, and unconsciously'.[43] Fortunately, we also have filmic surrogates like Anna and Mike or Streep and Irons, to make sure that we return to the present with some form of critical distance. Alas, it is not so easy for the actors themselves. While Anna is able to sustain a detached relationship to Sarah – her habitual gazing into mirrors allows her to retain a sense of herself as a distinct modern subject as opposed to a blurred composite of characters – Mike gets so caught up 'in the act' that his present identity (as well as his relationship with Anna) is irrevocably transformed.[44]

This first becomes apparent in the famous sequence where Mike and Anna are rehearsing an Undercliff scene where Sarah slips in the mud and Charles reaches out to break her fall. Although, at first, their exchanges are awkward, as if seemingly unprepared, it becomes readily apparent that they are completely committed to their characters. Indeed, as Ellen Handler Spitz rightly argues, 'In the glimpses we have of them, both Anna and Mike are portrayed as having a waking life wholly subservient to the inner frame, the film. They are artists living *for* as well as *in* their work; even their sexual intimacy seems inextricably linked with the film that they are making'.[45] It is thus very easy for Mike to lose himself in the persona of Sarah as Anna imperceptibly crosses over from her profession as actress to her Victorian character. Reisz expresses this switch through a seamless cut: Anna's modern-day dress is caught on a bramble, she moves toward Mike, and as she tries to move past him she slips ... and we slam cut to a close-up of Sarah slipping in the mud on the Undercliff.

This collapsing of different time frames through performance takes on added resonance as the film develops, because Mike starts to apply psychological and emotional elements of his modern relationship with Anna to his performance as Charles, and vice versa. For example, as

Sarah exits the barn following her secret liaison with Charles on Ware Commons, Reisz immediately cuts to Anna exiting her trailer, linking the two time periods through a smooth, logical continuity of reverse cutting. However, for Mike, there is an ironic disjuncture. While he has just kissed Anna/Sarah and is about to leave for London in the fictional deceit – indeed, he is still in costume as the cast and crew break for lunch – in the modern scenario he is temporarily 'losing' Anna (dressed in street clothes) as she is about to meet up with David in the capital. Mike's annoyance seems to spill over into his acting, for his irritability with Sam in the fictional hotel scene that follows seems completely over the top, as if it were motivated more by Mike's situation with Anna than by Charles's relationship with Sarah.

The import of 'commemorative rite' reaches its zenith in Pinter's twin endings, which have only an oblique relation to Fowles's existential alternatives. Deleting the novel's first, imagined ending altogether, the film cuts straight from London to Exeter station and Charles's rendezvous with Sarah at Endicott's Hotel. The film then closely follows the outline of the book until, after a gap of three years, we witness the final showdown between Charles and Sarah. Reisz and Pinter shift the denouement from the Rossetti House to Broad Leys on Lake Windermere, Charles F. A. Voysey's proto-modernist domestic masterpiece, where Sarah, now a gifted self-portrait artist, works as a governess to the children of an architect named Elliott. This is a logical change of location as it removes Sarah from the *retardataire* aesthetic ethos of the Pre-Raphaelites to a more progressive context reflective of her own artistic growth.

Unlike Fowles's second ending, where Sarah has deliberately refused to contact Charles, in Reisz and Pinter's version she actively instigates the meeting, for she has read Charles's advertisements in the newspaper and is eager to resurrect their relationship. As in the novel, Charles is self-righteously outraged, claiming that she has destroyed his life: 'You have planted a dagger in me and your "Damned Freedom" gives you license to twist it in my heart. Well no more!!' As he rushes towards the door, she seizes his arm, but he flings her roughly to the floor. Then, as if surprised by his violent strength, he moves solicitously to her side. She sits up slowly, trying desperately to compose her feelings: 'Mr Smithson. I called you here to ask your forgiveness. You loved me once. If you still love me, you can ... you can forgive me. I know it is your perfect right to damn me, but if you do still love me ... ' She breaks off hesitantly and they look deeply into each other's eyes. He hesitates before placing his hand under her chin: 'Then I must forgive you'. She takes his hand and affirms her love: 'Yes you must'. They kiss tenderly. Reisz dissolves to a long shot from inside the narrow tunnel leading

out from the neighbouring boathouse. Then, accompanied by the plaintive adagio from Mozart's Piano Sonata No. 17 in D, Charles and Sarah
row out onto the lake, reborn like twin souls from a shared womb. The
camera then zooms out to widen the arch of the tunnel to give a Gothic,
church-like frame to this bucolic scene, as if God himself were blessing
their renewed vows.

While the sentimentalism of this ending echoes the 'cloying violins'
of Fowles's equivalent, it is nonetheless far removed from the overt decla-
rations of mutual will-to-power in the novel. Moreover, Reisz undercuts
both the authenticity of the sequence and our willing suspension of
disbelief on several fronts. Firstly, we are aware of Sarah 'acting', so that
the true emotion of the scene becomes, once again, mere mockery. She
seems to have sensed that she cannot win Charles back with pure honesty,
so she must play the 'delicate female' one more time, feigning injury so
that he can feel in manly control. She woos him again and wins his love,
but her performance smacks too much of her Undercliff confessional
about her 'seduction' by Varguennes. Secondly, we notice that Sarah is
wearing an outfit that Anna had earlier picked out in a London store,
thus associating this touching fictional reunion with Anna's growing
'real life' estrangement from Mike. This bifurcation of centripetal and
centrifugal romantic forces is exacerbated by the fact that the Windermere sequences immediately follow Mike's garden party, when his
relationship with Anna is at its most frustrating.[46] That Mike has subli-
mated his anger into his performance as Charles becomes clear as he
throws Sarah to the floor. He overacts the violence, and immediately
checks himself, as if the tensions of the modern story have bled into the
visuals of the 'film within the film'. For Chatman, 'This is the unique
visual transgression: although dressed and performing as Charles,
Mike's frustration about Anna's "failure" to be Sarah is so great that his
anger gets the better of him, and he falls out of character. His passion
for Sarah – and his anger with Anna for not *being* Sarah – makes him
overdo the scene. Then, realizing that Anna might be seriously hurt, he
expresses his apprehension, which is relieved only when she nods and
smiles'.[47] Pushing the interpretation still further, Richard Corliss sees
this sequence as transcending clear-cut distinctions between period and
modern, between Fowles's Victorian story and the framing narrative,
operating instead on a third dramatic level. For Corliss, we are in the
'screening room' of Mike's increasingly fevered imagination. Mike has
become not only the respective on- and off-screen lovers, but the *film-
maker* as well. This almost clichéd final version of Fowles's *The French
Lieutenant's Woman* is the film *he* would have made to fulfil his own
desperate desires.[48]

Corliss's reading is borne out by Pinter's second ending, which solves the problem of the novel's necessary tendency towards repetition by setting the final denouement in the exact same Windermere location – the Voysey House – but in the present day, during the cast and crew's post-filming wrap party. Reisz uses the segue to repudiate the romanticism of the boating sequence by replacing the first ending's use of Mozart with the upbeat sounds of rock music from the party, thereby shattering the tranquil calm of the lake and disclosing the fleeting fragility of Mike's imagined artifice. Indeed, the unit party is in full swing: everyone is in modern clothes except Mike and Anna, who are still wearing their costumes from the previous scene, as if to signify their difficulty of separating fiction from reality. However, Anna is determined to make a clean break with Mike and return to her life with David in New York. After saying her goodbyes, she climbs the staircase of the Voysey House and enters her dressing room. After turning on the light, she sits and stares at herself in the mirror, creating a visual doppelgänger. Just as Sarah's red wig sits on its stand to the left of the dressing table, signifying both Anna's professional investment in the fictional character and her ability to discard it once the job is over, her mirror image acts as a comforting reassertion of her own self-identity. Anna knows that she can never be, nor wants to be, the fantasy figure that Mike seeks and desires. On the other hand, she also lacks the artistic self-realization of Sarah, communicated through the fictional character's painted self-portraits. Anna remains an empty cipher to the audience, and perhaps even unto herself.

Mike, in contrast, knows exactly what he wants: or at least he thinks he does. Noticing that Anna has suddenly disappeared from the party, he rushes towards the house, giving Lynsey Baxter/'Ernestina' an expeditious kiss on his way in.[49] Just as Charles had done in the period scene, Mike climbs the stairs before entering Anna's empty dressing room. To the strains of composer Carl Davis's lyrical viola theme (Sarah's recurring leitmotif) he touches the red wig before turning off the mirror lights. Is he in love with Anna or the representation of Sarah? Can he even tell the difference? We receive our answer when, on entering the location set of Charles's final rapprochement with Sarah, he suddenly hears the tell-tale sound of a car door slamming. He rushes towards the bay window, kneels on the window seat and looks out, just in time to see Anna driving away. But instead of crying 'Anna', he shouts 'Sarah!', just before Reisz zooms in to a tight close-up on his anguished face.[50] Mike's fusion with his Victorian counterpart is now complete: he has become so enveloped in the 'commemorative rite' of his craft that he can no longer discern the difference between fantasy and reality.

However, Mike also has the last laugh. Under the film's closing credits, Reisz returns us to the scene of the boathouse tunnel, as Charles and Sarah row out onto the lake. This time the zoom continues so that the tunnel arch disappears, projecting us into the full landscape, *sans* frame. This reprise of the earlier ending can be interpreted in several ways. Firstly, it acts as Reisz's Brechtian reminder to the audience of the fictional status of both the inner and outer stories of the film we have just viewed, effectively disavowing the 'reality effect' of the outer narrative as no more authentic than the inner one. Secondly, as Shoshana Knapp convincingly argues, 'the author of the film/dream ... is none other than Mike, who both recalls and re-directs the scene he has previously played, a scene that represents, at once, Charles's romantic fulfilment and Mike's unfulfilled yearning for an analogous happy ending. Mike mixes memory and desire – re-imagining a past plenitude capable of replacing and redeeming his present loss, and then making that past fuller and longer (53 seconds versus 15) than the version we have viewed'.[51] Mike even changes the original lake scene's background music, replacing Mozart with Carl Davis's romantic viola theme, thereby imbuing his mind-screen with the all-encompassing resonance of Sarah's constructed persona.

So is the film ultimately a paean to the imagination and its power to overcome primordial lack? Well, yes and no. For Knapp, 'Both Charles and Mike, persistently and destructively, attempt to reduce complexity to formula. To avoid sharing their error, the viewer must challenge the authority of their visions, as the two imperfect repetitions encourage one to do. Some dreams are less true than others'.[52] While this reading provides further evidence of Reisz's continuing theme of interpellation, it also, ironically, returns us to Fowles and the innate question of choice. It is ultimately up to the audience to decide whether they want to iden-tify with Mike's hopeless dream or not. However, this is less an existen-tial issue than a question of the redemptive power of art and artifice, for as Gaston suggests, isn't life, when it comes down to it, a matter of inventing fictions for ourselves in order to overcome the most extreme critical conditions?[53] Perhaps art is the only hope in a post-modern world where truth is contingent and desire exists not as an end in itself but rather travels along the byways of further desires. Which brings us, not by accident, to Tom O'Toole and Reisz's last feature, *Everybody Wins*.

Notes

1 John Fowles, quoted in James Campbell, 'An Interview with John Fowles', *Contemporary Literature*, Vol. 17, No. 4, Autumn 1976, p. 466.
2 Harold Pinter, in the programme of the 1960 performance of *The Room* and *The Dumbwaiter*, quoted in Beverle Houston and Marsha Kinder, 'The Losey-Pinter Collaboration', *Film Quarterly*, Vol. 32, No. 1, Fall 1978, p. 25.
3 Karel Reisz, 'Substance into Shadow', in Roger Manvell and R. K. Neilson, eds, *The Cinema 1952* (Harmondsworth, Penguin Books, 1952, reprinted New York, Arno Press, 1978), p. 204.
4 *Ibid.*
5 *Ibid.*, p. 189.
6 Reisz, quoted in Kennedy, 'Interview with Karel Reisz', p. 28.
7 Fowles, quoted in Campbell, 'An Interview with John Fowles', p. 466.
8 John Fowles, quoted in Richard Combs, 'In Search of the French Lieutenant's Woman', *Sight and Sound*, Vol. 50, No. 1, Winter 1980–81, p. 35.
9 Neil Sinyard, *Filming Literature: The Art of Screen Adaptation* (London and Sydney, Croom Helm Ltd, 1986), p. 135.
10 John Fowles, *The French Lieutenant's Woman* (Boston, New York and London, Little, Brown and Company, 1969 and 1998), p. 95.
11 Fortunately for the reactionary Victorian patriarchs, John Stuart Mill's parallel campaign for the emancipation of women was unsuccessful.
12 Freeman is a successful tea importer in the film, stressing his role as a symbol of mercantilism and labour exploitation.
13 Fowles, *The French Lieutenant's Woman*, p. 337.
14 *Ibid.*, p. 96.
15 Charles Scruggs, 'The Two Endings of *The French Lieutenant's Woman*', *Modern Fiction Studies*, Vol. 31, No. 1, Spring 1985, p. 98.
16 Barry N. Olshen, *John Fowles* (New York, Frederick Ungar, 1978), p. 57.
17 Fowles, *The French Lieutenant's Woman*, p. 448.
18 *Ibid.*, p. 450.
19 *Ibid.*, pp. 459–60.
20 *Ibid.*, p. 460.
21 *Ibid.*, p. 467.
22 Scruggs, 'The Two Endings of *The French Lieutenant's Woman*', p. 106.
23 Elizabeth D. Rankin, 'Cryptic Coloration in *The French Lieutenant's Woman*', *The Journal of Narrative Technique*, Vol. 3, No. 3, September 1973, p. 205.
24 Seymour Chatman, 'A New Kind of Film Adaptation: *The French Lieutenant's Woman*', in *Coming to Terms: The Rhetoric of Narrative in Fiction and Film* (Ithaca and London, Cornell University Press, 1990), p. 166.
25 Fowles, *The French Lieutenant's Woman*, p. 75.
26 *Ibid.*, p. 20.
27 John Fowles, 'Foreword' to Harold Pinter, *The Screenplay of* The French Lieutenant's Woman (London, Jonathan Cape), 1981, p. viii.
28 Combs, 'In Search of the French Lieutenant's Woman', p. 34.
29 Reisz, quoted in *ibid.*
30 Peter J. Conradi, '*The French Lieutenant's Woman*: Novel, Screenplay, Film', *Critical Quarterly*, Vol. 24, No. 1, Spring 1982, p. 47.
31 Fowles, 'Foreword' to Pinter, *The Screenplay of* The French Lieutenant's Woman, p. xii.
32 Reisz, quoted in Combs, 'In Search of the French Lieutenant's Woman', p. 35.
33 Harold Pinter, quoted in Leslie Garis, 'Translating Fowles into Film', *New York Times Magazine*, 30 August 1981, Section 6, p. 54.

34 Pinter, quoted in Richard Corliss, 'When Acting Becomes Alchemy', *Time*, Vol. 118, No. 10, 7 September 1981, p. 49.

35 Marc Silverstein, *Harold Pinter and the Language of Cultural Power* (Lewisburg PA, Bucknell University Press, 1993), p. 20.

36 Chatman, 'A New Kind of Film Adaptation: *The French Lieutenant's Woman*', p. 165.

37 Fowles, *The French Lieutenant's Woman*, pp. 144–5.

38 Homi Bhabha, 'Of Mimicry and Man: The Ambivalence of Colonial Discourse', in *The Location of Culture* (London and New York, Routledge, 1994), p. 86.

39 Peter Childs and Patrick Williams, *An Introduction to Post-Colonial Theory* (London, Prentice Hall, 1997), p. 131.

40 My UC Santa Barbara colleague, Helen Taschian, points out another important connection between Sarah and Rossetti's lover, Elizabeth Siddall. Citing Marcel Proust, Elizabeth 'had been loved tenderly, loved by the man and by the artist, which is to be loved twice, because painters have a tenderness for the creature that suddenly realizes for them, in an exquisite and living form, a long cherished dream, and lavish upon her a gaze that is more thoughtful, more intuitive and, to put it plainly, more charged with love than is possible for other men'. Marcel Proust, first published in *La Chronique des arts et de la curiosité*, 14 November 1903. Accessed 24 July 2005. www.yorktaylors.free-online.co.uk/rossetti.htm. In much the same way, Mike/Charles loves Anna/Sarah twice – as both an actor and as a man.

41 The interior film's 'Director' is K. Q. Rogers, Reisz's old *Sequence nom de plume*.

42 Reisz, quoted in Kennedy, 'Interview with Karel Reisz', p. 28.

43 Glen A. Mazis, 'The "Riteful" Play of Time in *The French Lieutenant's Woman*', *Soundings*, Vol. 67, No. 3, Fall 1983, p. 308.

44 The classic filmic instance of Mike's dilemma is George Cukor's *A Double Life* (1948), in which Ronald Colman plays a Shakespearean actor whose offstage life becomes murderously blurred with his on-stage role as Othello, with disastrous results.

45 Ellen Handler Spitz, 'On Interpretation of Film as Dream: *The French Lieutenant's Woman*', *Post Script: Essays in Film and the Humanities*, Vol. 2, No. 1, Fall 1982, p. 20.

46 It's interesting to note that both Pinter and Reisz assume that we expect all film scripts to be shot in chronological order, yet another of the picture's performative sleights of hand.

47 Chatman, 'A New Kind of Film Adaptation: *The French Lieutenant's Woman*', p. 179.

48 Corliss, 'When Acting Becomes Alchemy', p. 50.

49 'Ernestina' looks a little disappointed as she turns and walks towards the camera. Is there another modern love story going on here – an unrequited love/crush of 'Ernestina' for Mike?

50 It was actually John Fowles who suggested that the film's final line of dialogue be 'Sarah!', not 'Anna'. Corliss, 'When Acting Becomes Alchemy', p. 50.

51 Shoshana Knapp, 'Film as Dream II', *Post Script: Essays in Film and the Humanities*, Vol. 2, No. 3, Spring/Summer 1983, p. 60.

52 *Ibid.*, p. 61.

53 Georg Gaston, 'The French Lieutenant's Woman', *Film Quarterly*, Vol. 35, No. 2, Winter 1981–82, p. 55.

Theatre of the absurd: Arthur Miller's *Everybody Wins* (1990) and Samuel Beckett's *Act Without Words I* (2000)

10

Coherence in film remains distinctly secondary in importance to the enticing infantile riddle of sheer image itself. (Arthur Miller)[1]

The most complicated achievements of thought are possible without the assistance of consciousness. (Sigmund Freud)[2]

If I cannot bend the Higher Powers, I will move the Infernal Regions. (Virgil, *The Aeneid*, VII, 312)

Go on failing. Go on. Only next time, try to fail better. (Samuel Beckett)

It's a bright, sunny winter's day as goateed private dick, Tom O'Toole (Nick Nolte) drives his beat-up station wagon into the unfamiliar environs of Highbury, Connecticut, a picturesque yet tarnished New England industrial city, population 40,000. An ex-Boston cop, Tom has been living with his two sons and schoolteacher sister, Connie (Judith Ivey), since the premature death of his wife three years earlier. Although Tom's most recent cases have been mainly routine insurance investigations, he has a long-standing reputation as a hard-nosed advocate for the legal rights of the underdog, willing to exploit the muckraking tabloids and news media to take on City Hall and get wrongful sentences overturned. Tom is visiting Highbury to meet Angela Crispini (Debra Winger), an ardent follower of his investigative exploits who is hoping to interest him in representing Felix Daniels (Frank Military), currently doing time for the brutal stabbing murder of his uncle, Dr Victor Daniels. Although she had never met Felix until the trial, Angela has taken a personal interest in the case and hints to Tom that she knows the identity of the real killer. However, whether through fear for her own safety or general paranoia – Angela believes the Highbury police are watching her every move – she is reluctant to divulge everything she knows.

Embarrassed by Angela's fawning attentions, Tom is initially loathe to get involved, but after meeting with the gaunt, dispirited Felix in prison and reading the case file – a broken tooth from his comb is the only forensic evidence tying the young man to the crime scene – he agrees to make some inquiries. Tom's interest is piqued further when he discovers that the prosecutor on the case was his bitter rival, Charley Haggerty (Frank Converse), who once tried to have his license revoked. With his sights firmly set on a run for State Senate, Haggerty is not about to have his high-profile case overturned. Although Felix's new Defence Attorney (Timothy D. Wright) claims that Felix had incompetent counsel, the District Attorney strenuously fights the motion for a new trial and the appeal is rejected. Meanwhile Angela is working her own seductive magic on Tom. First, after admitting a personal connection to Daniels – he had been her doctor and a 'very wonderful friend' – she lets slip that the cops already know the identity of his killer. In fact, they had him in custody immediately after the murder but for some reason let him go. She is willing to talk to the authorities but there are still a few facts that she has yet to prove. That's where Tom comes in: 'You could wrap things up in a month. I know what to look for and where to look'. Then, as if Tom needed more inducement, she tells him that Felix is just the tip of the iceberg: the whole case goes right to the top of the State hierarchy, including Haggerty himself. After she slips into 'something more comfortable', Tom's three years of self-imposed celibacy meets its premature end and 'he is on her before his brain can begin to catch up'.[3]

Ignoring Connie's sensible warnings that Angela's 'loopy' behaviour is clouding his better judgement, Tom follows her first suggested lead to Amy (Kathleen Wilhoite), a skinny, strung out junky who lives in a run-down shack in the backwoods. Confirming Angela's story, Amy fingers her pony-tailed biker boyfriend Jerry (Will Patton) for the doctor's murder. Wracked by guilt, the Catholic-raised Jerry had gone to the cops and confessed to the crime but was immediately released, despite being covered in Daniels's blood. Tom tracks him down to an abandoned mill next to the river where Jerry has established his own 'church' to unburden the souls of his fellow sufferers, including Angela. 'Her thoughts are poisoning her, but she won't trust me enough to help her', bemoans the cult leader. Inside the mill, Tom discovers a bizarre tabernacle, dominated by the statue of Jerry's personal 'god', Major Jerome Seth McCall, a Civil War 'poet and soldier' who gave 'his life for the nation, 1825–1862'. Jerry has purloined the monument from its plinth in the local cemetery and created a do-it-yourself altarpiece by surrounding its head with a 'halo' of illuminated hubcaps. Jerry is obviously as mad as a hatter and fully capable of committing the murder.

Unfortunately, just as Tom's investigation is starting to make some real progress he is thwarted by, of all people, Angela. Stepping out from the shadows of the tabernacle, she suddenly berates him for attempting to contact Jerry and following up leads without prior consultation. To make matters worse, she has undergone a radical personality change, taking on the persona of 'Renata Sherwood', an affected society snob who seems curiously drawn to Jerry's cult and is clearly protecting someone connected to the case (Haggerty perhaps?). Reluctant to continue the investigation if Angela refuses to come clean – 'It's like chasing feathers in a tornado', complains Tom to his sister – the detective's confusion is further compounded when, while walking downtown after dark, he spots Angela being propositioned as a hooker by a passing motorist. Catching up with her on the street, he discovers that she has a black eye. She claims that the police roughed her up to keep her quiet. It seems that Tom's presence in Highbury has upset City Hall, a fact corroborated when he spots Chief of Police Bellanca (Mert Hatfield) closely monitoring their activities from a passing police cruiser. Yet, an obvious question remains. Is Angela really a prostitute or are we witnessing yet another of her multiple personalities? Bellanca asserts the former, for the next day in Haggerty's office he vindictively informs Tom that Angela has been a hooker for years and nothing she says can be trusted. However, a few days later, after admitting that, as a young girl, she had been repeatedly raped by her father, Angela undergoes what seems to be an authentic and unrehearsed personality change, this time metamorphosing without warning into the foul-mouthed prostitute, 'Leontine'. Clearly transported to another time and place, Tom has become a total stranger to her. Have the root causes of Angela's mood swings become the real mystery? Can we believe *anything* she says? What hope is there for Felix's release if the chief defence witness and informant is an untreated schizophrenic?

Tom turns in desperation to his friend, Judge Harry Murdoch (Jack Warden), who confirms that Haggerty is the party's choice for Senate and that he will fight tooth and nail for his political life on the Daniels case. Unless Angela tells everything she knows, Tom might as well drop the whole investigation. On the other hand, having read the trial transcript, Murdoch admits that she has a right to be upset: 'All they proved in court was that Felix was in the doctor's house. Nobody proved he killed anybody'. Reinvigorated, Tom once again puts the squeeze on Angela. It turns out that her multiple personalities are a defence mechanism unconsciously generated to cover up and dissimulate her own (and others') guilty involvement in the case. She finally admits to having been Dr Daniels's lover, and that Jerry acted as his main drug runner. In fact, she and Amy also acted as couriers, regularly running dope from Bimini to feed Victor's Connecticut drug empire. Jerry killed

Daniels because he thought he owed him money. The biker cultivated an ongoing fantasy that Victor would help him build his church, and when Daniels refused to finance the operation, Jerry went berserk and slashed his throat. The police failed to arrest him because Jerry knew all the local drug connections – from Daniels, to Bellanca, and ultimately to City Hall itself. Using Felix as an all-too-convenient patsy, Haggerty was complicit in deliberately trying a case that he knew was a frame-up from the beginning. Then Angela drops the bombshell – in addition to Daniels, she has also been sleeping with Haggerty himself! 'He nearly left his wife for me', says Angela. 'It was the best two years of my life ... until they made him rig the case against Felix'. Angela begged Haggerty not to send up an innocent man but he was in too deep with the local big wigs. Suppressing his astonishment, Tom presses his advantage: 'If we can get Jerry to unload in front of a lawyer, you've not only sprung that innocent kid but you've nailed the police department and Haggerty ... I think you owe this much to Felix'. But Angela is unwilling to sacrifice 'the love of her life'. Cornered, she once again slips into her 'Renata' persona and refuses to co-operate, as if her patrician identity were an over-determination of her more tenuous, real-life relationship to Haggerty and the New England establishment.

For his part, Haggerty is also aware that Angela holds vital evidence against him, specifically intimate letters that allude to his guilty involvement in the frame-up. After he subsequently roughs up Angela and ransacks her apartment, searching in vain for the incriminating documents, she once again turns to Tom for protection. This is the detective's last opportunity to get real evidence of the affair, but just as he is about to break open her safe, a hysterical 'Renata' intervenes, accusing him of stealing her property. The penny finally drops: 'You called me in to dig up just enough to get Felix out. Is that it? But without touching anybody else! And now you're asking me to protect the bastard that put him there? You've been trying to go north, south and powder your nose all at the same time! But that can't be done, baby, not with me!!' Tom finally gets the full truth from Jerry. Promising him full immunity if he will sign an affidavit, the detective coaxes out a detailed confession. Daniels, it seems, used to pay off everybody: Haggerty, Bellanca, you name it. 'He used to brag about it!', recalls Jerry. 'All I wanted to do was to talk to Daniels about building my new church, but he wouldn't listen to me. And he owed me money. But he wouldn't even open the Goddamn door ... And he had like, *five* locks!' However, as her lover, Daniels would always open the door for Angela. Thus Jerry, eager to confront Daniels about his funds, asked her along as a front so that he could gain entry into the house. Angela has been so guilt-stricken about Felix's indictment because she was a witness and party to the murder herself. After Tom takes this in, he convinces Jerry that a full confession will also see Angela in the clear, both with her own conscience and with the authorities. However, as they are driving back into Highbury, Jerry's feeling of moral liberation takes a terrifying grip. As he straddles his motorbike, 'Jerry seems to be floating in a dream, his innocence returned, his guilt flying out of him, arms still in the air, eyes closed'.[4] He drives headlong into an oncoming truck and is killed instantly.

With his key witness and perpetrator dead, Tom turns to Judge Murdoch to see if he can make a deal for Angela, who could still be indicted as an accessory to Daniels's homicide. The next day, Murdoch calls to tell Tom the good news: after talking with Angela they have agreed on a compromise. Better still, he is taking over the case himself. Felix is out on bail pending a new trial, and Angela has been spirited out of state for her own protection. When a gleeful Tom visits Murdoch at his home gym to offer his congratulations, he discovers that the estate grounds are being prepared for a garden party. 'You are unbelievable', effuses Tom. 'This thing's gonna bring the whole thing crashing down – on Haggerty, Bellanca, the whole damn police department, right?' 'I've sprung Felix, Tom – that'll have to be the end of it', replies the Judge, stepping off his exercise bike and heading for the shower. 'This woman has been through enough. And I must tell you, I think you've been damn rough on her ... This is a sensitive human being, a *deep* human being. I will not allow her to be tortured any further by this case'. Despite Tom's outrage, Murdoch stands firm: 'Felix is out and that's it. You can't save the Goddamn world'.

Tom discovers the real reasons for Murdoch's tactical retreat as soon as he steps outside. Far from being out of state, Angela is in fact getting ready for the garden party in the neighbouring guesthouse. She has obviously made a great impression on the Judge and is clearly about to add him to her already impressive list of sexual conquests ('From what I hear, it's her way of saying hello', quips Connie). Angela is full of righteous self-justification: 'Tom, you know what they would have done to me. We saved a man. It's the one good thing I've ever done, can you understand that?' Then she adds the kicker: 'This way everybody wins'. 'Almost, yeah', replies a disgusted Tom. Meanwhile, to the 1920s jazz strains of Leon Redbone crooning 'Hot Time in the Old Town Tonight', Murdoch makes his way through the assembled party guests – greeting Bellanca with easy familiarity on the way – to the guesthouse to pick up his date. When he knocks on the door, Angela stalls him so that she can sneak Tom out the back way to avoid any embarrassment ('He's a little old fashioned, he'll be upset', she explains). As a bewildered Tom heads

for his car, he runs into a grateful, teary-eyed Felix, who has arrived for
the party with his parents, and finally Charley Haggerty, who is there
to announce his upcoming campaign for Senate. At first, the two men
cross paths without recognition. Then they suddenly stop, turn and look
at one another. 'You're leaving early', observes Haggerty. 'How about a
drink?' Tom laughs, turns away and keeps walking towards us, smiling
incredulously until he disappears below the bottom of the frame. The
camera holds square on Haggerty as he makes his way towards the reassuring classical symmetry of Murdoch's house, all business as usual.

    Everybody Wins was adapted by Arthur Miller from his own two-char-
acter, one-act play, *Some Kind of Love Story*, which was first presented in
tandem with *Elegy for a Lady* in 1982, both starring Christine Lahti and
Charles Cioffi. The play ran for six weeks to sold-out audiences at the
Long Wharf in New Haven before eventually reaching the Old Vic in
London in 1989 with Helen Mirren and Bob Peck as Angela and Tom.
'In different ways both works are passionate voyages through the masks
of illusion to an ultimate reality', notes Miller. 'In *Some Kind of Love
Story* it is social reality and the corruption of justice which a delusionary
woman both conceals and unveils. The search in *Elegy for a Lady* is for
the shape and meaning of a sexual relationship that is being brought to
a close by a lover's probable death. In both the unreal is an agony to be
striven against and, at the same time, accepted as life's condition'.[5] The
subsequent expanded screenplay – Miller's first original script since
John Huston's *The Misfits* in 1962 – was originally titled *Almost Everybody Wins* and was loosely based on a 1973 Connecticut murder case in
which Peter Reilly, a Canaan teenager, was convicted of murdering and
sexually mutilating his fifty-one-year-old mother, Barbara Gibbons, in
a brutal stabbing at her home. Alone and without legal counsel, Reilly
underwent several hours of interrogation at police headquarters before
owning up to the gruesome crime. Convinced that detectives had coerced
the confession, friends and neighbours flocked to Reilly's aide, raising
money for his legal defence. Despite this unprecedented public show of
support, Peter was convicted of first-degree manslaughter, receiving a
sentence of six to sixteen years. The local community – including Miller
himself – was outraged, spurring the playwright to alert the national
press and push for the formation of a new defence team. However,
before a second trial could begin, the prosecutor died and his successor
discovered new evidence that prompted the state to drop its case. All
requests by Reilly and his attorneys to see the state police files have been
denied, sparking rumours that the evidence was wilfully destroyed.

    This lurid combination of an 'unsolved mystery' involving a savage
crime, a major miscarriage of justice, political cover-up and the Good

Samaritan efforts of local townspeople seemed like a strong commercial mix to the film's producer, Jeremy Thomas, who had just won a Best Picture Oscar for Bernardo Bertolucci's *The Last Emperor* (1987). Reisz agreed, seeing the film as 'a comedy-melodrama with film-noir tensions. It's really a small-town thriller, with a comic and ironic mixture of story-telling'.[6] Moreover, with Miller's involvement there was little problem attracting financing, and the film was eventually budgeted at a generous $19 million, with Norwich, Connecticut, standing in for Highbury, while interiors were shot in Wilmington, North Carolina. Both Thomas and Reisz felt that the New England milieu was a major asset because the insular small-town story could then be told through Tom's outsider eyes, while the images of Norwich's actual economic decay – the millworks have closed, creating a lost, undefined, post-industrial milieu – would provide a perfect backdrop and visual metaphor for Miller's richly over-determined language.

   While the film is admittedly not one of Reisz's strongest efforts, nothing could have prepared the film-makers for the disastrous box-office returns – the US gross was a mere $1,372,000 – or the almost uniform critical disdain (a notable exception was Pauline Kael, who waxed lyrical about Winger's bravura performance in the *New Yorker*). Very few people actually saw the film in the US as it opened without press screen-ings and, despite a strong cast and Miller's obvious marquee value, it was immediately dismissed as a commercial dud. The few reviews it did receive were generally negative, with Stanley Kauffmann describing Reisz's direction as 'relentlessly nondescript',[7] while in *Sight and Sound* Philip Kemp criticized the director's trademark attention to detail as 'ambience for its own sake, put to no dramatic purpose'. Besides, 'as any gambler knows, the trouble with everybody winning is that you end up with a pretty unsatisfactory pay-out'.[8] *Rolling Stone*'s Peter Travers complained that, 'Miller has buried a familiar story about small-town corruption under an avalanche of overblown dialogue ... Perhaps Reisz had all he could handle just keeping the threads of script from unrav-elling'.[9] Even worse, 'Miller borrows too many insights from himself: He's covered corruption in *All My Sons*, the little guy squashed by the system in *Death of a Salesman*, religious fanaticism in *The Crucible* and even sexual enthrallment in *After the Fall* (a thinly veiled autobiograph-ical play about Miller's marriage to Marilyn Monroe)'.[10]

   Travers makes a valid point, but Miller – himself a veteran of the Cold War and blacklist – was also aware of changing historical and cultural realities, that a film about political corruption set in 1990 is not going to have the same allegorical or moral ramifications as a similar script set in, say 1960. For example, one can easily read *The Misfits* (1961) retrospectively as a post-McCarthy era allegory of the trashing of the American Dream. Like Reisz and Robert Stone's *Dog Soldiers*, to which it bears uncanny similarities, Huston's film strips away the veneer of individualism – in this case the rapidly declining lifestyle of washed-up Nevada cowboys – to disclose the originary violence and corruption at its source, whereby one person's 'freedom' is always at the expense of another's. It also traces American society's inexorable degeneration from a myopic sense of Manifest Destiny to a stultifying conformity, spawned by Cold War paranoia and HUAC red baiting. In contrast, as Kemp argues, 'The new film could perhaps be taken as Miller's comment on the Reagan years, in which the evasions and hypocrisies, the rumours of disclosures and impeachments, finally fizzled away to nothing, with the chief culprit ambling off into the sunset with the same old amiable grin'.[11] It seems perfectly apt that Nick Nolte (a brilliant actor who in many ways epitomizes the corrupted 'All-American' innocence of the anti-war generation) links the two critical sensibilities, for the Samurai individualism of Hicks in *Dog Soldiers* – already disclosed as yet another counter-cultural anachronism – is now reprised as the dogged seeker of truth, Tom O'Toole, private investigator. Only the stakes have changed. Where there was once a moral 'norm' against which truth might be measured and ultimately prevail – the PI solves the case, nails the 'bad guys', restores order – now there is only contingency and deception. In effect, the realist *work* – and its political corollary – has become a post-structuralist *text*, impossible to decipher, remaining, like Sarah in *The French Lieutenant's Woman*, an ensnaring enigma. Unfortunately, as real-life politics began to slide into a cynical amoralism – the 1980s 'drugs-for-guns' covert operations of Oliver North replacing the 1970s public conscience of Sam Ervin and the Senate Watergate Committee – film audiences suddenly seemed to prefer their cinematic ethics in clearly distinct shades of black and white. As Kael lamented in her orig-inal review of Reisz's film, 'For a brief period in the late sixties and early seventies, moviegoers seemed willing to be guided through a movie by their intuition and imagination; if this slyly funny picture about the spread of corruption had been released then, it might have been considered a minor classic. It's satirical in an odd, hallucinatory way'.[12] Indeed, *Everybody Wins* is much closer to the narrative experimentation of Arthur Penn's *Night Moves* (1975), where Gene Hackman's private eye actually fails to solve the case, than the film's 1990s competition in the vein of more conservative plotters such as John Grisham and Tom Clancy.

Much of the film's post-structural enigma lies in the fact that, as Reisz himself puts it, 'The events – the violence, the betrayals – are largely off-screen. The story is about the undercurrents, the things undisclosed – what seems is not always what is'.[13] Instead of outward facts and concrete evidence, we get endless verbal dissimulation, especially from Angela. Debra Winger herself stressed the difficulties of reciting Miller's dialogue, because, 'Arthur's words don't always roll off the tongue. What we are doing and saying is secondary – all of these subtexts are the focal points'.[14] In other words, as in the case of *The French Lieutenant's Woman*, the film's performative register once again takes the form of an exaggerated 'cryptic coloration', where dialogue is spoken less to communicate the truth than to camouflage it, to bury it under a veneer of verbal mockery. This mockery also extends to the film's deconstruction of 'commemorative rite', for Winger not only has the difficult task of playing Angela, but she must also convincingly switch roles (often in mid-sentence) to 'inhabit' her character's other personalities, 'Renata' and 'Leontine'. As Kael points out, Angela is 'always acting things out on a stage of her own creation. She's out of control, and Winger makes her irrationality passionately real. Winger's Angela is soft and boneless and appealingly whory, with an automatic pretty smile. She wears slips and has breakdowns; she's all femininity and formlessness – she can become anything at any time'.[15]

This protean quality of the acting ritual is less of a problem in *The French Lieutenant's Woman*, where the 'film within the film' allows the characters of Mike and Anna to help the audience draw reasonably clear distinctions between the framing story and the fiction. Unfortunately, in Angela's case we are never sure whether her mood swings are part of her conscious or unconscious personality, which leads to considerable narrative confusion. However, this seems to have been Miller's intention all along, for it is clear that he uses the characters' dialogue – indeed verbal language in general – in much the same way as it exists in dreams, i.e. as another form of *image*. In this sense, 'cryptic coloration' in *Everybody Wins* closely resembles the structure of Freud's dream-work, specifically the four constituting elements of condensation, displacement, issues of representability and secondary revision, metaphorical and metonymic forms which have to be decoded into rational, scientific language. As the film's designated investigator, Tom takes on the role of therapist-cum-archaeologist, deciphering the manifest content of Angela's dream-like verbiage to disclose the latent, unconscious truths buried beneath the surface.

On this level at least, Angela is a classic psychoanalytic case study. If, as Freud suggests, 'Dreaming is a piece of infantile mental life that has been superseded',[16] we can find the root causes of Angela's multiple personality disorder in her childhood. Angela's defining Primal Scene is her alleged rape by her father. It hardly matters if the abuse actually happened, as long as it represents a powerful semiotic signifier that Angela has been forced to suppress. It is significant that in the original play, she regresses into a third persona – omitted from the film – an eight-year-old girl named Emily, who is fearful of her father's nightly visits. The Name of the Father (following Lacan, it is as much linguistic as 'real') is thus an extremely over-determined and ambivalent Oedipal symbol for Angela, as 'he' is associated simultaneously with both love and violent incestuous abuse. It is hardly surprising that later in life she sleeps with Dr Daniels and Charley Haggerty, leading establishment figures who stand in as convenient surrogate father figures. One could argue that Angela sets up Daniels's murder as an unconscious means of punishing the doctor as a proxy for her 'bad', abusive father. However, instead of getting the Oedipal monkey off her back, it adds another in the form of framing the innocent Felix, who is in many ways her own surrogate son. Feeling as if she has prostituted herself to the powers-that-be, she develops her identity as 'Leontine' as a form of ritual self-punishment. Meanwhile, Haggerty the DA takes on the role of the flawed but essentially 'good' father – literally the 'love of her life'. She can only reach atonement by using Tom to free Felix, but not at the expense of destroying her fragile Oedipal deceit. At the film's end, Judge Murdoch is in the process of becoming another father figure/possible lover. Like Haggerty, he helps her to sublimate her incestuous fears/ desires to the punishing law of the superego, effectively eradicating all residue of her original ego. Tom, in contrast, wants to destroy the superego – to blow the lid off City Hall – but Angela cannot co-operate because her unconscious identification with the Connecticut establishment is her only means for psychological recovery (thus explaining her censorious intercessions in the investigation as the patrician 'Renata').

All this is well and good, but it is a *rational* explanation of the filmic narrative, reducing complex issues of desire and psychic lines-of-flight to the central Freudian schema of the Primal Scene and the Oedipus Complex. That Miller does not share this perspective is clear from the Preface to the published screenplay, where he draws a clear analogy between the supremacy of the image (as opposed to dialogue) in the film and its direct relationship to the irrationality of dream, which would override any claim for cinema as the preferred medium of logical analysis:

> The film scene, even the apparently legato one, is always secretly in a hurry, much like its unacknowledged matrix, the dream scene, which flashes up in the sleeper and dies away in a matter of seconds. Dreams ... are almost never verbal. Sometimes a single emblematic word, or

perhaps two, may emerge in a dream scene as a clue (most likely ambig-uous) to its intent, but everyone knows the dream in which people are avidly talking, with no words coming from their mouths, thus creating the image of talk rather than talk itself ... The dreamer is essentially deaf, and this suggests that film's origins, like those of dream, reach back to archaic stages of our evolution, to a period antedating our capacity to understand language, when we communicated in the primitive sign language of infancy ... Coherence in film remains distinctly secondary in importance to the enticing infantile riddle of sheer image itself.[17]

Miller seems to be talking as much about the inherent ambiguities of *Everybody Wins* as an example of cinema in general as he is about the specific characters within the story itself. For Miller, 'dreaming and movie watching are essentially passive activities, something happening *to* us, rather than an active and wilful participation in another's imagi-nary world, as is the case with reading or even watching stage plays built on words instead of pictures'.[18] The playwright argues that the seductive pleasure of watching a film is based on its incoherent, unconscious and sensuous nature. This is equally true for the cinema audience as it is for Tom's attraction to Angela, who is the absolute epitome of incoherence and instability.

The film establishes this cryptic relationship from the beginning, for as Tom drives into Highbury he pops a cassette into his car stereo and the diegetic soundtrack underscores the opening credits with Leon Redbone's tongue-in-cheek rendition of 'I Wanna Be Seduced', as if the whole film were itself in ironical scare quotes. The lyrics are particularly suggestive, as they seem to represent the unconscious feelings of both Tom and the male spectator:

'I want to be seduced / want a woman to talk to me suggestively. / Make a point of touching me when she talks / leaving all the jealous men in the joint to mumble in their beer and gawk. / I know it only happens, when I'm napping / nodding in a reverie / that I find myself a woman who wouldn't mind seducing me'.

As the music ends, Angela appears on-screen for the first time, thus condensing three key thematic elements: the instigator of the narra-tive quest (i.e. Angela's pursuit of justice); Tom and the spectator as its willing agents; and the unconscious world of dream and desire. As the film's audience, we are thus confronted with an unusual paradox. If Tom is the film's nominal psychotherapist/ archaeologist, he is himself bewitched by dreams – he literally wants to be seduced by unconscious forces – thus making his ability to resist and decipher Angela's decep-tions impossible. He becomes inextricably caught in the imagistic slip-pages between condensation and displacement, to the point where, like

Mike in *The French Lieutenant's Woman*, he no longer has an ostensible grip on the real. Indeed, in a key line from the play, Tom concedes at one point that, 'I've got to stop looking for some red tag that says 'Real' on it; I don't have the education, but I have the feeling and I'm just going to have to follow my nose, wherever it takes me, y'know? – If it's real for me then that's the last question I can ask, right?'[19] However, this becomes extremely difficult when the power of the image 'for its own sake' overrides its interpretative meaning.

Angela, in contrast, has given herself up to the paradox, refusing to delineate a clear-cut course between dream and waking reality. Thus, as she and Tom drive to the prison for their first meeting with Felix, Angela puts a cigarette in her mouth but fails to light it. 'I'm bustin' my nuts tryin' to quit so I just kinda go through the motions', she explains. 'Everything in the world is suggestion, you know. Everything is just one step away from a dream'. Later, when Tom presses her on whether she went to the doctor's house with Jerry on the night of the murder, she says that she cannot be sure: 'Maybe I dreamed it all'. More importantly, she adds a key insight into her predicament: 'Maybe now you get the feeling ... that everything is possible and impossible at the same time, right? You feel it? This is what I live with all the time!' It is clear that Angela's problem is less one of sanity versus insanity than distinguishing between myth and reality, desire and fact. This leads her to live exclusively in the moment, to 'only depend on the next thing that happens', as Marilyn Monroe's character puts it in *The Misfits*. We are clearly faced with a slippage between significance – Lacan's linguistic 'real' – and the Real that lies concealed in the gaps of its chains of desire. This contradiction between art as pure intuition and art as rational exegesis is the same problem faced by Mike in *The French Lieutenant's Woman*, with extremely unsettling results. It is particularly unnerving in a detective story where the private eye is completely dependent upon his interpretation of clues gleaned from the phenomenological reality of his surroundings – both from people and objects – in order to decipher the case. If that reality is itself but a dream, there is nowhere left to go but into pure oneirism.

Given this all-encompassing dreamscape, Reisz's habitual use of mirrors now takes on a radically different tenor. Instead of expressing clear-cut distinctions between virtual and actual space (such as the *doppelgänger* motifs in *Saturday Night and Sunday Morning* and *The Gambler*), or providing a yardstick for consolidating a concrete sense of self-identity (Anna in *The French Lieutenant's Woman*), mirrors are now incorporated into a much broader surrealist vocabulary, as a constituent part of the dream-work itself. Jean Cocteau was the master of such *mise-*

en-scène (specifically *L'Orphée*, 1949), where mirrors act as portals and conduits, linking characters and images to other parts of the dream narrative to create a labyrinthine weave of metonymic connections. *Everybody Wins* follows a similar 'logic'. Thus, for example, Tom is 'captured' by this dream scenario as soon as he enters Highbury, for as Leon Redbone begins to sing, 'I want to be see-duced … ', Reisz cuts to a close-up of Tom's face in his rear-view mirror, thereby linking dream, desire and the crystalline in a single over-determined image. Similarly, the song ends just as Tom gets his first glimpse of Angela, approaching his car from the rear. Significantly, this view is not in 'real' space but, like Alexander Rodchenko's famous photographic portrait, *The Chauffeur*, is shot in the reverse image of his car's wing mirror (suggesting both duplicity and instability), while the tightly reduced frame-within-a-frame communicates an express need to keep Angela's (multiple) identities within bounds.

However, the mirror also links Tom and Angela to the de-territorializing oneiric circuit that weaves its way throughout the film, resurfacing at key moments through other crystalline reflections as if to indicated the 'return of repressed' in outward form. Thus, immediately after Angela admits to Tom that her father used to rape her, she walks across her living room and checks her make-up at her dressing table, so that we only see her mirror reflection. It is as if she were unconsciously connecting her adult waking reality to the Primal Scene of her repressed childhood. However, Tom is also reflected in the same mirror – in the extreme right background – jammed between Angela's virtual image and the reflected edge of the bedroom door, not only entrapping him spatially, but also sucking him in to the same dream-work circuit. Whether Tom likes it or not, his determination to keep Angela on track with the case, to stay focused on disclosing what she knows, is irrevocably linked to her unconscious (and therefore largely indecipherable) relationship to her past. Finally, this ensnaring circuit finally traps Judge Murdoch. While Tom is praising the Judge for having the guts to take on City Hall, Reisz 'doubles' Murdoch in a mirror shot next to the shower door, just as he delivers his line, 'I've sprung Felix, Tom – that'll have to be the end of it'. When Tom replies, 'What do you mean, Judge', Murdoch joins Tom in actual space, and repeats his line, as if for added emphasis. However, this is less a case of duplicity – the mirror shot expressing his collusion with Haggerty and City Hall, the actual shot his pragmatic solution to a difficult case – but instead an example of both 'worlds' existing in the same enveloping unconscious space. Tom might appear outraged, as if he were above such corrupt compromises, but he, like the film's spectator, has been ensnared in the dream-work from day one, a willing mechanism in its latent duplicities. Murdoch is exactly right: Tom 'can't save the Goddamn world' because he has no idea what that world is. Given its innate absurdity, maybe he simply dreamt the whole thing.

Although some commentators have argued that the commercial and critical failure of *Everybody Wins* compelled Reisz to eschew the cinema for the theatre throughout the rest of the decade, in a 1999 interview with Bob Cashill he cited other reasons for his artistic change of direction: 'Old age and senility, really', he explained, with an obvious chuckle. 'Mainly, there comes a point when you don't have anything to say to the 15–to-25 year-olds who are the basic movie-going audience. I've always loved theatre, and about five years ago I started directing shows. And I'm having a ball. The thing about the theatre is that you take your cue from the author, which is not the case with the movies. And the theatre is happening now, as you experience it – if it goes dead, it's not happening at all'.[20] In addition to reviving Tom Murphy's *The Gigli Concert* in 1992 and Terence Rattigan's *The Deep Blue Sea* (which won the 1993 Critics' Circle Award and an Olivier nomination), Reisz collaborated with his old cohort Harold Pinter on several plays, including the latter's *Moonlight* (1996), *Ashes to Ashes* (1999), *A Kind of Alaska* and *Landscape* (both 1998). More importantly, Reisz's return to the stage reacquainted him with the works of Samuel Beckett. 'I have read Beckett's novels for many years and I've seen the plays', says Reisz, 'but I also directed the stage version of *Happy Days* at the Gate, Dublin, with Rosaleen Linehan [in 1996], so I have one whole chunk of experience of working with the extraordinary demanding precision of the writing. So yes, I am an admirer'.[21] Reisz was thus an obvious candidate to direct one of the projects in Michael Colgan and Alan Moloney's ambitious 'Beckett on Film' television series. Funded by RTE, Channel 4, Bord Scannán na Eireann and Tyrone Productions, the series featured nineteen films by nineteen different directors, including Michael Lindsay-Hogg, David Mamet, Anthony Minghella, Atom Egoyan and Neil Jordan.

Shot in April 2000 at Ardmore Studios in Ireland, Reisz's contribution was the sixteen-minute *Act Without Words I*, Beckett's first published balletic mime. Written in French in 1956 with accompanying music by his cousin, John Beckett, this extremely stylized one-act play was originally conceived as part of a double bill (along with *Endgame*, 1957), receiving its first performance at London's Royal Court Theatre in 1957. 'It was an intriguing challenge to film a Beckett play', notes Reisz:

> You have to rethink and refeel everything, but it was a nice problem. I chose *Act Without Words* because of Beckett's clever use of the artifice of

theatre and the way he intermingles humour and pathos. *Act Without Words I* is a mime, with no dialogue at all. The artifice of the thing being set in the theatre is part of the pleasure of the piece. Now I have to find a way of making the artifice of the cinema part of the pleasure of the piece. It's a nice problem. I think it's a jeu d'esprit in a rather ambiguous, half-despairing way. But it's a very light piece for Beckett. As always with Beckett, in the agony there is pity, understanding and humanity. By using repetition, Beckett was trying to make sense of his own experience of the world. Right or wrong doesn't come into it.[22]

Like *Endgame* and *Waiting for Godot* (1952), the play emphasizes the problem of humans' relationship with an external world beyond their control that frustrates all their efforts to make it habitable and meaningful. As Arthur Marwick argues, 'Beckett asks, in effect, whether at any time life is worth having, and he presents this not as a question for debate (which would be pointless), but as a permanent doubt'.[23] The play thus provides an interesting coda, not only to Reisz's career as a whole (particularly the possibility of sustaining a viable resistant politics), but also his ongoing critique of existentialism in *The Gambler, Dog Soldiers* and *The French Lieutenant's Woman* as well as Tom O'Toole's futile quest for a meaningful 'truth' in *Everybody Wins*.

Using the edge of the filmic frame as analogous to the entrapping 'box' of the theatrical proscenium, Reisz establishes an inhospitable *mise-en-scène* from the beginning. The film opens on a stark desert set, dazzlingly lit against a cloudless blue sky, as if to symbolize humans' acute consciousness of their 'empty' condition – their 'being-in-the-world' against the horror of an all-encompassing nothingness. Then, as the wind whips up, we hear an off-screen gong as a Man (Sean Foley) is 'flung' into view from stage left, crying out as he tumbles head-over-heels onto the sand. He gets up, looks around, thoroughly bewildered. Suddenly, he hears the sound of a whistle from stage right. He runs towards it and for a split second exits the frame before being 'thrown' back into the space, as if by unseen forces. Then as he dusts himself off, he hears the whistle again, this time from stage left and once more tries to flee, with the exact same result. Finally, as the whistle sounds a third time, he ignores it, approaches the camera and slumps down on a small rise in the sand. It is a small victory: he is already beginning to learn not only that he cannot escape from his existence, but also that the world is governed by forces that are beyond his control and that maliciously love to tease him. The remainder of the film is a continuous sequence of further tempting offers – each announced by the whistle – and consequent dispiriting disappointments.

Thus, as the Man sits in desperate need of shade, his shirt pulled up over his close-cropped head, a welcoming palm tree descends from the top of the frame. He breathes a sigh of relief and relaxes in the cooling shadow of this makeshift oasis. Idly examining his hands, he notices that his fingernails could use a trim. As if on cue, the whistle blasts and a large pair of tailor's scissors descend on a wire from above. However, as he cuts his nails, the shade suddenly disappears and he looks around with dismay: the palm fronds have closed up, leaving him once again exposed to the blinding sun. Next, a small carafe labelled 'Water' descends and hovers some nine feet above the ground, tantalizingly out of his grasp. Reisz cuts to a high angle down as the Man jumps up, but he is unable to reach it from the ground. To make matters worse, he keeps falling to the sand, expending more energy than if there were no water at all. Fortunately, more help is at hand: a large cube descends from the upper left of the frame, falling to the ground with a thud. As one might expect, it is not quite large enough to help him reach the carafe, so he is presented with another, smaller cube to add to its height. It takes the Man a while to master the logistics – the boxes have to be stacked with the smaller on top of the larger rather than vice versa – but as soon as he figures out the correct balance the carafe is, you guessed it, withdrawn! When a third, even smaller cube appears, dancing tantalizingly in front of his nose, the Man stares at it with utter venom, forcing it to scurry away, frame right.

Although our hero is slowly learning to resist existence's teasing seductions, he cannot rid himself completely of attaching useful meaning to objects and their positive relation to human actions. Thus, when a knotted climbing rope is let down from the flies, he is filled with new hope. To the sounds of Michael Nyman's urgent, low-stringed arpeggios (as if to mimic the rush of blood coursing through his veins), he shins up the rope in order to reach for the water, only for it to collapse as he is mere inches from his goal. After vainly trying to lasso the carafe with the rope, the Man finally gives up, deciding to end it all by hanging himself from one of the horizontal branches of the palm tree. However, just as he is making a makeshift scaffold by placing the cubes under the tree, the bough droops. He slowly and wearily returns the two cubes back to their original positions, placing the rope on top of them. Suddenly he hears the whistle again and runs to exit the frame, stage left. Of course, this attempt is no more successful than the previous ones: he is 'flung' back onto the stage, taking his usual spill. When he hears another whistle from stage right, he resists the temptation to try and exit, staring instead at his fists. He unclasps them, looks at his hands, then picks up the scissors. He starts to trim one of his fingernails but stops to feel the sharpness of the blade. After placing the scissors on one of the cubes, he unbuttons the top of his shirt and feels the sweat on his neck: is he going to cut his own throat? The question becomes moot when the cube, rope and scissors are also withdrawn: Beckett denies him even the option of suicide. Thoroughly defeated, he sits down on the large cube to reflect on his lot, but this too proves to be a mistake: unseen forces pull the cube out from under him before yanking it up to the flies. The Man makes no effort to get up. Instead, he lies on the sand, his face towards the camera. Suddenly, the water carafe once more comes winging in from the background before hovering in front of his sweating face. However, this time he ignores it and the water disappears, stage right. The bough of the tree returns to its horizontal position and the palm fronds open to bring back the shade, but again the Man refuses temptation. Finally, the tree is removed and he is left completely alone, staring at his hands. Fade to black.

Several Beckett scholars have pointed out that the Man's situation in *Act Without Words I* is not dissimilar to that of the mythological figure, Tantalus, the son of Zeus and king of Sipylos, from whom we get the word, 'tantalize'. Accused of stealing ambrosia from the gods, he was condemned to an eternity of hunger and thirst in Tartarus, the underworld zone of punishment. Immersed up to his neck in a pool of water, every time he attempted to slake his thirst by bending his neck to drink, it drained tantalizingly away. To add insult to injury, overhanging the pool were boughs laden with luscious fruit. However, each time Tantalus stretched to pluck this juicy sustenance, the winds blew the boughs beyond his reach. In the case of Beckett's protagonist, the full reality of this 'torture' becomes clear to him only gradually. He will never be able to receive any substantial benefit from the gratifications that are proffered, and to pursue them will only lead to greater frustration. This is largely because Beckett's individual has no grasp of his actions, or indeed why he exists in the first place. It is highly significant that the Man is 'flung' onto the stage, for it relates the drama to the philosophy of Martin Heidegger (an acknowledged Beckett source), whose notion of *Geworfenheit*, the state of being 'thrown' or 'flung' into existence, refers to the basic existential situation of humankind. As George Steiner points out, 'The world into which we are thrown, without personal choice, with no previous knowledge ... was there before us and will be there after us'.[24] Humans thus find themselves alive and conscious in a world they did not choose and with various specific limitations over which they have no control. This constitutes what Heidegger calls humans' *Faktizität* or 'facticity'. In the play, this 'facticity' is that of a person who finds himself thrust into a human condition that makes him thirsty and hot, and thus in serious need of water and shade. However, far from attaining his basic needs, the protagonist ultimately realizes that to pursue his desires by appropriating what the world has to offer is ultimately futile.

It is significant, given Reisz's attraction to the play, that *Act Without Words I* is one of Beckett's least well received works. Ruby Cohn sees it as 'almost too explicit', Ihab Hassan says the mime is 'a little too obvious and pat', while John Spurling, comparing the play to *Godot*, felt that the play is 'over-explicit, over-emphasized and even, unless redeemed by its performer, so unparticularized as to verge on the banal'.[25] However, Beckett scholar S. E. Gontarski correctly makes a much stronger case for the work. He directly relates the playwright's 'primitive theatre' to Nietzsche's Dionysian drama and Antonin Artaud's Theatre of Cruelty: 'Beckett has created here one of his most subtle and compact images of the birth of existential humanity, of the existential artist, with all the ironies inherent in the coincidence of birth and death'.[26] For Gontarski, this is Beckett's closest acknowledgement of Artaud's demand for a theatre of 'pure theatrical language which does without words, a language of signs, gestures and attitudes having an ideographic value'.[27] In this case, gestures come to represent ideas, attitudes of mind and aspects of nature in a concrete manner, much like hieroglyphs. Beckett sees his protagonist as 'human meat – or bones' and associates him with Clov in *Endgame*, 'thinking and stumbling and sweating, under our noses, like Clov about Hamm, but gone from refuge'.[28]

However, unlike traditional interpretations of *Endgame* and *Godot*, which suggest that existence is cyclical and that existential struggle is doomed to play the same futile games without end, *Act Without Words I* is a defiantly linear fable.[29] 'Clearly birth (or being "thrown" into "being") is a point of origination', notes Gontarski, 'and it takes a Procrustean reading of the ending to fit the mime into the circular patterns of *Waiting for Godot* or *Endgame*. Its futility is finally of another, quite linear order'.[30] Thus although the Man regresses towards immobility at the film's end, he doesn't deteriorate into complete helplessness, bad conscience or *ressentiment*. The next day he is presumably ready for more of the same – but on different lines and perhaps with different outcomes – suggesting that his final immobility is willed rather than accepted as a fatalistic default. Although the inferior force (Man) is ultimately defeated by its superior (Existence), it does not mean that the Man in the play ceases to rebel against the force of Being – he may still refuse to obey as an expression of his own becoming:

> Ironically then, the protagonist is most active, most potent when inert, and his life acquires meaning as it closes. In this refusal, this cutting of the umbilical rope, a second birth occurs, the birth of Man. The

protagonist has finally acquired, earned, a name, Mankind or hu-Manity
(another M, in any case). As he refuses the bidding of the outside force,
as he refuses to act predictably, in his own self-interest, as he refuses the
struggle for the most elemental of man's needs, he breaks free of need
the way Murphy never could.[31]

Unlike Reisz's other existential characters, Axel Freed, Ray Hicks and
Sarah Woodruff, each of whom are dependent upon a willed action in
order to assert their will-to-power, Beckett's protagonist creates himself,
and frees himself of need and survival by refusing to act at all. In this
sense, he is a pure artist. His struggles and inventions fail, all the better
to produce an artistic success as pure line of flight, much like the pure
freedom of Nietzsche's Zarathustra. It is as if Reisz were saying, when
all else fails, we always have the boundless absurdity of art itself to help
us fail even better. In other words, sit back, roll film, and enjoy ...

Notes

1 Arthur Miller, 'Preface' to *Everybody Wins* (New York, Grove Weidenfeld, 1990),
   p. xi.
2 Sigmund Freud, *The Interpretation of Dreams*, The Penguin Freud Library, Vol. 4,
   trans. James Strachey (Harmondsworth, Penguin Books, 1976), p. 751.
3 Miller, *Everybody Wins*, p. 22.
4 *Ibid.*, p. 88.
5 Arthur Miller, 'Introduction' to *Two-Way Mirror* (London, Methuen, 1984), unpag-
   inated.
6 Karel Reisz, quoted in Kirk Johnson, 'Arthur Miller's Vision of Love Becomes a
   Movie', *New York Times*, 11 June 1989, Section 2, p. 22. The fact that two of the
   film's main protagonists, Tom and Jerry, are also the names of famous cartoon
   characters, should not escape our notice.
7 Stanley Kauffmann, 'The Woman in the Case', *New Republic*, Vol. 202, No. 10, 5
   March 1990, p. 26.
8 Philip Kemp, 'Maybe Baby', *Sight and Sound*, Vol. 59, No. 2, Spring 1990, p. 136.
9 Peter Travers, '*Everybody Wins*', *Rolling Stone*, 22 February 1990, p. 39.
10 *Ibid.*
11 Kemp, 'Maybe Baby', p. 136.
12 Pauline Kael, 'The Current Cinema: New Age Daydreams', *New Yorker*, 17
   December 1990, p. 121.
13 Reisz, quoted in Johnson, 'Arthur Miller's Vision of Love Becomes a Movie',
   p. 19.
14 Debra Winger, quoted in *ibid.*, p. 23.
15 Kael, 'The Current Cinema: New Age Daydreams', p. 120.
16 Freud, *The Interpretation of Dreams*, p. 721.
17 Miller, 'Preface' to *Everybody Wins*, p. xi.
18 *Ibid.*, p. xii.
19 Miller, *Some Kind of Love Story* in *Two-Way Mirror*, p. 62.
20 Quoted in Bob Cashill, 'Director Karel Reisz Sifts Through Pinter's *Ashes*', *Playbill*, 8 February 1999. Accessed 16 March 2005. www.playbill.com/features/
   article/64863.html.

21 Interview: Reisz on Beckett. Accessed 30 August 2005. www.beckettonfilm.com/plays/actwithoutwordsone/text_only/interview_reisz_text.html.
22 *Ibid.*
23 Arthur Marwick, *Culture in Britain Since 1945* (Oxford, Basil Blackwell, 1991), p. 34.
24 George Steiner, *Martin Heidegger* (Chicago, University of Chicago Press, 1978) p. 87.
25 All quoted in S. E. Gontarski, '"Birth Astride of a Grave": Samuel Beckett's *Act Without Words I*', in S. E. Gontarski, ed., *The Beckett Studies Reader* (Gainesville, University of Florida Press, 1993), p. 29.
26 *Ibid.*, p. 30.
27 Antonin Artaud, *The Theater and Its Double*, trans. Mary Caroline Richards (New York, Grove Press, 1958), p. 39.
28 Beckett, quoted in Gontarski, '"Birth Astride of a Grave"', p. 31.
29 For a radically revised, ontologically affirmative reading of Beckett, see Gilles Deleuze, 'The Exhausted', trans. Anthony Uhlmann, *SubStance*, No. 78, Vol. 24, No. 3, 1995, pp. 3–28.
30 Gontarski, '"Birth Astride of a Grave"', p. 31.
31 *Ibid.*, p. 32.

Conclusion

11

> What I want my films to have is sobriety. I want to make interesting the *trivia* of everyday life. (Karel Reisz)[1]

The month following Karel Reisz's death at the age of seventy-six in November 2002, the *London Review of Books* decided to orchestrate a tribute to 'this most elegant and spirited of men' by publishing a series of tributes from his friends and colleagues. Director Roger Spottiswoode (*Under Fire*, 1983, *Tomorrow Never Dies*, 1997, *Ripley Under Ground*, 2005), related a particularly telling anecdote that perfectly encapsulated the integrity of the man while also helping to explain his unfortunate paucity of output:

> Some thirty years ago, I found myself locked in a London cutting-room with him for several months as we edited *The Gambler*. One day, he took a phone call from Los Angeles. It was unusually long and when he finally hung up, he had a bewildered expression on his face. 'They want me to remake *Woman in the Dunes*,' he said. He went on: 'I told them there had been a rather exquisite film of that title quite recently. Just a few months ago, in fact. "Yes," they told me, "but now so-and-so wants to do the part."' He mentioned a well known L.A. actress. Karel went on: 'So I asked them, what about the existing film, won't that be a problem? And they said: "Certainly not, so-and-so is going to buy all the prints and burn them. End of problem."' There was a moment's pause, then the smile returned to his face, and he laughed. 'Amazing, isn't it?' he said. 'Nice to be reminded why it's so much simpler to live here and not there.'[2]

Playwright John Guare tells a similar story, recalling that when Reisz was approached with a view to directing one of the *Star Wars* sequels, he refused without hesitation: 'The idea of doing something emotionally inert just for the technical exercise wasn't for Karel'.[3]

Instead, Reisz's chief motivator as a director, which radically limited the number and types of projects he chose to film, but at the same time guaranteed a clear line of continuity in his own work, was the interior life of his *characters*. This interest led to his movement away from documentary realism to a more personal, hybrid mode of film-making. Discussing the drawbacks of deliberately propagating a so-called directorial 'signature', Reisz noted to Stephen Zito that, 'A very dangerous thing happens to filmmakers – they start believing their own myths and start working and reworking the things critics say that they're good at. You just have to lay yourself open to the characters – and then, of course, it always comes out as part of your own work'.[4] According to the late Gavin Lambert, the kind of character that most interested Reisz gives an important clue to his own personality, which was essentially closely guarded: 'On the surface he seemed (and in many ways was) exceptionally reasonable and balanced. But he was also a passionate underground subversive, something that emerges in all his most personal movies, *Saturday Night and Sunday Morning*, *Isadora*, *The Gambler* and *Dog Soldiers/Who'll Stop the Rain*). It also accounts for a private mystery. In her vivid and engaging memoir, *The Memory of All That*, Betsy Blair writes she fell in love with Karel not just on account of his charm and wit and intelligence, but because "I know I'll always be interested in him, intrigued by him."'[5] For Lambert, the chief characteristic of Reisz's films is that they are essentially 'portrait films', each constructed around a central character who is also an adventurer – an 'irreconcilable enemy of law' – who doesn't simply 'buck the system' but invigorates both individual and social history with the revolutionary spirit of nonconformity. Although Reisz retained a sceptical attitude towards such activity – as we have noted, he kept a firm critical distance from his characters' self-interpellating 'madness', whether it be Arthur Seaton's self-destructive womanizing, Morgan's animalism, Axel Freed's gambling addiction, or Angela Crispini's multiple personalities – he was also an obvious admirer of the outsider's will-to-power and the subjective, often dreamlike world (*Morgan*, *Isadora*, *Everybody Wins*) that they construct for themselves outside the prevailing *Zeitgeist*.

More importantly, Reisz was able to sustain this enquiry by radically transforming the nature of cinematic realism as a viable critical medium. Although many critics have cited the important legacy of Reisz and Lindsay Anderson's kitchen sink films on the subsequent generation of British realist film-makers – most notably Ken Loach, Mike Leigh, Alan Clarke and Stephen Frears (Reisz's assistant director on *Morgan*) – many of these directors would probably have emerged, like Michael Apted, from regional television regardless of the mainstream success of their Free Cinema brethren. In any case, Reisz's realism rapidly developed away from its kitchen sink roots into a more individual, hybrid style. This fused elements of naturalist *mise-en-scène* (through authentic, class-based locations, whether it be working-class Nottingham or the French Riviera), with the more 'formal' vocabulary of French cinema, specifically the historical legacy of poetic realism (Marcel Carné) and surrealism (Jean Cocteau and Jean Vigo) and the more contemporary applications of Brechtian distanciation (Jean-Luc Godard) and dislocated temporal montage (Alain Resnais). The pictorial 'glue' that holds these widely differing influences together is Reisz's commitment to the expressive qualities of everyday trivia as objective correlatives of his characters' subjectivities. Thus Arthur Seaton's neatly arranged, well-tailored suits; Morgan's assorted bric-à-brac, ranging from his portraits of Trotsky and Stalin to his gorilla suit and Mickey Mouse alarm clock; Charles Smithson's meticulously ordered collection of antiquarian books and fossils; Mrs Poulteney's sturdy, leather-clad Bible; and Patsy Cline's 'down-home' Virginia kitchen – each tells us as much about their characters' desires and interests than any amount of adventurous 'derring-do'.

Moreover, Reisz also knew, almost instinctively, when to let the art direction do the work, and when to move the camera in order to open up shifting correlatives within a single take. Thus, for example, Morgan is an *animator* of his surroundings. The trivia of his everyday life has little significance in and of itself without his anarchic spirit to give it life. Thus his shaving cream is simply a tool for his morning toilette until he uses it to dab the nose of the constable, committing a 'technical assault' in the process. Similarly, his gorilla suit is a mere empty shell lying around his studio until he dons it as a useful piece of wardrobe for gate-crashing Leonie's wedding. In contrast, in *Everybody Wins*, the surroundings *animate the character*, creating an objective correlative of their shifting mental states. Thus, each time that Tom visits Jerry at the old mill, Reisz employs a master shot, filmed in long, continuous takes, during which he dollies the camera in 90° or 180° arcs, using Tom as the ostensible fulcrum or pivot in the centre of the circle. This acts as his springboard for cutting in to punctuating shot/reverse-shot close-ups for the purpose of subjective emphasis. In this way, Jerry is captured largely from Tom's point-of-view (even though Tom may also be in the shot), but he defies a stable positioning because the figure/ground relationship is constantly changing as the camera moves in relation to his body. As a result, the background behind the cult leader keeps shifting throughout the conversation, even though Jerry himself is barely moving, much like a constantly changing back-projection. At one point he may be 'framed' by the statue of Major McCall, at another by his strange metal sculptures, at others by the cracked and broken skylights of the mill itself, and finally by the visually overwhelming junk of his garage-cum-workshop. Thus in one economical sequence, Reisz is able to relate Jerry's unstable personality to all the components of his life – from religious leader to artist to biker mechanic – without minimizing the importance of any one specific correlative. All the so-called 'trivia' of his surroundings contribute to the same psychic jigsaw puzzle. In effect, we are reminded of an earlier observation made by Lionel Trilling, quoted by Reisz as the epigraph of his own article on Lewis Milestone, that 'Ideology is not acquired by thought, but by breathing the haunted air',[6] a fitting epitaph for Reisz's own artistic approach to the cinema.

Notes

1 Quoted in Oakes, 'New Reputations: Karel Reisz, Break for Commercial', p. 861.
2 Roger Spottiswoode, quoted in Andrew O'Hagan, 'Karel Reisz Remembered'. Accessed 5 January 2005. www.lrb.co.uk/v24/n24/mult03_.html.
3 John Guare, quoted in *ibid.*
4 Reisz, quoted in Zito, '*Dog Soldiers*: Novel into Film', p. 12.
5 Gavin Lambert, 'The Rebel Inside', *The Guardian*, 20 June 2003.
6 Quoted in Reisz, 'Milestone and War', p. 12.

Appendix

Karel Reisz's seasons as Programmes Officer at the National Film Theatre[1]

1953 (attendance 159,157)

Origins of the Western; Great Comedians – The Silent Screen; German Cinema Classics; Mexican Programme; Hitchcock; Silent Film in Russia; De Sica; Silent Film in France; The Coronation; Ealing Comedy; Silent Film in Britain; He, She and It; Documentary Tradition; Beginnings of the Cinema; Chaplin Programme; Christmas Comedy.

1954 (attendance 181,905)

Erich von Stroheim – Director and Actor; Carol Reed and Humphrey Jennings; Ballet; Gaumont-British Library Anniversary; The Child Actor; British and American Musical; World Cinema; Films from Asia; 50 Years of Film; Musicals.

1955 (attendance 202,714)

From the Stage to the Screen; Musicals and Comedies; W. C. Fields; Laurel and Hardy; Homage to United Artists; Luis Buñuel; Special; Cukor and Lang; Méliès and Four Comedies; John Huston; Sixty Years of Cinema; John Ford; Hitchcock Thrillers; Drama in the Big City; Fable, Fairytale and Fantasy.

Free Cinema Programmes, February 1956–March 1959

Programme 1: 5–8 February, 1956

O Dreamland (Lindsay Anderson, UK, 1953, 12 mins)

Together (Lorenza Mazzetti, UK, 1953, 52 mins)
Momma Don't Allow (Karel Reisz and Tony Richardson, UK, 1956, 22 mins)

Programme 2: 9–12 September, 1956

Le Sang des Bêtes (Georges Franju, France 1948, 20 mins)
Neighbours (Norman McLaren, Canada, 1952, 8 mins)
On the Bowery (Lionel Ragosin, US, 1955, 65 mins)

Programme 3: 'Look at Britain', 25–29 May, 1957

The Singing Street (N. McIsaac, J. T. R. Ritchie, R. Townsend, UK, 1952, 18 mins, extract only)
Wakefield Express (Lindsay Anderson, UK, 1952, 30 mins, extract only)
Every Day Except Christmas (Lindsay Anderson, UK, 1957, 40 mins)
Nice Time (Claude Goretta and Alain Tanner, UK, 1957, 17 mins)

Programme 4: 'Polish Voices', 3–6 September, 1958

Paragraph Zero (Wlodzimierz Borowik, Poland, 1956, 17 mins)
Where the Devil Says Good-night (Kazimierz Karabasz, Poland, 1956, 11 mins)
House of Old Women (Jan Lomniki, Poland, 1957, 9 mins)
Once Upon a Time (Walerian Borowczyk, Poland, 1957, 9 mins)
Two Men and a Wardrobe (Roman Polanski, Poland, 1957, 15 mins)
Dom (Jan Lenica, Poland, 1958, 12 mins)

Programme 5: 'French Renewal', 7–9 September, 1958

Les Mistons (François Truffaut, France, 1957, 28 mins)
Le Beau Serge (Claude Chabrol, France, 1958, 97 mins)

Programme 6: 'The Last Free Cinema', 18–22 March, 1959

Food for a Blush (Elizabeth Russell, UK, 1955, 30 mins)
Enginemen (Michael Grigsby, UK, 1957, 21 mins)
Refuge England (Robert Vas, UK, 1959, 27 mins)
We Are the Lambeth Boys (Karel Reisz, UK, 1959, 52 mins)

Karel Reisz's top ten films of all time

1963 (*Films & Filming* 'Desert Island Films')[2]

Earth (Alexander Dovzhenko, 1930)
The General (Buster Keaton, 1926)
L'Age d'Or (Luis Buñuel, 1930)
Une Partie de Campagne (Jean Renoir, 1936)
Young Mr. Lincoln (John Ford, 1939)
Red River (Howard Hawks, 1948)
Palm Beach Story (Preston Sturges, 1942)
Meet Me in St. Louis (Vincente Minnelli, 1944)
Two Pennyworth of Hope (Renato Castellani, 1952)
L'Avventura (Michelangelo Antonioni, 1960)

2002 (*Sight and Sound*'s Top Ten Poll)[3]

The Discreet Charm of the Bourgeoisie (Luis Buñuel, 1972)
Earth (Alexander Dovzhenko, 1930)
Fires Were Started (Humphrey Jennings, 1943)
The Lady Eve (Preston Sturges, 1941)
Nashville (Robert Altman, 1975)
Raging Bull (Martin Scorsese, 1980)
La Règle du Jeu (Jean Renoir, 1939)
Strangers on a Train (Alfred Hitchcock, 1951)
They Were Expendable (John Ford, 1945)
Tokyo Story (Yasujiro Ozu, 1953)

Notes

1 From Ivan Butler, *'To Encourage the Art of the Film': The Story of the British Film Institute* (London, Robert Hale, 1971), p. 187.
2 From 'Desert Island Films', *Films & Filming*, Vol. 9, No. 11, August 1963, pp. 11–13.
3 www.bfi.org.uk/sightandsound/topten/poll/voter.php?forename=Karel&surname=Reisz.

Filmography and theatre credits

As producer

Every Day Except Christmas, 1957, 40 mins, b/w

Production company: Graphic Films, for the Ford Motor Company. First film of the series, 'Look at Britain'
Producers: Karel Reisz and Leon Clore
Director: Lindsay Anderson
Photography: Walter Lassally
Editing/Sound: John Fletcher
Music: Daniel Paris
Commentary: Alun Owen

I Want to Go to School, 1960, 30 mins, b/w

Production company: Graphic Films, for the National Union of Teachers
Producers: Karel Reisz and Leon Clore
Director and screenplay: John Krish

This Sporting Life, 1963, 134 mins, b/w

Production company: Independent Artists
Executive producers: Julian Wintle and Leslie Parkyn
Producer: Karel Reisz
Director: Lindsay Anderson
Screenplay: David Storey, adapted from his novel
Photography: Denys Coop
Art director: Alan Withy
Set decoration: Peter Lamont
Production director: Albert Fennell
Editing: Peter Taylor
Music/Musical director: Roberto Gerhard
Costumes: Sophie Devine
Casting: Miriam Brickman
Continuity: Pamela Mann

Sound editing: Chris Greenham
Sound recording: John W. Mitchell and Gordon K. McCallum
Leading players: Richard Harris (Frank Machin), Rachel Roberts (Margaret Hammond), Alan Badel (Weaver), William Hartnell (Johnson), Colin Blakely (Maurice Braithwaite), Vanda Godsell (Mrs Weaver), Anne Cunningham (Judith), Jack Watson (Len Miller), Arthur Lowe (Slomer), Harry Markham (Wade), George Sewell (Jeff), Leonard Rossiter (Phillips), Katharine Parr (Mrs Farrer), Bernadette Benson (Lynda), Andrew Nolan (Ian), Peter Duguid (Doctor), Wallas Eaton (Waiter), Anthony Woodruff (Head waiter), Michael Logan (Riley), Murray Evans (Hooker), Tom Clegg (Gower), Ken Traill (Trainer), Frank Windsor (Dentist), John Gill (Cameron).

As director

Momma Don't Allow, 1956, 22 mins, b/w (co-directed with Tony Richardson)

Production company: British Institute, Experimental Film Production Fund
Co-director: Tony Richardson
Photography: Walter Lassally
Editing/Sound: John Fletcher
Music: The Chris Barber Band, with Chris Barber (trombone), Pat Halcox (trumpet), Monty Sunshine (clarinet), Lonnie Donegan (guitar), Jim Bray (counterbass), Ron Bowden (drums), Ottilie Patterson (vocals)

March to Aldermaston, 1959, 33 mins, b/w

Production company: Contemporary Films
Producer: Derrick Knight
Production assistants: Karel Reisz, Lindsay Anderson, Christopher Brunel, Charles Cooper, Allan Forbes, Derrick Knight, Kurt Lewenhak, Lewis McLeod, Eda Segal, Elizabeth Russell, Stephen Peet, Derek York.
Editing: Mary Beales and Lindsay Anderson
Commentary written by Christopher Logue and Lindsay Anderson, read by Richard Burton

We Are the Lambeth Boys, 1959, 52 mins, b/w

Production company: Graphic Films, for the Ford Motor Company. Second film of the series, 'Look at Britain'
Executive Producer: Robert Adams
Producer: Leon Clore
Assistants: Louis Wolfers, Raoul Sobel
Photography: Walter Lassally
Editing: John Fletcher

Music: John Dankworth and his Orchestra
Commentary: Jon Rollason

Saturday Night and Sunday Morning, 1960, 89 mins, b/w

Production company: Woodfall Film Productions
Executive Producer: Harry Saltzman
Producer: Tony Richardson
Screenplay: Alan Sillitoe, from his novel
Photography: Freddie Francis
Art director: Ted Marshall
Set decoration: Timothy O'Brien
Production manager: Jack Rix
Editing: Seth Holt
Music: Johnny Dankworth and his Orchestra. Special lyrics by David Dear-
     love
Wardrobe: Sophie Devine, Barbara Gillett
Continuity: Pamela Mann
Sound recording: Peter Handford, Bob Jones
Sound editing: Chris Greenham
Leading players: Albert Finney (Arthur Seaton), Shirley Anne Field (Doreen
     Gretton), Rachel Roberts (Brenda), Hylda Baker (Aunt Ada), Norman
     Rossington (Bert), Bryan Pringle (Jack), Robert Cawdron (Robboe),
     Edna Morris (Mrs Bull), Elsie Wagstaff (Mrs Seaton), Frank Pettitt
     (Harold Seaton), Avis Bunnage (Blousy woman), Colin Blakely (Loud-
     mouth), Irene Richmond (Mrs Gretton), Louise Dunn (Betty), Peter
     Madden (Drunken man), Cameron Hall (Mr Bull), Alister Williamson
     (Policeman), Anne Blake (Civil defence officer)

Night Must Fall, 1964, 101 mins, b/w

Production company: MGM
Executive producer: Laurence P. Bachman
Producers: Albert Finney, Karel Reisz
Screenplay: Clive Exton, adapted from the play by Emlyn Williams
Photography: Freddie Francis
Art director: Lionel Couch
Set decoration: Timothy O'Brien
Production director: Timothy Burrill
Editing: Fergus McDonell, Philip Barnikel
Music/Musical director: Ron Grainer
Sound editing: Malcolm Cooke
Sound mixing: J. B. Smith
Leading players: Albert Finney (Danny), Mona Washbourne (Mrs Bramson),
     Susan Hampshire (Olivia), Sheila Hancock (Dora), Michael Medwin
     (Derek), Joe Gladwin (Dodge), Martin Wyldeck (Inspector Willett), John
     Gill (Foster)

Morgan: A Suitable Case for Treatment, 1966, 97 mins, b/w

Production company: Quintra Productions, British Lion Films
Producer: Leon Clore
Screenplay: David Mercer, adapted from his teleplay, *A Suitable Case for Treatment*
Photography: Larry Pizer, Gerry Turpin, gorilla material filmed by Alan Root, Bernard Grzimek
Art director: Philip Harrison
Production manager: Roy Baird
Editing: Tom Priestley
Music: Johnny Dankworth
Costumes: Jocelyn Rickards
Casting: Miriam Brickman
Continuity: Pat Moon
Sound recording: Peter Handford
Dubbing mixer: Hugh Strain
Dubbing editor: John Crome
Leading players: Vanessa Redgrave (Leonie Henderson), David Warner (Morgan Delt), Robert Stephens (Charles Napier), Irene Handl (Mrs Delt), Newton Blick (Mr Henderson), Nan Munro (Mrs Henderson), Bernard Bresslaw (Policeman), Arthur Mullard (Wally), Graham Crowden (Counsel), Peter Cellier (Second counsel), John Rae (Judge), Angus MacKay (Best man), Peter Collingwood (Geoffrey), John Garrie (Tipstaff), Marvis Edwards (Maid), Robert Bridges (Ticket collector)

Isadora, 1968, 153 mins (director's cut), 177 mins (original release print), col.

Production company: Universal
Producers: Robert and Raymond Hakim
Screenplay: Melvyn Bragg, Clive Exton, additional dialogue by Margaret Drabble
Adaptation: Melvyn Bragg
Photography: Larry Pizer (Eastmancolor)
Art directors: Michael Seymour, Miso Senesis, Ralph Brinton
Production designer: Jocelyn Herbert
Set decoration: Bryan Graves, Harry Cordwell, Jocelyn Herbert
Production manager: Eric Rattray
Production manager in Yugoslavia, Italy and France: Henri Baum
Editing: Tom Priestley
Music: Original music composed and conducted by Maurice Jarre; music for the modern dance sequences composed by Anthony Bowles; music for the classic dance sequences arranged and conducted by Anthony Bowles
Choreography: Litz Pisk
Continuity: Ann Skinner

Sound recording: Ken Ritchie, Maurice Askew
Sound editing: Terry Rawlings
Dialogue editing: Jim Atkinson
Leading players: Vanessa Redgrave (Isadora), John Fraser (Roger Thornton), James Fox (Edward Gordon Craig), Jason Robards (Paris Singer), Ivan Tchenko (Essenin), Vladimir Leskova (Bugatti), Cynthia Harris (Mary Desti), Bessie Love (Mrs Duncan), Tony Vogel (Raymond Duncan), Libby Glenn (Elizabeth Duncan), Ronnie Gilbert (Miss Chase), Wallas Eaton (Archer), Nicholas Pennell (Bedford), John Quentin (Pim), Christian Duvaleix (Armand), David Healy (Sullivan, manager of Chicago theatre), Lucinda Chambers (Deirdre), Simon Lutton Davies (Patrick), Noel Davis (Doctor), Ina de la Haye (Russian teacher), Constantine Yranski (Russian companion), Stefan Gryff (Russian party interpreter), John Brandon (Gospel Billy), Margaret Courtenay, Arthur White, Iza Teller, John Warner, Alan Gifford, Zuleika Robson, Arnold Diamond, Anthony Gardner, Sally Travers, Mark Dignam, Robin Lloyd, Lucy Saroyan, Jan Conrad, Hal Galili, Roy Stephens, Cal McCord, Richard Marner

On the High Road (TV, 1973), 47 mins, col.

Production company: BBC Television
Producers: Gavin Millar, Melvyn Bragg
Screenplay: English adaptation by Jeremy Brooks, Kitty Hunter Blair, from a one-act play by Anton Chekhov
Photography: Brian Tufano (Eastmancolor)
Design: Tony Abbott
Editing: David Martin
Music arrangement: Anthony Bowles; accordion by Henry Krein
Costumes: Robin Fraser-Paye
Sound: Michael Turner, Stan Morcomb
Leading players: Colin Blakely (Merik), Graham Crowden (Bortsov), David Baker (Fedya), Bob Hoskins (Kuzma), Barry Keegan (Tikhon), Peter Madden (Savva), Vanda Godsell (Maria), Lucy Griffiths (Efimova), Natalie Kent (Nazarovna), Jimmy Gardner (a traveller), David Sterne (Coachman)

The Gambler, 1974, 111 mins, col.

Production company: Paramount
Producers: Irwin Winkler, Robert Chartoff
Screenplay: James Toback
Photography: Victor J. Kemper (Eastmancolor)
Production designer: Philip Rosenberg
Production manager: Hal Polaire
Editing: Roger Spottiswoode

Music: Jerry Fielding, based on Symphony No. 1 by Gustav Mahler. 'Una Furtiva Lagrima' sung by Enrico Caruso
Costumes: Albert Wolsky
Casting: Cis Corman
Continuity: Julia Tucker
Sound mixer: Dennis Maitland
Sound editor: Terry Rawlings
Dialogue editor: Derek Holding
Sound re-recordist: Doug Turner
Leading players: James Caan (Axel Freed), Paul Sorvino (Hips), Lauren Hutton (Billie), Morris Carnovsky (A. R. Lowenthal), Jacqueline Brookes (Naomi), Burt Young (Carmine), Carmine Caridi (Jimmy), Carl W. Crudup (Spencer), Vic Tayback (One), Steven Keats (Howie), London Lee (Monkey), Antonio Fargas (Pimp), Stuart Margolin (Cowboy), William Andrews (Basketball coach), Joseph Attles (Singer in park), Ernest Butler (Vernon), Sully Boyar (Uncle Hy), Gregory Rozakis (Joe), Starletta De Paur (Monique), Ed Kovens (Ricky), Lucille Patton (Ricky's wife), Mitch Stein and Jonathan Koshner (College announcers), Charles Polk (Harlem bartender), M. Emmett Walsh (Las Vegas gambler), James Woods (Bank officer), Joel Wolfe (Moe), Allen Rich (Bernie), Ric Mancini (Sal), Raymond Serra (Benny), Baron Wilson (Basketball janitor), Richard Foronji (Donny), Frank Sivero (Donny's driver), Philip Sterling (Sidney), Patricia Fay (Bank teller), Beatrice Winde (Hospital receptionist), Leon Pinkney (Street basketball boy), Alisha Fontaine (Howie's girl), Presley Caton (Monkey's girl), Dick Schaap (Television announcer), Chick Hearn (Radio announcer)

Dog Soldiers (aka *Who'll Stop the Rain* in the US), 1978, 126 mins, col.

Production company: United Artists
Producers: Herb Jaffe, Gabriel Katzka
Screenplay: Judith Rascoe, Robert Stone, based on the novel *Dog Soldiers* by Robert Stone
Photography: Richard H. Kline (Technicolor)
Additional photography: Ron Taylor
Production designer: Dale Hennesy. In Mexico, Augustin Ytuarte.
Set designer: Dianne Wager
Set decorator: Robert DeVestel. In Mexico, Enrique Estevez
Production manager: Sheldon Schrager. In Mexico, Alberto Ferrer
Supervising Editor: John Bloom
Assistant film editors: Chris Ridsdale, Mark Conte, Peter Boyle. In Mexico, Carlos Puente Portillo
Special effects: Paul Stewart, Jerry Williams, Kenneth Pepiot, Chuck Dolan
Music: Laurence Rosenthal
Source music advisor: Tom Nolan. Songs: 'Philadelphia Fillies' by Del Reeves; 'Put a Little Love in Your Heart' by Jackie DeShannon; 'American

Pie' by Don McLean; 'I'll Step Down' by Slim Whitman; 'Hey Tonight', 'Who'll Stop the Rain' and 'Proud Mary' by Creedence Clearwater Revival; 'Gimme Some Lovin' by The Spencer Davis Group; 'Golden Rocket' by Hank Snow

Costumes: William Theiss

Casting: Jennifer Shull

Script supervisor: Kathy Thomas. In Mexico, Ana Maria Quintana

Production sound mixer: Chris Newman. In Mexico, José B. Carles

Re-recording mixer: Bill Rowe

Sound editing: Don Sharpe

Leading players: Nick Nolte (Ray Hicks), Tuesday Weld (Marge Converse), Michael Moriarty (John Converse), Anthony Zerbe (Antheil), Richard Masur (Danskin), Ray Sharkey (Smitty), Gail Strickland (Charmian), Charles Haid (Eddie Peace), David Opatoshu (Bender), James Cranna (Gerald), Timothy Blake (Jody), Joaquin Martinez (Angel), Shelby Balik (Janey), Jean Howell (Edna), Jose Carlos Ruiz (Galindez), John Durren (Alex), Bobby Kosser (Hippie), Wings Hauser (Marine driver), Jonathan Banks (Marine), Michael Bair (Blinded man), Derrel Maury (Soldier), Jan Burrell (Mother), Stuart Wilson (Father), James Gavin (Helicopter pilot), Bill Cross (Radio operator)

The French Lieutenant's Woman, 1981, 123 mins, col.

Production company: United Artists

Producer: Leon Clore

Screenplay: Harold Pinter, from the novel by John Fowles

Photography: Freddie Francis (Technicolor)

Production designer: Assheton Gorton

Art directors: Norman Dorme, Terry Pritchard, Allan Cameron

Set decorator: Ann Mollo

Editing: John Bloom

Assistant editors: Jeremy Hume, Chris Ridsdale

Special effects: Alan Bryce, Nobby Clarke

Music: Carl Davis. Adagio from Mozart's Sonata in D, K 576, played by John Lill

Costume designer: Tom Rand

Casting director: Patsy Pollock

Continuity: Kay Fenton

Sound recordist: Ivan Sharrock

Sound re-recordist: Bill Rowe

Sound editing: Don Sharpe

Leading players: Meryl Streep (Sarah Woodruff/Anna), Jeremy Irons (Charles Smithson/Mike), Hilton McRae (Sam), Emily Morgan (Mary), Charlotte Mitchell (Mrs Tranter), Lynsey Baxter (Ernestina Freeman), Peter Vaughan (Mr Freeman), Patience Collier (Mrs Poulteney), Leo McKern (Dr Grogan), Colin Jeavons (Vicar), Penelope Wilton (Sonia), Jean Faulds (Cook), Liz Smith (Mrs Fairley), Michael Elwyn (Montague),

David Warner (Murphy), Gerald Falconetti (Davide), John Barrett (Dairyman), Arabella Weir (Girl on undercliff), Ben Forster (Boy on undercliff), Catherine Willmer (Dr Grogan's housekeeper), Anthony Langdon (Asylum keeper), Edward Duke (Nathaniel), Richard Griffiths (Sir Tom), Graham Fletcher-Cook (Delivery boy), Richard Hope (3rd assistant), Toni Palmer (Mrs Endicott), Cecily Hobbs (Betty Anne), Doreen Mantle (Lady on train), Alun Armstrong (Grimes), Joanna Joseph (Lizzie), Judith Alderson (Red-haired prostitute), Cora Kinnaird (2nd prostitute), Orlando Fraser (Tom Elliott), Fredrike Morton (Girl), Alice Maschler (2nd girl), Matthew Morton, Vicky Ireland, Claire Travers Deacon, Harriet Walter, Janet Rawson, Mia Soteriou, Mary MacLeod, Peter Fraser, Rayner Newmark

Sweet Dreams, 1985, 115 mins, col.

Production company: HBO Pictures, Silver Screen Partners
Producers: Bernard Schwartz, Charles Mulvehill
Screenplay: Robert Getchell
Photography: Robbie Greenberg (Technicolor)
Production designer: Albert Brenner
Art director: David M. Haber
Set design: Frances W. Wells, Kandy Stern
Set decorator: Garrett Lewis
Production manager: Charles Mulvehill
Editing: Malcolm Cooke
Special effects: Burt Dalton, Rodney M. Byrd
Music: Charles Gross
Music consultant: Gregg Perry
Music editor: George Brand
Choreographer: Susan Scanlan
Costumes: Ann Roth
Casting: Ellen Chenoweth
Script supervisor: Wilma Garscadden-Gahret
Sound recording: Jeff Wexler, Don Coufal, James Stuebe
Sound re-recording mixer: Bill Rowe
Sound editors: Derek Holding, Colin Miller
Leading players: Jessica Lange (Patsy Cline), Ed Harris (Charlie Dick), Ann Wedgeworth (Hilda Hensley), David Clennon (Randy Hughes), Gary Basaraba (Woodhouse), John Goodman (Otis), P. J. Soles (Wanda), James Staley (Gerald Cline), Terri Gardner (Girl singer), Courtney Parker (Older Julie), Caitlin Kelch (Sylvia Hensley), Robert L. Dasch (John Hensley), Colton Edwards (Baby Randy), Holly Filler (Madrine), Bruce Kirby (Arthur Godfrey), Jerry Haynes (Owen Bradley), Kenneth White (Big Bill Shawley), Stonewall Jackson (Announcer at Opry), Jake T. Robinson (Biker), Boxcar Willie (Old man in jail), Tony Frank (Bartender), Charlie Walker (Cowboy Copas), Frank Knapp Jr. (Hawkshaw Hawkins), Richard J. Kidney (TV technician), Jack Slater (Recording engineer), Missy

Proulx (Girlfriend at fair), Aleda Pope (Girlfriend at fair), Carlton Cuse (Sergeant), John E. Davis (Skip Cartmill), John Walter Davis (Stone), Toni Sawyer (Baby nurse), Robert Rothwell (Plastic surgeon), Patricia Allison (Surgery nurse), Patsy's band: William Byrd (bass), John R. Smarr (acoustic guitar), Fred K. Young (drums), Curtis Young (singer/guitar), Michael David Black (singer/guitar)

Everybody Wins, 1990, 98 mins, col.

Production company: Film Trustees Ltd.
Executive producers: Linda Yellen, Terry Glinwood
Producers: Jeremy Thomas and Ezra Swerdlow
Screenplay: Arthur Miller, adapted from his play, *Some Kind of Love Story*
Photography: Ian Baker (Panavision)
Production designer: Peter Larkin
Art director: Charley Beal
Editing: John Bloom
Music: Mark Isham, additional music by Leon Redbone
Script supervisor: Sandy McLeod
Casting: Ellen Chenoweth
Costume design: Ann Roth
Sound editor: Don Sharp
Sound mixer: Ivan Sharrock
Leading players: Debra Winger (Angela Crispini), Nick Nolte (Tom O'Toole), Will Patton (Jerry), Judith Ivey (Connie), Kathleen Wilhoite (Amy), Jack Warden (Judge Harry Murdoch), Frank Converse (Charley Haggerty), Frank Military (Felix Daniels), Steven Skybell (Father Mancini), Mary Louise Wilson (Jean), Mert Hatfield (Bellanca), Peter Appel (Sonny), Sean Weil (Montana), Timothy D. Wright (Defence Attorney), Elizabeth Ann Klein (Judge), James Parisi (Reporter), R. M. Haley (Driver), T. M. Nelson George (Judge #2), David Ellis (Stunt co-ordinator), Tim Davison, Don Pulford, Richard Allison (Utility stunts)

Act Without Words I, 2000, 16 mins, col.

Production company: RTE, Channel 4, Bord Scannán na Eireann and Tyrone Productions
Executive producers: Joan Egan, Joe Mulhollan and Rod Stoneman
Producers: Michael Colgan and Alan Moloney
Script: Samuel Beckett
Photography: Seamus Deasy
Art director: Clodagh Conroy
Production designer: Charles Garrad
Editing: Lesley Walker
Music: Michael Nyman
Costumes: Joan Bergin
Script supervisor: Renee Foley-Burke
Leading player: Sean Foley (Man)

As director, theatre productions

Gardenia, 1982, by John Guare, with James Woods, JoBeth Williams and Sam Waterston. Manhattan Theater Club, New York.

The Gigli Concert, 1992, by Tom Murphy, with Tony Doyle and Barry Foster. Almeida Theatre, London.

A Doll's House, 1993, by Henrik Ibsen, with Niamh Cusack. Gate Theatre, Dublin.

The Deep Blue Sea, 1993, by Terence Rattigan, with Penelope Wilton and Linus Roache. Almeida Theatre, London. With Penelope Wilton and Colin Firth at the Apollo Theatre, London (Critics' Circle Award and an Olivier nomination). The Apollo production was filmed as a BBC TV play in their 'Performance' series, broadcast 12 November 1994.

Moonlight, 1995, by Harold Pinter, with Blythe Danner and Jason Robards. Roundabout Theatre, New York.

Happy Days, 1996, by Samuel Beckett, with Rosaleen Linehan. Beckett Festival at the Lincoln Center, New York and the Almeida Theatre, London.

A Kind of Alaska, 1998, by Harold Pinter, with Penelope Wilton and Bill Nighy. Donmar Warehouse Theatre, London.

Long Day's Journey into Night, 1998, by Eugene O'Neill, with Donald Moffat and Rosaleen Linehan. Gate Theatre, Dublin.

Ashes to Ashes, 1998–99, by Harold Pinter, with Lindsay Duncan and David Straithairn. Roundabout Theatre/Gramercy Theatre, New York.

A Kind of Alaska, 2001, by Harold Pinter, with Brid Brennan, Stephen Brennan and Penelope Wilton. Pinter Festival at the Lincoln Center, New York.

Landscape, 2001, by Harold Pinter, with Stephen Brennan and Penelope Wilton. Pinter Festival at the Lincoln Center, New York.

The Yalta Game, 2001, by Brian Friel, adapted from Chekhov's 1899 story, *The Lady with the Lapdog*, with Ciarán Hinds and Kelly Reilly. Dublin Festival.

Bibliography

Works by Karel Reisz

Books

The Technique of Film Editing, Second Enlarged Edition with Gavin Millar, New York, Focal Press Ltd, 1953, and Hastings House Publishers, 1968.

Articles and reviews in *Sequence* (1950–52)

'*The Search*' (Fred Zinnemann), No. 10, New Year 1950, p. 152.
'*Young Man of Music*' (Michael Curtiz), No. 11, Summer 1950, pp. 14–15.
'*The Wooden Horse*' (Jack Lee), No. 12, Autumn 1950, p. 18.
'*La Terra Trema*' (Luchino Visconti), No. 12, Autumn 1950, pp. 38–40.
'*The Breaking Point*' (Michael Curtiz), No. 13, New Year 1951, p. 16.
(as Quentin Rogers), 'Doublethink', review of *Vitezny Film* (*The Victorious Cinema*), No. 13, New Year 1951, pp. 44–5.
'The Later Films of William Wyler', No. 13, New Year 1951, pp. 19–30.
'Milestone and War', No. 14, New Year 1952, pp. 12–16.
'Ophuls and *La Ronde*', No. 14, New Year 1952, pp. 33–5.

Articles and reviews in *Sight and Sound* (1950–58)

'Editing', February 1950, p. 32.
'Editing', Vol. 19, No. 2, April 1950, p. 79.
'Editing', Vol. 19, No. 5, July 1950, p. 209.
'Editing', Vol. 19, No. 8, December 1950, pp. 335 and 339.
'Editing', Vol. 19, No. 10, February 1951, p. 415.
'Editing', Vol. 19, No. 12, April 1951, p. 476.
'The Editor: Jack Harris', Vol. 20, No. 1, May 1951, p. 16.
'Editing: Unfair to Eisenstein?', Vol. 20, No. 2, June 1951, pp. 54–5, 65.
'Review of Sergei Eisenstein's *Film Form*', Vol. 21, No. 1, August–September 1951, pp. 44–5.
'Interview with Huston', Vol. 21, No. 3, January–March 1952, pp. 130–2.

'*A Place in the Sun*' (George Stevens), Vol. 21, No. 3, January–March 1952, pp. 120–2.

'*A Streetcar Named Desire*' (Elia Kazan), Vol. 21, No. 4, April–June 1952, pp. 170–1.

'*The Importance of Being Earnest*' (Anthony Asquith), Vol. 22, No. 1, July–September 1952, p. 28.

'Hollywood's Anti-Red Boomerang: Apple Pie, Love and Endurance Versus the Commies', Vol. 22, No. 3, January–March 1953, pp. 132–7, 148.

'*The Member of the Wedding*' (Fred Zinnemann), Vol. 22, No. 4, April–June 1953, pp. 197–8.

'*Man on a Tightrope*' (Elia Kazan), Vol. 23, No. 1, July–September 1953, p. 32.

'In the Picture: Reports from the Festivals – Berlin', Vol. 23, No. 2, October–December 1953, p. 60.

'*Umberto D*' (Vittorio de Sica), Vol. 23, No. 2, October–December 1953, pp. 87–8.

'*From Here to Eternity*' (Fred Zinnemann), Vol. 23, No. 3, January–March 1954, pp. 145–6.

'*Stroheim in London*', Vol. 23, No. 4, April–June 1954, pp. 172–3.

'*Le Salaire de la Peur*' (Henri-Georges Clouzot), Vol. 23, No. 4, April–June 1954, pp. 197–8.

'*The Maggie*' (Alexander Mackendrick), Vol. 23, No. 4, April–June 1954, pp. 199–200.

'*The Knave of Hearts*' (René Clément), Vol. 24, No. 1, July–September 1954, p. 31.

'*Sabrina Fair*' (Billy Wilder), Vol. 24, No. 2, October–December 1954, p. 91.

'*Riot in Cell Block 11*' (Don Siegel), Vol. 24, No. 3, January–March 1955, p. 143.

'*The Little Fugitive*' (Ray Ashley, Morris Engel, Ruth Orkin), Vol. 24, No. 3, January–March 1955, pp. 145–6.

'*Death of a Cyclist*' (Juan Antonio Bardem), Vol. 26, No. 1, Summer 1956, p. 32.

'*A Girl in Black*' (Michael Cacoyannis), Vol. 26, No. 3, Winter 1956–57, p. 154.

'*A Face in the Crowd*' (Elia Kazan), Vol. 27, No. 2, Autumn 1957, p. 89.

'The Festivals: Experiment at Brussels', Vol. 27, No. 5, Summer 1958, pp. 231–4.

Miscellaneous articles, 1951–58

'The Showman Producer', in Roger Manvell and R. K. Neilson, eds, *The Cinema 1951*, Harmondsworth, Penguin Books, 1951, pp. 160–7.

'Substance into Shadow', in Roger Manvell and R. K. Neilson, eds, *The Cinema 1952*, Harmondsworth, Penguin Books, 1952, reprinted New York, Arno Press, 1978, pp. 188–205.

'A Use for Documentary', *Universities and Left Review*, No. 3, Winter 1958, pp. 23–4, 65–6.

General bibliography and works cited

Adair, Gilbert, *Hollywood's Vietnam*, London, Heinemann, 1989.

Aldgate, Anthony, *Censorship and the Permissive Society: British Cinema and Theatre, 1955–1965*, Oxford, Clarendon Press, 1995.

—— and Jeffrey Richards, *Best of British: Cinema and Society from 1930 to the Present*, London and New York, I. B. Tauris, 1999.

Allsop, Kenneth, *The Angry Decade: A Survey of the Cultural Revolt of the Nineteen-Fifties*, London, Peter Owen Ltd, 1958.

Althusser, Louis, *Lenin and Philosophy and Other Essays*, trans. Ben Brewster, London, New Left Books and New York, Monthly Review Press, 1971

Anderson, Lindsay, 'Angles of Approach', *Sequence* No. 2, Winter 1947, pp. 5–8.

—— 'A Possible Solution', *Sequence* No. 3, Spring 1948, pp. 7–10.

—— 'The Director's Cinema?', *Sequence* No. 12, Autumn 1950, pp. 6–11, 37.

—— 'Only Connect: Some Aspects of the Work of Humphrey Jennings', *Sight and Sound*, Vol. 23, No. 4, April–June 1954, pp. 181–6.

—— 'Stand Up! Stand Up!', *Sight and Sound*, Vol. 26, No. 2, Autumn 1956, pp. 63–9, reprinted as 'Commitment in Cinema Criticism', *Universities and Left Review*, No. 1, Spring 1957, pp. 44–8.

—— 'Free Cinema', *Universities and Left Review*, No. 2, Autumn 1957, pp. 51–2.

—— 'Get Out and Push!', in Tom Maschler, ed., *Declaration*, New York, E. P. Dutton and Co., 1958, pp. 137–60.

—— 'Sport, Life and Art', *Films & Filming*, Vol. 9, No. 5, February 1963, pp. 15–18.

—— 'John Ford: A Monograph', *Cinema*, Vol. 6, No. 3, 1971.

—— 'Free Cinema (1 and 2)', National Film Theatre Programme Notes, 15 August 1977.

—— *About John Ford*, London, Plexus, 1981 and 1999.

Andrew, Dudley, *Mists of Regret: Culture and Sensibility in Classic French Film*, Princeton NJ, Princeton University Press, 1995.

Anonymous, 'From Free Cinema to Feature Film: Mr. Karel Reisz Talks about the Change', *The Times*, 19 May 1960, p. 18.

—— 'Karel Reisz: Free Czech', *Films & Filming*, Vol. 7, February 1961, p. 5.

—— 'Desert Island Films', *Films & Filming*, Vol. 9, No. 11, August 1963, pp. 11–13.

—— 'David Mercer on Why He Writes the Plays He Does', *The Times*, 27 July 1966, p. 6.

—— 'Free Cinema at the NFT', 22 March 2001. British Film Institute. www.bfi.org.uk/showing/nft/interviews/freecinema.

Archer, Robin *et al.*, *Out of Apathy: Voices of the New Left Thirty Years On*, London and New York, Verso, 1989.

Armes, Roy, *A Critical History of the British Cinema*, New York, Oxford University Press, 1978.

Artaud, Antonin, *The Theater and Its Double*, trans. Mary Caroline Richards, New York, Grove Press, 1958.

Ashby, Justine and Andrew Higson, *British Cinema, Past and Present*, London and New York, Routledge, 2000.

Auster, Albert and Leonard Quart, *How the War Was Remembered: Hollywood & Vietnam*, New York, Praeger Publishers, 1988.

Baker, Peter G., 'Re-Presentation (*March to Aldermaston*)', *Films & Filming*, Vol. 5, No. 7, April 1959, p. 25.

Barnum, Carol M., 'An Interview with John Fowles', *Modern Fiction Studies*, Vol. 31, No. 1, Spring 1985, pp. 187–203.

Barr, Charles, ed., *All Our Yesterdays: 90 Years of British Cinema*, London, BFI, 1986.

Barsam, Richard Meran, *Nonfiction Film: A Critical History*, New York, E. P. Dutton, 1973.

Bazin, André, *What Is Cinema? Vol. 1*, trans. Hugh Gray, Berkeley and Los Angeles, University of California Press, 1967.

Bhabha, Homi, 'Of Mimicry and Man: The Ambivalence of Colonial Discourse', in *The Location of Culture*, London and New York, Routledge, 1994.

Bigsby, Christopher, *The Cambridge Companion to Arthur Miller*, Cambridge, Cambridge University Press, 1997.

Biskind, Peter, 'Muscular Contractions', *Sight and Sound*, Vol. 15, No. 2, February 2005, pp. 24–6.

Blair, Betsy, *The Memory of All That: Love and Politics in New York, Hollywood, and Paris*, New York, Alfred A. Knopf, 2003.

Bond, Ralph, 'Not So Free Cinema', *Film & TV Technician*, June–July 1957.

Brantlinger, Patrick, Ian Adam and Sheldon Rothblatt, '*The French Lieutenant's Woman*: A Discussion', *Victorian Studies*, Vol. 15, No. 3, March 1972, pp. 339–56.

Brater, Enoch, '*The French Lieutenant's Woman*: Screenplay and Adaptation', in Steven H. Gale, ed., *Harold Pinter: Critical Approaches*, London and Toronto, Associated University Presses, 1986, pp. 139–52.

Braunstein, Peter and Michael William Doyle, eds, *Imagine Nation: The American Counterculture of the 1960s and '70s*, New York and London, Routledge, 2002.

Brock, Hugh, 'Evolution of the Aldermaston Resistance', *Peace News*, No. 1182, 20 February 1959, Supplement, p. III.

Bülow, Louis, 'Nicholas Winton: Schindler of Britain'. www.auschwitz.dk/Winton.htm.

Butler, Ivan, '*To Encourage the Art of the Film*': The Story of the British Film Institute, London, Robert Hale, 1971.

Cameron, Ian, ed., *Movie Reader*, New York and Washington, Praeger Publishers, 1972.

Campbell, James, 'An Interview with John Fowles', *Contemporary Literature*, Vol. 17, No. 4, Autumn 1976, pp. 454–69.

Canby, Vincent, '*The Loves of Isadora*', *New York Times*, 28 April 1969, p. 33:1.

—— '*The Loves of Isadora*', *New York Times*, 4 May 1969, p. II:1:6.

—— '*The Gambler*', *New York Times*, 3 October 1974, p. 50:1.

Cashill, Bob, 'Director Karel Reisz Sifts Through Pinter's *Ashes*', *Playbill*, 8 February 1999. www.playbill.com/features/article/64863.html.

Caughie, John and Kevin Rockett, *The Companion to British and Irish Cinema*, London, BFI/Cassell, 1966.

Caute, David, *The Year of the Barricades: A Journey Through 1968*, New York, Harper and Row, 1988.

Changas, Estelle, '*Isadora*', *Film Quarterly*, Summer 1969, pp. 45–8.

Charlton, Leigh, 'Who'll Stop the Director', *Village Voice*, 23, 4 September 1978

Chartoff, Robert and Irwin Winkler, 'Dialogue on Film', *American Film*, Vol. 2, No. 3, December–January 1977, pp. 37–52.

Chatman, Seymour, 'A New Kind of Film Adaptation: *The French Lieutenant's Woman*', in *Coming to Terms: The Rhetoric of Narrative in Fiction and Film*, Ithaca and London, Cornell University Press, 1990, pp. 161–83.

Chekhov, Anton, 'On the High Road', in '*The Vaudevilles' and Other Short Works*, trans. Carol Rocamora, Lyme NH, Smith and Kraus, 1998.

Childs, Peter and Patrick Williams, *An Introduction to Post-Colonial Theory*, London, Prentice Hall, 1997.

Cohen, Philip, 'Postmodernist Technique in *The French Lieutenant's Woman*', *Western Humanities Review*, Vol. 38, No. 2, Summer 1984, pp. 148–61.

Coleman, John, '*Night Must Fall*', *New Statesman*, Vol. 67, 15 May 1964, p. 782.

—— 'Mercer's Monkey', *New Statesman*, Vol. 71, 15 April 1966, p. 549.

—— 'Bitter Rice', *New Statesman*, Vol. 89, No. 2299, 11 April 1975, p. 492.

—— 'Turn Up For the Book (*The French Lieutenant's Woman*)', *New Statesman*, Vol. 102, No. 2639, 16 October 1981, pp. 28–9.

Combs, Richard, '*Dog Soldiers*', *Monthly Film Bulletin*, Vol. 45, No. 539, December 1978, pp. 238–9.

—— 'In Search of the French Lieutenant's Woman', *Sight and Sound*, Vol. 50, No. 1, Winter 1980–81, pp. 34–5, and 39.

—— 'Through a Glass Darkly', *Sight and Sound*, Vol. 50, No. 4, Autumn 1981, p. 277.

—— 'Angst and Abstraction' (*Dog Soldiers*), *The Listener*, Vol. 117, No. 3014, 4 June 1987, p. 52.

—— '*Everybody Wins*', *Sight and Sound*, Vol. 1, No. 1, May 1991, pp. 47–8.

Conradi, Peter J., '*The French Lieutenant's Woman*: Novel, Screenplay, Film', *Critical Quarterly*, Vol. 24, No. 1, Spring 1982, pp. 41–57.

Cooke, Alan, 'Free Cinema', *Sequence* No. 13, New Year 1951, pp. 11–13.

Cooper, D. E., 'Looking Back on Anger', in Vernon Bogdanor and Robert Skidelsky, eds, *The Age of Affluence 1951–1964*, London, MacMillan, 1970, pp. 254–87.

Corliss, Richard, 'When Acting Becomes Alchemy' (*The French Lieutenant's Woman*), *Time*, Vol. 118, No. 10, 7 September 1981, pp. 48–50.

Curran, James and Vincent Porter, *British Cinema History*, London, Weidenfeld and Nicolson, 1983.

Cutts, John, '*Night Must Fall*', *Films & Filming*, Vol. 10, June 1964, pp. 21–2.

Deleuze, Gilles, 'The Exhausted', trans. Anthony Uhlmann, *SubStance* No. 78, Vol. 24, No. 3, 1995, pp. 3–28.

Deleuze, Gilles and Félix Guattari, *Anti-Oedipus: Capitalism and Schizophrenia*, trans. Robert Hurley, Mark Seem and Helen R. Lane, Minneapolis, University of Minnesota Press, 1983.

Demby, Betty Jeffries, 'Festivals: Cannes 1978', *Filmmakers Newsletter*, Vol. 11, No. 11, September 1978, p. 64.

Dempsey, Michael, '*The Gambler*', *Film Quarterly*, Vol. 28, No. 3, Spring 1975, pp. 49–54.

Dodson, Mary Lynn, '*The French Lieutenant's Woman*: Pinter and Reisz's Adaptation of Fowles's Adaptation', *Literature/Film Quarterly*, Vol. 26, No. 4, 1998, pp. 296–303.

Donner, Clive, 'Memories of Karel', 'Directors Guild of Great Britain', 2003. www.dggb.co.uk/publications/article12_127.html.

Dostoyevsky, Fyodor, *Notes from Underground*, trans. Andrew R. MacAndrew, New York, Signet Classics, 1961.

Drabble, Margaret, 'Isadora the Good' (Review of Francis Steegmuller, ed., *Your Isadora: The Love Story of Isadora Duncan and Gordon Craig*), *The Listener*, Vol. 93, No. 2392, 6 February 1975, pp. 185–6.

Duncan, Isadora, *My Life*, New York, Liveright, 1927 and 1995.

Dupin, Christophe, 'Early Days of Short Film Production at the British Film Institute: Origins and Evolution of the BFI Experimental Film Fund (1952–66)', *Journal of Media Practice*, Vol. 4, No.2, 2003, pp. 77–91

Durgnat, Raymond, '*Morgan – A Suitable Case for Treatment*', *Films & Filming* 12, June 1966, pp. 6, 10.

—— *A Mirror for England: British Movies from Austerity to Affluence*, London, Faber and Faber, 1970.

—— 'Britannia Waives the Rules: The Angry Young Cinema Grows Out', *Film Comment*, Vol. 12, No. 4, July–August 1976, pp. 50–9.

Eagleton, Terry, *Literary Theory: An Introduction*, Minneapolis, University of Minnesota Press, 1983.

Ellis, Jack C., 'Changing the Guard: From the Grierson Documentary to Free Cinema', *Quarterly Review of Film Studies*, Vol. 7, No. 1, Winter 1982, pp. 23–35.

—— *The Documentary Idea: A Critical History of English Language Documentary Film and Video*, Englewood Cliffs NJ, Prentice Hall, 1989.

Ellis, John, ed., *1951–1976: British Film Institute Productions,* London, BFI, 1977.

Emanuel, Muriel and Vera Gissing, *Nicholas Winton and the Rescued Generation*, London, Vallentine Mitchell, 2002.

Farber, Stephen, 'Artists in Love and War', *Hudson Review*, Vol. 22, No. 2, Summer 1969, pp. 295–306.

Feuer, Jane, *The Hollywood Musical*, Bloomington and Indianapolis, Indiana University Press, Second Edition, 1993.

Fowles, John, *The French Lieutenant's Woman*, Boston, New York and London, Little, Brown and Company, 1969 and 1998.

—— 'On Writing a Novel', *The Cornhill*, No. 1060, Summer 1969, pp. 281–95.

—— 'Notes on an Unfinished Novel', in Thomas McCormack, ed., *Afterwords: Novelists on Their Novels*, New York and Evanston, Harper and Row, 1969, pp. 160–75.

—— 'Foreword' to Harold Pinter, *The Screenplay of The French Lieutenant's Woman*, London, Jonathan Cape, 1981, pp. vii–xv.

—— 'The French Lieutenant's Diary', *Granta*, No. 86, Summer 2004, pp. 7–36.

French, Philip, 'Alphaville of Admass', *Sight and Sound*, Vol. 35, No. 3, Summer 1966, p. 110.

Freud, Sigmund, *The Interpretation of Dreams*, The Penguin Freud Library, Vol. 4, trans. James Strachey, Harmondsworth, Penguin Books, 1976.

—— 'Beyond the Pleasure Principle' (1920), in *On Metapsychology*, The Penguin Freud Library, Vol. 11, trans. James Strachey, Harmondsworth, Penguin Books, 1984, pp. 275–338.

—— 'Delusions and Dreams in Jensen's *Gradiva*', in The Penguin Freud Library, Vol. 14, trans. James Strachey, Harmondsworth, Penguin Books, 1985.

Friedman, Lester, ed., *Fires Were Started: British Cinema and Thatcherism*, Minneapolis, University of Minnesota Press, 1993.

Gale, Steven H., 'Harold Pinter's *The French Lieutenant's Woman*: A Masterpiece of Cinematic Adaptation', in Steven H. Gale, ed., *The Films of Harold Pinter*, Albany, State University of New York Press, 2001, pp. 69–86.

Garis, Leslie, 'Translating Fowles into Film', *New York Times Magazine*, 30 August 1981, Section 6, pp. 24, 48–54, 69.

Garner, Dwight, 'The Apostle of the Strung-Out: The *Salon* Interview, Robert Stone', 14 April 1997. www.salon.com/april97/stone970414.html.

Gaston, Georg, *Karel Reisz*, Boston, Twayne Publishers, 1980.

—— '*The French Lieutenant's Woman*', *Film Quarterly*, Vol. 35, No. 2, Winter 1981–82, pp. 51–6.

Gitlin, Todd, *The Sixties: Years of Hope, Days of Rage*, New York, Bantam Books, 1987.

Gontarski, S. E., '"Birth Astride of a Grave": Samuel Beckett's *Act Without Words I*', in S. E. Gontarski, ed., *The Beckett Studies Reader*, Gainesville, University of Florida Press, 1993, pp. 29–34.

Gow, Gordon, '*Isadora*', *Films & Filming*, Vol. 15, No. 8, May 1969, pp. 52–3.

—— '*The Gambler*', *Films & Filming*, Vol. 21, No. 7, April 1975, pp. 39, 42.

—— 'Outsiders: Karel Reisz in an Interview with Gordon Gow', *Films & Filming*, Vol. 25, No. 4, January 1979, pp. 12–17.

—— '*Dog Soldiers*', *Films & Filming*, Vol. 25, No. 4, January 1979, p. 32.

Graham, Allison, *Lindsay Anderson*, Boston, Twayne, 1981.

Grierson, John, *Grierson on Documentary*, Forsyth Hardy, ed., London, Faber and Faber, 1966.

Gussow, Mel, *Conversations with Pinter*, New York, Limelight Editions, 1994.

Hachem, Samir, 'Sweet Dreams', Horizon, Vol. 28, No. 8, October 1985, pp. 30–2.

Hall, Stuart, 'In the No Man's Land', Universities and Left Review, No. 3, Winter 1958, pp. 86–7.

—— 'Culture, the Media, and the "Ideological Effect"', in Mass Communication and Society, James Curran, Michael Gurevitch and Janet Woollacott, eds, London, Edward Arnold, 1977 and 1979, pp. 315–48.

—— 'Cultural Studies and its Theoretical Legacies', in Cultural Studies, Lawrence Grossberg, Cary Nelson and Paula A. Treichler, eds, New York and London, Routledge, 1992, pp. 277–94.

—— and Tony Jefferson, eds, Resistance through Rituals: Youth Subcultures in Post-War Britain, London, HarperCollins, 1975.

Hallam, Julia and Margaret Marshment, Realism and Popular Cinema, Manchester and New York, Manchester University Press, 2000.

Hanson, Cynthia, 'The Hollywood Musical Biopic and the Regressive Performer', Wide Angle, Vol. 10, No. 2, 1988, pp. 15–23.

Hewison, Robert, In Anger: Culture in the Cold War, 1945–60, London, Weidenfeld and Nicolson, 1981.

Higson, Andrew, 'Britain's Outstanding Contribution to the Film: The Documentary-Realist Tradition', in Charles Barr, ed., All Our Yesterdays: 90 Years of British Cinema, London, BFI, 1986, pp. 72–97.

—— 'Waving the Flag: Constructing a National Cinema in Britain, Oxford, Clarendon Press, 1995.

—— ed., Dissolving Views: Key Writings on British Cinema, London, Cassell, 1996.

Hill, Derek, 'Failure on the March (March to Aldermaston)', The Tribune, 27 February 1959, p. 11.

Hill, John, Sex, Class and Realism: British Cinema 1956–1963, London, BFI, 1986.

Hogenkamp, Bert, Film, Television and the Left in Britain 1950 to 1970, London, Lawrence and Wishart, 2000.

Hoggart, Richard, The Uses of Literacy: Aspects of Working-Class Life with Special Reference to Publications and Entertainments, London, Chatto and Windus/Penguin, 1957.

—— 'We Are the Lambeth Boys', Sight and Sound, Vol. 28, Nos. 3–4, Summer–Autumn 1959, pp. 164–5.

—— 'Lambeth Boys', Sight and Sound, Vol. 54, No. 2, Spring 1985, pp. 106–9.

Houston, Beverle and Marsha Kinder, "The Losey-Pinter Collaboration," Film Quarterly, Vol. 32, No. 1, Fall 1978.

Houston, Penelope, 'March to Aldermaston', Sight and Sound, Vol. 28, No. 2, Spring 1959, p. 89.

—— 'Keeping Up with the Antonionis', Sight and Sound, Vol. 33, No. 4, Autumn 1964, pp. 163–8.

Hutcheon, Linda, 'Freedom through Artifice: The French Lieutenant's Woman', in Narcissistic Narrative: The Metafictional Paradox, New York and London, Methuen, 1980 and 1984, pp. 57–70.

Jacob, Lewis, 'Free Cinema 1', *Film Culture*, Vol. 4, No. 2, February 1958.

Jarman, Francis, 'Birth of a Playwriting Man' (Interview with David Mercer), *Theatre Quarterly*, Vol. 3, No. 9, January–March 1973, pp. 43–55.

Jefferson, Tony, 'Cultural Responses of the Teds', in Stuart Hall and Tony Jefferson, eds, *Resistance through Rituals: Youth Subcultures in Post-War Britain*, London, HarperCollins, 1975, pp. 81–6.

Johnson, Kirk, 'Arthur Miller's Vision of Love Becomes a Movie', *New York Times*, 11 June 1989, Section 2, pp. 19, 22–3.

Jones, Malcolm, 'Introduction' to Fyodor Dostoyevsky, *Notes from the Under-ground* and *The Gambler*, trans. Jane Kentish, Oxford, Oxford University Press, 1991, and 1999, pp. vii–xxiii.

Kael, Pauline, 'Commitment and the Straitjacket', in *I Lost It at the Movies*, Boston, Little, Brown and Co., 1965, pp. 62–78.

—— 'So Off-Beat We Lost the Beat', in *Kiss Kiss, Bang Bang*, Boston, Little, Brown and Co., 1968, pp. 20–5.

—— 'The Current Cinema: The Actor and the Star' (*The Gambler*), *New Yorker*, 14 October 1974, pp. 174–5.

—— 'The Current Cinema' (*The French Lieutenant's Woman*), *New Yorker*, 12 October 1981, pp. 158–62.

—— 'The Current Cinema: Heroines' (*Sweet Dreams*), *New Yorker*, 21 October 1985, pp. 122–3.

—— 'The Current Cinema: New Age Daydreams' (*Everybody Wins*), *New Yorker*, 17 December 1990, pp. 120–1.

Karagueuzian, Maureen, 'Irony in Robert Stone's *Dog Soldiers*', *Critique: Studies in Modern Fiction*, Vol. 24, No. 2, Winter 1983, pp. 65–73.

Katzman, Jason, 'From Outcast to Cliché: How Film Shaped, Warped and Developed the Image of the Vietnam Veteran, 1967–1990', *Journal of American Culture*, Vol. 16, No. 1, Spring 1993, pp. 7–24.

Kauffmann, Stanley, 'The Woman in the Case' (*Everybody Wins*), *New Republic*, Vol. 202, No. 10, 5 March 1990, p. 26.

Kemp, Philip, 'Maybe Baby' (*Everybody Wins*), *Sight and Sound*, Vol. 59, No. 2, Spring 1990, pp. 135–6.

Kennedy, Harlan, 'The Czech Director's Woman' and 'Interview with Karel Reisz', *Film Comment*, Vol. 17, No. 5, September–October 1981, pp. 26–31.

—— 'Minute Reisz: Six Earlier Films', *Film Comment*, Vol. 17, No. 5, September–October 1981, p. 29.

Klein, Joanne, *Making Pictures: The Pinter Screenplays*, Columbus, Ohio State University Press, 1985.

Knapp, Shoshana, 'Film as Dream II', *Post Script: Essays in Film and the Humanities*, Vol. 2, No. 3, Spring/Summer 1983, pp. 60–1.

Knox, Stephen H., 'A Cup of Salt for an O.D.: *Dog Soldiers* as Anti-Apocalypse', *The Journal of General Education*, Vol. 34, No. 1, Spring 1982, pp. 60–8.

Kopkind, Andrew, '*Sweet Dreams*', *Nation*, Vol. 241, No. 16, 16 November 1985, pp. 531–3.

Krauss, Rosalind, 'Corpus Delecti', in *L'Amour Fou: Photography and Surre-alism*, New York, Abbeville Press, 1985, pp. 57–100.

Kroll, Jack, 'Lusty Queen of Country (*Sweet Dreams*), *Newsweek*, Vol. 106, 7 October 1985, p. 88.

Kustow, Michael, '*Morgan, a Suitable Case for Treatment*', *Sight and Sound*, Vol. 35, No. 3, Summer 1966, p. 144.

Laing, R. D., *The Politics of Experience and The Bird of Paradise*, London, Penguin Books, 1967.

Laing, Stuart, *Representations of Working Class Life 1957–1964*, Basingstoke, Macmillan, 1986.

Lambert, Gavin, 'Your Critic – Right or Wrong!', in Roger Manvell, ed., *The Cinema 1952*, Harmondsworth, Penguin Books, 1952, reprinted New York, Arno Press, 1978, pp. 140–8.

—— 'A Last Look Round', *Sequence* No. 14, New Year 1952, pp. 4–8.

—— 'Who Wants True?' *Sight and Sound*, Vol. 21, No. 4, April–June 1952, pp. 148–51.

—— 'Free Cinema', *Sight and Sound*, Vol. 25, No. 4, Spring 1956, pp. 173–7.

—— *Mainly About Lindsay Anderson*, New York, Alfred A. Knopf, 2000.

—— 'The Rebel Inside', *The Guardian*, 20 June 2003.

Lassally, Walter, 'The Dead Hand', *Sight and Sound*, Vol. 29, No. 3, Summer 1960, pp. 113–15.

Leach, Jim, 'David Mercer: British Writer', The Museum of Broadcast Communications. www.museum.tv/archives/etv/M/htmlM/mercer-david/mercerdavid.htm.

Lee, Martin A., and Bruce Shlain, *Acid Dreams: The CIA, LSD and the Sixties Rebellion*, New York, Grove Press, 1985.

Lichtenstein, Claude and Thomas Schregenberger, eds, *As Found: The Discovery of The Ordinary*, Zürich Museum of Design, Lars Müller Publishers, 2001.

Logue, Christopher and Lindsay Anderson, '*March to Aldermaston* (complete commentary)', *Peace News*, No. 1182, 20 February 1959, Supplement, pp. I–II.

Lorsch, Susan E., 'Pinter Fails Fowles: Narration in *The French Lieutenant's Woman*', *Literature/Film Quarterly*, Vol. 16, No. 3, 1988, pp. 144–54.

Lovell, Alan, 'March Against Madness', *Peace News*, No. 1182, 20 February 1959, Supplement, p. IV.

—— 'Film Chronicle' (*Saturday Night and Sunday Morning*), *New Left Review*, No. 7, January–February 1961, pp. 52–3.

—— 'Karel Reisz's Experiment' (*Night Must Fall*), *Peace News*, 5 June 1964, p. 8.

—— 'Free Cinema', in Alan Lovell and Jim Hillier, *Studies in Documentary*, New York, Viking Press, 1972, pp. 133–72.

—— and Jim Hillier, *Studies in Documentary*, New York, Viking Press, 1972.

Lovell, Terry, 'Landscape and Stories in 1960s British Realism', *Screen*, Vol. 31, No. 4, 1990, pp. 347–76.

Luckett, Moya, 'Travel and Mobility: Femininity and National Identity in Swinging London Films', in Justine Ashby and Andrew Higson, *British Cinema, Past and Present*, London and New York, Routledge, 2000, pp. 233–45.

MacCabe, Colin, 'Realism and the Cinema: Notes on Some Brechtian Theses', *Screen*, Vol. 15, No. 2, Summer 1974.

McCarthy, Matt, 'Free Cinema – In Chains', *Films & Filming*, Vol. 5, No. 5, February 1959, pp. 10 and 17.

McCoy, Alfred W., *The Politics of Heroin: CIA Complicity in the Global Drug Trade*, New York, Lawrence Hill Books, 1991.

McFarlane, Brian, '*The French Lieutenant's Woman*', *Cinema Papers*, January–February 1982, pp. 73–4.

—— 'A Literary Cinema? British Films and British Novels', in Charles Barr, ed., *All Our Yesterdays: 90 Years of British Cinema*, London, BFI, 1986, pp. 120–42.

—— 'Sequence: "Saying Exactly What We Liked"', *Filmviews*, No. 135, Autumn 1988, pp. 31–4.

—— *An Autobiography of British Cinema*, London, Methuen, 1997.

Manvell, Roger, ed., *The Cinema 1952*, Harmondsworth, Penguin Books, 1952, reprinted New York, Arno Press, 1978.

—— and R. K. Neilson, eds, *The Cinema 1951*, Harmondsworth, Penguin Books, 1951.

Marcuse, Herbert, with Barrington Moore and Robert Paul Wolff, *A Critique of Pure Tolerance*, Boston, Beacon Press, 1965.

Marwick, Arthur, '*Room at the Top, Saturday Night and Sunday Morning*, and the "Cultural Revolution" in Britain', *Journal of Contemporary History*, Vol. 19, No. 1, January 1984, pp. 127–51.

—— *Culture in Britain Since 1945*, Oxford, Basil Blackwell, 1991.

Maschler, Tom, ed., *Declaration*, New York, E. P. Dutton and Co., 1958.

Mazis, Glen A., 'The "Riteful" Play of Time in *The French Lieutenant's Woman*', *Soundings*, Vol. 67, No. 3, Fall 1983, pp. 296–318.

Mekas, Jonas, 'Cinema of the New Generation: Part One, Free Cinema and the Nouvelle Vague', *Film Culture*, No. 21, Summer 1960, pp. 1–6.

Mercer, David, *A Suitable Case for Treatment*, in *Collected T.V. Plays, Volume Two*, London, John Calder, 1981, pp. 7–45.

Miller, Arthur, *Some Kind of Love Story*, in *Two-Way Mirror*, London, Methuen, 1984, pp. 23–66.

—— *Everybody Wins*, New York, Grove Weidenfeld, 1990.

Milne, Tom, '*Night Must Fall*', *Sight and Sound*, Vol. 33, No. 3, Summer 1964, p. 144.

—— '*The French Lieutenant's Woman*', *Monthly Film Bulletin*, Vol. 48, No. 573, October 1981, pp. 199–200.

—— '*Sweet Dreams*', *Monthly Film Bulletin*, Vol. 53, No. 626, March 1986, pp. 85–6.

Moore-Gilbert, Bart, and John Seed, eds, *Cultural Revolution? The Challenge of the Arts in the 1960s*, London and New York, Routledge, 1992.

Murphy, Robert, *Sixties British Cinema*, London, BFI, 1992.

—— ed., *The British Cinema Book*, London, BFI, 1997.

Nietzsche, Friedrich, *The Birth of Tragedy*, trans. Walter Kaufmann, New York, Vintage, 1967.

—— *On the Genealogy of Morals*, trans. Walter Kaufmann and R. J. Hollingdale, New York, Vintage, 1989.

Oakes, Philip, 'New Reputations: Karel Reisz, Break for Commercial', *Punch*, Vol. 240, No. 1299, 7 June 1961, pp. 858–61.

O'Hagan, Andrew, ed., 'Karel Reisz Remembered', *London Review of Books*, Vol. 24, No. 24, 12 December 2002. www.lrb.co.uk/v24/n24/mult03_.html.

Olshen, Barry N., *John Fowles*, New York, Frederick Ungar, 1978.

Orbanz, Eva, *Journey to a Legend and Back: The British Realistic Film*, Berlin, Edition Volker Spiess, 1977.

Paletz, David, '*Morgan*', *Film Quarterly*, Vol. 20, No. 1, Fall 1966, pp. 51–5.

Palmer, R. Barton, 'What Was New in the British New Wave?', *Journal of Popular Film and Television*, Vol. 14, No. 3, pp. 125–35.

Perkins, V. F., 'The British Cinema', in Ian Cameron, ed., *Movie Reader*, New York and Washington, Praeger Books, 1972, pp. 7–11.

Phillips, Gene D., 'An Interview with Karel Reisz,' *Cinema* (Beverly Hills), Vol. 4, No. 2, Summer 1968, pp. 53–4.

—— *The Movie Makers: Artists in an Industry*, Chicago, Nelson-Hall Company, 1973.

Pinter, Harold, *The Screenplay of* The French Lieutenant's Woman, London, Jonathan Cape, 1981.

Prince, Rod, '*Saturday Night and Sunday Morning*', *New Left Review*, Vol. 1, No. 6, November–December 1960, pp. 14–17.

Quigly, Isabel, 'Out of the Bag', *Spectator*, No. 6835, 26 June 1959, p. 911.

Rankin, Elizabeth D., 'Cryptic Coloration in *The French Lieutenant's Woman*', *The Journal of Narrative Technique*, Vol. 3, No. 3, September 1973, pp. 193–207.

Read, Daniel and Peter Roelofsma, 'Hard Choices and Weak Wills: The Theory of Intrapersonal Dilemmas', *Philosophical Psychology*, Vol. 12, No. 3, September, 1999, pp. 341–56.

Richards, Jeffrey, 'New Waves and Old Myths: British Cinema in the 1960s,' in Bart Moore-Gilbert and John Seed, eds, *Cultural Revolution? The Challenge of the Arts in the 1960s*, London and New York, Routledge, 1992, pp. 218–35.

Richards, Jeffrey and Anthony Aldgate, *Best of British: Cinema and Society 1930–1970*, Oxford, Basil Blackwell, 1983.

Richardson, Tony, *The Long Distance Runner: An Autobiography*, New York, William Morrow, 1993.

Ritchie, Harry, *Success Stories: Literature and the Media in England 1950–1959*, London, Faber and Faber, 1988.

Robbins, David, ed., *Independent Group: Postwar Britain and the Aesthetics of Plenty*, Cambridge MA, The MIT Press, 1990.

Roginski, Ed, 'Who'll Stop the Rain', Film Quarterly, Vol. 32, No. 2, Winter 1978–79, pp. 57–61.

Roszak, Theodore, The Making of a Counter Culture: Reflections of the Technocratic Society and Its Youthful Opposition, Garden City NY, Doubleday and Company, Inc., 1969, p. 49.

Saltzman, Harry, 'New Wave Hits British Films', Films & Filming, Vol. 6, No. 7, April 1960, pp. 11 and 28.

Sarris, Andrew, 'Metaphor in Search of a Movie', Village Voice, 9–15 September 1981, p. 49.

Sarup, Madan, An Introductory Guide to Post-Structuralism and Postmodernism, Second Edition, Athens, University of Georgia Press, 1988 and 1993.

Scruggs, Charles, 'The Two Endings of The French Lieutenant's Woman', Modern Fiction Studies, Vol. 31, No. 1, Spring 1985, pp. 95–113.

Shelton, Frank W., 'Robert Stone's Dog Soldiers: Vietnam Comes Home to America', Critique: Studies in Modern Fiction, Vol. 24, No. 2, Winter 1983, pp. 74–81.

Sigal, Clancy, 'Vietnam Wound' (Dog Soldiers), The Listener, Vol. 112, No. 2870, 9 August 1984, p. 33.

Sillitoe, Alan, Saturday Night and Sunday Morning, New York, Alfred A. Knopf and Plume Books, 1958 and 1992.

—— 'What Comes on Monday?', New Left Review, Vol. 1, No. 4, July–August 1960, pp. 58–59.

—— 'The Long Piece', in Mountains and Caverns, London, W. H. Allen, 1975, pp. 9–40.

Silverstein, Marc, Harold Pinter and the Language of Cultural Power, Lewisburg PA, Bucknell University Press, 1993.

Sinfield, Alan, Literature, Politics and Culture in Postwar Britain, Oxford, Basil Blackwell, 1989.

Sinyard, Neil, Filming Literature: The Art of Screen Adaptation, London and Sydney, Croom Helm Ltd, 1986.

Spitz, Ellen Handler, 'On Interpretation of Film as Dream: The French Lieutenant's Woman', Post Script: Essays in Film and the Humanities, Vol. 2, No. 1, Fall 1982, pp. 13–29.

Stein, Ruthe B., 'The Loves of Isadora', Cinéaste, Vol. 3, No. 1, Summer 1969, pp. 20–1.

Steiner, George, Martin Heidegger, Chicago, University of Chicago Press, 1978.

Stokes, Sewell, Isadora Duncan: An Intimate Portrait, London, Brentano's, 1928.

Stone, Robert, Dog Soldiers, Boston and New York, Houghton Mifflin Company, 1973.

Sulik, Boleslaw, 'Saturday Night and Sunday Morning', in Masterworks of the British Cinema, New York, Harper and Row, 1974, pp. 348–52.

Sussex, Elizabeth, Lindsay Anderson, London, Studio Vista Ltd, 1969.

—— The Rise and Fall of British Documentary: The Story of the Film Movement

Founded by John Grierson, Berkeley and Los Angeles, University of California Press, 1975.

Swingewood, Alan, *The Myth of Mass Culture*, London, Macmillan, 1977.

Taylor, John Russell, 'Tomorrow the World: Some Reflections on the Un-Englishness of English Films', *Sight and Sound*, Vol. 43, No. 2, Spring 1974, pp. 80–3.

Travers, Peter, '*Everybody Wins*', *Rolling Stone*, 22 February 1990, p. 39.

Turim, Maureen, 'Poetic Realism as Psychoanalytical and Ideological Operation: Marcel Carné's *Le Jour se Lève*', in Susan Hayward and Ginette Vincendeau, eds, *French Film: Texts and Contexts*, London and New York, Routledge, 1990, pp. 103–16.

Turk, Edward Baron, *Child of Paradise: Marcel Carné and the Golden Age of French Cinema*, Cambridge MA and London, Harvard University Press, 1989.

Vallance, Tom, 'Karel Reisz: Director of *Saturday Night and Sunday Morning*', Obituary in *The Independent*, 28 November 2002.

Walker, Alexander, *Hollywood, England: The British Film Industry in the Sixties*, London, Harrap, 1974 and 1986.

—— *National Heroes: British Cinema in the Seventies and Eighties*, London, Harrap, 1985.

Welsh, James M., 'The Man Who Made *The French Lieutenant's Woman*', *Literature/Film Quarterly*, Vol. 10, No. 1, 1982, pp. 65–7.

—— and John C. Tibbetts, eds, *The Cinema of Tony Richardson: Essays and Interviews*, Albany, State University of New York Press, 1999.

Whall, Tony, 'Karel Reisz's *The French Lieutenant's Woman*: Only the Name Remains the Same', *Literature/Film Quarterly*, Vol. 10, No. 2, 1982, pp. 75–81.

Whitebait, William (i.e. George Stonier), 'Bombardment', *New Statesman*, Vol. 55, No. 1412, 5 April 1958, p. 452.

—— 'Aldermaston', *New Statesman*, Vol. 57, No. 1458, 21 February 1959, p. 255.

Williams, Emlyn, *Night Must Fall*, New York and Los Angeles, Samuel French Inc., 1935.

—— *Emlyn: An Early Autobiography, 1927–1935*, London, The Bodley Head, 1973.

Wolfe, Tom, *The Electric Kool-Aid Acid Test*, New York, Farrar, Straus and Giroux, 1968.

Wollen, Peter, 'The Last New Wave: Modernism in the British Films of the Thatcher Era', in Lester Friedman, ed., *Fires Were Started: British Cinema and Thatcherism*, Minneapolis, University of Minnesota Press, 1993, pp. 35–51.

Wood, Jennifer M., 'Invitation to a Head Fracture: Straight Talk from Maverick *Harvard Man* James Toback, *Moviemaker*, Vol. 2, No. 7, 2002. www.moviemaker.com/hop/15/directing.html.

Zito, Stephen, '*Dog Soldiers*: Novel into Film', *American Film*, September 1977, pp. 8–15.

Foreign language publications

Benayoun, Robert, 'Cannes Vingt: Olé' (*Morgan*), *Positif*, No. 79, October 1966, p. 85.

Bloch-Morhange, Lise, '*The French Lieutenant's Woman*: Entretien avec Karel Reisz', *Cahiers du Cinéma*, No. 332, February 1982, Supplément: *Le Journal des Cahiers*, pp. 3–4.

Cattini, Alberto, 'Karel Reisz', *La Nuova Italia*, January–February 1985.

Chevrie, Marc, 'A Voix Perdue' (*Sweet Dreams*), *Cahiers du Cinéma*, No. 381, March 1986, pp. 60–1.

Ciment, Michel, 'Un Festival Bien Ordonné (Cannes en 1969)' (*Isadora*), *Positif*, No. 107, Summer 1969, pp. 41–2.

—— 'Rencontre avec Karel Reisz', *Positif*, No. 115, April 1970, p. 45.

—— 'Nouvel Entretien avec Karel Reisz (à propos de *Who'll Stop the Rain?*)', *Positif*, No. 212, November 1978, pp. 12–19.

—— 'Entretien avec Karel Reisz,' *Positif*, No. 252, March 1982, pp. 22–30.

Delahaye, Michel, 'Carrefours' (*Isadora*), *Cahiers du Cinéma*, No. 214, July–August 1969, pp. 60–3.

Pérez, Michel, 'Elle a Dansé le Meilleur de sa Vie...' (*Isadora*), *Positif*, No. 109, October 1969, pp. 63–5.

Seguin, Louis, 'Un Tours de Vache' (*We Are the Lambeth Boys*), *Positif*, No. 32, February 1960, pp. 25–30.

Sineux, Michel, 'L'Adieu aux Armes (*Guerriers de l'Enfer*)', *Positif*, No. 212, November 1978, pp. 4–5.

—— 'Le Désir Triangulaire (*La Maîtresse du Lieutenant Français*), *Positif*, No. 252, March 1982, pp. 13–16.

Thirard, Paul-Louis, 'Les Fils de Famille' (*Night Must Fall* and *Morgan*), *Positif*, No. 83, April 1967, pp. 37–40.

Török, Jean-Paul, 'Le "Lugubre" Cinéma Anglais' (*Saturday Night and Sunday Morning*), *Positif*, No. 43, January 1962, pp. 35–45.

—— 'Qu'est-ce que le Free Cinema?', *Positif*, No. 49, December 1962, pp. 13–20.

—— '*Isadora*', *Positif*, No. 115, April 1970, p. 39.

—— 'Le Démon de la Perversité' (*The Gambler*), *Positif*, No. 170, June 1975, pp. 66–8.

—— 'To Stand Outside and to Risk', *Positif*, No. 212, November 1978, pp. 2–3.

—— 'Entretien avec Karel Reisz (à propos de *The Gambler*)', *Positif*, No. 212, November 1978, pp. 6–11.

Viviani, Christian, '*Who'll Stop the Rain* ou *Dog Soldiers*', *Positif*, No. 208–9, July–August 1978, p. 100.

Index

Note: Page numbers in *italics* refer to illustrations, while 'n.' after a page reference indicates the number of a note on that page. Titles of films and literary works can be found under their authors' names where the names are also mentioned in the text.